Also in the Variorum Collected Studies Series:

R.B. SERGEANT
Farmers and Fishermen in Arabia
Studies in Customery Law and Practice

WAEL B. HALLAQ
Law and Legal Theory in Classical and Medieval Islam

DAVID AYALON
Islam and the Abode of War
Military Slaves and the Adversaries of Islam

C.F. BECKINGHAM
Between Islam and Christendom
Travellers, Facts and Legends in the Middle Ages and the Renaissance

NICHOLAS LOWICK
Coinage and History of the Islamic World

JEAN MAURICE FIEY
Communautés syriaques en Iran et Irak des origines à 1552

GEORGES VAJDA
Études de théologie et de philosophie arabo-islamiques à l'époque classique

ANDREW S. EHRENKREUTZ
Monetary Change and Economic History in the Medieval Muslim World

GEORGE MAKDISI
Religion, Law and Learning in Classical Islam

WILFERD MADELUNG
Religious and Ethnic Movements in Medieval Islam

WILFERD MADELUNG
Religious Schools and Sects in Medieval Islam

ROGER M. SAVORY
Studies on the History of Ṣafawid Iran

M.J. KISTER
Society and Religion from Jāhiliyya to Islam

COLLECTED STUDIES SERIES

From Zoroastrian Iran to Islam

Shaul Shaked

From Zoroastrian Iran to Islam

Studies in Religious History and Intercultural Contacts

VARIORUM
1995

Published by VARIORUM
Ashgate Publishing Limited
Gower House, Croft Road,
Aldershot, Hampshire GU11 3HR
Great Britain

Ashgate Publishing Company
Old Post Road,
Brookfield, Vermont 05036
USA

ISBN 0–86078–539–4

British Library CIP Data
Shaked, Shaul.
From Zoroastrian Iran to Islam: Studies in Religious
History and Intercultural Contacts.
(Variorum Collected Studies Series; CS505)
I. Title. II. Series.
295. 0955

US Library of Congress CIP Data
Shaked, Shaul.
From Zoroastrian Iran to Islam: Studies in Religious History
and Intercultural Contacts / Shaul Shaked.
p. cm. -- (Collected Studies Series; CS505). Includes Bibliographical
References and Index.
ISBN 0–86078–439–4 (hardback: alk. Paper)
1. Zoroastrianism--History. 2. Zoroastrianism--Influence. 3. Iran--
Religion. 4. Zoroastrianism--Relations--Islam. 5. Islam--Relations--
Zoroastrianism.
I. Title. II. Series: Collected Studies; CS505.
BL1525. S43 1995 95–4597
295' .09--dc20 CIP

The paper used in this publication meets the minimum requirements of the
American National Standard for Information Sciences – Permanence
of Paper for Printed Library Materials, ANSI Z39.48-1984. ∞ ™

Printed by Galliard (Printers) Ltd, Great Yarmouth, Norfolk, Great Britain

COLLECTED STUDIES SERIES CS505

CONTENTS

This volume contains x + 321 pages

PREFACE

The collection of articles selected for this volume reflects two main topics: interpretations of Sasanian Zoroastrianism and the transmission of Sasanian Zoroastrian ideas into Islam. The two themes are interconnected: we learn a substantial amount about Sasanian Zoroastrianism from the reflection of Sasanian ideas in the Arabic compositions, and we can appreciate how much Islam benefited from the influx of Iranian ideas by carefully analyzing the contents of Sasanian lore as transmitted in various channels, both Iranian and Islamic.

The studies published here have been printed originally over several years in different journals and collective works, and I hope they will gain from being set side by side.

Some more recent work relating to these topics has not been included in this collection. I refer particularly to the paper 'Some Islamic reports concerning Zoroastrianism', *Jerusalem Studies in Arabic and Islam* 17 (1994):43–84, which complements the discussion of Zurvanism in Study V. Many of the themes discussed in the articles that constitute the first part of this collection have been touched upon also in my recent book *Dualism in transformation*, London 1994.

It may be noted that references to the Addenda in the index are marked by "A" where one would expect to find the page number.

My wife, Miriam, has as usual given me a helping hand in preparing the volume. She is particularly responsible for the preparation of the index.

The volume was largely prepared when I enjoyed the hospitality of NIAS, the Netherlands Institute for Advanced Study in the Humanities and Social Sciences, at Wassenaar during the year 1994/5. I should like to thank the directors of that institute for making it a productive and enjoyable year.

I should like to thank also the publishers who have agreed to allow me to reproduce the articles first printed by them.

SHAUL SHAKED

NIAS, Wassenaar
April, 1995

PUBLISHER'S NOTE

The articles in this volume, as in all others in the Collected Studies Series, have not been given a new, continuous pagination. In order to avoid confusion, and to facilitate their use where these same studies have been referred to elsewhere, the original pagination has been maintained wherever possible.

Each article has been given a Roman number in order of appearance, as listed in the Contents. This number is repeated in each page and is quoted in the index entries.

Corrections and additions noted in the Addenda have been marked by an asterisk in the margin corresponding to the relevant text to be amended.

ACKNOWLEDGEMENTS

Grateful acknowledgement is made to the following persons, institutions and publishers for their kind permission to reproduce the articles included in this volume: Dr Meir Zadok, Director of The Israel Academy of Sciences and Humanities, Jerusalem (for article I); Per Kværne, Editor of *Acta Orientalia* (II); Dan Benovici, Director of The Magnes Press, Jerusalem (III); Professor Yohanan Friedmann on behalf of *Jerusalem Studies in Arabic and Islam* (IV, VI, VII, IX, XI); Georg Siebeck, J.C.B. Mohr, Tübingen (V); Professor Philippe Gignoux on behalf of the Association pour l'Avancement des Études Iraniennes, Paris (VIII, XII); E.J. Brill, Leiden (X).

I

ESOTERIC TRENDS IN ZOROASTRIANISM

SCHOLARS DEALING WITH the history of the Zoroastrian religion have tended to fall broadly into two categories. On the one hand, there are the scholars who incline to believe that the Zoroastrian religion indulged in mystery cults and ecstatic practices, and they include in particular those who hold it possible to discover in Iran the origins of certain doctrines which are found in the Hellenistic world, such as the mysteries and gnosticism, or esoteric beliefs, which have, in general, an exotic or Oriental flavour. The approach of the other group is more sceptical; they rely, by and large, more closely on the evidence of the extant Iranian texts themselves, where extravagant ideas of the type just referred to, if they can at all be shown to exist, are not found in any abundance and are marginal. In the first category, one may mention the names of Reitzenstein, Schaeder [1] and Götze, [2] who tried mainly to establish connections between Iran and Greece, as well as that of Nyberg, who has compared Zarathushtra's religion to shamanistic rites.[3]

1 R. Reitzenstein, *Das iranische Erlösungsmysterium*, Bonn 1921; R. Reitzenstein & H. H. Schaeder, *Studien zum antiken Synkretismus aus Iran und Griechenland*, Leipzig–Berlin 1926.

2 A. Götze, 'Persische Weisheit in griechischem Gewande—Ein Beitrag zur Geschichte der Mikrokosmos-Idee', *Zeitschrift für Indologie und Iranistik*, II (1923), pp. 60–98, 167–177.

3 H. S. Nyberg, *Die Religionen des alten Iran*, Leipzig 1938 (reprinted Osnabrück 1966). This book has aroused much justified criticism; one may refer to: R. C. Zaehner, *JRAS* (1940), pp. 210–212; O. Paul, *ARW*, XXXV (1939), pp. 215–234; W. Wüst, *ibid.*, pp. 234–249; G. Dumézil, *RHR*, CXXIII (1941), pp. 206–210; J. Tavadia, *ZDMG*, C (1950), pp. 205–245; K. Rudolph, *Numen*, VIII (1961), pp. 104 ff. W.B. Henning severely censured Nyberg's reconstructions in his book: *Zoroaster—Politician or Witch-Doctor?* London 1951. But cf. Mary Boyce in her obituary of Henning, *BSOAS*, XXX (1967), p. 783.

This general trend of research has been continued by S. Wikander[4] and G. Widengren,[5] who emphasize what seems to them to be the evidence for mystery associations and ecstatic practices. Widengren has also been one of the main protagonists of the Iranian origin of gnosticism.[6]
A competent and lucid criticism of many of these views was made by the Rev. Father Jean de Menasce in a paper read at the Eranos meeting of 1944; his conclusion denies the existence of any form of esoteric preaching in Zoroastrianism:

> There is nothing in the Mazdean tradition of revelation to suggest a selective and occult initiation. So open is the Mazdean preaching that it provides an appropriate basis for the holy war waged in the name of the faith by defenders well-armed with the temporal sword. Moreover, the Mazdeans frequently attack other religions for propagating themselves in a fashion that is secret, hidden, and hence shameful.[7]

In the following pages I shall try to show that this total denial of a secret element in the Zoroastrian religion of the Sasanian period is not entirely justified, although it is perfectly true that in that period it did address itself to all mankind. Passages such as the following stress its universal character:

> dādār-ōhrmazd ēn dēn ne ēwāz (ī) ō ērān šahr be ō hamāg gēhān ud harw srādag fristēd, ud andar hamāg abēzagīhā ku gumēzagīhā rawāg kard ēstēd: mēnōgīhā pad cihrīg ⟨ī⟩ dānāg ⟨ī⟩ rāst-menišnīh ⟨ī⟩ rāst-gōwišnīh; gētīgīhā pad rāst-kunišnīh andar kadāmjān-ez-ē a'ōn rawāg ku ēn-ez ī ag-dēn-tar kas ēn dēn wuzurg-mādagīhā pad-eš. be andar ēn ēdōn gumēzagīh

4 S. Wikander, *Der arische Männerbund,* Lund 1938; idem, *Feuerpriester in Kleinasien und Iran,* Lund 1946.

5 G. Widengren, *Hochgottglaube im alten Iran,* Uppsala 1938; idem, *The Great Vohu Manah and the Apostle of God,* Uppsala 1945; idem, *Die Religionen Irans,* Stuttgart 1965.

6 Idem, 'Der iranische Hintergrund der Gnosis', *Zeitschrift für Religions- und Geistesgeschichte,* IV (1952), pp. 97–114; idem, 'Les origines du gnosticisme et l'histoire des religions', in: *Studies in the History of Religions* (Supplements to *Numen*), XII: *The Origins of Gnosticism — Colloquium of Messina 13–18 April 1966,* Leiden 1967, pp. 28–60, for which cf. the critical remarks by U. Bianchi, *ibid.,* pp. 716 ff. Cf. the survey of literature on this question in: Duchesne-Guillemin, *Religion,* pp. 267 ff.

7 'Les mystères et la religion de l'Iran', *Eranos Jahrbuch, 1944,* XI, Zurich 1945, pp. 185–186. The passage is here quoted in the English translation which was published in: J. Campbell (ed.), *The Mysteries — Papers from the Eranos Yearbooks (Bollingen Series,* XXX, 2), New York 1955, p. 148.

hamāg abēzagīhā rawāg būd⟨an⟩ rāy be kōšišnīg šāyēd, ud +hamāg ēn dēn abzāyišnīg u-š ham-bidīg kāhišnīg bawēd, tā dēn ō bawandag rawāgīh ud pad-eš gēhān ō abēzagīh rasēd.[8]

The Creator Ohrmazd sends this religion not only to the Kingdom of Iran but to the whole world and to every variety [of human beings]. In the whole he has made widespread pure things, where mixed things [are found]; in *mēnōg*,[9] through the nature of a wise man, who thinks truth and speaks truth, and in *gētīg*, through doing truth; he [has made it] current in every one in such a manner that even a person who is most attached to bad religion has within him the great tenets[10] of this religion. But in order that all purity should be current in this mixture which is such, it is meet to struggle: [then] all this religion will become increased and its adversary diminished, until the religion will attain complete propagation and the world will come by that to purity.

From its style, the passage seems to be late.[11] Its contents, however, reflect good Sasanian doctrines: an active proselytizing effort appears to have prevailed in Sasanian Iran, being perhaps mainly provoked as a competition against the zealous propaganda carried on by the numerous religious movements which tried to win adherents from each other and from the official State religion. This can be seen from the inscriptions of the Sasanian kings, and especially from those of Kardēr,[12] as well as from other Pahlavi texts.[13]

8 *DkM*, p. 460, ll. 8–18; *Dk. Facs.*, pp. [359] f. (The symbol + is here used to signify that the following word has been emended.)

9 The notions of *mēnōg* and *gētīg* stand for the non-perceptible aspect of the world and the perceptible one, respectively. Cf. S. Shaked, 'The Notions *mēnōg* and *gētīg* in the Pahlavi Texts and their Relation to Eschatology', *Acta Orientalia* (in press).

10 This sentence could also be translated approximately as follows: '. . . [has within him this religion] in large quantity', or '. . . as far as its big contents are concerned [that is, merely in so far as the general outline is concerned]', taking *wuzurg-mādagīhā*, in both these possibilities, as being an adverbial phrase rather than a noun in the plural. Although syntactically it is more desirable to interpret such a form in Pahlavi as an adverb, we have here other similar forms which must be taken as plural nouns. The sense obtained in the translation offered above is more satisfactory.

11 Cf. the use of forms in *-īhā* as plurals.

12 Cf. M. Sprengling, *Third Century Iran—Sapor and Kartir*, Chicago 1953. For the Naqš-i Rajab inscription, cf. R. N. Frye, *IIJ*, VIII (1965), pp. 211–225; for Ka'ba-ye Zardušt, cf. M.-L. Chaumont, *JA*, CCXLVIII (1960), pp. 339–379; for Sar Mašhad, cf. R. N. Frye, *Harvard Journal of Asiatic Studies*, XX (1957), pp. 702–708.

13 E.g. *Pahlavi Rivâyat Accompanying the Dâdistân-î Dînîk*, ed. B. N. Dhabhar, Bombay 1913, p. 9:

If, therefore, there is any ground for talking about an esoteric element in the Zoroastrian religion of the Sasanian period, we cannot assume it to affect the open character of the religion as such (although at least one passage in contemporary Christian literature seems to complain about the secret nature of Sasanian Zoroastrianism in general).[14] It would be more natural, and perhaps more in keeping with the spirit of the period, to find evidence which shows that a certain conception or interpretation of the religion, which shows variation from the common aspect of it, was regarded as a secret. There is, indeed, convincing testimony for the existence in Iran of a conception of classes or grades of people, forming a hierarchy as respects the propagation of religious knowledge. An assembly of sayings which illustrates the general conception of a hierarchy is found in Book VI of *Dēnkard*—the gnomic part of a book which has been characterized as 'a Zoroastrian encyclopedia'.[15]

[204] u-šān ēn-ez a'ōn dāšt ku mardom 3 ēwēnag, ēwag buxt, ēwag anēraxt, ēwag ēraxt. buxt hān ke ciš az yazdān +ašnawēd ud pad kār dārēd, anēraxt hān ke az pas ī awe ke ciš ašnūd, ēraxt hān ke ⟨az⟩ dastwarān be wardēd.

[205] u-šān ēn-ez a'ōn dāšt ku mardom ēn 3 ēwēnag ō wahišt rasēnd, ēwag hān ī dānāg, ēwag hān ī dānāg-hayyār, ēwag hān ī dānāg-ne-hamēmār.

[206] u-šān ēn-ez a'ōn dāšt ku mardom ēn 3 ēwēnag, ēwag gāhānīg, ēwag haδa-mānθrīg, ēwag dādīg. awe ī gāhānīg hamīh abāg yazdān, ⟨u-š⟩ wizihīdagīh az dēwān ud druzān ⟨u-š⟩ xwāstag paymān az šām ud sūr, ud pad wināh ī kunēd šarm ud awwēnišn pādifrāh.

> ag-dēn-ē kirbag ēn meh ka az dād ī ag-dēnīh be ō weh-dēn āyēd.
>
> This is the greatest virtuous deed of a follower of evil religion: when he comes from evil religion over to the Good Religion.

Further material on the subject of proselytization among the Zoroastrians can be seen in M. N. Dhalla, *History of Zoroastrianism*, Bombay 1963, p. 325.

14 Cf. P. Bedjan (ed.), *Histoire de Mar Jabalaha, de trois autres patriarches, d'un prêtre et de deux laïques, nestoriens*, Paris–Leipzig 1895. In the story of Mar Yazīdpanāh's martyrdom, the following argument is presented in favour of the Christian religion and against that of the *mōbad*s:

> Everything that is open is truth, and what is hidden is falsehood. If, indeed, the religion of the Magi is the truth, and if they worship the true god, why do you hide your religion? If it is not the truth, why do you persecute the Christians with injustice and villany? (p. 403).

Cf. also F. Nau, *RHR*, XCV (1927), pp. 177 f.

15 Menasce, *Encyclopédie*.

ud hān ī haδa-manθrīg hamīh abāg ahlawān, u-š wizihīdagīh az druwandān, u-š xwāstag paymān hān ī frārōn kunihēd, ud pad wināh ī kunēnd aštar ī srōšōcaranām ud xrafstar ōzadan ud wad-axwān tuxtan pādifrāh.

ud hān ī dādīg hamīh abāg ērān, u-š wizihīdagīh az anērān, u-š xwāstag paymān az ⟨hān⟩ +be ku dādīhā šāyēd kardan, ud pad wināh ī kunēnd kūg zīwišn ud +nihang rōz pādifrāh.[16]

[204] They held this, too, thus: People are of three types: one is saved, one is not guilty and one is guilty. Saved is one who hears the thing from the gods and performs it; not guilty is one who follows the man who heard the thing; guilty is one who turns away from the [religious] authorities.

[205] They held this, too, thus: These three kinds of men reach paradise: one, a man who is wise; one, a man who is a helper of the wise; and one, a man who is a non-opposer of the wise.

[206] They held this, too, thus: People are of these three kinds: one, those of the *Gāθā;* one, those of the *Haδa-mānθra;* and one, those of the *Dād.*

The association of the *Gāθā* people is with the gods, their separation is from the demons and devils. The measure of their desired possession is some [?] evening and morning meals. The punishment for sins which they commit is shame and reproof.

The association of the *Haδa-mānθra* people is with the righteous and their separation is from the wicked. The measure of their desired possession is that which is done righteously. The punishment for sins which they commit is the *sraošō-čaranā* whip, the killing of reptiles and atonement through evil existence.

The association of the *Dād* people is with Iranians and their separation is from non-Iranians. The measure of their desired possession is [what issues] from what one may lawfully do. The punishment for sins which they commit is a short life and a brief day.

Each one of these three passages describes a different division of people into classes, and it is clear from this divergence that the several hierarchies do not in any way reflect generally accepted social distinctions within the

16 *DkM*, pp. 516 f.; *Dk. Facs.*, pp. [404] f. (Variants, discussions of single words and fuller references for quotations from *Dēnkard* VI are reserved for a planned edition of that text.)

community. The separation of people into groups seems here to be a figure of speech rather than a social reality.

At the same time, one may draw from these passages the safe conclusion that it was a current notion, in the period when they were composed, to regard the generality of the faithful believers and of the righteous followers of the law not as a homogeneous society of people having equal standing in religion but as consisting of a number of groups having different degrees of knowledge and obligations which they felt imposed on them for action. The emphasis in the three passages quoted is on religious practice, rather than on any form of perception, although we hear in *Dēnkard* VI, 205 of 'the wise', the highest class, to follow whom, or even not to oppose them, is a virtue. A basic distinction can also be noticed between people who 'associate' directly with gods, or 'hear a thing from them', and those who associate with other people, whatever be the precise significance of this difference.

Another passage in *Dēnkard* VI gives a threefold division of faithful Zoroastrians which is based on a different criterion:

* [70] u-šān ēn-ez a'ōn dāšt ku andēšišn ī mēnōgīg az druwandīh gāhānīgān, ud hān ī gētīgīg az duš-srawīh haδag-mānθrīgān, ud tars az puhl ud pazd ī pādixšāy dādīgān be pāyēnd.[17]

They held this, too, thus: The apprehension of *mēnōg* protects the people of the *Gāθā* from wickedness; the apprehension of *gētīg* protects the people of *Haδa-mānθra* from ill-fame. Fear protects the people of *Dād* from the punishment and chastisement of the ruler.

In this passage, the difference between the classes of believers is said to consist in the nature of their 'fear' or 'apprehension'. What a *mēnōg* or 'spiritual' type of fear implies, as opposed to *gētīg* ('material') fear, we may deduce from the type of thing from which they respectively help to save people: *mēnōg* fear is concerned with righteousness and wickedness, *gētīg* fear with the social reactions which obtain through Man's actions. The three divisions of the Avesta are a favourite device for labelling the three classes of people according to their relative position within the community. But the significance of each one of the Avestan divisions does not seem to be tightly fixed; it is used rather more as an *ad hoc* device and is adapted to the context in which it happens to occur. Thus, for example, the definition of the middle section, *Haδa-mānθra,* varies: it is easy enough to fit the *Gāθā* section, on the one hand, and

17 *DkM,* p. 485; *Dk. Facs.,* p. [377]; MS K 43, foll. 186r f.

the *Dād* section, on the other, to the dualistic division between *mēnōg* and *gētīg*, but where does the middle section belong? In the last passage quoted, it represents the approach of 'this world' (*gētīg*).[18] Another passage, in *Dēnkard* III, by contrast, firmly puts *Haδa-mānθra* on the side of *Gāθā* in the category of *mēnōg*. It has the following sentence:

[197] ēwag hān ī dādīg dād ward-pānag-ez ī abar ō haδag-mānθrīg ⟨ud⟩ gāhānīg dād ī pad-eš abēzagīh ī weh-dahišnān bawēd rāy ōstīgān-tar mehēnīdan ud waxšēnīdan.[19]

One, to enlarge and increase more firmly the law of *Dād*, even as the guardian which protects from change the law of *Haδa-mānθra* and *Gāθā*, through which is [obtained] the purity of the good creations.

The interpretation of this text in terms of *mēnōg* and *gētīg* emerges from the parallel which occurs in the following chapter of *Dēnkard* III, which gives the opposite of the above text. The passage just quoted is paraphrased as follows:

[198] ēn ī gētīg dād pad-ez ward-pānagīh ī ō hān ī mēnōg dād stāyīdan ōstīgānēnīdan waxšēnīdan.[20]

To praise, make firm and increase this law of *gētīg* even as that which guards that law of *mēnōg* from change.

Here we have contrasting opinions as to the position of *Haδa-mānθra*; but a third passage can also be quoted, in which a compromise attitude is offered. It occurs at the beginning of *Dēnkard* VIII:

[1] +ōšmurišn ī dēn ī mazdēsn bazišn 3. gāhān ī ast +abērdar mēnōg-dānišnīh mēnōg-kārīh, ud dād ī ast abērdar gētīg-dānišnīh ud gētīg-kārīh, ud haδag-mānθrīg ī ast abērdar āgāhīh ud kār ī abar hān ī miyān ⟨ī⟩ ēd 2.[21]

The division in the categories of the Mazdean religion is into three: *Gāθā*, which is principally knowledge of *mēnōg* and action of *mēnōg*; *Dād*, which is principally knowledge of *gētīg*

18 In *Dk*. VI, 206, quoted above, no attempt is made to form a correspondence between the threefold division of the Avesta and the dualistic one of the universe.

19 *DkM*, p. 212, ll. 19–22; *Dk. Facs.*, p. [166], ll. 6 f. I know of no other occurrence of the expression *ward-pānag(īh)* which is found here and in the following passage. Reading *rad pānag(īh)* is, however, less satisfactory.

20 *DkM*, p. 214, ll. 10 f.; *Dk. Facs.*, p. [167], ll. 11 f.

21 *DkM*, p. 677, ll. 11–14; *Dk. Facs.*, p. [526], ll. 12–15; cf. *SBE*, XXXVII, p. 4; Molé, *Culte*, pp. 62 f.

> and action of *gētīg;* and *Haδa-mānθra,* which is principally the awareness and action which are according to that which is between these two.

Juxtaposition of the passages shows, I believe, that the differing attributions and identifications should not be taken as literally binding statements. They do, however, bring out the fact that three basic notions of Sasanian religion are from time to time related to each other and are used on occasion to make a rhetorical point. The three sets of ideas are: the three divisions of the Avesta used as symbols; the distinction in the structure of the universe between *mēnōg* and *gētīg*; and the notion of classes of people forming a religious hierarchy.[22]

This notion of a religious hierarchy in Zoroastrianism, which can be supported by further material,[23] should be examined in connection

22 The existence of this notion of religious classes has already been noticed by the late Molé (*Culte,* pp. 26 ff., and especially pp. 61 ff.). Molé tried to apply this information to the problem of the divergence between the religion of the Achaemenids and the Zoroastrian religion as known to us from literature. According to his suggestion, the religion professed by the Achaemenid kings would be Zoroastrian, if we agree to recognize three different shapes of Zoroastrianism depending on the religious class of the individual. The Achaemenid kings would be members of the *Dād* class, and would have a code of law different from that applied to the higher classes in the religion, governed as they are by the scriptures. This solution seems, however, to oversimplify the issue. The texts do not authorize us to talk of religious classes which are socially fixed. What is more, the differences reflected in the texts between the 'classes' do not seem to affect the universal requirement to observe the precepts of the religion or to believe in the Zoroastrian doctrines. The difference would only show presumably in the level of religious experience attained by the individual, while all 'classes' adhere to the same basic code. The old Achaemenid problem, which springs from the fact that the Achaemenids had different practices, for example, in the matter of burial, must therefore be said to remain unresolved. It may be remarked in this connection that Molé's interpretation of the Gathic doctrine (to which he attributes an esoteric aspect, but without explaining his intention, on p. 70 of his book) is done almost exclusively in terms of a mystical renovation. Although his discussion contains several illuminating remarks, the approach must be regarded as a personal one.

* 23 It is evident in Iranian traditions which have been preserved in Arabic literature of the *adab* type. One important Arabic source of this kind is Miskawayh's *Jāwīdān Xirad,* the value of which has been recognized by W. B. Henning, 'Eine arabische Version mittelpersischer Weisheitsschriften', *ZDMG,* CVI (1956), pp. 72–77. A passage there reads as follows:

> وعلى العاقل ان يجعل الناس طبقتين متباينتين ويلبس لهم لباسين مختلفين . فطبقة من العامة يلبس لهم لباس انقباض وانحجاز وتحرز في كل كلمة . وطبقة من الخاصة يخلع عندهم التحرز ويلبس لهم لباس الامنة واللطف والمفاوضة . ولا يدخل في هذه الطبقة الا واحداً من الف ليكون كلهم ذوي فضل في الرأي وثقة في المودة وامانة في السرور ووفاء بالاخاء (p. 72).

with a collection of sayings, which is also found in *Dēnkard* VI, and which enjoin a hierarchy of teaching or of the diffusion of religious knowledge. The first of these passages is the following:

[55] u-šān ēn-ez a'ōn dāšt ku wāzag ō ōstwārān gōwišn ud dēn andar hamdēnān uskārišn ud kirbag ud bazag ō harw kas gōwišn.[24] *

They held this, too, thus: One ought to say the word to reliable people, to consider religion among those of the same religion, and to speak of good deeds and sins to everyone.

'Good deeds and sins' are the openest subject for discussion, 'religion' and 'the word' are progressively more confined. The term *dēn* 'religion' is ambiguous. It could, in principle, refer either to the subjective notion of religious faith or to an objective reality of religion. *Hamdēnān* would, accordingly, mean people who share the same religious attitude, who

> The wise man should treat people as two distinct classes and don two different garments for them. One class is the common folk, for whom he ought to don a garment of contraction, restraint and wariness in every word. The other class are the elect, for whom he ought to cast off wariness and don a garment of sincerity, kindness and shared discussion. Only one in a thousand is admitted into this class, so that they all possess distinction of judgment, reliability in friendship, loyalty in joy and fidelity in brotherhood.

The distinction between the common folk and the elect cannot here be interpreted in terms of a social hierarchy; it represents the tendency of forming closed *élite* groups whose opinions are kept in secret from the common folk.

A similar doctrine was, of course, also typical of the Sasanian social and political structure in general, and it served as the underlying theory behind the rigid class system in Iran. An example illustrating this point, which shows at the same time the difference between the two types of sayings, may be quoted from an Arabic source which refers to a Sasanian tradition:

> وقال بزرجمهر سوسوا احرار الناس بمحض المودة والعامة بالرغبة والرهبة والسفلة بالمخافة
> (Al-Ṭurṭūšī, *Sirāj al-Mulūk*, Cairo 1935, p. 114; a slight variant is found in Muḥ. b. 'Abdallāh al-Xaṭīb al-Iskāfī, *Luṭf al-tadbīr*, ed. A. 'Abd al-Bāqī, Cairo 1964, p. 4; Ibn Qutayba, *'Uyūn al-axbār*, Cairo 1963, I, p. 8).
>
> Buzurjmihr said: Lead the noble with sheer friendliness, common folk by desire and apprehension, and low people by terror.

This is advice given to a ruler, who should use a different method of government for each of the classes which compose society; the number of classes is here, too, given as three. The expression *aḥrār al-nās* 'free people', hence 'noblemen', seems to reflect Pahlavi *āzādān*, a word which possesses a similar ambiguity. The same doctrine is propounded in the Sasanian source preserved in the *Letter of Tansar*, cf. *Tansar's Epistle*, ed. M. Minovi, Tehran 1932, p. 18; transl. M. Boyce, Rome 1968, p. 43.

24 *DkM*, p. 483; *Dk. Facs.*, p. [375]; MS K 43, fol. 184v.

are in the same religious group. The term *wāzag* 'the word' is obscure in this context. Some further material on it can be drawn from the passage immediately following the one just quoted:

[56] u-šān ēn-ez a'ōn dāšt ku wāzag ⟨ō⟩ awe gōwišn ke wīr a'ōn ku frāz gīrēd, ud huš a'ōn ku be ne jūyēd, ud xrad a'ōn ku awe ī did weh tawān kardan.[25]

They held this, too, thus: One ought to say the word to a person who has such comprehension that he grasps it, and who has such awareness that he does not forget [?], and who has such wisdom that he is capable of doing good to his fellow.

This text defines the meaning of *ōstwārān* 'reliable people' in the previous passage. It does so in terms which are, so to speak, both intellectual and ethical: the man to be trusted ought to be one who is capable of grasping what he is told, retaining it, and putting it to good use. The three functions which are mentioned in the passage are defined in their turn in a text which comes not long after the one just quoted, and which shows the consistency with which the terms are used in the text:

[64] u-šān ēn-ez a'ōn dāšt ku wīr kār ēd ciš xwāstan, ud huš kār ēd ganzwarīh kardan ud ciš ī wīr xwāhēd nigāh dāštan, ud xrad kār ēd wizīdārīh kardan ud weh ud wattar šnāxtan ud hān ī weh kardan ud hān ī wattar hištan.[26]

They held this, too, thus: The work of comprehension is this, to be a treasurer and to guard the thing which comprehension seeks. The work of wisdom is this, to discriminate, to recognize the good and the evil, to do that which is good and to abandon that which is evil.

The basic intellectual accent of all three functions emerges from this passage with particular emphasis. This is not contradicted by the fact that *xrad* 'wisdom' is here described as being concerned with discriminations of ethical character, such as must be put into practice.[27]

25 *DkM*, p. 483; *Dk. Facs.*, p. [375]; MS K 43, fol. 184v.

26 *DkM*, p. 484; *Dk. Facs.*, p. [376]; MS K 43, fol. 185v.

27 The concept of *xrad* 'wisdom' is particularly closely connected to religious and ethical practice. This is evident in the work entitled *Mēnōg ī Xrad*, but also in such sayings as the following from *Dēnkard* VI:

[C 83] ēn-ez paydāg ku ēdōn ce'ōn zamīg kadag ī āb ud āb pērāyag ī warz ud warz abzāyišn ī gēhān ud az-eš be bar dāštārīh ī kišwar, ēdōn-ez dānāgīh kadag ī wehīh ud wehīh tan ī xrad ud xrad abzāyēnīdār ī gēhān (*DkM*, p. 567; *Dk. Facs.*, p. [448]).

The text of *Dēnkard* VI, 55, quoted above, should be associated with another passage in the same book, where the terms used are more explicit. This text has a hierarchy of a similar nature:

[254] u-šān ēn-ez a'ōn dāšt ku āštīh ud mihr andar harw dām dahišn, kirbag ō harw kas gōwišn, ud zand pad šabestān cāšišn, ud rāz ō ōstwārān gōwišn. ud srōšīgīh ud dādestānīgīh andar anjaman dārišn, ud rāmišn andar myazd gāh, ud yazišn ī yazdān pad škōyišn kunišn.[28]

They held this, too, thus: One should instruct[29] peace and love in every creature, speak good deeds to every person, teach *Zand* in the household,[30] and tell the secret to reliable people. One should keep obedience and lawfulness in the assembly, joy in the place of the *myazd* [ritual], and perform the worship of the gods in confinement (?).[31]

The passage consists of two series of sentences which must originally have been separate. The two parts of the passage consist each of a rising hierarchy. The first section has the series 'peace and love', 'good deeds', '*Zand*' and 'secret' (*rāz*, perhaps better translated as 'mystery'). The three items that follow are only joined to the first series artificially: in themselves they form another hierarchy, which again begins with the most open and exoteric item: 'obedience and lawfulness', which are

This, too, is manifest: In the same way as the earth is the abode of water, and water is the ornament of husbandry, and husbandry is the increase of the world, and the fruit from it is the preservation of the climes — so also knowledge is the abode of goodness, and goodness is the body of wisdom, and wisdom is that which furthers the world.

28 *DkM*, p. 528; *Dk. Facs.*, p. [416]; MS K 43, fol. 202v.

29 The word *dahišn* 'instruction, knowledge' is to be discussed separately. The reading of the Copenhagen manuscript is *dārišn*, which is also possible; *dahišn*, however, besides being a *lectio difficilior* in the sense suggested here, fits better as it forms part of a series of verbs which all denote verbal communication.

30 The word *šabestān* means literally 'sleeping quarters, harem'. It occurs in such a meaning in the story 'Xusrau ī Kawādān ud Rēdag', *PhlT*, p. 33, § 63 (cf. M. J. Unvala, *The Pahlavi Text 'King Husrav and His Boy'*, Paris [no date], p. 29; Bailey, *Zor. Pr.*, p. 114, n.); *PhlT*, p. 35, § 100 (Unvala, *ibid.*, p. 36): *bārag ī šabestānīg* 'the riding beast of the *šabestān*'. *Šabestān* is also the title of a dignity; cf. *PhlT*, p. 20, § 18 (?); *PhlT*, p. 85, § 1. For the occurrences of this title on seals and in Persian and Parthian inscriptions (Ka'ba-ye Zardušt, where the Greek equivalent is εὐνοῦχος); cf. W. B. Henning, *Handbuch der Orientalistik*, Part I, Volume IV: *Iranistik*, I, Leiden–Cologne 1958, p. 45.

31 The meaning of *škōyišn* (or *škandišn*?) can only be guessed from the contexts in which it occurs. Cf. *Dk.* VI, 240, 254, C 83e; *DkM*, p. 206, l. 10; R. C. Zaehner, *BSOS*, IX (1937–1939), p. 315.

held in the 'assembly', that is, in public; this is followed by 'joy', which is restricted to the specific ritual mentioned (and perhaps to those entitled to take part in it, for example, priests); and the series is concluded with 'the worship of the gods' which apparently must be done in private. The difference between the two hierarchies appears to be that the first consists of a set of pious actions which involve some relationship with other people, particularly through the communication of religious knowledge on various levels, whereas the second enumerates three modes of worship or attitudes towards the gods. The first series rises, therefore, from the universal to the extremely restricted circle of people, the second moves from the 'assembly' to the private.

If we then take the first set of sentences by itself and confront it with the series contained in *Dēnkard* VI, 55–56, we gain a much more definite idea of the mode and meaning of the restrictions imposed on the dissemination of certain aspects of the faith. The one point which must again be stressed is that the hierarchies which occur here are not 'institutional'; they are not part of the structure of society. This is plain from the fact that the division in *Dēnkard* VI, 55 is into three levels, and there are four levels in *Dēnkard* VI, 254.[32] We cannot, therefore, expect to find literal parallels between the two texts, but the correspondence is nevertheless close and enlightening. The first item of *Dēnkard* VI, 254 does not occur in VI, 55, but the other three can be easily compared:

Dk. VI, 254	*Dk*. VI, 55
(a) āštīh ud mihr andar harw dām dahišn	(a) —
(b) kirbag ō harw kas gōwišn	(b) kirbag ud bazag ō harw kas gōwišn
(c) zand pad šabestān cāšišn	(c) dēn andar ham-dēnān uskārišn
(d) rāz ō ōstwārān gōwišn	(d) wāzag ō ōstwārān gōwišn
(a) instruction of peace and love in every creature	(a) —
(b) speaking of good deeds to every person	(b) speaking of good deeds and sins to every person
(c) teaching of *Zand* in the household	(c) consideration of religion among those of the same religion
(d) telling *rāz* to reliable people	(d) telling the word to reliable people

32 This is not an important difference, admittedly; the first item in *Dk*. VI, 254, can be disregarded, as it does not refer to human society.

The comparison is particularly striking in the last two items, where we notice the juxtaposition of *Zand*/*dēn* and the illuminating parallel of *rāz*/*wāzag*.

Leaving aside for the moment the latter pair, we notice that a grave restriction affects the teaching of *Zand*, the commentary on and interpretation of the sacred scriptures. This restriction is described by the Arabic writer al-Bīrūnī in the following terms: *

> Knowledge of what is in the Avesta, brought by him [scil. by Zoroaster?], is only released to a person from among them [that is, from among the Zoroastrians] whose religion is trusted and whose [religious] manner is praised by people of their [= the Zoroastrian] religion. That [knowledge] is only expanded before him after a certificate has been written for him which can be brought as evidence concerning the release of that [knowledge] to him by masters of the religion.[33]

33 وليس يطلق علم مـا في الابستا الذي جـاء به الا لرجل منهم يوثق بدينه وتحمد طريقته عند اصحاب دينهـم ولا يوسّـع له في ذلـك الا بعد ان يكتب له سجل يحتج به في اطلاق ارباب الدين ذلـك له (J. Fück, 'Sechs Ergänzungen zu Sachaus Ausgabe von al-Bīrūnis "Chronologie Orientalischer Völker" ', in: J. Fück (ed.), *Documenta Islamica Inedita*, Berlin 1952, p. 76).

The *Letter of Tansar* also mentions as one of the main crimes for which a man is to be punished the act of employing 'in the religion' unlawful interpretations (*dar dīn ta'vīlha-yi nā-mašrū' nihad;* ed. M. Minovi [cf. above, n. 23], p. 22; transl. M. Boyce, p. 47).

Similar statements in Mas'ūdī:

وجمع اهل مملكته على دين المجوسية ومنعهم النظر والخلاف والحجاج في الملل (*Murūj al-Dhahab*, ed. Y. A. Dāghir, Beirut 1965, I, p. 290).

> He [scil. Anūšarwān] incorporated the entire population of his kingdom into the Magian religion and prevented them from reflection, controversy and polemics concerning sects.

In Tha'ālibī: ومنـع من تعلمه العـامة (*Histoire des rois des Perses*, ed. H. Zotenberg, Paris 1900 [reprint Tehran 1963]) 'and the common folk were barred from learning it [scil. Zoroaster's book of revelation]'.

Al-'Āmirī apparently possesses a similar historical tradition when he tries to explain why the Persians, although intelligent by nature, had never attained to the knowledge of the good religion. One of the two reasons for this, according to him, is the fact that the *mōbad*s prevented the people by force from obtaining Divine Wisdom. As a second reason al-'Āmirī gives the enslavement of the people to their rulers. 'There is no doubt', he says, 'that the subjugation [read: *tasxīr*] of a freeborn intelligent person . . . , and pushing him away from the acquisition of the highest aim and from desiring, through expending his effort, to reach the high rank and dignity which he desires, are [acts of] the utmost humiliation and vileness [read: . . . *ilā mā yatamannāhu min al-jāhi wa-l-'uluwwi huwa l-ġāyatu min al-ittiḍā'i wa-l-xissati*]'. Cf. text in J.C. Vadet, 'Le souvenir de l'ancienne Perse chez le philosophe Abū l-Ḥasan al-'Āmirī (m. 381 H.)', *Arabica*, XI (1964), p. 262.

It is possible to assume that the expression 'knowledge of what is in the Avesta' refers to the understanding, or interpretation, of the Avesta, and not necessarily to the text of the Avesta itself. If this assumption is correct, it is interesting to note the expression *yūθaqu bi-dīnihi* '[a man] whose religion is trusted', which can be taken as an echo of the Pahlavi term *ham-dēn* 'a man who shares the same religion', in *Dēnkard* VI, 55. It is also noteworthy that al-Bīrūnī mentions a written certificate (*sijill*) which must be issued to a man before he is entitled to have the knowledge revealed to him. This detail is not corroborated from other sources.

The reason for the restriction on the teaching of *Zand* can be explained by reference to the Arabic historian al-Mas'ūdī, who gives the following information in a much-quoted passage:

> In the days of Mani the name *'Zindaqa'* appeared . . . in the following manner: When Zoroaster son of Spitama . . . brought the Persians their book, known as Avesta, written in the first language of Persian, and he made a commentary [*tafsīr*] for it, which is the *Zand,* and to this commentary he made an interpretation [*šarḥ*], which he called *Pāzand* as we said before, *Zand* being an explanation in order to interpret that which was revealed earlier; if anyone came forth in their religion with something which contradicted the revealed message, which is the Avesta, and deviated towards the interpretation, which is the *Zand,* they [the Persians] would say: 'He is a *Zandī,'* using an attribute related to the interpretation, alluding to the fact that he has strayed from the manifest matters which derive from that which is revealed towards an interpretation which is contradictory to the revelation.[34]

Despite the attempts made to interpret the relationship between Avesta and *Zand* in a different manner,[35] there is no reason to doubt the basic accuracy of the information given here, viz., that *Zand* was the inter-

34 Mas'ūdi, *op. cit.* (above, n. 33), p. 275.

35 S. Wikander, *Feuerpriester in Kleinasien und Iran,* Lund 1946, pp. 125 ff., esp. 140 ff.; followed by J. C. Tavadia, *Die mittelpersische Sprache und Literatur der Zarathustrier*, Leipzig 1956, pp. 24–27; G. Widengren, *Die Religionen Irans,* pp. 245 ff. The question is complicated by the additional problem whether the Avesta existed as a written book in the Sasanian period; cf. F. Nau, 'Etude historique sur la transmission de l'Avesta et sur l'époque probable de sa dernière rédaction', *RHR,* XCV (1927), pp. 149–199; H. S. Nyberg, *Journal of the K. R. Cama Oriental Institute,* XXXIX (1958), pp. 21 ff.; Bailey, *Zor. Pr.,* pp. 149 ff.; Duchesne-Guillemin, *Religion,* pp. 40 ff. The relationship between Avesta and *Zand* is explained in *Dēnkard* III, 204 as that of a text and its interpretation; see Appendix A.

pretation of the Avesta, and that *Pāzand* was a way of rendering this interpretation more intelligible.[36]

It is interesting to note that *Zand* was attributed to Zoroaster himself, while, in the same breath and in an apparently self-contradictory manner, the interpretation is taken to go against the revelation. This muddle in presenting the interpretation of *zandīq*[37] strengthens the feeling that it was not produced by the Islamic author, but that it forms part of his Iranian source, which he merely renders as he received it.

The important point to be gleaned from Mas'ūdī, viz., that *Zand* or the interpretation of the Holy Scriptures was considered to be the main tool of heretics, finds full support in the Zoroastrian literature. A passage in *Dēnkard* VI says:

[C 26] ēn-ez ēdōn: zand kār ud dādestān juttar ne gōwišn ud kunišn ud rāyēnišn ce'ōn hān ī pōryōtkēšān ⟨guft ud⟩ kard ud cāšt ud ul āwurd. ce-š ahlamōgīh pad-eš ō gēhān āyēd ke zand kār ud dādestān juttar cāšēd ud gōwēd ud kunēd ce'ōn hān ī pōryōtkēšān guft ud kard ud cāšt ud ul āwurd.[38]

This, too, thus: One ought not to speak, do or arrange the business of *Zand* differently from what the original orthodox [spoke,] did, taught and brought forth. For heresy comes to the world by one who teaches, speaks or does the business of *Zand* differently from what the orthodox spoke, did, taught and brought forth.

The warning given here specifies that a free manipulation of *Zand*, which does not faithfully reproduce the received *Zand* of old, opens

36 Thus also al-Bīrūnī in connection with the Mazdakites: لان زند هو التفسير عندهم وبايزند هو التاويل (J. Fück, *op. cit.*, above, n. 33, p. 79); Mas'ūdī, *Al-Tanbīh wa-l Išrāf*, ed. M. J. de Goeje, Leiden 1894 (reprint Beirut 1965), pp. 91 f.

37 On the term *zandīq, zindīq*, cf. H. H. Schaeder, *Iranische Beiträge*, I, Halle 1930, pp. 274 ff.; Menasce, *Apologétique*, pp. 228–244; idem, *Encyclopédie*, pp. 66 f.; Molé, *Oriens*, XIII/XIV (1960–1961), pp. 1–11; O. Klíma, *Mazdak*, Prague 1957, pp. 201–203. For the 'Abbasid period cf. G. Vajda, 'Les zindiqs en pays d'Islam au début de la période abbaside', *RSO*, XVII (1938), pp. 173–229. In the pre-Islamic period the term was applied to followers of Mazdak; Ibn Sa'īd, *Našwat al-Ṭarab*, quoted in: M. J. Kister, 'Al-Ḥīra', *Arabica*, XV (1968), p. 145. 'Abd al-Jabbār describes how Mani used the interpretation *(tafsīr)* of the Avesta so as to delude people into believing him to be the Messenger of Light; cf. S. Pines, 'The Jewish Christians of the Early Centuries of Christianity According to a New Source', *Proceedings of the Israel Academy of Sciences and Humanities*, Vol. II, No. 13, Jerusalem 1966, pp. [67] f.

38 *DkM*, p. 558; *Dk. Facs.*, p. [441]; MS K 43, fol. 231v.

up the danger of heresy. This passage is followed by two others,[39] which warn particularly against learning the Avesta and *Zand* from wicked people and teaching it to them.[40] By discussing the Avesta and *Zand* with wicked people one is likely to put weapons in their hands, with which they can attack the religion from within, and by learning from them one is liable to be influenced by heretical opinions. Fear of heretics is so considerable that people are enjoined not to enter into controversy with them, apart from a person in a position of religious authority, whose duty it is to conduct a polemic.[41]

As the peculiarity of the danger of heresy is that it threatens from within, it is possible to envisage the Avesta and *Zand* as constituting a barrier against it, in so far as knowledge of these texts can be kept from people who are suspect of heretical leanings.[42]

Although there was seen to be a danger in disseminating either Avesta or *Zand* indiscriminately, the danger was considered to be greater with regard to *Zand*. An explicit injunction is contained in the *Zand ī Wahman Yasn*, and is characteristically connected to the story of Mazdak:

39 *Dk*. VI, C27–C28 = *DkM*, pp. 558 f.; *Dk. Facs.*, p. [441]; MS K 43, foll. 231v f.

40 In a similar vein we have in *DkM*, p. 834, ll. 19–21:

> andarz ī ō mardomān abar pahrēz ī az pasīh ī awe ī ahlamōg, ne niyōšīdan ud ne xwāstan ī az-eš +dahišn ī abastāg ud zand.
>
> An advice to men to beware of following a heretic: not to hear and not to seek from him the instruction of Avesta and *Zand*.

Cf. also Molé, *Culte*, pp. 216 f. The same idea also occurs in the Pahlavi interpretation of *Yasna* xxxi:18 (cf. Molé, *loc. cit.*).

41 *Dk*. VI, 231 = *DkM*, p. 523; *Dk. Facs.*, p. [411].

42 Cf. the following text in *Dēnkard* VI:

> [215] u-šān ēn-ez a'ōn dāšt ku dēn 7 parisp ast, az-ešān hān ī bēdom mānθr ud zand.
>
> [216] u-šān ēn-ez a'ōn dāšt ku kas-ez nēst ke ēn dēn petyārag-tar hēnd ce'ōn hān ī ahlamōg ce +jud az hān ī ahlamōgān kas-ez nēst +ke +tar ī parisp ast ī +az be-z ō dēn bēdom andar tawān āmadan, awe ī ahlamōg pad jām ī mānθrbarīh tar ī parisp ī bēdom andar āmad, ast ī +az be-z ō dēn xwadīh ud nazdīh rasēd (*DkM*, p. 519; *Dk. Facs.*, p. [407]).
>
> [215] They held this, too, thus: Religion consists of seven walls. The farthest out among them is the sacred word and the *Zand*.
>
> [216] They held this, too, thus: There is no one who is a more serious opponent to the religion than the heretic. For apart from heretics there is no one at the other side of the wall who can come from the outside into the farthest end of religion. The heretic came inside across the farthest wall, wearing the garment of a carrier of the holy word. There are some who come from the outside into the [very] selfness and nearness of religion.

> ēw bār gujastag mazdak ī bāmdādān dēn petyārag ō paydāgīh āmad. u-šān petyārag pad dēn ⟨ī⟩ yazdān kard. hān anōšag-ruwān xusrō [. . .] may-⁺windādān, ud weh-šāpūr, ⁺ud[?] dād-ōhrmazd ī ādurbādagān dastwar, ud ādur-farn-bag ī a-drōg, ud ādurbād ud ādurmihr ud baxt-āfrīd ō pēš xwāst, u-š paymān az-eš xwāst ku ēn yasnīhā pad nihān ma dārēd, be pad paywand ī šmāh zand ma cāšēd. awēšān andar xusrō paymān kard.[43]

> At one time the opposition to the religion of Mazdak, son of Bāmdād, became manifest. They presented opposition to the religion of the gods. Khusrau of Immortal Soul called to his presence [. . .] son of May-Windād, Weh-Šāpūr, Dād-Ohrmazd, the religious authority of Azerbaijan, Adurfarnbag the non-liar, Ādurbād, Ādurmihr, and Baxt-Āfrīd. He asked them to give him a promise, saying: 'Do not keep these *Yasnas* in secret. Do not teach *Zand* outside your kinsmen.' They gave Khusrau the promise.

That knowledge of *Zand* was in effect more restricted than knowledge of the Avesta, at least in the ninth century, is seen from two passages of the *Dādestān ī Dēnīg,* where questions which concern technical points of ritual are raised. The situation described is one of an *ērbad* who knows by heart both Avesta and *Zand,* as opposed to a *hāwišt,* who has only the Avesta but no *Zand.*[44] At the same time, it should

43 *ZWY* ii:1–4 (p. 5). The first name may perhaps be read May-Windādān Weh-Šāpūr, with the patronymic preceding the person's name; in that case no omission need be postulated. On the text cf. the remarks by J. C. Tavadia, *Die mittelpersische Sprache und Literatur der Zarathustrier,* Leipzig 1956, pp. 122 f. K. Czeglédy, *Acta Orient. Hung.,* VIII (1958), pp. 34 f., would regard the restriction on the teaching of *Zand* mentioned in this passage as a characteristic feature of apocalyptic literature. It seems, however, to reflect the injunction of *Yašt* iv:9.

44 See *Dd.,* Questions XLIV–LXV (below, Appendix B).
Very interesting instructions are found in Saddar Nasr:

> īnki bihdīnān-rā mī-bāyad ki xaṭṭ-i avastā bi-āmōzand pēš-i hērbadān va ōstādān tā dar xᵛāndan-i niyāyiš va yašt xaṭā na-ravad (Chap. 98).

> It is incumbent on believers in the Good Religion to learn the script of the Avesta so that they may not make errors in the recitation of the *Niyāyiš* and the *Yašt.*

> īnki mōbadān va dastūrān va radān va hērbadān rā na-šāyad ki hama kas rā pahlavī āmōzand. ki zartušt az hōrmizd pursīd ki pahlavī āmōxtan mar kasān rā šāyad. hōrmizd ba-afzōnī javāb dād ki har ki az nasl-i tu bāšad mōbad va dastūr va hērbad-ē ki xiradmand bāšad, dīgar hēč kas rā na-šāyad juz az īnki gufta-am. agar dīgarān rā āmōzad ō-rā 'aẓīm gunāh bāšad. agar bisyār kār kirfa karda bāšad farjām-i ō-rā ba-dōzax buvad (Chap. 99).

not be supposed that either Avesta or *Zand* was really held in great secrecy: priests chant them loudly in the open while doing their work,[45] and texts state that Avesta and *Zand* must be taught widely in the world.[46] We even read of the *Zand* as being more widespread than the Avesta.[47] The duty of going to the *ērbadestān,* the religious school,

> It is not allowed to *mōbad*s, *dastwar*s, *rad*s and *hērbad*s to teach Pahlavi to all people. Zoroaster asked Ohrmazd: Is it allowed to teach Pahlavi to people? Ohrmazd answered with bounty, [it is allowed to teach it] to every person who is of your descendants, a *mōbad,* a *dastwar* and a *hērbad* who is endowed with wisdom. It is not allowed [to teach it] to any person apart from what I said. If one teaches it to other people, it will be a great sin to one; even if that person does many virtuous deeds, his end will be in hell.

The Pahlavi script was perhaps meant to be a cryptography; cf. P. Peeters, *Recherches d'histoire et de philologie orientales,* I, Brussels 1951, pp. 191 f.

45 Cf. *Dk.* VI, D3, D5 = *DkM,* pp. 569 f., 571 f.

46

> ēdōn weh guft ōhrmazd ō spitāmān zardušt ku be xwān ud warm be kun, pad zand ud pāzand wizārišn be cāš, ō ērbadān ud hāwištān gōw, ud pad gēhān frāz gōwēnd (*ZWY* iv:67 [p. 37]).

> Thus spoke Ohrmazd well to Zoroaster son of Spitama: Read and memorize, teach the interpretation by *Zand* and *Pāzand,* say it to the *ērbad*s and *hāwišt*s, and they shall speak it forth in the world.

The opening words to *Dēnkard* VIII, which contains a summary of the Avesta, make the following statement:

> haštom abar hangerdīgīh ī hān ī andar naskīhā ī dēn ī mazdēsn jud jud ēdar ayād. hān ī andar šādurwān ī ēn nāmag abar ōšmarišn ī weh-dēn ō āgāhīh ī wasān nibišt ud niwēgēnīd az zand, hān ī dēn, pad āgāh-dahišnīh ī ō ēd pādram dastwar, pad xwad ēwāz ī dēn nibišt (*DkM,* p. 677, ll. 2–7; *Dk. Facs.,* p. [526]; cf. Molé, *Culte,* pp. 61 f.).

> The Eighth [book]; a summary of that which occurs in the *nask*s of the Mazdean religion. A memory of each one separately is [found] here. That which is found within the binding of this book concerning the categories of the Good Religion, was written for the knowledge of the many and was communicated from the *Zand,* which is the religion. It was written as an authority for teaching knowledge to this mass of people, by the word of religion itself.

The phrase *pad zand, hān ī dēn* may refer to the fact that the technical term *andar dēn* serves to introduce a quotation from *Zand.*

47 In an answer to a query of a Christian, Buxt-Mahrē, the wonder of the Avesta is extolled, and it is stated that it goes beyond the comprehension of men. Of the *Zand* we read in the answer:

> ud zand pad ēwēnag-ē guft ēstēd pad miyān ī gēhān rawāg-tar ud andar gēhān āšnāg-tar ⟨az⟩ xwad abastāg (*DkM,* p. 459, ll. 11–12; *Dk. Facs.,* p. [359]; cf. Bailey, *Zor. Pr.,* p. 162).

> *Zand* has been said to serve as a mirror [of the Avesta]. It is more current in the world and better known in the world than the Avesta itself.

there to learn the *Zand,* it is said, falls on every one who lives in this world.[48]

The restrictions of teaching which we have quoted so far are generally not such as to give Zoroastrianism the character of an esoteric religion. They are merely measures taken out of caution and self-defence. They were evidently not universally observed. Nevertheless, our previous quotations have indicated that, besides the general and public religion, or probably within it, there was a certain element which was to be confined to a small group of reliable people.[49] In the passages quoted, this element was designated by the words *rāz* and *wāzag,* and it was seen to be more restricted than the *Zand.* The word *rāz* is used several times in the Pahlavi books in connection with a group of religious mysteries, which seem to be usually related to the fields of creation and eschatology as well as to the knowledge of the proper way of fighting the demons.[50] It should, however, be remarked that this word does not necessarily designate in many of its occurrences a secret piece of knowledge or a doctrine which must be kept hidden; it seems often to denote a hidden cause, a latent factor, a connection which is not immediately evident. Such is the use of the term, for example, when it is said that the 'secret' why the Jews rest on the Sabbath is the fact that God rested on the seventh day of creation.[51]

Armed with these observations, one may perhaps try to guess at the contents of the secret mentioned in the passages of *Dēnkard* VI, where its teaching was restricted to those who are 'reliable'. What follows is an attempt to form a correlation between this idea of a restricted teaching of one part or aspect of the religion and the structure of Sasanian theology, as it is reflected in the Pahlavi texts, and especially in the *Dēnkard.* It seems fairly certain, at any rate, that the popular view of the Zoroastrian religion, as far as it can be reconstructed from the texts, Iranian and foreign, and from archaeological monuments, differed quite con-

48 ce harw ke andar gētīg and-cand yašt-ē kardan ud wināh ī andar dast ud pāy be dānistan abāyēd be ke karr ayāb gung ēnyā. ne pādixšāy be ka kunihēd ēn-ez, ērbadestān be kardan ud zand be dānistan (*PhlT,* p. 46, §33).

For every one in this world, except one who is blind or deaf, ought to perform so many *yašt* and to know the sins which are in the hand and foot. But one is not capable of that unless this, too, is done: to attend the *ērbadestān* and to know the *Zand.*

49 The existence of secret doctrines, or of restrictions in the dissemination of religious truths, can already be noticed in certain Avestic texts. Cf. *Yasna* xlviii: 3; *Yašt* iv: 9 and xiv: 46. *

50 On *rāz,* see Appendix C.

51 See the text of *ŠGV* xiii: 14, quoted in Appendix C §XI.

siderably from the theological conception. It may, therefore, be plausible to assume that certain parts of this theological conception were deemed unsuitable for general propagation among simple believers.

Apart from the ethical dualism which characterized it, Zoroastrianism was also marked by a dualism of a different kind, which affected its view of the world. The twin concepts in this cosmological dualism are *mēnōg* and *gētīg,* the former term designating the non-material, largely invisible, world, the latter the sensible and visible aspect. From the point of view of creation, *mēnōg* is primary and *gētīg* derivative, the second having been formed from the first, which served as a prototype for the creation of the material world. The *gētīg* world is dependent on *mēnōg* in the sense that it is foreshadowed by it and also in the sense that *mēnōg* elements cause the *gētīg* world to move and live and that *mēnōg* powers can come at will and clothe themselves in *gētīg* forms. The existence of *gētīg* is, at the same time, essential for the conception of the world, because the fight between the two great deities, good and evil, cannot take place and cannot be ultimately decided except on the plane of *gētīg; mēnōg* serves at this stage, in its turn, as a reflection of what goes on in *gētīg,* as, for example, in the fact that, in the final judgment of the individual, his *gētīg* ethical self is reflected by a *mēnōg* figure, *dēn.* The two notions are thus seen to be intertwined and mutually dependent to a large degree.[52]

One of the interesting points about this theological conception of Zoroastrianism is the statement that Ahreman and the powers of evil have their existence only in *mēnōg; gētīg* is a world which belongs entirely to Ohrmazd and his host, although it has been contaminated and made imperfect by the intrusion of evil. This point is also attested by the fact that Ahreman has his holding in this *gētīg* world only in so far as he is present, parasitically as it were, in the minds of some people. He can be removed from this world by making all people renounce him.[53] The gods themselves, to whom the whole material world belongs, appear to exist mainly as abstract qualities which can be realized by good people in their daily life (and which are apparently also visible in fires, plants, perhaps also water and other manifestations of the elements). Their presence in this world seems to hang largely on the effort and striving of *gētīg* beings. The highest aim of the good man in

52 These observations on *mēnōg* and *gētīg* are a summary of some of the conclusions reached in the study devoted to these concepts (see above, n.9).

53 On this question see S. Shaked, 'Ahreman, the Evil Spirit, and his Creation', in: *Studies in Mysticism and Religion, Presented to G. Scholem,* Jerusalem 1967, pp. 227–234.

his life is to become united to the gods, a goal to be reached by developing in oneself the qualities and powers which represent the gods within oneself.[54] Some extracts from the texts in *Dēnkard* VI may be quoted to illustrate this point:

[236] u-šān ēn-ez a'ōn dāšt ku xīr ī yazdān hagrez pad menišn az-eš be ne ēstēd, ud a'ōn abar ēstišn ku hān ī abārōn ciš hagrez pad menišn ne menīdan. +ce ōš (ī) mardomān andar harw zaman zaman frāz rasēd, ud bīm +ēwāz pad hān gāh ī ka ōš frāz rasēd ēg mard ciš ī abārōn hamē +menēd, ōh-ez pēš ī +hān mard frārōn-kunišn bawēd ēg ruwān-dušmen be bawēd. ce hamē tā mard kirbag ud ahlāyīh menēd ēg yazd andar tan (andar tan) mānēnd ud dēwān staw bawēnd ud be šawēnd, ud ka ciš ī abārōn menēd ēg dēw andar ō tan dwārēnd. . .[55]

They held this, too, thus: Never depart from the things of the gods in your thought. One should stand upon them in such a way that one never thinks a sinful thing in one's thought. For death comes to men at every hour, but fear comes only at that time when, upon the coming of death, the man thinks a sinful thing. Thus, before that man becomes a doer of righteous deeds he becomes an enemy of the soul. For as long as a man thinks good deeds and righteousness, the gods remain in his body and the demons become stupefied and depart, and when he thinks a sinful thing the demons rush into his body. . .

The impression that one gets from this passage is that the effort of a righteous man during his life is dedicated to the task of providing a hospitable abode for the gods in his body. The whole good effort can come to naught at any moment through his failure to ward off the sinful thoughts which come flocking to him constantly, and this may encourage the demons to rush into his body. The fear alluded to in this passage is the fear of judgment after death. The conclusion which can be drawn from this passage is formulated in a positive manner in *Dēnkard* VI in the following injunction:

[20] u-šān hān ciš ēn guft ⟨ku⟩ ke yazdān dōst-ē bawēd hagrez menišn az dōstīh ī yazdān be ne +wisānēd.[56]

They said this [concerning] that thing: He who becomes a friend of the gods never separates his thought from the friendship of the gods.

54 This aspect of Zoroastrian theology is to be treated separately.

55 *DkM*, pp. 524 f.; *Dk. Facs.*, pp. [412] f.

56 *DkM*, p. 476; *Dk. Facs.*, p. [370]; MS K 43, fol. 180r.

The type of religion advocated by these and similar texts is one which is based on constant meditation and devotion to the gods, and this is ultimately believed to bring about close and intimate relationship between man and the gods.[57]

The degree of identification which a righteous man can attain with the gods is probably higher than that which can be guessed from these quotations. The following passage, also in *Dēnkard* VI, should be considered in this connection:

[77] u-šān ēn-ez a'ōn dāšt ku kas-ez mardom nēst ke az mād zāyēd u-š ēn 6 mēnōg abar ne kōšēnd: wahman ud akōman, srōš ud xešm, spandarmad ud druz ī tarōmad.

[78] u-šān ēn-ez a'ōn dāšt ku ke wahman pad tan mehmān ēg-eš ēn daxšag ku taftīg bawēd pad kirbag ud hu-paywand bawēd abāg wehān ud +hugar bawēd pad āštīh ud ne-angadīhān [?] jādag-gōwīh, ud xwad rād bawēd. ud ke akōman pad tan mehmān ēg-eš ēn daxšag ku absard bawēd pad kirbag ud duš-paywand bawēd abāg wehān ud dušwār bawēd ⟨pad⟩ āštīh kardan ud ne-angadīh [?] petyārag ud xwad ⟨pan⟩ bawēd.

ud ke srōš pad tan mehmān ēg-eš daxšag ēn ku andar harw gāh saxwan abāg šāyēd guftan ud ka gōwēnd ōh niyōšēd ud ka āhōg abāz gōwēnd padīrēd ud wirāyēd ud kasān rāy drōg ne gōwēd ud hān ī +ōh abē-wināh ne zanēd ud hān ī wināhgār pad paymān zanēd. ud ke xešm pad tan mehmān ēg-eš daxšag ēn ku harw gāh ciš ne šāyēd abāg guftan ud ka gōwēnd ne niyōšēd ud ka kōdag-ez āhōg-ez gōwēnd ēg-eš āhīd bawēd ud ne wirāyēd ud kasān rāy drōg was gōwēd ud hān ī abē-wināh was zanēd.

ud ke spandarmad pad tan mehmān ēg-eš daxšag ēn ku bawandag-menišn bawēd u-š ka sārēnēnd ne sārihēd u-š ka was-ez pad xīr ī gētīg bahr abar rasēd ēg-ez az xīr ī yazdān be ne wardēd ud kirbag pādāšn az mēnōgān xwāhēd ne az gētīgān. ud ke druz ī tarōmad pad tan mehmān ēg-eš daxšag ēn ku sabuk-menišn bawēd u-š ka sārēnēnd sārihēd u-š ka andak-ez pad xīr ī gētīg bahr rasēd ēg-ez az +xīr ī yazdān be ēstēd ud kirbag pādāšn az gētīgān xwāhēd ne az mēnōgān.[58]

[77] They held this, too, thus: There is not one man born of a mother over whom these six spirits do not wage war: Wahman ['Good

57 Cf. *Dk*. VI, 221 f. = *DkM*, p. 520; *Dk. Facs.*, pp. [408] f.; and *Dk*. VI, E1 = *DkM*, p. 575; *Dk. Facs.*, p. [455].

58 *DkM*, pp. 487 f.; *Dk. Facs.*, pp. [378] f.; MS K43, foll. 187v–188v.

Mind'] and Akōman ['Bad Mind']; Srōš ['Obedience'] and Xešm ['Anger']; Spandarmad ['Humility'] and the demon Tarōmad ['Arrogance'].

[78] They held this, too, thus: A man whose body is inhabited by Wahman this is his mark. He is ardent as regards good works, is well-connected with good people, is easy in [making] peace, with regard to people devoid of wealth he [practises] intercession, by himself he is generous. He whose body is inhabited by Akōman this is his mark. He is cool as regards good works, has bad relation with good people, is difficult in making peace, is an adversary of those who have no wealth, by himself he is [avaricious].

He whose body is inhabited by Srōš this is his mark. It is possible to talk to him everywhere, when he is talked to he listens, when he is told of a fault he accepts and corrects it, he does not tell a lie to people, he does not chastise an innocent person, and he chastises a sinful person with measure. He whose body is inhabited by Xešm this is his mark. It is not possible to talk to him at any place, when he is talked to he does not listen, when he is told of even a small fault he is offended and does not correct it, he tells many lies to people, and he inflicts much chastisement on an innocent person.

He whose body is inhabited by Spandarmad this is his mark. He has reverence, when he is incited he is not aroused, even when a large share falls to him from the things of this world he does not turn away from the things of the gods, he desires the reward of good deeds from the spirits, not from earthly beings. He whose body is inhabited by the demon Tarōmad this is his mark. He is light-minded, when he is incited he is aroused, even when a small share falls to him from the things of this world he stands away from the things of the gods, and he seeks the reward for good deeds from earthly beings, not from the spirits.

This passage is typical of the theological attitude of the Pahlavi books; it represents the connection between Man and the main gods as reflected in his attitude and action. The particular relationship which can be formed between Man and a god or a demon is one in which Man is activated from within by the spirit. The spirit, god or demon, stands for a quality of mental attitude and its inherence in Man is visible by the fact that his behaviour conforms to it. In the Zoroastrian religious system the believer is encouraged to strive towards 'union' with the gods;[59] this union can be realized by the man's identifying himself as closely as that is possible with the character typified by the gods.[60] The theological conception of the gods and of the demons seems thus to have differed from the popular and mythological ones in that it regarded the deities as abstractions of qualities — that is, in a manner quite close to what they were originally in the *Gāθās* and to what they correctly represented by the meaning of their names. The immanent character of the notion of god in this group of writings comes out in a particularly striking manner in the following passage from *Dēnkard* VI, where the scope of the term *yazd* 'god' is widened beyond what we would normally expect:

[237] u-šān ēn-ez a'ōn dāšt ku abd-ez ḥād hān ī yazd-ē harw panāh aweš kunēd ud parastēd ud tarsagāh bawēd ēg az anāgīh be bōzēd. u-š awe yazd rāy guft ēd bawēd ruwān ī xwēš.[61]

They held this, too, thus: There will be wonder to him who gives every protection to a god, worships him and is reverent towards him; he [the god] then saves him from evil. He said concerning that god: it is one's own soul.

Although it is not easy to quote other examples for one's own soul being called god, the saying here is in keeping with the view that the gods are spirits inherent in Man and with the repeated warnings that a man should do everything for the sake of his own soul.[62] The passage presents a

59 A text from *Dēnkard* VI which represents this attitude may be quoted as an example:

[43] In religion there are three principal things: union (*hamīh*), separation (*wizihīdagīh*) and the measure (*paymān*). Union is this: one who, in thought, speech and deed, in every righteousness, is together with the gods, and the good ones. This union never perishes (*DkM*, p. 480).

There follow definitions of the other two terms, separation meaning being removed from sin and the demons. 'Gods and the good ones' is a frequent combination in the Pahlavi texts.

60 The expression *yazdān-xēm mardom* 'a man of godly character, one who has the character of the gods', is found to designate a person who has a special relationship with the gods in *Dk*. VI, 221–222 = *DkM*, p. 520.

61 *DkM*, p. 525; *Dk. Facs.*, p. [413].

62 *ruwān ī xwēš rāy*, cf. for example, *Dk*. VI, 210, A2; a sinful person is called *ruwān-dušmen* 'an enemy of the soul'; cf. *Dk*. VI, 236. The expression corresponds to 'for the sake of the gods' in the saying in *Dēnkard* VI:

[273] ke harw ce kunēd ēwāz yazdān rāy kunēd, harw ce'ōn kunēd pad-eš ahlaw bawēd (*DkM*, p. 533; *Dk. Facs.*, p. [420]; MS K43, fol. 212v).

A man who does everything for the sake of the gods alone, in whatever manner he does it he becomes righteous through it.

good example of the method of literary expression which is common in *Dēnkard* VI: it tends to use hints and allusions, sometimes only half explained, as well as riddles, and is reminiscent of the techniques often used in the Jewish midrashic literature or, somewhat less strongly, of the riddle as a teaching device in Indian literature.[63]

One sometimes has the impression in *Dēnkard* VI, that the allusion or riddle technique serves partly to hide the complete meaning of the author, perhaps when themes which were considered to reflect the esoteric contents of this system of thought were touched upon. We occasionally find what may be considered to be an attempt to interpret the basic precepts of the Zoroastrian religion or of eschatology in an allegorical or spiritualized manner,[64] but this sort of guess is speculative by nature and extremely hard to prove.

The important differences between the theological and the mythological or popular trends in Zoroastrianism (and those which were most likely to cause a deliberate restriction on the teaching of the theological), were presumably such as could have affected the religious practices and the

63 Cf. L. Renou, 'The Enigma in the Ancient Literature of India', *Diogenes,* XXIX (1960), pp. 32–41.

64 A few examples from the *Dēnkard* VI may be quoted: *

[57] There is that thing which he who is in it does not move away (*ayāsēd*) from it, and he who is not in it moves towards it (*DkM*, p. 483).

The riddle is solved in the next section (VI, 58) where it is revealed that the object referred to is 'the religion' (=*dēn*). Allegorical interpretations are found, for example, in the following passage:

[108] People have three things which are very good, these are, drinking *haoma,* drinking wine and carrying the sacred girdle. Drinking *haoma* is this: when one stands upon one's essential being [*axw*]. Drinking wine is this: when one stands on peace (*āštīh*). Carrying the sacred girdle is this: when one is separated from the wicked (*DkM*, p. 496).

The existence of people who use allegorical interpretations with regard to the basic facts̜ of the Zoroastrian religion is corroborated by al-Bīrūni. He states that those people, whom he calls *aṣḥābu l-ta'wīlāt min al-furs,* have allegorizing interpretations for the different holidays.

> Those among the Persians who use allegorical interpretations extracted from these days parables to serve as allegories. They established the *Mihrajān* as an indication of the resurrection and the end of the world, because plants reach their end at that period and the materials of growth are withheld from them, and because animals abstain from reproduction. They also established *Nowrōz* as an indication of the beginning of the world, because the opposite of these conditions exists then (Al-Bêrûnî, *Chronologie orientalischer Völker,* ed. Ed. Sachau, Leipzig 1923, p. 223).

simple faith of the uninitiated. Thus, for example, the idea that Ahreman and his powers have no *gētīg* aspect of their own might seem to stand in contradiction to the general idea about the presence of the evil creatures in this world. It was apparently an ancient Iranian idea (of Magian origin?) that they represent the powers of evil in the world and that it is a virtue to kill as many of them as possible.[65] One would not expect all this to be rejected out of hand in what one may call 'higher Zoroastrianism', but it loses much of its meaning and seems to be thrust into the background. In *Dēnkard* VI, the killing of reptiles is only mentioned as a punishment for the sins of people who belong to the *Haδa-mānθra* or middle section in the threefold division of religious society.[66]
Speculation as to the nature of the theological religion of Zoroastrianism may be left at this point. What does seem quite tenable is that the notion of a hierarchy of religious truths, which existed in the Pahlavi literature, was associated with the notion of the religious hierarchy of the believers in the religion, and that these two hierarchies had some relationship to the division of the Zoroastrian community into folk religion, on the one side, and a more sophisticated type of religion, developed by the learned, on the other. The weight of the evidence tends, I believe, to favour an interpretation of the restricted religion of the *Dēnkard* not as a mystery religion, as this term has come to be used, but as a system of thought which is fairly intellectual and spiritualized in character. A religion of this type would not be an isolated phenomenon in the Near East in the Sasanian period. Analogous traits can be found in the two monotheistic religions and more closely in Manichaeism, as well as in India, in the higher forms of Brahmanism and Buddhism.

65 Cf. Herodotus, I, 140; Plutarch, *De Iside et Osiride*, 46; *Vendidad* xviii: 65.

66 *Dk.* VI, 206; cf. above pp. [5–6]. The killing of noxious creatures as an atonement of sins committed is found in *Vendidad* xiv: 5 f.; xviii: 73.

Appendix A

A PAHLAVI TEXT ON THE QUALITIES OF AVESTA AND *ZAND*

(see above, p. [14], n. 35)

⟨1⟩ abar ⁺wāspuhragānīh ī abastāg ⟨ud⟩ hān ī zand, az nigēz ī weh-dēn.
⟨2⟩ hād-šān pad hampursagīh ī āgnēn āgāhīh ⟨ī⟩ mēnōg barišnīg pad dānišn xwadīh. u-šān ō mardom āgāhīh ⟨ī⟩ waxš abar-barišnīg az hān ce-šān gōwišn ō hamargān mardom. ⁺u-šān waxš abar-barišnīh ī ō mardom pad hām-srādag ēwāz ham-barišnīgān bawēd.
⟨3⟩ az abastāg ⁺wāspuhragānīh ēwag. hām-srādag mardom ham-barišnīg gōwišn ī yazdān ⟨ud⟩ dēn ī mazdēsn ēwāz.
⟨4⟩ az zand wāspuhragānīh ēwag. wēnēnd andar-eš ēwag ēwag wāzag dārmag ud miyānag ud stabr ud wēnišnān-ez dānišn (ī) frahaxtišnīg pad bōzišn ī jud jud.[1]

1. On the qualities proper to Avesta and *Zand*. From the instruction of the Good Religion.
2. To them[2] [viz. to the sages?] awareness of *mēnōg* is carried into the selfness of knowledge through the joint consultation [of people]. In their view, [the statement that] the awareness of the spirit[3] is being carried over to men [emerges] from that, namely, that their [= the gods'?] discourse is addressed to all people. The carrying over of [the knowledge of] the spirit to men is [done], according to them, through corporate[4] words of all kinds.
3. There is one quality proper to Avesta: The corporate discourse of the gods and the word of the Mazdean religion is [addressed to] all manner of people.

1 *Dk*. III, 204 = *DkM*, p. 224; *Dk. Facs.*, pp. [175] f.; Molé, *Culte*, pp. 502 f. The above tentative rendering differs from Molé's in a number of points.

2 *-šān* has caused considerable trouble, being written in the same way as *yazdān*. The present reading seems the only one which gives good sense throughout the passage.

3 *waxš*, literally: 'a word', is often used as a synonym for *mēnōg*. Cf. H. W. Bailey, *BSOS*, VI (1930–1932), pp. 280 f.; idem, *Zor. Pr.*, p. 105, n. 1. The phrase *āgāhīh ī waxš* seems here to be merely a stylistic variant of the phrase *āgāhīh ī mēnōg*.

4 For *ham-barišnīg(ān)*, cf. New Persian *ham-bar(a)* 'friend, companion'.

202

4. There is one quality proper to *Zand:* They see in each one of its[5] utterances that which is subtle, medium or coarse. The knowledge of [these] acts of seeing is instructive for the salvation of each person separately.

5 Viz., the Avesta's.

Appendix B

KNOWLEDGE OF AVESTA AND *ZAND*, AND THE TERMS *ĒRBAD* AND *HĀWIŠT*

(see above, p. [17], n. 44)

I

Dādestān ī Dēnīg, Question XLIV[1]

⟨1⟩ 44-om pursišn hān ī pursīd ku ērbadīh ayāb hāwištīh, kadām ērbad-ē bawēd kadām hāwišt, kadām hān ī pad ērbadīh kadām hān ī pad hāwištīh abāyēd dāštan.
⟨2⟩ passox ēn ku ērbadīh hāwištīh hamband, mādiyānīhā ērbadān āmōzēnd hāwištān āmōzēnd dānišn ī dēn ī ast abastāg ud zand.
⟨3⟩ ērbadān hāwištān būd hēnd pad āmōxtan ī az xwēš ērbad. hāwišt-ez amwašt-bawīh ērbad bawēnd abāg āmōxtār. andar ēwag tan bawēd ērbadīh ud hāwištīh. ⟨4⟩ pad hān ī hāwištagīhā āmōxtēd az ērbad ī dānāg-tar, az xwēš-tan ērbadīh āmōzēd ō hāwišt ī āmōxtār-kāmag ke-š āmōzišn niyāz. az-ez awe ka andar xwēš ērbad hāwišt, abar xwēš (ērbad)[2] hāwišt ērbad ast. ⟨5⟩ ce'ōn gōwihēd-ez ku pārs āhrōnān pēšag framādār abar +ōstādān ud mōbadān-ez, pārs sārār pēšōbāy ī dēn wāš kard, +ēdōn be wizīd pēšīhā ī andar dēn: ērbad abar zand āgāhišn, hāwišt abar abast⟨āg⟩. ⟨6⟩ awēšān +waxšag-tar ērbad frāz az yašt ud wisprad ud hād nērōg abzār ud abzār ī pad zand. hāwištān frāz az nīrang ī yazišn ud pādyābīh ud a-pādyābīh, ud pāk⟨īh⟩ ud rīmanīh ud wināh pad društag be šnāxt abzār ī pad abastāg. ⟨7⟩ ud harw 2 pēšag az harw astīh, hamēyīg-astīh, hamāg-wehīh ud frazām pērōzīh ī yazdān, nēst ⟨ud hamāg⟩ wattarīh (ud hamāg wehīh) ud +absihēnišn ī +dēwān [?] be šnāxtan, yazdān dōstīhā hān ī āhrōn hamist āmōxtan ud kardan ud dāštan frēzbānīg meh-dādestān dāštār.
1. The forty-fourth question. He asked: The position of *ērbad* or that of *hāwišt:* which one becomes *ērbad* and which one *hāwišt,* *
which one should we regard as *ērbad* and which one as *hāwišt?*
2. This is the answer. The position of *ērbad* is closely related to that of *hāwišt*. In principle both *ērbad*s and *hāwišt*s learn the know-

1 MS K 35, foll. 161r–162r; cf. *SBE,* XVIII, pp. 151–153. West's division of the text into sections has been retained.

2 This seems to be a case of dittography.

ledge of religion, which is the Avesta and *Zand*. 3. The *ērbad*s have been *hāwišt*s in that they learned from their own *ērbad*. The *hāwišt*s, too, become collectively *ērbad*s, [when they are] with a disciple. Being *ērbad* and being *hāwišt* is within one body, 4. in the sense that he who learns as a *hāwišt* from the *ērbad* who is more knowledgeable [than himself] teaches of himself in the capacity of an *ērbad* to a *hāwišt* who desires to be taught and who requires tuition. From this, too, [the identity of the two functions is seen]: one who is a *hāwišt* with regard to his own *ērbad*, as regards his *hāwišt* he is an *ērbad*. 5. As it is said that the chief of the calling of the priests of Pārs controls also the *ōstād*s and the *mōbad*s, and the ruler of Pārs is made the leader of the vehicle of religion, so also the foremost positions in the religion are chosen: the *ērbad* controls the knowledge of *Zand*, the *hāwišt* that of the Avesta. 6. The *ērbad* is more spiritual [?] among them. He has the instrument which springs from the power of *Yašt*, *Vispered* and the *Hā*s, and the instrument which is contained in *Zand*. The *hāwišt* has the instrument which springs from the firm knowledge of the ritual [*nīrang*] of worship, ablution and non-ablution, purity and defilement and sin, [viz., knowledge which is secured] by the Avesta. 7. Both callings have it imposed upon them to know of all [the following]: the existence, eternal existence, all-goodness and ultimate victory of the gods, the non-existence, [all-]evil, and the annihilation of the demons [?]; and also to teach, do and keep, together with the *āhrōn*s, the friendship of the gods, and to be keepers of the great matter.

II

Dādestān ī Dēnīg, Question LXV[1]

The theme of this chapter concerns a conflict between an *ērbad* who knows by heart only five *fragard*s (chapters) of *Nīrangestān*, Avesta with *Zand*, and who is a magus *(u-š ērbad-ē ke-š dōst āmad, nīrangestān 5 fragard abastāg pad zand warm ast, ud pad mōmardīh hamē rawēd)*, and a *hāwišt*, who knows all the five *nask*s ('books') of the Avesta by heart but knows no *Zand (ud az hāwištān mard-ē ke-š abastāg 5 nask warm u-š zand ciš-ez ne warm)*. The conflict arises over a man who desires to order a recitation of the whole sacred text *(dēn)*, but who has promised the lucrative function to the *ērbad* who knows much less of the Avestan text than the *hāwišt*.

1 MS K 35, foll. 178r ff.; cf. *SBE*, XVIII, pp. 201 ff.

III

It would seem from the two previous texts that *Zand* was regarded as the speciality of *ērbad*s, as opposed to *hāwišt*s. The current translation of *hāwišt* by 'pupil' or 'disciple' is not always appropriate; *hāwišt* appears to be a term for a rank of priests who were not so fully qualified as the *ērbad*s were expected to be, but who functioned as priests and who could vie with the *ērbad*s over priestly functions. In the same vein it is possible to refer to a number of further texts. In *Zand ī Wahman Yasn,* for example, it is said that one of the signs of the tenth century, near the end of the world, will be the following:

> awēšān ke pad ērbadīh ud hāwištīh nām barēnd ēwag ō did rāy wad xwāhēnd ud āhōg gōwēnd ud āhōg abar nigerēnd (*ZWY* iv:39).
>
> Those who are known to be in the positions of *ērbad* and *hāwišt* will wish evil to each other and will talk of [each other's] faults and see faults [in each other].

Both *ērbad* and *hāwišt* acted as preceptors and were, it appears, mostly engaged in teaching; cf., for example, *ZWY* iv:67 (above, n.46). This is not to deny that *hāwišt* often designates specifically an apprentice or disciple with regard to *ērbad;* cf., for example, *Dk.* III, 338 = *DkM,* p. 330, rendered by M. Molé, *Oriens,* XIII/XIV (1961), pp. 9 f.

Appendix C

THE TERM *RĀZ* IN THE PAHLAVI TEXTS

(see above, p. [19], n. 50)

* In the following pages some significant passages in which the word *rāz* is used in a religious sense are collected.

I

az madan ī tāzīgān ō (ī) ērān-šahr rawāgēnīd ī-šān duš-dēnīh ⟨ud⟩ duš-xwāhīh, (ī) az kayān hu-dēnīh ud az dēn-burdārān āzarmīgīh ānāft, ud rāzān ⟨ī⟩ būd ud bawēd, ⟨ud⟩ saxwanān ⟨ī⟩ +wahīh [?] ī zufr ī +abdēn, ⟨ud⟩ hu-+cimīgīh cišān, menišn ⟨ī⟩ weh ud kunišn ī rāst ⟨ud⟩ cim saxwan az ayādagīh ud dānišn ī pādram uzīd. wad-zamānīh rāy awe-z ⟨ī⟩ az dūdag ī abar-+māndagān ud kayān ud dēn-burdārān ō +brahm ud ristag ī awēšān duš-dēnān gumixt ud pad abrang, hān ī hu-dēnān saxwan ud brahm ud parastišn ud kardag pad āhōg ud ērang dāšt hēnd. awe-z ke-š pad ēn frahang ud rāz āmōxtan kāmag būd, az gyāg gyāg pad arg ud ranz ⟨ud⟩ +duš-pāragīh [?] ō xwēš kardan šāyast⟨an⟩ ne tawān būd (*GBd.*, p. 1, 1.10–p. 2, 1.7).

Following the coming of the Arabs to the Kingdom of Iran, their bad religion and ill-will found currency; the Good Religion weakened away from the noblemen and honour from the carriers of the religion. The secrets of that which was and will be,[1] profound and marvellous words of wisdom [?],[2] well-founded things, good thought, right action and word of reason — [all these] went out from the memory and knowledge of the populace. Owing to the evil time, even those who belonged to the highly-placed families, noblemen and carriers of the religion,

1 *rāzān ī būd ud bawēd* should be interpreted, one imagines, as referring to the mysteries of creation and eschatology.

2 Cf. the Manichaean Middle Persian word *whyẖ* 'wisdom', in F. C. Andreas & W. Henning, *Mitteliranische Manichaica aus Chinesisch-Turkestan*, II (*Sitzungsberichte der Preussischen Akademie der Wissenschaften, phil.-hist. Klasse, 1933*, VII), Berlin 1933, p. 343. This may be the correct interpretation of the word in *Dk*. VI, C83, rendered above, pp. [10] f., n. 27, 'goodness'.

mixed themselves in the custom and manner of those of evil religion and held [the evil religion] in splendour, while they held the words, custom, worship and deed of those of the Good Religion as faulty and condemned. A person who had the desire to be instructed in this lore and mystery could not appropriate them even [by collecting them] from various places through effort and trouble and difficulty [?].[3]

II

hān 5 rōz ī gāhānīg pad ham rōzan be āyēd ud be šawēd, rōz ī ne guft ēstēd, ce agar be guft hād dēwān rāz be dānist hād ud +wizand handāxt hād (*GBd.*, p. 56, ll. 6–9).

Those five *gāhān*-days come in and go out through the same 'window'. They are the days which are not spoken of, for, if they were spoken of, the demons would know the secret and would commit harm.

III

ud pas az hān pādašxwārgar az nazdīkīh ī drayāb bār mard-ē mihr yazd be wēnēd ud mihr yazd was rāz ī nihān ō hān mard gōwēd (*Ayādgār ī Zāmāspīg*, XVI, 43, in: G. Messina, *Libro apocalittico persiano Ayātkār i Žāmāspīk*, Rome 1939, p. 73; H. W. Bailey, *BSOS*, VI, 1930–1932, p. 584).

Afterwards in Pādašxwārgar, near the sea-shore, a man will see the god Mithra and the god Mithra will tell many hidden secrets to that man.

The context of this passage which is taken from an apocalypse recounting the events of eschatological times, leaves very little room for doubt as to the nature of the secrets revealed by Mithra to that man; they must be connected with the wars of the last days.

IV

hān ī ahlawān (ī) pad andar be-widīrišnīh ī gētīgīg dard-widār. pas-ez az be-widīrišnīh tā be-+widaštan ī-š pad hān ⟨ī⟩ škift āmār-ez +waštār. ud pas az āmār pad hān ī xwēš gāh urwāhmen, ⟨ud⟩ pad hān ī ka-š ham-+bāzān ī andar gētīg ke-šān hān ī

3 Literally: 'having a bad lot'(?).

mēnōgān rāz anāyāft ud hān ī awe gāh a-šnāxt gētīg-cihrīhā andar grōhīg andōhōmand ⟨ud⟩ abar yazdān abaxšāyišnēnāg. mēnōgān, mēnōg ī dahišn ⟨ud mēnōg ī yazišn ī⟩ dēn ī mazdēsnān, mēnōg ī weh ī andar gētīgīg, ke-šān awe-z ahlaw andar gētīg stāyīdār ud warzīdār ⟨ud⟩ rāyēnīdār ud pānag ud pahrēzēnāg ud hayyār bawēd, abar hān ahlaw ī az gētīgīg pānagīh ō pahrēz ⟨ud⟩ hayyār-dahišnīh apparihēd appardār garzišn, ⟨ud⟩ abar pādāšn paywandišn ud abar-eš nōg pānag ⟨ud⟩ ārāstār xwāyišn ō dādār kunēnd (*Dd.*. XXI, 2–3; cf. M. Molé, *RHR,* CLVII, 1960, pp. 179 f., where the translation is different).

The righteous undergo pain when they depart from *gētīg*. After having departed [from *gētīg*] and until they have gone through that frightful reckoning, they have joy in their place and also in the fact that their mates in *gētīg,* who have not obtained the secret of the spirits and are not aware of their place, are worried [about them] in company, in the nature of *gētīg,* and arouse the gods to pity [them]. The spirits, the spirit of creation [and the spirit of the worship of] the Mazdean religion, the good spirit within *gētīg,* for whom that righteous man is in *gētīg* the one who praises, works, arranges, protects, serves and helps—[these spirits, who are] those who have snatched [him out of this world] make a complaint to him who has snatched [him] concerning that righteous man who has been snatched away from the guardianship of *gētīg* to service and the giving of help [to the gods?] and they make a plea with regard to [his] reward. They also make supplication to the Creator concerning their new protector and arranger.

'The secret of the spirits' in this passage is specifically the knowledge of the eschatological reward due to the righteous.

V

wirāst kardan ī rist-āxēz abāg abd-passaxtīh ud wuzurgīh, pas-ez škift sahišnīh abar dāmān ke anāgāh hēnd. hān ī xwābar dādār rāzān cišān, ce'ōn harw nihuft rāz, be xwad awe ⟨ī⟩ harw-dānišn ī purr-āgāh ⟨ī⟩ wispān wisp ēnyā, hēc az gētīgān ud mēnōgān anaspurr ne dānist (*Dd.,* XXXVI, 2).

Making the resurrection arranged [goes together] with wondrous constitution and greatness. Then this seems extraordinary to creatures who are ignorant. None of the imperfect *gētīg* and *mēnōg* beings have known the secret things of the beneficient

Creator (which are as every hidden secret)—excepting Him himself, the all-knower, who is full of the knowledge of all that is in all.

VI

u-š pad wuzurg rāz ī purr-abdīh dūrīg a-margīh ō zīndagān dād ⁺zahag-paywandīh, hān ī weh ud abardom ast a-margīh ī petyāragōmandīh. ce hamē-zīndag (ī) petyāragōmand jāyēdān dard. awe škift zōr ī āyāft-paywand, hamē juwān pad paywand ud nāf ud āwādagān ī weh andar petyāragōmandīh. ud hamē-yīgīh ī zīndagīh, ku-šān pad xwēš frazand ⟨ud⟩ āwādag zīndagīh paywandihēd, jāyēdān (*Dd.*, XXXVI, 29; cf. Molé, *RHR*, CLV, 1959, p. 149).

Through the great mystery, full of marvel, he gave to living [people] long immortality: the descent of offspring, that which is the best and most excellent immortality of that which has adversity. For an eternal being which has adversity suffers always pain. That one has wondrous power who has been endowed with offspring, he is constantly young in adversity thanks to [his] good offspring, family and descendants. The constancy of [his] life is eternal. [A gloss adds: that is, their living continues through their children and descendants.]

Here *rāz* describes the mysterious knowledge of how a man may actually continue his earthly life after his departure from it, and why this method of eternal life is deemed superior to one by which the life of the individual in this world would be continued indefinitely.

VII

az wuzurg warz ud xwarr ī dādār abar burd pad tanōmandīh ō dušaxw mad ud 13 zamistān andar dušaxw pad dēw-karbīh raft, ud rāz ud abzār ke pad-eš dēw wānihēnd ud az mardom pādixšāyēnd warzāwand nēzumān-cārīhā az dēwān ul burd, ud dēwān pad xwad abzār zad ud wānīd ud az mardom a-pādixšāyēnīd ud dūrēnīd (*DkM*, p. 296, l. 17–p. 297, l. 1; *Dk. Facs.*, p. [226], ll. 8–12; the text is differently construed in Zaehner, *Zurvan*, pp. 250–263).

He [Yima] took some of the great miracle and fortune of the Creator, went in bodily form to hell and spent thirteen winters in hell in the form of a demon. By miraculous and skilful means he took away from the demons the secret and weapon by which the demons can be vanquished and made powerless over Man. He smote and vanquished the demons by this very weapon, made them lose their power over Man and removed them away from Man.

VIII

ud mad ō kay-syāwaxš ī bāmīg, ⟨ud⟩ pad-eš dēsīd kang-diz ī abd-kard pad hugar-dārišnīh ⟨ud⟩ pānagīh ⟨ī⟩ was warz ud xwarr ud rāz ī dēn, (ī) az-eš wirāyišn ī āwām ud abāz-⁺ārāstārīh ī ērān xwadāyīh ud abāz-paywandišnīh ī amāwandīh ⟨ud⟩ pērōzgarīh ō hān ī ōhrmazd dēn paydāg (*DkM*, p. 598, ll. 15–20; *Dk. Facs.*, p. [475], ll. 9–13; cf. Bailey, *Zor. Pr.*, p. 28; Zaehner, *BSOAS*, X, 1940–1942, p. 614).

And it [scil. *waxš* 'the spirit', mentioned in *DkM*, p. 594, l. 10] came to Kay Syāwaxš the Brilliant. He built for it Kang-diz, the wondrously-made, for the beneficent keeping and protection of the numerous miracles, fortunes and mysteries of the religion. From this was manifest the organization of time, the restitution of the rule of Iran, and the re-attachment of power and victory to the religion of Ohrmazd.

IX

andar ham zamān ōhrmazd nērōsang yazd ō mān ī wištāsp pad aštagīh ō ašawahišt amahraspand, xwārēnīdan ī ō wištāsp hān jān cašm pad abar-wēnišnīh ī ō mēnōgān axwān rōšngar xwarišn, ke rāy-eš dīd wištāsp wuzurg xwarr ud rāz (*DkM*, p. 642, ll. 3–7; cf. Widengren, 'Stand und Aufgaben der iranischen Religionsgeschichte', *Numen*, II, 1955, pp. 67 f.; idem, *Die Religionen Irans*, Stuttgart 1965, p. 70).

At the same time the Creator Ohrmazd [sent] the god Neryosang to the house of Vištāspa on a mission to the *Amahraspand* Aša-Vahišta, so as to feed the soul's eye of Vištāspa with the luminous food of looking above to the worlds of the spirits. For this reason Vištāspa saw great fortune and mystery.

The context is somewhat obscure, particularly as the text relies on a lost Avestan original. But the mystery seems to refer to what one sees in the world of the spirits.

X

u-šān ēn-ez a'ōn dāšt ku arzānīg bawišn pad harw rāz ⟨ī pay⟩-gār ī yazd ud yazdān *'dyn'y,* ce'ōn ⟨ka⟩ mard arzānīg bawēd ēg yazdān xwad az rāz +ī paygār ī xwēš āgāh kunēnd, ce yazd ganzwar ī ōstwār xwāhēnd. *'dynyx* ⟨ī⟩ yazdān ud rāz ⟨ī⟩ paygār ī xwēš az kas-ez nihān nēst, ce dānēh ku cand mardom wēš dānēnd yazd pādixšā-tar bawēnd. u-šān arzānīgān būd⟨an⟩ ēd guft ēdōn weh mard bawēd ku-šān yazdān rāh ō tan bawēd ud rāz ⟨ī⟩ xīr ⟨ī⟩ xwēš aweš nimāyēnd (*Dk.* VI, 214 = *DkM,* pp. 518 f.; *Dk. Facs.*, p. [407]).

They held this, too, thus: One ought to be worthy with regard to every mystery of the battle of the gods and to the gods' secrecy [?], for when a man is worthy, the gods themselves inform him of the secret of their battle, for the gods seek a reliable treasurer. The secrecy [?] of the gods and the mystery of their battle are not hidden from any one, for you ought to know that, as much as people know [them] better, the gods are more powerful. They [scil. the sages] said: 'To be worthy' means this: the man is so good that the gods have a way into his body and they show him the mystery of their things.

The phrase *ku-šān* in the last sentence, if it refers to *mard,* seems strange. There is an apparent contradiction between the first part of the passage, which talks of secrets and of selective disclosure of them to 'worthy' people, and the sentence which says that these same secrets are not hidden from any one. This, however, need not imply real inconsistency in thought: it is necessary to restrict the propagation of the knowledge implied in the 'secret' out of caution, but ideally everyone should know it, as it helps in the fight of the gods against the demons. The same sentiment is clearly seen in other passages in the Pahlavi books. For example:

They held this, too: The desire of Ohrmazd the Lord from people is this: Know me, for He knows: if they know me, every one will follow me. The desire of Ahreman is this: Do not know me, for he knows: if they know me, no one will follow me (*Dk.* VI, 31 = *DkM,* p. 479; *Dk. Facs.,* pp. [372] f.; also in *MX* 40, ll. 24–28; an Arabic version, attributed to Buzurjmihr, is found in Miskawayh, *Jāwīdān Xirad,* p. 38, ll. 18–19).

Knowledge obviously constitutes the power of Ohrmazd, but it has its dangers.

The word *'dyn'y, 'dynyx* is translated 'secrecy' on the assumption that

it is related to a similar-looking word in other passages of *Dēnkard.* In *DkM,* p. 329, l. 5 (cf. Menasce, *Encyclopédie,* p. 45, List D, No. 13), *'yn'yx* is used to designate a vice which is the excess of the virtue *nihānīh* 'humility, discretion', and is opposed to the virtue *arwandīh* 'courage, promptness'; *'yn'yx* may, therefore, designate 'secretiveness, extreme reticence'. In *DkM,* p. 58, l. 21 (cf. Menasce, *Encyclopédie,* p. 42, List B, No. 18), *''ynyx* is the vice which is the excess of *burdīh* 'patience, forbearance'; it can therefore signify 'secretiveness', hence 'concealment of grudge'. The vice which corresponds to it at the other extreme is *xešm* 'wrath, anger' (cf. *ibid.,* No. 2). In *DkM,* p. 67, l. 5; p. 329, l. 3; p. 371, l. 18, the compound *(')yn'-menišnīh* occurs as a vice of excess to the virtue *bawandag-menišnīh* 'humility', and the sense of 'reticence, secretiveness' fits in well.
It thus seems plausible that our word *'dyn'y, 'dynyx,* if it is the same word, means 'secrecy, concealment'.

XI

The various passages quoted above show two main characteristics of the mystery designated by the word *rāz*: the secret of the battle of the gods with the demons, which goes together with the knowledge of how to vanquish the demons; and the secret of eschatology.
Apart from these passages, where the word *rāz* seems to have a special religious meaning, the same word occurs of course also in contexts where it has the commonplace connotations of 'secret'. Such are, for example, the following sentences from *Andarz ī Ādurbād ī Mahraspandān: rāz ō zanān ma bar* (*PhlT,* p. 59, §11): 'Do not carry a secret to women' (cf. the Arabic translation which occurs in Miskawayh, *Jāwīdān Xirad,* p. 26, l. 14: لا تستعمل الثقة بالنساء، ولا تُفش اليهن سراً. Cf. in the same vein also *Dk.* VI, B44, B48; or: *abāg halag-gōwišn mard rāz ma kun* (*PhlT,* p. 61, § 35) 'Do not contract a secret with a babbler'.
A more significant occurrence can be seen in *ŠGV* xiii:14: *pa ã ham rāž nunca zuhūdã rōž i šunbaṯ aspīmand* 'For this same secret the Jews rest on the day of Sabbath even now'. The 'secret' here is the reason that God rested on the seventh day after He had created the world.
It may not be superfluous to note that *rāz* is a frequent concept in the Manichaean writings in Middle Persian and Parthian, and it designates the mysteries of the religion. A book of Mani's by the name of *The Book of Mysteries* (in Arabic, in the Fihrist and elsewhere: *sifr al-asrār*) is known to have formed part of the Manichaean canon (cf. P. Alfaric, *Les écritures manichéennes,* II, Paris 1919, pp. 17 ff.).
Similarly, in the system attributed to Mazdak by Šahrastānī, the highest

world is governed by its ruler through characters the combination of which makes 'the greatest name' *(al-ism al-a'ẓam)*. A man who fashions something in his imagination from these characters has 'the greatest secret' opened to him *(wa-man taṣawwara min tilka l-ḥurūfi šay'an infataḥa lahu l-sirru l-akbar;* Šahrastānī, *Kitāb al-milal wa-l-niḥal,* ed. Muḥammad Badrān, I^2, Cairo 1956?, p. 230). Mani's doctrine is gnostic in character, and Mazdak is probably strongly indebted to Greek thought (cf. F. Altheim & R. Stiehl, *Geschichte der Hunnen,* III. Berlin 1961, pp. 61 ff.; O. Klíma, *Mazdak—Geschichte einer sozialen Bewegung im sassanidischen Persien,* Prague 1957, pp. 208 ff.). For our purpose here it is, however, mainly interesting to note the common use of the notion of secret in two sects which flourished in Sasanian Iran, in both of which the term designates an inner core of the religion.

Appendix D

SECRET RELIGION AND HERESY IN THE SASANIAN THEORY OF GOVERNMENT

A text, known as the Testament of Ardashīr, an Arabic version of an original Sasanian composition, has recently been published twice, by two scholars, each independently of the other.[1] It contains instructions for governing the State in the best manner, and refers several times to problems affecting the relationship of the king to men of religion and religious sects. Some passages are of particular importance for our subject, and it will be useful to quote them in translation.

I

> Know that kingship and religion are twin brothers, no one of which can be maintained without the other. For religion is the foundation of kingship, and kingship is the guardian of religion.[2] Kingship cannot subsist without its foundation, and religion cannot subsist without its guardian. For that which has no guardian is lost, and that which has no foundation crumbles. The main thing of which I fear for your sakes is that the low people should rush and outdo you in the study of the religion,[3] in its interpretation[4] and in becoming expert in it, while trust in the power of authority should lead you towards scorning it [scil. religion]. [As a result] there would emerge secret chieftainships among the low people, the peasants and the rabble that you have harassed, tyrannized, deprived, terrorized and belittled. Know that there can never be in one kingdom both a secret chief in religion and a manifest chief in kingship without the chief in religion snatching away that which is in the hands of the chief in kingship. For religion is the founda-

1 *'Ahd Ardašīr*, edited by I. 'Abbās, Beirut 1967; this text will be used, unless otherwise noted. M. Grignaschi, 'Quelques spécimens de la littérature sassanide conservés dans les bibliothèques d'Istanbul', *JA*, CCLIV (1966), pp. 1–142; text and translation of the Testament of Ardašīr on pp. 46–90. The two editors will hereafter be referred to as IA and MG, respectively.

2 MG's text seems preferable here.

3 Here Arabic *dīn* presumably renders Middle Persian *dēn*, which means, in such a context, the Zoroastrian scriptures.

4 The reading *wa-ta'wīlihi wa-l-tafaqquhi fīhi* seems to me preferable, as it can be taken to reflect a Zoroastrian idiom such as *(*āmōzišn ī dēn*) *u-š wizārišn*. . .

> tion and kingship is the pillar, and the possessor of the foundation has more claim to the whole building than the possessor of the pillar (IA ed., pp. 53 f.; MG ed., text on p. 49; translation on p. 70).[5]

The main points of this passage for our purpose are that it contains a justification, from the point of view of the king, for restricting the instruction of religion among lower-class people, and a realization of the actual danger that religious groups should be formed which would not be under the jurisdiction of the king, though presumably within the confines of the State religion and adhering to the same scriptures. Such groups would have their own secret chiefs.

II

> In the past before us there have been kings [each] one of whom would impose the commentary on the totality [of people] and the instruction on the community, and set to work those who are unemployed, just as he would take care of his body by cutting excessive hair and nails and by washing the impurities. . . (IA ed., p. 54; MG ed., text on pp. 49 f.; translation on p. 70).[6]

This passage, which follows immediately the one first quoted, seems related to it in subject-matter. Both deal with the danger of the formation of heresies or secret religious groupings. Such heresies occur, as we have noted, as deviations from the approved commentary on the scriptures, and it is the king's duty to see to it that only one interpretation should reign. One method of securing uniformity of interpretation is to abolish unemployment. This point is made more explicitly in the following section of the same work:

> Know that the decay of dynasties begins by [the king] neglecting the subjects without [setting them to do] known works and recognized labours. If unemployment becomes rampant among people, there is produced from it consideration of [various] matters and thought about fundamentals. When they consider this, they consider it with different natures, and as a result their schools [of thought] become different. From the differences of their schools there is produced enmity and hatred [of each other] among them, while they are all united in disliking the kings . . . (IA ed., pp. 60 f.; MG ed., text on p. 53; translation on p. 73).

5 MG's translation of this passage is in some points different.

6 MG interprets this passage differently.

III

> The king ought not to acknowledge the pious, the ascetic and the devout to be closer to the religion, more devoted to it or more zealous for it than he is; he ought not to allow the ascetic and others than the ascetic to conduct their asceticism and religion outside what is enjoined and forbidden [7] to them. For the departure of the ascetics from what is enjoined and forbidden is a blemish on the kings and the kingdom, an imperfection for the people to ride upon, the harm from which, for the king and his successors, is evident (IA ed., pp. 56 f.; MG ed., text on p. 51; translation on pp. 71 f.).

If this passage is interpreted correctly, the following points of interest can be elicited from it. There seem to have existed circles of devout and pious people with a view of religion which differed from that of the State authorities, and with a claim to know the religion better. It is also possible to conclude that they differed from the mass of the people in certain practices, if the expression *al-amr wa-l-nahy* refers, as it seems to do, to religious precepts. The main fear in all the passages so far quoted is that views of religion deviating from the accepted ones may be formed; the people among whom this danger is possible are *al-sifla* or lower-class people in the first passage quoted, and *al-'ubbād wa-l-nussāk* 'the pious and the ascetic' in this passage. The author of the Testament may have the same groups of people in mind in both cases.

IV

> Have discourse with people of rank, give presents to the warriors, show joyful countenance to people of religion and confide your secrets to people who undertake the good and the evil of that, its beauty and ugliness (IA ed., p. 72; MG ed., text on p. 60; translation on p. 78).

This is a royal, secular version of the various sayings which present a hierarchy of people with whom one ought to converse and in what way. I must admit that the description of the people to whom one can tell secrets is not clear to me; the reference may be to people whom one can trust, who can take the consequences of their involvement. 'Men of

7 *al-amr wa-l-nahy* usually has a specific religious connotation in Arabic, and it can be taken to reflect the Zoroastrian dual notion of *kirbag ud wināh* 'good deeds and sins'. The phrasing here seems to suggest that it is the king who specifies what is to be observed.

religion' occupy third place here after *ahl al-marātib,* which probably refers to the aristocracy, and *ahl al-jihād,* the warriors.

V

> Among the subjects there is a kind of people who outwardly show humility, but are inwardly full of pride. A man who belongs to this type would exhort the kings and upbraid them, finding this the easier of the two methods of stabbing them.[8] He and many others call this [way of action] being a guardian of religion. If the king seeks to humiliate them, he knows of no sin for which they can be humiliated; if he wants to honour them—this is a position which they have taken for themselves against the king's desire; if he wants to silence them, the rumour will be that it was difficult for the king to accept their observance of the religion; if he orders them to speak, they will say things harmful and not helpful. These are the enemies of the dynasties and the misfortune of kings. The best advice for the king is to bring them closer to this world; [after all,] they strive towards this world and work for it. Once they are soiled with it, their ignominy will be manifest; in what they will do there will be an excuse for the king to kill them (IA ed., pp. 76 f.; MG ed., text on p. 62; translation on p. 80).

The people discussed in this passage belong to the general category of those who bring the ruler into conflict over matters of religion, but they seem to differ essentially from those who formed the subject of I and III above: those referred to here are hypocrites, while in the preceding passages the problem arose of people regarded as sincere. The people mentioned in the preceding passages are ascetics, while the hypocrites of the present passage do not include abstinence among their pretensions.

VI

The following section is quoted from a composition entitled *Āyīn li-Ardašīr,* published by M. Grignaschi from the same manuscript in which the Testament of Ardašīr occurs. A passage in the text of the *Āyīn,* which is a kind of book of social manners imposed by the king, describes how people were divided by Ardašīr into four classes, differentiated from each other by a graduated restriction on the use of gold,

8 One method being by sword and the other by words.

silver and gems.[9] The uppermost class was allowed the use of all three types of material for ornament, and the lowest was forbidden the use of any of them. The reason for this procedure is given as follows:

> What we forbade in this respect was not done out of paucity of wealth,[10] nor was it because in the eyes of those who have insight into matters and their final result, into the future life and the expectation of death, whatever people of this world do in this world is worthless. As, however, there is no other way for all the people of this world but to be either prosperous or destitute or in a middle position, we wanted people to be divided into these [same] divisions (*JA*, CCLIV, 1966, text on pp. 94 f.; translation on pp. 114 f.).

This text refers to ascetics, who deny any value to the material goods of this world. The king, the alleged author of this text, evidently respects this approach, but prefers to disregard it for practical reasons, as it goes against human nature. He decides to establish a classification of society based on the common practice. The ascetics in this passage, as well as in other passages quoted, represent good orthodox religion. This does not stand in contradiction to the conceptions of orthodox Sasanian Zoroastrianism known to us from the Pahlavi texts, as is sometimes erroneously assumed.[11] The only concern of the kings with

* 9 An interesting point of this passage is that silver is considered as more precious than gold. Silver was, in fact, the metal used as currency in Persia in the Sasanian period; cf. A. Mez, *Die Renaissance des Islams,* Heidelberg 1922, p. 445; B. Spuler, *Iran in frühislamischer Zeit,* Wiesbaden 1952, pp. 408–410. Most of the productions of Sasanian artistic metalwork were in silver; cf., e.g., O. Grabar, *Sasanian Silver—Late Antique and Early Mediaeval Arts of Luxury from Iran,* Michigan 1967, p. 79; R. Ghirshman, *Iran—Parthians and Sassanians,* London 1962, p. 204. Reports from the early Islamic period confirm this state of affairs. I am indebted to Prof. M.J. Kister for the following reference: 'Abd al-Razzāq states in his *Al-Muṣannaf fī l-ḥadīth* (MS Murad Molla 604, fol. 110a) that 'Umar levied taxes in silver from Iraq, 'which is a land of silver (*arḍ warq*),' and in gold from Syria, 'which is a land of gold.' Our text should be rendered as follows:

> As there were established among the people accepted conditions, agreed to by all, we allowed all vessels [read: *āniya*] of gold, silver and gems to one section of people, while we interdicted gems in particular to one section, and we interdicted gems ⟨and silver⟩ [read: *xāṣṣat al-jawhar* ⟨*wa-l-fiḍḍa*⟩] in particular to another, but allowed that section [the use of] gold, and we interdicted in particular to another section [the use of] gold, silver and gems.

10 Read: *jida.*

11 The contrast between 'orthodox' Zoroastrianism and an austere way of life undertaken out of devotion is purely illusory. All the evidence tends to show that the austerities of the devout were common in Sasanian times and did not clash with the Zoroas-

regard to ascetics, as we have seen (above, III), is not to be outdone by them in piety and not to let them run counter to the commonly accepted religious precepts. It was suggested, as will be recalled, that there were groups of religious people who indulged in allegorical interpretations of the practices of Zoroastrianism. If the devout ascetics of the passages collected here can be associated with the people who formed the subject of the present paper, we gain a more detailed view of the structure of Sasanian religion. It would seem that the pious people of these texts were at variance both with the State and the established clerical hierarchy; this can be seen from certain passages of *Dēnkard* VI.[12] Although they were by no means heretical, they could conceivably serve as a convenient breeding-ground for the numerous heresies which were such a common phenomenon of the Sasanian period.[13] The reservation felt towards them in the remnants of Sasanian court literature quoted here is, therefore, quite understandable.

trian view of the world; this view frequently alludes to this world as an inn, a temporary habitation, which should not be indulged in overmuch. Cf. the remarks of M. Molé, 'Un ascétisme moral dans les livres pehlevis?', *RHR*, CLV (1959), pp. 145–190. I hope to come back to this theme in another connexion.

12 Cf., e.g., *Dk.* VI, D2, D3, D5 = *DkM*, pp. 569 ff.; Mlle. Chaumont quotes these passages, but not quite accurately; see M. L. Chaumont, 'Vestiges d'un courant ascétique dans le zoroastrisme sassanide d'après le VIe livre du Dēnkart', *RHR*, CLVI (1959), pp. 1–23.

13 It is not always easy to identify the various heresies mentioned. Cf., e.g., Ibn Miskawayh, *Tajārib al-umam* (*E. J. W. Gibb Memorial Series*, Vol. VII, Part 1), Leiden 1909, pp. 190 f. (facsimile); text reproduced by M. Muḥammadī, *Al-tarjama wa-l-naql 'an al-fārisiyya fī l-qurūn al-islāmiyya al-ūlā*, I, Beirut 1964, pp. 62 f.; translation by M. Grignaschi, *JA*, CCLIV (1966), pp. 18 f.

I

List of Abbreviations

ARW = *Archiv für Religionswissenschaft*

Bailey, *Zor. Pr.* = H.W. Bailey, *Zoroastrian Problems in the Ninth-Century Books (Ratanbai Katrak Lectures)*, Oxford 1943

BSOAS = *Bulletin of the School of Oriental and African Studies*

BSOS = *Bulletin of the School of Oriental Studies*

Dd. = *Dādestān ī Dēnig* = *The Datistan-i Dinik*, Part I: *Pusrsishn I–XL*, ed. T.D. Anklesaria, Bombay [no date]. The text is quoted according to the divisions marked by Anklesaria (and not according to those introduced by E.W. West in his translation of the text, *SBE*, XVIII). The second part of the book, *Pursišn XLI–XCII*, is quoted from MS K 35; the inner divisions of the text are marked according to E.W. West, *ibid.*

Dk. = *Dēnkard*

Dk. III = *Dēnkard*, Book III. Chapter numbering according to that given in *Dīnkard*, ed. and transl. P.B. & D.P. Sanjana, I–XIX, Bombay 1874–1928; and in Menasce, *Encyclopédie*, pp. 82 ff.

Dk. VI = *Dēnkard*, Book VI. Section numbering according to Sanjana's edition (see *Dk.* III)

Dk. Facs. = *Dēnkart—A Pahlavi Text, Facsimile Edition of the Manuscript B of the K.R. Cama Oriental Institute Bombay*, ed. M.J. Dresden, Wiesbaden 1966

DkM = *The Complete Text of the Dinkard*, I–II, ed. D.M. Madan, Bombay 1911

Duchesne-Guillemin, *Religion* = Jacques Duchesne-Guillemin, *La religion de l'Iran ancien ('Mana'—Introduction à l'histoire des religions*, I, III), Paris 1962

GBd. = *Greater Bundahišn*, quoted from *The Bûndahishn—Being a Facsimile of the TD Manuscript No. 2*, ed. T.D. Anklesaria, Bombay 1908. The following edition has been compared: *Zand-Akāsīh—Iranian or Greater Bundahišn* (transliteration and translation by B.T. Anklesaria), Bombay 1956

IIJ = *Indo-Iranian Journal*

JA = *Journal Asiatique*

JRAS = *Journal of the Royal Asiatic Society*

Menasce, *Apologétique* = Pierre-Jean de Menasce (ed. & transl.), *Une apologétique mazdéenne du IXe Siècle, Škand-Gumānīk Vičār—La solution décisive des doutes (Collectanea Friburgensia*, NS XXX), Fribourg en Suisse 1945

Menasce, *Encyclopédie* = Pierre-Jean de Menasce, *Une encyclopédie mazdéenne—Le Dēnkart (Bibliothèque de l'Ecole des Hautes Etudes, Sciences religieuses*, LXIX), Paris 1958

Miskawayh, *Jāwīdān Xirad* = Abū 'Alī Aḥmad Ibn Muḥammad Miskawayh, *Al-Ḥikma al-Khālida—Jāwīdān Xirad*, ed. 'Abdurraḥmān Badawī (*Dirāsāt Islāmiyya*, XIII), Cairo 1952

Molé, *Culte* = Marijan Molé, *Culte, mythe et cosmologie dans l'Iran ancien—Le problème zoroastrien et la tradition mazdéenne (Annales du Musée Guimet, Bibliothèque d'Etudes*, LXIX), Paris 1963

MS K 35 = *Codices Avestici et Pahlavici Bibliothecae Universitatis Hafniensis*, III: *The Pahlavi Codex K 35*, First Part, Copenhagen 1934

MSK43 = *Codices Avestici et Pahlavici Bibliothecae Universitatis Hafniensis*, V: *The Pahlavi Codex K 43*, First Part, Copenhagen 1936

MX = *Mēnōg ī Xrad*, quoted according to *Dânâk-u Mainyô-î Khard*, ed. T. D. Anklesaria, Bombay 1913

PhlT = *Pahlavi Texts*, I–II, ed. Jamaspji Dastur M. Jamasp-Asana, Bombay 1897

RHR = *Revue de l'Histoire des Religions*

RSO = *Rivista degli Studi Orientali*

Saddar Naṣr = *Saddar Naṣr and Saddar Bundehesh*, ed. B. N. Dhabbar, Bombay 1909

SBE = F. Max Müller (ed.), *The Sacred Books of the East*, V, XVIII, XXIV, XXXVII, XLVII: *Pahlavi Texts*, I–V (transl. by E. W. West), Oxford 1880–1897 (reprinted Delhi 1965)

ŠGV = *Shikand-gûmânik Vijâr — The Pâzand-Sanskrit Text*, ed. Hôshang Dastûr J. Jâmâsp Äsânâ & E. W. West, Bombay 1887; cf. also Menasce, *Apologétique*

Zaehner, *Zurvan* = R. C. Zaehner, *Zurvan — A Zoroastrian Dilemma*, Oxford 1955

ZDMG = *Zeitschrift der deutschen morgenländischen Gesellschaft*

ZWY = *Zand ī Wahman Yasn*, quoted from *Zand-î Vohûman Yasn and Two Pahlavi Fragments*, ed. B. T. Anklesaria, Bombay 1957

II

THE NOTIONS *mēnōg* AND *gētīg* IN THE PAHLAVI TEXTS AND THEIR RELATION TO ESCHATOLOGY

The Zoroastrian religion is primarily known as dualistic in the sense that the opposition between the powers of good and the powers of evil occupies in its thought a central position. In addition to this opposition there is, however, in Zoroastrianism another pair of notions, which is no less important for a proper understanding of Zoroastrian ideas: the contrast between the notions of *mēnōg*, Avestan *mainyava-*, 'that which is non-material, non-sensual, intelligible', sometimes best translated 'ideal' in the sense of a conceptual prototype of a concrete existence, on the one hand, and *gētīg*,[1] Avestan *gaēiθya-*,[2] 'the material, earthly (world), that which can be apprehended through the senses', on the other. This pair of contrasting notions is neutral to the ethical dualism

[1] The word is often spelled in the Pahlavi texts *gyt'x*, and was read by H. S. Nyberg **gētāh* or *gētēh*, to distinguish between the substantive and the adjective, read by him *gētīk*; cf. *Hilfsbuch des Pehlevi*, II, Uppsala 1931, 80f., and *Journal Asiatique*, 219 (1931), p. 31ff. There is however no evidence for a vocalization *-ā-* in Middle or New Persian texts. Pāzand *gētī*, *gēθī*, *gīθī*, NP *gētī*, MPT *gytyg*, can all be best explained as reflecting a MP *gētīg*. The fact that an additional suffix *-yk* is usually added to the word in order to form the adjective (to be read *gētīgīg*) shows that the basic word had no formal distinction between substantive and adjective as Nyberg suggests, in the same way as *mēnōg* is a substantivized adjective, with a secondary adjectival form *mēnōgīg*. (In this I believe I am following the view of W. B. Henning.)

[2] In the Avestan text the same opposition was often expressed by other words. It is found already in the Gāthās, expressed for example as follows: *dāvōi ahvā astvatasčā hyatčā manaŋhō*, Y 28,2 (and similarly Y 43,3).

of Zoroastrianism and cuts through it. As it occupies a prominent position in the Zoroastrian religion, and particularly in the later literature, it has not been neglected by modern research, and a discussion of the terms can be found in the various general descriptions of the Zoroastrian religion.[3] Even so, some of the main aspects connected with them still require a detailed exposition; a thorough historical study of these concepts is called for, as well as a systematic description of their theological position in the Pahlavi writings. The twin concepts are crucial for understanding the mythological as well as the theological texts, and as they underwent considerable change of sense and usage from the Avestan period until the ninth century, when most of the extant Pahlavi texts were committed to writing, it is necessary to show how they developed; there is no doubt that they absorbed at least some amount of outside influence.[4] Leaving the historical problems aside, we shall here content ourselves with making some observations of a more general nature, with the aim of elucidating the theoretical position which this pair of opposites occupies in the

[3] The fullest discussion of this subject, as far as the Avestan material is concerned, was done by H. Lommel, *Die Religion Zarathustras nach dem Awesta dargestellt*, Tübingen 1930, 93 ff. Cf. also L.-C. Casartelli, *La philosophie religieuse du mazdéisme sous les Sassanides*, Paris-Bonn-Londres 1884, 63 ff.; R. C. Zaehner, *The dawn and twilight of Zoroastrianism*, London 1961, 200 ff.; J. Duchesne-Guillemin, *La religion de l'Iran ancien*, Paris 1962, 311 ff., and the remarks of H. S. Nyberg, *Die Religionen des alten Iran*, Osnabrück 1966 (Neudruck der Ausgabe 1938), 20f., and in *Journal Asiatique*, 219 (1931), p. 31–36. [Also G. Gnoli, *AION*, N.S. 13 (1963), p. 163–193, which came to my attention when the article was in press.]

[4] Cf. P. J. de Menasce in his edition of *Škand-gumānīk Vičār*, Fribourg 1945, p. 102f.; R. C. Zaehner, *Dawn and twilight*, p. 200f. It is not quite clear to me how it is possible to arrive (as Zaehner does) at the conclusion that *mēnōg*, in the sense of "the totally unformed primal matter of Aristotelian philosophy", was considered a third principle, besides the two spirits of orthodox theology. There is no evidence for this, apart from the general statement made by Eznik that some Zoroastrians accept three principles, a statement which can be better explained in other ways. It is, on the other hand, improbable that a philosophically inclined Zoroastrian, who defined *mēnōg* as meaning "a single, uncompounded substance without parts, invisible and intangible" (ibid., p. 200), would at the same time regard it as a member in a triad; even more so when we consider that the two other members of this group are supposed to be the two principles of good and evil—notions of a completely different order.

structure of late orthodox Zoroastrianism, as it is seen in the Pahlavi books.

In Pahlavi the terms have two distinct usages, which in the Avestan language were kept separate by a morphological distinction between *mainyava-* (adj.) and *mainyu-* (m. substantive). When used as adjectives or abstract nouns, they denote, first, two modes of being as cosmological ideas, the non-material as opposed to the material. When used as substantives they denote classes of beings.

The essential difference between the two modes of being is usually expressed by the contrast between visible *gētīg* and invisible *mēnōg*, but this criterion does not seem to hold in every case. Thus, for example, the clouds are said to be *mēnōg* beings carrying in them *gētīg* water;[5] the sky is held to be *mēnōg*;[6] the sun is apparently considered *mēnōg*, at least in one passage.[7] There are also various references to 'seeing *mēnōg*', as with regard to Zoroaster,[8] or when a new-born child is said to have the capa-

[5] GBd 222.9f.; *Pahlavi Rivāyat*, ed. Dhabhar, p. 163.14f.

[6] GBd 221.15. I am not sure of the precise meaning of the phrase: *u-š dāštārīh (ī) gētīg nēst*, Pahl. Rivāyat, p. 128.11, where it refers to *asmān*, and op. cit. p. 129.7f., where it refers to *zamīg*.

[7] DkM 42.20f.; cf. Appendix B, note 12 (below, p. 97).

[8] DkM 645.16. In a Middle Persian passage which is found in the *Pâzend Texts* (ed. E. K. Antiâ, Bombay 1909, p. 62ff.) immediately after the Bundahišn, and which follows in the Munich manuscript M6 the book *Šāyast ne šāyast* (cf. *Pahlavi Texts*, translated by E. W. West, Part I, Sacred Books of the East, vol. V, p. 372ff.), Zoroaster addresses Ohrmazd saying: 'Thy head, hands, feet, hair, face, and tongue are in my eyes just like those even which are my own, and you have the clothing men have; give me a hand, so that I may grasp thy hand' (West's translation). Ohrmazd's answer is: *man mainyū agarftār ham dasti man gərəftan na tuā*. "I am an intangible spirit. It is not possible to grasp my hand". Zoroaster is worried by the fact that Ohrmazd and the Amahraspands are intangible: when he departs from the presence of Ohrmazd and will no longer see him, there will be no way of experiencing the divinity by the senses. Ohrmazd's answer to this is that the specific material creations of Ohrmazd and of each of the Amahraspands (righteous man, cattle, fire, metal, earth and virtuous woman, water and vegetation) represent their concrete presence in the world, even when they themselves are invisible. Another text shows Zoroaster's capacity to see *mēnōg* with regard to the *druj*: he is said to have been the only one who saw the onslaught of the demon (although the text can be construed differently): *ka druz ō dām dwārist be zardušt az gētīgān kas-ez ne dīd* (*Pahlavi Rivāyat*, p. 130.6f).

city to see *mēnōg*.[9] Ohrmazd is said to see the spirit of men, 'for Ohrmazd sees everything'.[10]

There is, however, no justification, as far as I can see, for saying, as H. S. Nyberg does,[11] that *mēnōg* was conceived to be corporeal, and to have a body and a form. When a *mēnōg* being makes an apparition in front of a human being it is said to put on a bodily form, and this form, one can generally deduce from the context, does not belong to it organically. A characteristic example is found in the story of Wahman who came towards Zoroaster in the form of a man:

> *ka az hān ul raft zardušt, ā-š mard dīd ka raft az *rapiθwin-tar nēmag. hān būd wahman, ud hān awe sahist wahman pēš-karb, ku pad-tan-cašm-tar bawēd, ud pēš-nēwag, ku pad harw ciš pēš būd, hān awe sahist wahman cand hān ī 3-mard-nēzag bālāy* ... (DkM 624.8–12; facsimile edition, p. [496]).[12]
>
> "When Zoroaster went up from there, he saw a man who was going from the southern direction. That was Wahman. Wahman seemed to him as one who has the form in front, so that he might be more visible to bodily eye, and as one who has goodness in front, namely, he was to the fore in everything. Wahman seemed to him to have the height of three spears of a man . . ."

The text seems, by its syntax and by the fact that it contains epithets which require a somewhat strained interpretation in Pahlavi, to be a translation from an Avestan original.

The same type of conception is seen with regard to the mythical figure of Vərəθraγna, who assumes a number of forms according to Yašt 14,[13] and also with regard to the various incarnations of

[9] DkM 747.8f.; cf. Bailey, *Zoroastrian problems in the ninth-century books*, Oxford 1943, p. 98 n. 1.

[10] Dādestān ī Dēnīg XXX, 6 (this text is quoted according to the divisions in the edition of Anklesaria).

[11] *Journal Asiatique*, 219 (1931), p. 33.

[12] Cf. G. Widengren, *The Great Vohu Manah and the Apostle of God*, Uppsala 1945, p. 60. (In transcriptions from Pahlavi I have not generally noted *W* or *Y* added to or omitted from the text.)

[13] Cf. B. Geiger, *WZKM*, 40 (1933), p. 98–100; E. Benveniste and L. Renou, *Vṛtra et Vṛθragna. Etude de mythologie indoiranienne*, Paris 1934, p. 32f.

Xwarr, the concept of fortune.[14] Similarly, Ohrmazd is said to have put omniscient wisdom in Zoroaster's hand "in the form of water", which Zoroaster was made to drink.[15] *Dēn*, Avestan *daēnā*, is another instance for this phenomenon. It appears in the form of a maiden in eschatological scenes and has to declare its identity to the man whose religious ego it represents: it is apparently not supposed to be recognized by its mere form.[16]

Notwithstanding these observations, the contrast between *mēnōg* and *gētīg* is regularly defined by the adjectives 'invisible' as against 'visible' in the Pahlavi writings.

> *wimand ī gētīg wēnišnīg gīrišnōmand ciš. harw ce pad pad tan cašm wēnišnīg ud pad tan dast gīrišnōmand gētīg* (DkM 120.20–22; reading corrected from facsimile edition, p. [90].13–15) [cf. de Menasce, *Pratidānam* (Festschr. Kuiper), p. 194.]
>
> "The definition of *gētīg* is: a visible, tangible thing. Whatever is visible with bodily eye and tangible with bodily hand is *gētīg*."[17]

Or similarly in another text:

> *a-wēnišnīg mēnōg a-gumēzišn ō wēnāfdāg stī ud wēnišnīg nimūnag, mēnōg-waxšag ruwān andar gētīg-rawišnīg tan nēwag xwadāy kard* (Dādestān ī Dēnīg II, 13).
>
> "He made the unseen and unmixed *mēnōg* over to visible existence,[18] a model perceptible by sight. He made the soul, existing in *mēnōg*,[19] the good lord in the body, flourishing in *gētīg*".[20]

---

[14] H. W. Bailey, *Zoroastrian Problems*, p. 29 ff.

[15] *Zand-ī Vohûman Yasn*, ed. B. T. Anklesaria, Bombay 1957, p. 8; cf. Bailey, op. cit., p. 29, n. 2.

[16] Cf. the texts collected by Jal Dastur Cursetji Pavry, *The Zoroastrian doctrine of a future life*, New York 1926, p. 33 ff., and M. Molé, "Daēnā, le pont Činvat et l'initiation dans le Mazdéisme", *RHR*, 157 (1960), p. 155–185.

[17] Cf. for this passage especially the remarks made by P. J. de Menasce in his edition of *Škand-gumānīk Vičār*, p. 102 f., where further passages are discussed. Dēnkard III, chapter 123 (DkM 119 ff.), also defines *gētīg* in these terms.

[18] On the term *stī* cf. Appendix B, below p. 89 ff.

[19] The expression *mēnōg-waxšag* as opposed to *gētīg-rawišnīg*, is discussed in Appendix A, below p. 87 ff.

[20] The translations of this passage by M. Molé, in his book *Culte, mythe et cos-*

These two modes are also conceived of as being two realms or domains, differentiated as it were geographically, as in the phrase which occurs in the famous catechism of the *Pand-Nāmag*:

> *az mēnōg mad hēm, ayāb pad gētīg būd hēm*? (Pahlavi Texts, ed. Jamasp-Asana, p. 41).
>
> 'Have I come from *mēnōg* or have I been originated in *gētīg*?' (The proper Zoroastrian answer to this question is, of course, the first alternative).

In this text, however, the underlying meaning of the two terms cannot be made clear only by reference to a cosmological difference between two zones or spheres of existence. There is also a certain value symbolism attached to the two concepts: the first, *mēnōg*, stands for the religious values, and the second represents the secular world. This difference is connected with the idea that *mēnōg* is also a term for the eschatological world and for what it stands for: the trial of the spirits, reward and punishment. A person can be said to attach himself to *mēnōg* as opposed to *gētīg* in the sense that he leads a life dedicated to virtue, constantly meditating about the final judgement.[21]

Apart from this abstract usage of the two terms, they can also denote two classes of individual beings belonging respectively to the two modes of existence. To this category of usage belong phrases like *mēnōgān ud gētīgān*, '*mēnōg* and *gētīg* beings';

---

mologie dans l'Iran ancien, Paris 1963, p. 478, and M. F. Kanga in *J. M. Unvala Memorial Volume*, Bombay 1964, p. 134, differ from the one offered here. The sense of this passage is close to the one in Škand-gumānīk Vičār VIII, 33: *nun acārī šāyaṯ dānastan ku īn gəθī i vīnašnī gīrašnī až mainyō i avīnašnī agīrašnī dāṯ būṯ əstəṯ* "It is now possible to know with certainty that this visible and tangible *gētīg* was created from an invisible and intangible *mēnōg*". The same meaning of *mēnōg* and *gētīg* is also seen in the passage Dēnkard VI, 79 (DkM 488.7–14) about Ardwahišt who is seven months in *gētīg* and five months of the year in *mēnōg*, a statement which is interpreted as referring to the "manifestation" or non-manifestation of the plants.

[21] A typical text illustrating this point is: *xīr ī gētīg a-paymān ne ārāyišn, ce gētīg a-paymān-ārāy mard mēnōg-wišōb bawēd* (Dēnkard VI, 149; = DkM 505). "One ought not to embellish the things of *gētīg* in excess of the measure, for a man who embellishes *gētīg* in excess of the measure becomes one who corrupts *mēnōg*".

mēnōgān yazdān, 'the *mēnōg* ones, the gods'; or the expression *mēnōg* when applied to the two antagonistic spirits, Ohrmazd and Ahreman.[22]

So much for the definition of the two terms. When they are examined as used in the context of creation,[23] we notice that the *Greater Bundahišn* describes the process by which the world came into being as consisting of three stages. The relevant passage runs as follows:

> *ōhrmazd pad amahraspandān brīnōmand mad ka-š dād būd hēnd 3 rad. ce-š abāz ō gētīg abāyast dādan, u-š nōg-tar pad tan ī pasēn anāgīh az-eš be a-paydāg burdan. u-š dām ī mēnōg mēnōgīhā dārēd, u-š dām ī gētīg mēnōgīhā dād, u-š did be ō gētīgīhā dād* (GBd 13.7–13). "Ohrmazd came to be a possessor of time divisions, three periods, through the *amahraspands*, when he created them. For he had to create them back into *gētīg*, and then again to extinguish evil from them in the future body. He holds *mēnōg* creation in *mēnōg* form, he created *gētīg* creation in *mēnōg* form, and he created it again into *gētīg* form".[24]

We seem to have here two alternative interpretations of an earlier, presumably Avestan, tradition concerning the three periods connected with the creation of the Amahraspands. The first version is incomplete: a reference to the first creation, in *mēnōg*, is missing. This omission can be explained either as the result of a scribal error, or preferably as an ellipse, made by the author, of an obvious idea which the reader is certain to complete for himself. The three stages should be, according to the first

---

[22] Examples for this can be seen in H. S. Nyberg, *Hilfsbuch des Pehlevi*, II, p. 150.

[23] The main Pahlavi texts which deal with the double creation, *mēnōg* and *gētīg*, have been discussed more than once, but they still await definitive publication. They are most conveniently given in transcription and translation in R. C. Zaehner, *Zurvan: a Zoroastrian dilemma*, Oxford 1955, p. 276ff., where references to earlier literature will be found. Of subsequent publications, some of the remarks on textual matters in M. Molé's article entitled "Le problème zurvanite", *Journal Asiatique*, 247 (1959), p. 431–469, are particularly important. Interesting observations are also made by U. Bianchi, *Zamān i Ōhrmazd*, Torino 1958, p. 95ff.

[24] Cf. M. Molé, loc. cit., p. 438f., where a somewhat different translation is given.

version: (creation in *mēnōg*), creation in *gētīg*, the eschatological period.

The alternative interpretation tries to distinguish between three moments in creation by itself, without taking eschatology into account. The three stages thus obtained are: (1) *mēnōg* creation in *mēnōg*; then *gētīg* creation (2) first in *mēnōg*, (3) then in *gētīg*. The first, or pure *mēnōg* creation, may not involve a creation strictly speaking at all, for the verb used is *dārēd* "holds". The first moment here indicates a state of existence before any material creation of the world is envisaged; this is followed by a first stage of 'real' creation: the prototype of the material world being fashioned in "ideal" form, which is then translated into *gētīg*. The two interpretations have in common the fact that one of the "three periods" falls outside the proper existence of this world: in the first it is eschatology, in the second it is the period preceding the proper existence of the universe. Both interpretations of this tradition depend upon the statement that the three periods came into being with the creation of the Amahraspands, which statement belonged, so it seems, to the original Avestan sacred text on which the Pahlavi elaboration is based.

The text of the first chapter of the Bundahišn is in fact based on a conception of creation in three stages, on the lines of this second interpretation.[25] It also presents the creation of the world as a process in which the Amahraspands take part.[26] The essential trait of the Bundahišn's description is that the world was first formed in a *mēnōg* form, and that this conceptual or *mēnōg* world was later translated into a visible and tangible form, into *gētīg*. This mythology of creation seems to interpret in temporal terms a duality of existence which is taken to characterize life in the world. The *mēnōg* world is taken here to precede *gētīg*. *Gētīg* does not exist on its own. It is foreshadowed by a *mēnōg* prototype, from which it is derived and on which it continues to be in a sense dependent.

The same type of relationship between *mēnōg* and *gētīg* in the context of creation is formulated in theological terms in a

---

[25] This point is made by M. Molé in his analysis of the chapter, loc. cit., p. 442–445.

[26] GBd p. 14, ch. I (§ 33–35 in Zaehner's numbering).

number of texts in the third book of the *Dēnkard.* To quote a fairly short but representative chapter:[27]

abar dām mēnōgīg āfurdan, az mēnōgīh ō gētīgīh rasīdan paydāgīh. az nigēz ī weh-dēn.

(1) *hād mēnōg āfurišn bawišn ast ī a-hambūd wāspuhragānīh ast ī a-wēnišnīg a-gīrišnīg, ud bun ast ī gētīg.*

(2) *ud gētīg dahišn ham-bawišnīg ī bawišn ī mēnōg, ud dahīg ud paydāgīh ast ī mēnōg, u-š wāspuhragānīh ast ī wēnišnīg gīrišnōmand.*

(3) *ud ēd paydāg ku mēnōg bun ī gētīg. ēn-ez paydāgīh ka gētīg ciš az ham-bawišnīh ciš wišāyihēd abāz ō bawišn mēnōg rasēd ī-š ast bun.*

(4) *ud mēnōg bawišn ēwag ast ī a-bahr, ōh-ez mēnōg, dādār fradom azešīg āfurišn ī xwānihēd bawišn.*

(5) *ud gētīg ham-bawēnišnīh dahišn *ast *ī dādār az fradom azešīg āfurišn bawišn ham-bawēnīd.*

(6) *ud dām fradom pad mēnōg dād, az mēnōgīh gētīgīh āwurd. weh-dēn nigēz ēn-ez paydāgīh.*

"On creating the creatures in *mēnōg*, their manifestation coming from *mēnōg* to *gētīg*. From the instruction of the Good Religion.

(1) *Mēnōg* creation is 'becoming' (*bawišn*), without adversary. It has a special quality:[28] invisible and intangible. It is the root of *gētīg*.[29]

(2) *Gētīg* production[30] is a 'co-existent' (*ham-bawišnīg*)[31] of

---

[27] Dēnkard III, chapter 416; DkM 398f.; facsimile edition, p. [310]f. The text corresponds partly to the first part of chapter 105; DkM 98f.; facsimile edition, p. [72]f. [Cf. Gnoli, *AION* N.S. 13 (1963), 187].

[28] The latest discussion of the word *wāspuhragān* 'special, particular' is by W. B. Henning in *Indo-Iranica, Mélanges Morgenstierne*, Wiesbaden 1964, p. 95–97. Numerous occurrences are recorded, especially in Dēnkard and *Škand-gumānīk Vičār* (VII, 2, the abstracts *pasāxtaī ciharanīdaī vāspuhargānī*, 'being fashioned, being given nature and having special qualities', stand in juxtaposition; and similarly further in the same chapter).

[29] This simile occurs more than once. Thus in *Škand-gumānīk Vičar* VIII, 24: *gəθī bar i mainyō vaš mainyō bun*, '*Gētīg* is the fruit of *mēnōg*, *mēnōg* is its root'.

[30] There is a consistent terminological distinction between *āfrīdan* (*āfurdan*), which is the verb reserved for *mēnōg* creation, and *dādan, dahišn*, a verb which

mēnōg 'becoming'. It is a product[32] and a manifestation of *mēnōg*. It has a special quality: being visible and tangible.

(3) This is revealed: *mēnōg* is the root of *gētīg*. This is also a revelation: when a *gētīg* thing is loosened from 'co-existence', it comes back to 'becoming', *mēnōg*, which is its root.

(4) *Mēnōg*, viz. 'becoming', is one, undivided. Even this is *mēnōg*, the first originated[33] creation of the Creator, called 'becoming'.

---

is used when the secondary character of *gētīg* production is to be emphasized. The etymology of *āfrīdan* favours a spiritual connotation; cf. W. B. Henning, 'Das Verbum des Mittelpersischen der Turfanfragmente', *Zeitschrift für Indologie und Iranistik*, IX, 1933, p. 200f. This verb was exclusively used in the Manichaean texts for expressing the idea of creation, conveyed in Syriac by the verb *qerā*, 'to call'; see F. C. Andreas and W. B. Henning, *Mitteliranische Manichaica aus Chinesisch-Turkestan*, I, Berlin 1932 (Sitzungsberichte der preussischen Akademie der Wissenschaften, phil.-hist. Klasse, 1932), p. 179 n. 5. H. Junker (*Vorträge der Bibliothek Warburg*, 1921–22, p. 134) reads this word *āwurišn*, but this is unfounded. The verb *dādan* was perhaps chosen for *gētīg* creation because it could convey the notion of a transference or 'giving over' of what has previously existed in *mēnōg*. In the last sentence of our text the verb *āwurd* in which the idea of motion is even more stressed, is substituted. In that phrase it comes in opposition to *dād*, which designates there *mēnōg* creation (*dād* being also used as the general word for creation). [Cf. Gnoli, op. cit., p. 174 and n. 37.]

31 The precise meaning of *hambawišn* can be deduced from *hambūd* 'that which exists together, a rival'. In DkM 99.5ff. we read: *ud rōšn mēnōg ... az a-ham-būd mēnōg bawišn ō ham-bawišn ī hān gētīg waštan šāyēd* "the luminary *mēnōg* ... can turn from *mēnōg* 'being' lacking a rival into the 'co-existence' of that *gētīg*". The word is used with a different emphasis in the following passage: *dādār ēwag ēwag stī az bun ī stī nērōg ud waxš az bun ī waxš zōr abāz xwāst, ud ēwēnagōmand ud karbōmand pad abēzagīh ō-z ruwān ham-bawēnēd, abāg-ez ruwān anōšagēnēd* (DkM 345.15ff.). "The Creator has sought back each *stī* from the root of the force of *stī* and each spirit (*waxš*) from the root of the force of the spirit, and he joins them in purity, equipped with *ēwēnag* and *karb*, to the soul, and he makes them immortal, together with the soul". The precise sense in which this verb and its derivatives are used to designate a stage in the development of the embryo escapes me. It may denote the stage of the embryo's 'differentiation' or 'materialization'. Cf. GBd p. 16, and Zaehner, *Zurvan*, p. 305, note to line 173.

32 *dahīg* 'product' is frequent in the Dēnkard. Cf., e.g., DkM 202.22; 203.2, 5, 6, 8; 208.4, 7; 350.8; 384.5; 417.18; 420.20; 421.5.

33 *azešīg* 'originated, derived': the existence of this adjective shows that the postposition *az-eš* is not considered merely as a preposition with an enclitic pronoun but constitutes a separate lexeme. On the use of the postposition cf. M. Boyce,

(5) *Gētīg* is a production brought into 'co-existence', which the Creator caused to come into co-existence from the first originated creation, 'becoming'.

(6) He produced the creatures first in *mēnōg*; from *mēnōg*-ness he brought out *gētīg*-ness.
This too is a revelation from the instruction of the Good Religion."

The chapter seems to present here the twofold scheme familiar to us now from the Bundahišn. There is the basic opposition between *mēnōg*-creation and *gētīg*-creation, which are designated by the traditional technical terms *bawišn* and *ham-bawišn*, 'becoming' and 'co-existence'. The first term in this twofold scheme, *bawišn*, occupies also the first stage in a fourfold conception of creation, which consists of *bawišn*, *bawišn-rawišnīh*, *bawišn-astišnīh*, *stī*.[34] The underlying idea in our chapter is however very close to the one which distinguishes three stages of creation, just like the Bundahišn text discussed above.

It does not seem as if this type of text dealing with cosmogony attaches any greater moral value to one of the two concepts, *mēnōg* or *gētīg*. The only warranted statement which can be made on the basis of these texts is that *mēnōg* is primary and *gētīg* is secondary, not only in the chronological sense, but also in the logical order of things. Thus, *mēnōg* is a datum, a pre-existent fact; it is the root. *Gētīg*, being created, is in need of explanation or justification, and this is done by stating the functions for which it was created.[35] Even texts of a more mythological character, in which, for example, the fire or the frawahrs express their

---

'Some Middle Persian and Parthian constructions with governed pronouns', *Dr. Unvala Memorial Volume*, Bombay 1964, p. 49–56.

[34] This scheme is briefly discussed in Appendix B.

[35] Thus, for instance, in Dēnkard III, chapter 365 (DkM 350.5–7): "From the 'wheel' (proceeded) the hot-moist 'becoming' possessed of wind; for arresting the demons which reside in *mēnōg*, it is, with assembled forces, the begetter of *gētīg* creations, the seed of seeds" (cf. Appendix D). Zaehner's translation of this passage, *Zurvan*, p. 374, is quite different. The reason given here for engendering *gētīg* creations is the need to check the progress of evil and ultimately to vanquish it; cf. also below, notes 40 and 41.

refusal to be created into the material world and have to be coaxed into willingness,[36] cannot be adduced as a proof of the inferior position of *gētīg*. Life in the material world is full of hardship because of the interference of the evil power, but it is not said to be bad by itself. In fact, as we shall see, evil has no 'real' existence in the material world.

A discussion of the position and constitution of *gētīg* occurs in Dēnkard III, chapter 123, which begins with the following definition:[37]

> "*gētīg* is a (mode of) being (*stī*)[38] which is visible and tangible in corporeality. Its creation was for that which wages battle against [the oppression and] the oppressor, which itself is repelling the opponent of creation.[39] It is connected to the eternal good motion (*jāyēdānīg nēwag-rawišnīh*).
>
> Its work is that for which it was created. This, too, is revealed of it: when there are no *gētīg* creations, the work of repelling the oppressor is not accomplished (lit. the work is bare of repelling the oppressor).[40]

According to this text (and this is a commonplace idea in the Pahlavi literature),[41] the object of the material creation is to

---

[36] For the fire, cf. *Pahlavi Rivāyat*, p. 58 ff., and DkM 796.17 ff.; on the frawahrs, GBd 38.14 ff.

[37] DkM 120.15–20, facsimile edition, p. [90]. The text of the chapter is transcribed completely in H. W. Bailey, *Zoroastrian problems*, p. 205–209, but the reading can now be revised in some points. I had the privilege to read this chapter, as well as other texts, with the Rev. Father J. de Menasce in the winter of 1963, and wish warmly to acknowledge the benefit I derived from him. [Cf. now translation of ch. 123 by de Menasce in *Pratidānam* (Festschrift Kuiper), The Hague-Paris 1968, pp. 193–200.]

[38] See P. J. de Menasce, *ŠGV*, p. 102. Bailey's reading, *gētīk hast gētīk*, is not intelligible. The difficulty in reading is caused by the word *stī*, which resembles *gētīg*. The scribes do however distinguish between them by writing *sty* for *stī* and *st'x* (*gyt'x*) for *gētīg*. See Appendix B.

[39] Reading: *u-š dahišn ō kōxšišnīg ī ōštāb ud ōštābāg ī xwad ast dahišn-hamēstār-spōzīh*. The words *ōštāb ud ōštābāg* appear to be a dittography; the original scribe may have meant to cross out *ōštāb* when he supposedly replaced it by *ōštābāg*.

[40] *ka nēst hēc gētīg-dahišnān kār brahnag az ōštāb-spōzīh*.

[41] The idea is expressed also in a Pahlavi text which summarizes a lost Avestan original, the Dām-dāt Nask. It says: *abar kunišn *ī dādārīh ud dādan ī dām pahlom*.

serve as the battle-ground for the fight against evil. It is in fact the only plane on which the struggle can at all be favorably decided. It is for this reason that it is crucially important to have a continuous existence of the material world, and for this reason it is also promised that there never will be a period in which man will not exist in the material world,[42] man being the main carrier of the battle against the evil spirits.[43] We thus see here a certain dialectic relationship obtaining between *mēnōg* and *gētīg*. *Mēnōg* is the primary existence, but as it is invisible and immovable, it lacks an aspect of reality. The real clash between the good *mēnōg* and the evil *mēnōg* can only occur on a *gētīg* level. At the same time, however, the fight which takes place between the two parties is not conceived to be a straigtforward war between equal rivals. Only Ohrmazd and his creations 'really' exist in *gētīg*, while Ahreman and the demons have no *gētīg* at all,[44] and they only participate in the life of *gētīg* in a secondary way, parasitically as it were:

> *dām ī ōhrmazd mēnōg ud gētīg-ez. awe ī druz nēst gētīg, be wad ī mēnōgīh abyōzēd ō gētīg. ce'ōn sam ī hāwandīh-ez drāz andar ēwag, a'ōn abarwēzīh paydāg ī mēnōgān ud gētīgān ī weh abar mēnōgān ī wad* (Dd XXXVI, 51; cf. M. Molé,

fradom pad mēnōgīh, cand ud ce'ōn dāštan ī pad mēnōg, waštan ī az-eš, gētīg cihrēnīdag ud sāxtag ō andar ēbgadīg kōšišn, pattūdan ud rāyēnīdan ud paywastag šāyastan ō frazām ī drang ī ēbgadīgīh (DkM 681.11–15; facsmile edition, p. [529]f.; cf. Molé, *Culte, mythe et cosmologie*, p. 390, for a slightly different transcription and rendering). "On the making of creation, and creating the creatures best. First in *mēnōg*; how much and in what manner it was kept in *mēnōg*; its being turned away from it; *gētīg* being originated and fashioned for the fight against the Assault; its enduring, its being ordered, and the possibility of its being joined to the end of the period of the Assault". On *drang*, 'period, duration', cf. R. C. Zaehner, *BSOS*, 9 (1937/39), p. 319. See also note 35 above.

42 Cf. Dādestān i Dēnīg, pursišn XXXIV, 2 (ed. T. D. Anklesaria, p. 71): *ēn gētīg hamēšag az āfurišn tā-z ō abēzag fraškardārīh hagrez abē-mardom ne būd ne-z bawēd*. "This *gētīg* (world), from its creation to the pure rehabilitation, never was and never will be without man". The whole chapter is transcribed and translated by M. Molé in *RHR*, 155 (1959), p. 157f.

43 Cf. the texts collected by Molé in *Culte, mythe et cosmologie*, p. 469ff.

44 The theme is discussed in some detail in *Studies in Mysticism and Religion presented to G. Scholem*, Jerusalem 1967, p. 227–234.

> *Journal Asiatique*, 247 [1959], p. 453. I have used here some of the variants which seem preferable to Anklesaria's text).
>
> "The creation of Ohrmazd is both *mēnōg* and *gētīg*, while that of the demon has no *gētīg*: but the evil of *mēnōg* is joined to *gētīg*. Just as there is long fear of (their) having equal power in one (of the contenders), so the victory of the good *mēnōg* and *gētīg* beings over the evil *mēnōg* ones is manifest".

If the function of *gētīg* is to serve as the decisive battle ground between the two powers, it is clear that it was created for this purpose because it affords undeniable superiority to Ohrmazd. *Gētīg* is the place where the existence of Ahreman can be ontologically denied, and where the outcome of the battle can be foreseen with confidence, despite the fear which the apparent equality of powers arouses.

Gētīg is thus the stage where the proper activity of the world takes place, *mēnōg* in a sense becoming, after the stage of creation, a derivative mode of being: it is affected by the events of *gētīg* and seems merely to echo the happenings which go on in *gētīg*.[45]

[45] This idea is expressed in Zātspram, chapters XXXIIf.: *ce'ōn nimūd pad handāzag ud andar nibīgān ī *hanbūdīgān* (?) *ku awe ke-š andar gētīg kunišn-ē ayāb tawān-*nērōgīh-ē ayāb mehīh-ē ayāb xwēškārīh-ē pad-eš sazāgīg, u-š bandihēd pad rāstīh *ud dārēd pad sūd ud sazēnēd, hān ēwēnag dānišn ud tawān-nērōgīh ud mehīh ud xwēškārīh ō hān ī awe ruwān paywandēnd, u-š pad-ez mēnōg ham-brahmagīh pad-eš bawēd.* "As was shown by analogy and in the composite (?) writings, a person who is worthy in the *gētīg* of action, craftsmanship, dignity or a vocation, and by whom it is performed (lit. tied) in truth, and who possesses it for (causing) benefit, and who makes it seemly, the same kind of knowledge, craftsmanship, dignity and vocation will be joined to his soul, and even in *mēnōg* the same manner will be in him". The implication is that one's worth in fulfilling one's vocation in *gētīg* is reflected in one's *mēnōg* position. The observations made by R. C. Zaehner (*Zurvan*, p. 259) are not borne out by the text, even if his reading were accepted. (Incidentally, the membership of the four classes being assigned to the category of *kunišn*, mentioned by Zaehner in this connection, does not presumably mean the fact of *belonging* to the class, which would be absurd, for this is decided by birth; it means rather fulfilling the functions of one's class properly.) The next chapter in Zātspram ends in a statement which phrases this idea sharply: *a'ōn ce'ōn pad gētīg āb-tāzīdār būd, hān ī mēnōgīg wārān kardār* (p. 134): "Just as if one was in *gētīg* a pourer of water, and in *mēnōg* a maker of rain". The texts are discussed also by Molé, *Culte, mythe et cosmologie*, p. 107, who shows the continuity of orthodox tradition on these points.

This aspect of the relationship between *mēnōg* and *gētīg* is particularly prominent in the eschatological descriptions.

The original primacy of *mēnōg* is however not in doubt. All good in this, the *gētīg* world, derives from *mēnōg*, and all evil likewise.[46] Good and evil in this world are not only derivative, and therefore lacking, as it were, original force, they are also subject to the special condition of this *gētīg* world, which is that of being in a state of 'mixture', *gumēzagīh*. For this reason neither good nor evil can be experienced in this world in their full force, in purity. They are here inextricably welded together. They are blended in such a way that they can only be conceived separate in *mēnōg* or in eschatology: the eschatological moment in this contrast is naturally brought into play for answering questions of theodicy.[47]

How good and evil are conceived to be mixed in *gētīg* can be seen from a passage which describes the evil experienced by the wicked in hell:

> *u-š nēst andar hēc āsānīh ud xwašīh ud urwahmīh, u-š andar ast hamāg gandagīh ud rīmanīh ud anāgīh ud dušxwārīh. u-š ne hangōšīdag hēc gandagīh ud rīmanīh ud dard ud anāgīh ī gētīgīg, ce ne hangōšīdag gumēzag anāgīh ī gētīgīg ō hān ī-š a-jumāy nēwagīh, u-š* dmšn *az bun-kadag ī anāgīh* (Dd XXVI, 3–5; p. 54). "There is no comfort or pleasure or joy in it. There is in it all stench and pollution and pain and evil and discomfort. No stench and pollution and pain and evil of *gētīg* is similar to it, because the mixed evil of *gētīg* is not similar to that with which there is no goodness, and which issues (?)[48] from the source of evil".

The text of this chapter, which denies the similarity between the evil of hell, which is *mēnōg* and pure, and that found in the

[46] This is clearly stated, for example, in chapter VIII of *Škand-gumānīk Vičār*.

[47] This is the theme of *Dādestān ī Dēnīg*, pursišn V, which tries to answer the question: 'Why does evil always come more to the good than to the wicked'. One of the ways to answer this question is to accept the existence of a balance of reward between *mēnōg* and *gētīg*; according to this view one person cannot get reward or punishment twice, on both planes. The idea is also present in the famous 'joyful thoughts' of Ādurbād (DkM 572f., and parallels).

[48] On the word *dmšn* see Appendix C.

gētīg world, has a parallel in the preceding chapter of *Dādestān ī Dēnīg,*[49] where a similar idea is expressed with regard to the goodness of paradise in relationship to this world.

In a non-theological context[50] the same thought occurs in a story which can here be paraphrased: Weh-dād ī Ādur-Ohrmazdān, who was a chief *mōbad,* saw in a place by which he happened to pass two priests (*ērbad*) who carried fire-wood from a mountain on their backs, chanting together the Avesta and the Zand. He questioned them as to the reason for their action, and they answered: As every person must undergo the evil created by Ahreman either in *gētīg* or in *mēnōg,* it seems to us better to go through our share of evil in *gētīg,* where we see, at the same time as we suffer evil, the sun and the moon, where we get food and possessions and remedy for maladies, rather than undergo it in *mēnōg,* in hell, where nothing good is intermixed with the evil.[51]

The relationship between *mēnōg* and *gētīg* is also expressed in spatial and temporal terms. *Mēnōg* is unlimited, *gētīg* is limited; *mēnōg* is intransient, *gētīg* is transient:

> *be pad āgāh-dārīh ī ō gētīgān nimūnag guftan ud nimūdan ī az gētīg ēnyā kanāragōmand abāg a-kanārag, ud a-sazišnīg abāg sazišnīg, ud kahišnīg abāg a-kahišnīg ham-hangōšīdag ne bawēd. ud gētīg ast kanāragōmand ud sazišnīg ud kahišnīg, hān ī a-sar-rōšnīh ast a-sazišnīg ud a-kahišnīg* (*Dādestān ī Dēnīg* XXX, 18f.). "Except for the purpose of making known to the people of *gētīg,* telling them and showing them an example taken from *gētīg,* there is no likeness between that which is limited and that which is unlimited, that which is constant and that which is transient, that which diminishes and that which is undiminishing. *Gētīg* is limited, transient,

---

[49] Chapter XXV, discussed in Appendix C.

[50] DkM 571f.; Dk VI, D5. An edition with a translation of Dēnkard, Book Six, is in press.

[51] The same idea about the joy of paradise is also found in Dd XXX, 17. On a cruder level of reasoning, the fact that *xīr ī gētīg*, 'the things of this, the material, world', are less perfect than *xīr ī mēnōg*, is explained (in *Mēnōg ī Xrad*, Chapter 12) as due to the influence of the planets on *gētīg*.

diminishing, and the endless light is intransient and undiminishing".

One should perhaps add that these epithets are applied to the contrast between *gētīg* in the meaning of the actual, transient, life in this world, as against *mēnōg*, the world of eschatology. In GBd, p. 9, the term *mēnōg a-be-wardišnīh*, "the non-reversibility of *mēnōg*", occurs, as one of the phases in the process through which creation came into being.[51a]

The distinction between the two concepts of *mēnōg* and *gētīg*, it may be not superfluous to point out, is not equivalent to any contrast between divine and human beings or between creating powers and the created world. Such a contrast seems alien to Zoroastrianism.[52] The world was first created in *mēnōg*, and thus an aspect of creation falls under *mēnōg*. In *gētīg*, on the other hand, there are also divine beings. Thus the usual formula for gods refers to 'gods (*yazdān*), both *mēnōg* ones and *gētīg* ones'.[53]

The two worlds, the ideal world of *mēnōg* and the material world of *gētīg*, are thus separate from each other only on the plane of creation and eschatology. In the actual world the separation can only be done by intellectual analysis. Although this is never explicitly said, the actual world could perhaps be described as one of mixture in this sense too, that *mēnōg* and *gētīg* are blended in it together.[54] This mixture is indeed stated

---

[51a] Cf. Molé, *JA*, 247 (1959), p. 435f.

[52] H.S. Nyberg, *Journal Asiatique*, 219 (1931), p. 34, seems to be wrong when he applies to *mēnōg* the label 'divine'.

[53] Cf., e.g., *Škand-gumānīk Vičār* I, 4; *Pahl. Rivāyat*, p. 72.14: *yazdān ī mēnōgān ud yazdān ī gētīgān*. The formula is already Avestan; cf. *xšnūmaine yazatanąm ašaonąm mainyavanąm gaēθyanąm* in Yasna 7, 4; *Altiranisches Wörterbuch*, column 1279.

[54] Cf. DkM 140.11ff.; facsimile edition, p. [106]: *andar gumēzagīh gētīg ud mēnōg bahrān winārišn ud kārīgīh pad ham-yuxtīh ud paywastag-zōrīh ī ēwag abāg did būd* (- - -) *u-šān az wiškanišn ī zōr ēwag az did wišōbišn ud a-kārīh paydāg*. "In the "mixture" the arrangement and the effectiveness of the parts of *gētīg* and *mēnōg* are (attained) by their being joined together and having their powers united with each other. . . . From the separation of their forces from each other there is manifest disintegration and loss of effectiveness". The term "mixture" here, as elsewhere, refers to the state of the present world, where good and evil are mixed together; the subject-matter of the chapter, however, is the need to enable the

to be an essential condition for its proper functioning. The parables adduced for the way in which *mēnōg* is invisibly present in the *gētīg* world are those of the raw material from which a material object is made, such as the wool from which the woolen garment is fashioned or the parent's seed in the offspring.[55]

Every material object, as well as every intellectual concept, seems to be represented by a *mēnōg* prototype or to have a *mēnōg* counterpart.[56] At the same time, on the other hand, *mēnōg* ideas have their visible incarnations, as we have seen above.

Various material bodies are said to have a *mēnōg* which dwells in them. It is difficult as a rule to decide whether a *mēnōg* which is associated with a particular object is a 'prototype', which exists separately, or a cosmic *mēnōg* which is inherent in that individual. Sharp differentiation is never made in the texts between the different categories of *mēnōg*, and the distinction may be taken to be irrelevant to the Zoroastrian authors. Separate but inherent *mēnōgs* can however sometimes be clearly noticed in the texts. As an example, the following passage may be quoted. To the question whether Ohrmazd can be seen by the spirits after death a negative answer is given, and the reason is this:

> *be hān ī ka pad wuzurg-andēšīh ī dādār mēnōgān gētīgīg-wēnišnīhā paymōzēnd ayāb ō gētīgān mēnōg-sōhišnīg wēnišn abyōzēnd ēnyā, axw pad gētīg-sōhišn mēnōgān dīdan pad hān hangōšīdag tawān ce'ōn ka tanīhā wēnēnd ke-š ruwān andar,*

---

mēnōg and the *gētīg* components of this world to work in harmony and assist each other. That both elements are given equal standing is evident from the discussion which follows in the chapter, where various *gētīg* and *mēnōg* concepts which are dependent upon each other are listed, and a table is drawn to make the point clear.

[55] The text which presents the theory around the presence of *mēnōg* within *gētīg* in the clearest manner is chapter 191 of Dēnkard III (DkM 202f.; facsimile edition, p. [157]f.); it is given in Appendix D. The idea occurs also in chapter 194 (DkM 207f.; facsimile edition p. [161]ff.), and in chapter 276 (DkM 290; facsimile edition, p. [221]).

[56] Examples are: 'the spirit of the body' of man, *Dādestān ī dēnīg* XV, 7: *mēnōg ī tan ud abārīg weh mēnōgān* (also ibid. XVI, 4, 13). 'The spirit of creation' (*mēnōg ī dahišn*) and 'the spirit of the worship of the religion of the Mazdeans' (*mēnōg ī yazišn ī dēn ī mazdēsnān*) are mentioned in Dd XXI, 1. 'The spirit of the Gāthās', DkM 790.14; 'the spirit of the wind', Zātspram III, 10, 11; 'the spirit of the sky', GBd 18.13.

> *ayāb ka ātaxš wēnēnd ke-š warhrān andar, ayāb āb wēnēnd ke-š xwēš mēnōg andar ast* (Dādestān ī Dēnīg XXX, 5).[57]
>
> "Except in cases when through the great consideration of the Creator, the spirits are clothed in visible *gētīg*, or when *gētīg* people are endowed with sight which is in the nature of *mēnōg* perception, the self (of men) can see the spirits with *gētīg* perception by that similitude, like when bodies are seen in which there is soul, or fire in which there is Warhrām, or water in which its spirit is found". *

Every group of objects seems to have its collective *mēnōg* representation.[58] Such are, for example, the Amahraspands, who represent the 'elements' of this world, each of which is a species of beings. The Amahraspands are described in one place as the *mēnōg* and the *xwadīh*, 'selfness', of *gētīg* beings:

> *ud abārīg-ez gētīg dahišnān pad hān ī-šān mēnōg amahraspand ke-šān ast xwadīh a-marg, ud pad dēsag sāwišnōmand hēnd, pad ham-dar dādestān hān ī mardom* (DkM 43.11–14, facsimile ed. [32].6–8). "And the other *gētīg* creations, as to their *mēnōg*, the Amahraspand, who are their selfness, are immortal, and as to their form are corruptible. Man is in the same category."[59]

In addition to the previous categories of *mēnōg*, every group of *mēnōgs* may have a *mēnōg* idea or chief of its own.[60] We thus

---

[57] Cf. H. W. Bailey, *Zoroastrian Problems*, p. 112f.

[58] A *mēnōg* which represents the totality of a species can be often defined either as denoting a collective of beings or a corresponding abstract notion. Nyberg's contention that all abstracts in Iranian are merely 'disguised' collective nouns (*Die Religionen des alten Iran*, p. 87) does not carry conviction. The opposite can be claimed with equal validity.

[59] The original Avestan term for this idea is *ratu-* (cf. Yasna 12), sometimes reflected in the Pahlavi term *rad*. Cf. the note of J. Darmesteter in his *Zend-Avesta*, (Reproduction photographique) Paris 1960, I, p. 122f., n. 1.

[60] This is a probable, though not entirely proven, deduction from certain references which are found in the texts. Thus, in a passage which is concerned with repentance from a sin committed by a person, 'the demon in front of whom he committed that sin' (*hān druz ke pēš wināh kard*) has to depart from the body

obtain several layers of *mēnōg*, which differ from each other by the distance by which they are removed from the material world.[61] Ohrmazd is regarded, in accordance with this conception, as the *mēnōg* of (all) the *mēnōgs*, the ideal prototype of all *mēnōg* existence.[62] The pure *mēnōg* world, the world of Ohrmazd and the Amahraspands, as well as that of Ahreman and his host, is stated to be eternal. But there must be numerous *mēnōgs* whose existence is ephemeral, or who are at least generated in time. These are, for example, the spirits of the good deeds and of the

---

of that man and to come in front of the *mēnōg* demon (*druz ī mēnōg*: Dēnkard VI, 315; DkM 544). The *mēnōg* demon seems to be a prototype of the individual demons, themselves *mēnōg* beings representing the sins committed by individual people. The arch-demon would seem to be called *mēnōg* to distinguish it from those individual demons which are 'inherent' in the *gētīg* world. Cf. also with regard to Ohrmazd, *infra*, note 62.

[61] We encounter such epithets as: *hān ī ōhrmazdīg xrad, hān ī mēnōgīg xrad* (*Dādestān ī Dēnīg* XXXVI, 13, p. 78) 'The wisdom of Ohrmazd, the *mēnōg* wisdom'. Since every wisdom is a *mēnōg* concept, the epithet may in this case stress the particularly elevated *mōnōg* character attributed to the wisdom of Ohrmazd. *Gētīg* seems also to have several layers of concreteness. In Dēnkard III, 365, the expression 'the finest (or thinnest, keenest: *dārmag-tom*) *gētīg* self' is found, cf. Appendix D.

[62] *ōhrmazd ī weh dahagān dādār andar-ez mēnōgān mēnōg, u-š mēnōgān-ez wēnišn ōh *dīdan ī mēnōgān abar gētīgān paydāg* (*Dādestān ī Dēnīg* XXX; 4, Anklesaria's edition, p. 59): 'Ohrmazd, the Creator of the good creatures, is a *mēnōg* even among *mēnōgs*. His being seen by the spirits is similar to what is known of the spirits being seen to *gētīg* beings'. The same idea is expressed ibid., XVIII, 3: *ōhrmazd-ez andar mēnōgān mēnōg*, and XXXVI, 10: *awe ī abartom rōšnān xwadāyān xwadāy-tom mēnōgān mēnōg-tom wispagān ōhrmazd ī dādār*. "He who is the highest of the luminaries, the most lord of the lords, the most spirit of the spirits, Ohrmazd the creator of all"—the peculiar syntax here may suggest an Avestan original to the formula (*wispagān* should be a genitive depending on *dādār* by analogy with *weh dahagān dādār* in Dd XXX, 4, quoted above). The context makes it clear that what is meant is that Ohrmazd stands in the same relationship to *mēnōg* beings as the latter in their turn stand with regard to the visible world. In *Škand-gumānīk Vičār* I, 2, *andarica mainyuā mainyō*, we should therefore translate accurately: "he is a *mēnōg* even with regard to the (other) *mēnōgs*", who are like *gētīg* in relation to him. (The translation '*mēnōg* entre les *mēnōgān*', does not bring this point out with sufficient clarity). Chapter 206 of Dēnkard III (DkM p. 225f., facsimile ed., p. [176]f.; cf. Appendix D) presents a scheme according to which the *mēnōg* and *gētīg* products of Ohrmazd occupy each a supreme position in its class. Among all *mēnōg* beings the *mēnōg* product of Ohrmazd is endowed most with *mēnōg*-ness; and the some applies to the *gētīg* product of Ohrmazd.

bad deeds of man.[63] We do not know whether predestination was taken to such an extreme position as to require the pre-existence of all the *mēnōg* correspondences relating to the individual person, or of single events, but it is reasonable to assume that such individual *mēnōgs* were considered to be manifestations of a general and eternal 'idea'.[64]

Man constitutes a problem by itself in this scheme. Here, as in other fields, man represents on a smaller scale the same structural relationship, in this case between *mēnōg* and *gētīg*, which obtains in the world. Man's existence in this world is preceded by a *mēnōg* prototype, which seems to be eternally pre-existent, the *fravaši*, or *frawahr* in Pahlavi: the way in which the *frawahr* is transferred from *mēnōg* existence to 'being clad in flesh' in the *gētīg* world is described in some detail in Dd XXXVI, 25 f.[65] His material existence in the actual world is a blend of a

---

[63] *mēnōg ī kirbag* is mentioned in an eschatological rôle in Dd XXX, 2. The three spirits, representing the good thought, speech and deed of a wicked person, come to comfort him during the first three nights after his death, according to Dd XXVI, 4. Above, note 60, the expression 'that demon in front of whom the sin was done' was noticed. In Dk VI, 290 (DkM 535), we encounter the idea of a light (*rōšnīh*) which emerges from a good thought, speech or action, leading the man towards *dēn*, and likewise a darkness which is the outcome of an opposite situation. This idea has probably some affinity with that of a *mēnōg* which represents pious deeds or sins, although it shows that the system of thought is not very tight in this respect.

[64] The ambiguity is striking, and may be conscious, in chapter 137 of Dēnkard III (DkM 140–142; facsimile ed., p. [106] f.). Thus, for example, where there is a scheme of *gētīg-mēnōg* correspondences in the life of the individual person: *gētīg tan* (body) corresponds to *mēnōg ruwān* (soul); similarly *xwāstag* (possession), in *gētīg*, corresponds to *kirbag* (pious work) in *mēnōg*; *āzarm* (honour) to *frārōn-tuxšāgīh* (righteous effort); *pādexšāyīh* (rule) to *dēn* (religion); *hudahišn* (good instruction; *dahišn*, 'instruction', is to be discussed in another publication), to *dānāgīh* (knowledge). *Mēnōg* in these correspondences, it should be noticed, is not the 'idea' of its *gētīg* pair, but its pious counterpart.

[65] The passage is treated in Appendix B. Of the extensive literature on the subject of the *fravaši*, H. Lommel's introduction to Yt. 13 in his *Die Yäšt's des Awesta, übersetzt und eingeleitet*, Göttingen-Leipzig 1927, p. 101 ff., and R. C. Zaehner, *The dawn and twilight of Zoroastrianism*, p. 146 f., may be pointed out. That *frawahr* is a permanent *mēnōg* existence of man can best be seen in the passage of GBd 34.10 ff. (text and translation in Bailey, *Zoroastrian problems*, p. 112): 'When during the period of the Assault people die, the body is joined to the earth, the *jān* to the wind, the *ēwēnag* to the sun, the soul (*ruwān*) to the *frawahr*'.

purely material body, *tan*, also termed *karb*, and a 'form', *ēwēnag*,[66] with a soul which marks his existence in the actual world, *ruwān*, the two being linked together by a vital soul, *jān*.[67]

Man is defined as consisting of *tan* and *ruwān*, the latter perhaps signifying in this context all the *mēnōg* forces in man, in the following passage:

> *ud hān ke xwadīh a-marg u-š paymōzan sāwišnīh hamargānīhā mardom ī pad hān ī-šān xwadīh ruwān a-marg, ud paymōzan ī tan andar gumēzagīh sāwišnōmand, pad hamīh ī āgnēn xwānihēd mardom ī pahlom hēnd gētīg dahišnān* (DkM 43.5ff.; facsimile edition, p. [32].2ff.). "That whose self is immortal and whose clothing is corruptible is the totality of men, in whom the self, viz. the soul, is immortal, and the clothing, viz. the body, is corruptible in the state of mixture. They are called men by the combination of both. They are the best of the *gētīg* creations".

Further in the chapter *ruwān* is called 'the guardian of the body' (*ruwān ī pānag ī tan*, DkM 43.15, facsimile edition [32],9). in the moral literature, the opposition between *tan* and *ruwān* denotes the contrast between wordly values and the higher aims of religion, representing the contrast between *gētīg* and *mēnōg* inside man.[68]

---

[66] For the constitution of man in general we have a thorough study with a most valuable discussion of sources in the chapter entitled 'Martōm', p. 78ff., of H. W. Bailey's *Zoroastrian problems*. On the terms *tan*, *karb*, *ēwēnag* see op. cit., p. 96 (where the three are apparently taken to be identical), and p. 118; the identity of *tan* and *karb* is certain. The two terms never come together, and they interchange as variants (cf. GBd 72.11, where DH has *klp'* for the text's *tn'*). The term *ēwēnag* seems however to be a distinct concept, though close in significance to the other two. The frequent occurrence of the pair *karb ud ēwēnag*, or in reversed order (cf. Bailey, *loc. cit.*) shows that the two are not identical. *Tan* and *ēwēnag* also come side by side, as for example: *tan abāz wirāyēd, ēg-šān ēwēnag be dahēnd* (GBd 223.8; Bailey, p. 97): "He restores the body, then *ēwēnag* is given to them". It may be assumed that *tan* or *karb* both mean the physical body, while *ēwēnag* means perhaps the 'shape' of the body. This would explain why *ēwēnag* 'is implied' in the *karb*, as noticed by Professor Bailey (loc. cit.).

[67] The way in which *jān* and *ruwān* come from "*mēnōg* existence" to "being clad in *gētīg*" is described in Dd XXVII, 2.

[68] Cf., e.g., *Pahlavi Texts*, ed. Jamasp-Asana, p. 148f., 153 § 76; p. 50 § 55.

The function of *jān* is defined in the following manner:

> *ōh-ez guft *pēšēnīg frazānagān ku jān ast mēnōg ī zīwēnāg andarg ruwān ud tan. tā ruwān ham-kadag ī tan zīndagīh dārēd tan, widard tan zīndagīh ī ruwān ast* (Dd XXII, 4).
>
> "The ancient wise men said thus too: *jān* is the vivifying spirit between *ruwān* and *tan*. As long as the *ruwān* is a dweller of the body, it (*jān*) keeps the body alive. Once the body has departed, it is the life of the *ruwān*".

In the scheme which occurs in chapter 137 of Dēnkard III,[69] visualized in the table given at the end of that chapter, *jān* occupies a mediating position between *tan* and *ruwān*, and also, interestingly, between *gētīg* and *mēnōg*. *Jān* has an affinity with the wind, *wād*,[70] which itself occupies an ambiguous position in the division of the world into *mēnōg* and *gētīg*: it is not directly visible, but it is perceptible through its action.

The ethical or religious self of man has its own representation in the form of *dēn*, which also plays a part in his judgement after death, but which is at the same time an objective existence of a social and perhaps also cosmic nature.[71] Man's activity in the actual world is marked by several *mēnōg* beings; there is, as it were, a *mēnōg* echo or reflection to every thought, speech or deed of man in the actual world.[72] As a species man is represented in *mēnōg* by Ohrmazd,[73] just as the other earthly elements are

---

[69] DkM 140–142; facsimile edition, p. [106]f.; above, note 64, for a partial summary.

[70] Cf., e.g., GBd 34.10ff., quoted above, note 65.

[71] The ambiguity is already Avestan. The attempts to distinguish between two separate concepts miss a characteristic point of Zoroastrian thought, for this ambiguity is typical of *mēnōg* notions. On *daēnā* cf. above, note 16. As opposed to the *fravaši*, which is an eternal *mēnōg* person, *dēn* is chiefly man's religious consciousness in this world and his moral self after death.

[72] Above, note 63.

[73] GBd 33.15ff., 163.8f.: *u-š gētīg daxšag mard ī ahlaw ke mard ī ahlaw rāmēnīd ayāb bēšīd ēg-eš ōhrmazd rāmēnīd ayāb bēšīd bawēd.* "His (sc. Ohrmazd's) *gētīg* mark is the righteous man. Whoever has caused a righteous man joy or affliction, has caused joy or affliction to Ohrmazd". Cf. Lommel, *Die Religion Zarathustras*, p. 106f. On the mythological plane man is represented by Gayōmard.

represented by the Amahraspands.[74] At the same time, however, by a different approach, every part of man is said to belong to a particular *mēnōg*: man's non-material faculties belong to Ohrmazd, while the components of his body are divided between the Amahraspands.[75]

Apart from these instances, which belong to what may be called the *mēnōg* accompaniment to man's earthly existence, there is also man's involvement with the world of *mēnōg* beings, his relationship to the cosmic beings on the *mēnōg* plane. Man's function on earth is to fight the demons and to help the good spirits,[76] and the relationship formed between man and the cosmic spirits is quite intimate. The spirits, apparently both good and evil, wish to reside in man, and man's duty is to try and drive away the evil spirits from him while making the good spirits take dwelling in him.[77] The phrase 'a man's *Srōš*', occurs, *Srōš* being the spirit of obedience, one of the major divinities of Zoroastrianism.[78] Such a phrase makes it possible to assume that the conception of divine spirits should be taken in a more abstract

[74] Cf. Lommel, loc. cit.

[75] GBd 196.1–5; cf. A. Götze, *ZII*, 2 (1923), p. 70; G. Widengren, *The Great Vohu Manah*, p. 53.

[76] *ōhrmazd ī xwadāy harw dām ēn-ez 2 sūd rāy dād, ēbgad pad-eš absihēnīdan ud gugāhīh ī xwēš rāy* (DkM 502.12ff.; facsimile ed., p. [392].7ff.; Ms. K43, fol. 199v). "The Lord Ohrmazd created every creature even for these two benefits, in order to annihilate through it the Assault, and so as to have a witness for himself". According to Ādurbād son of Zardušt every person should know the answer to a number of questions, one of which is: "For what purpose am I here (sc. in this world)?" (*cim ēdar hēm*). The correct answer is, "I am here in order to make the demons powerless" (*a-pādexšāy kardan ī druz rāy ēdar hēm*): DkM 573.18ff.; facsimile ed., p. [454].

[77] To quote but one example: ... *hamē tā mard kirbag ud ahlāyīh menēd ēg yazd ī andar tan andar tan mānēnd ud dēwān staw bawēnd ud be šawēnd* (DkM 524.18ff.; facsimile ed., p. [412]f.). "As long as a man thinks pious deeds and righteousness, the gods which are in his body remain in the body, and the demons are beaten and depart".

[78] Cf. the following quotation from Dēnkard VI, 90: "Just as among vessels of gold, silver and other metals, those which are purer and freer from defects have sweeter sound, so also a man who is purer in the things of the gods and freer from defects in himself, ... his Srōš produces the best sound ..." (*ēg-eš srōš wāng ī pahlom barēd*, DkM 491; facsimile ed., p. [382]; Ms K43, fol. 191r.). An alternative rendering of the latter phrase could be: "Srōš produces for him the best sound", which does not go against the observations offered here.

manner than the apparent wording of many passages suggest; one must reckon with the possibility that certain mythological formulations were understood in a figurative sense. There is, it should be remembered, a high degree of abstraction in Zoroastrian literature right from the *Gāthā*, where the whole pantheon consists of terms which denote abstract ideas. Even when they are conceived in the most personified manner, they never seem to lose their character as concepts, as general abstractions.[79] On the other hand, it is very likely that on the lower level of religion these expressions were taken literally, and the concepts of demonology, as well as those connected to the relationship between man and the good spirits, were understood in concrete form.

Man in the actual world is thus presented as the main battleground for the spirits. The outcome of the battle is in fact entirely dependent on man, the ultimate victory is effected by man's ability to vanquish the demons within himself.[80] In this we have another instance to the 'echo' character of *mēnōg*: the fate of the *mēnōg* world is determined by the battle conducted here by man.

The relationship between *mēnōg* and *gētīg*, as we have seen it work in the actual world, can now be examined against the conception of eschatology. Eschatology presents a well-known problem in the history of religions, which I believe can be solved in the context of Iranian religion by reference to the structure outlined above. It consists in the Pahlavi texts[81] of three distinct themes: individual eschatology (i.e., life after death, individual judgement and reward, paradise and hell), apocalypse (the cataclysm leading to the end of the world and the figure of the Saviour), and universal eschatology (resurrection, universal judgement, the rehabilitation of the world).

The problem arises from the duplication of events,—the double ordeal, judgement and reward, resurrection coming after what

---

[79] This observation does not include, of course, the divine persons which do not form part of the original Zoroastrian system, such as Mithra, Anāhitā etc., or the mythological figures, such as Gayōmard etc.

[80] Cf. Dēnkard VI, 130 (DkM 501; K43, fol. 198v.f.); 264 (DkM 530f.; K43, fol. 211r.).

[81] As well as in the fully developed Judaeo-Christian tradition. The clearest general account of the events of eschatology according to the Pahlavi sources is to be found in R. C. Zaehner, *The dawn and twilight of Zoroastrianism*, p. 302 ff. Several pertinent remarks are made by Molé, *RHR* 162 (1962), p. 211 ff.

seems like eternal bliss in paradise for the righteous, etc. To quote J. Duchesne-Guillemin: 'Les âmes jouissent de la béatitude dans la Maison du Chant, dans la lumière, dans la présence de Dieu. Pourquoi faut-il alors qu'il y ait une résurrection? A quoi bon le corps, instrument de lutte, quand la lutte est finie?' That author concludes: 'Deux doctrines, évidemment, ont cherché à se combiner: celle de l'immortalité de l'âme et celle de la résurrection des corps' (*La religion de l'Iran ancien*, p. 352).[82]

When we consider, however, that in the field of eschatology, just as in the parallel subject of creation, the interplay between *mēnōg* and *gētīg* must have occupied an important position in Iran, whether completely consciously or only partly so, the conception of Zoroastrian eschatology may seem more coherent.

Interpreted in these terms, the first, or individual stage in eschatology means a transference of man, at death, from the material world into *mēnōg*. This removal follows a certain period of transition, during which it is apparently not entirely clear whether the separation of man's *mēnōg* aspect, notably the soul, and his body, is going to be final. This transition of the *mēnōg* parts of man at death back to the *mēnōg* world is compared to the birth of man, at which the same *mēnōg* constituents move from *mēnōg* to settle in *gētīg* existence. In both cases this is a critical process, fraught with danger, and should be accompanied by the appropriate religious rites.[83] Death is thus regarded as an inverse reflection of birth; it is the individual's birth into *mēnōg*.

---

[82] The problem was earlier formulated by H. W. Bailey, *Zoroastrian Problems*, p. 116f. One ought however to remark that the observations on *Dādestān ī Dēnīg* XXX, 9, on p. 117 of *Zoroastrian Problems* (followed by Duchesne-Guillemin), are not quite accurate. The text is: *ud āmār ī pad wināh ud kirbag abar wahištīgān ne bawēd. xwad andar ēn mādiyān škift pursišnīh, ce ruwān ī widardagān be ō wahišt kard-āmārīh ud tuxt-*wināhīh ēdōn rasēd *ku-š tā fraškard anōh gāh ud ō nōg āmār a-niyāz.* "There is no reckoning for sins or pious deeds with the people of paradise. The question itself in this matter is surprising, for the souls of the departed reach paradise having their reckoning done and having their sins atoned for, in such a way that they have their place there until the Renovation and there is no need for a new reckoning". The question asked of Mānuščihr at the beginning of this chapter clearly referred to the problem of whether the just in paradise undergo reckoning while they are there, and Mānuščihr regards this as a 'surprising' question. There is no talk here of the problem of the double judgement.

[83] Cf. Dd XXVII.

When death in *gētīg* is total, the life of the soul after death begins, this being a summary and a judgement of life on earth. The descriptions of it in the Pahlavi literature suggest a dramatic reflection of man's ethical accomplishment in actual life. This stage of eschatology, conducted as it is in purely *mēnōg* terms, consists essentially of an ethical echo of one's *gētīg* life.

Universal eschatology, on the other hand, is entirely enacted in *gētīg*. The events leading to the rehabilitation of the world, the events of the apocalypse, constitute a phase in the history of the world in which the battle between the two ethical principles becomes fiercest, and the conditions of material life sink lowest. The world undergoes a considerable worsening of its situation. This stage in the life of the world is comparable to the death pangs in the life of the individual. Then comes the final stage of eschatology. The world does not cease to be, nor does it stop being *gētīg*. But *gētīg* existence itself undergoes profound change. It is no longer a 'mixture' but is purified from evil and elevated.

> *ōhrmazd abāg srōš-ahlaw ul ēstēd ud srōš-ahlāyīh āz be zanēd, ōhrmazd gannāg-mēnōg . . . yašt-ē be kunēd ud zamīg 3 nēzag bālāy ul šawēd . . . pad panjom yašt ō star pāyag rasēd ud garōdmān az hān gyāg frōd ō star-pāyag āyēd* (Pahlavi Rivāyat accompanying Dd, p. 156f.).[84]
>
> "Ohrmazd will stand up together with Srōš the Righteous. Srōš's Righteousness will smite (the demon) Āz (concupiscence), and Ohrmazd will smite the Evil Spirit. He will perform a sacrifice, and the earth will rise to the height of three spears . . ., at the fifth sacrifice, it will reach the station of the stars and Garōdmān (the highest paradise) will descend from its place down to the station of the stars".

The text goes on to say that Ohrmazd, the Amahraspands, all the gods and men will be together in one place. At the same time the world also sheds away some of the distinctive marks of

---

[84] Cf. Bailey, *Zoroastrian Problems*, p. 117; Molé, *Culte, mythe et cosmologie*, p. 89. The same idea occurs also in DkM 824.11 ff.; West(*SBE*, XXXVII, p. 235) and Widengren (*Hochgottglaube*, p. 119) understood the passage as containing a reference to Mithra, but this is unfounded. *

materiality. There is no more hunger, thirst, old age or death. There is sexual satisfaction without procreation:

> *mardom pad tan dād ī 40 sālag humānāg hamāg a-ōš ud a-marg ud a-zarmān ud a-sūyišn ud a-pūyišn* (Pahlavi Rivāyat, p. 157.10ff.);
>
> *ka-šān pas az hān gōšt-xwarišnīh ne abāyēd pad hān cim rāy ce-šān pad harw zamān mazag xwašīh ī hamāg gōšt andar dahān ēstēd* (ibid., p. 158.8ff.).
>
> "They will not need to eat meat, because they will have the sweet taste of meat always in their mouth";[85]
>
> *ud mard ud zan ēwag abāg did kāmag bawēd rāyēnēnd ud kunēnd be-šān zāyišn ne bawēd* (ibid., p. 158.12ff.).
>
> "men and women will have desire for each other and will satisfy it, but they will have no offspring".[86]

In these details it is clear that the change that occurs in the eschatological existence does not imply a transformation in the essential nature of *gētīg*; only what may be termed the unpleasant weight of *gētīg* existence is removed, while pleasurable experiences lose nothing from their effect. The elevation or purification of *gētīg* in eschatological times does not imply any negative attitude towards earthly pleasures, as has sometimes been concluded by scholars.[87] This is *gētīg* existence, one might say, which has become nearly *mēnōg*; or, more accurately, it has come as close to *mēnōg* as it is possible to do without ceasing to be *gētīg*. For Zoroastrianism, the ideal type of existence is one which combines 'the best of both worlds', in a very literal sense.

Thus, if our interpretation is correct, there is a parallel movement in individual and universal eschatology. The individual moves form *gētīg* existence (made worse by death pangs) over to *mēnōg*; the world moves from *gētīg* existence (through a debased stage) over to a purified, *mēnōg*-like, *gētīg* eschatological epoch.

---

[85] Cf. also Dd XXXIV, 3.

[86] Cf. also *Pahlavi Texts*, p. 107.

[87] See R. C. Zaehner, *The dawn and twilight of Zoroastrianism*. p. 313.

In addition, however, the human *mēnōg* returns, in resurrection, to the purified *gētīg* of the world, and thus comes to its ultimate fulfilment, which is an existence in an elevated kind of *gētīg* where the distinction between *mēnōg* and *gētīg* is perhaps neutralized. The whole history of the world is seen as a kind of dialectic movement: from *mēnōg* creation into *gētīg* actuality, and thence into the reality of *gētīg* endowed with the advantages of *mēnōg*.[88]

APPENDIX A

mēnōg-waxš(ag)

The fixed idiomatic expression *mēnōg-waxš*, *mēnōg-waxšag* (or *waxšīg*), which occurs in *Dādestān ī Dēnīg* II, 13 (cf. above, p. 63), where it comes in antithesis to *gētīg-rawišnīg*, deserves to be noticed in detail.[1] It seems to be characteristic of the style of Mānušcihr, though it occurs at least once outside the treatise *Dādestān ī Dēnīg*, in DkM 350.5–7.[2] The following passages help to establish the precise meaning of this expression.

> *jān ud ruwān ka az mēnōg-waxš be ō gētīg-paymōgīh rasēd* (Dd XXVII, 2): "When the *jān* and the soul come from *mēnōg* existence to being clad in *gētīg*".

[88] If this attempt at a structural interpretation of Zoroastrian eschatology in terms of *gētīg* and *mēnōg* is accepted, it may conceivably be used as an argument in the old debate about the possibility of Iranian influence in the development of Judaeo-Christian eschatology. The fact that the duplication of eschatological events makes good sense in Iran, forming as it seems to do an essential part of an organic whole, and the complementary fact that this is not the case in Judaism, should not be regarded as less significant than the observation, so often made in this connection, that certain eschatological themes are not to be found in the scanty remains of ancient Zoroastrian literature. There can be little doubt that the choice of themes which have survived in the fragments of the Avesta is not comprehensive.

[1] Several examples are quoted by H. W. Bailey, *Zoroastrian Problems*, p. 118f. For the word *waxš* and its derivatives cf. also H. W. Bailey, *BSOS*, 6 (1930/32), p. 280f.; *Zoroastrian Problems*, p. 105, note 1 (in the example from GBd 178.15ff., quoted there, it would seem more natural to take *waxšagīh* as the antithesis to **tanēgirdīh*).

[2] The whole chapter is given in Appendix D; it also contains similar expressions, such as: *waxšōmand mēnōgān* (DkM 349.10f.); *mēnōg ī wāxš-nērōg*, opposed to *mēnōg ī cihr-nērōg* (ib., lines 7–8).

In this passage an idiomatic play on words occurs, similar to the one which can be noticed in Dd II, 13. The material counterpart to *mēnōg-waxš* here is *gētīg-paymōgīh*.

> *az hān ce'ōn pāsbānīh ud pānagīh ī gētīgān az dādār framān srōš-ahlāy xwēškārīh, ud āmārgar-ez pad setōš ēwag srōš-ahlāy, hān ī ruwān 3 rōz ud šab mēnōg-waxš gāh andar gētīg pānagihēd pad hān ī srōš pādārīh ud āmārihēd pad-ez hān ī srōš āmārīh* (Dādestān ī Dēnīg XXVII, 6): "As the preservation of and guardianship over *gētīg* creatures is the work of Srōš the Righteous, by the Creator's command, and the one who does the reckoning during the three days following death is also Srōš the Righteous alone—that soul [of a person who has just died] is guarded by the guardianship of Srōš and is reckoned with through the reckoning of Srōš for three days and nights, a period of *mēnōg* existence inside *gētīg*".

We notice here again that *mēnōg-waxš* comes in close relationship to *gētīg*, though they do not form here a parallel.

> *harw 3 andar dāmān meh, u-š mehmānīh pad pahlomīgān mardān ahlawān, mēnōgīg, pad hān ī abēzag frawahr mēnōg-waxšīhā ō druz kōxšāg ud spōzāg ud wānāg ud ānābāg, hān ī yazdān spāh zōrēnāg, mēnōg xwadāyīh ī ōhrmazd. gētīgīhā, pad gētīg paymōgīh, hambandīh ī tan ud jān* (Dd I, 3): "All three are the greatest among the creatures. In *mēnōg* their residence in the best righteous men is by the fact that the pure *frawahr* is, in *mēnōg* existence, a fighter against the demons, one who rejects them, vanquishes them and weakens them, one who strengthens the army of the gods, the *mēnōg* lordship of Ohrmazd. In *gētīg* (their function is) to connect the body to the *jān* by being clad in *gētīg*".[3]

This passage is particularly illuminating as we have in it, besides the contrast *mēnōg-waxšīhā*: *pad gētīg-paymōgīh*, also the explicatory opposition *mēnōgīg* — *mēnōg-waxšīhā*, which parallell *gētīgīhā* — *pad gētīg-paymōgīh*.

---

[3] Cf. for this passage M. Molé, *Culte, mythe et cosmologie*, p. 475; M. F. Kanga, in *Indo-Iranica, Mélanges G. Morgenstierne*, Wiesbaden 1964, p. 100.

Another relevant passage is somewhat more difficult to interpret. The following reading is offered tentatively:

> *anōh haspihast ud ēstēd mēnōg-waxšīg hān ī band-drubuštīh ke-š harwisp bandān nigāh *ud aweš xwad ast wuzurg xwarr ke-š harwisp bandān nigāh ud dēn ī abēzag ī gumān-wizār brāzihast bāmīg ud dūr-pērōg ce'ōn a-sazišn-yazdān* (?), *star-pēsīd mēnōgān-tāšīd weh-dēn ī mazdēsnān, ēdōn-ez brāzīd rōšnān ī purr-xwarrān* (Dd XXXVI, 35): "There (sc. in *Garōdmān*) came to rest[4] and there stands in *mēnōg* existence that barricade-fortress which has the supervision of all barricades, and to it itself (belongs) the great splendour (*xwarr*), which has the supervision of all barricades; the pure religion, resolving doubts, shone, lustrous and with far-reaching radiance,[5] like the incorruptible gods (?),—the good religion of the Mazdaeans, star-ornamented, fashioned by the spirits, thus also shone the luminaries full of splendour".[6]

The passage is by no means lucid, partly because it is not easy to assign each of the epithets which it contains to its appropriate owner. It seems, however, that the 'barricade-fortress' in *Garōdmān*, the supreme heaven, is meant to represent the Mazdaean religion, mentioned at the end of this passage. *

APPENDIX B

stī[1]

The word *stī* has two distinct uses. It designates an abstract notion, 'existence, being', as well as the individual possessor of

[4] For the verb *haspih-* cf. R. C. Zaehner, *BSOS*, 9 (1937–39), p. 901. The reading here is assured by the occurrence of the corresponding noun in a similar context earlier in the same chapter, in § 17 (Dd, ed. Anklesaria, p. 81): *ud ēwarzēnd ō haspēn pad hān ī amahraspandān abāgīh ud hān ī dādār xwarr*: 'and they arrive for resting in the company of the Amahraspands and the *xwarr* of the Creator".

[5] The word *pērōg* 'radiance' has two alternative spellings in the Pahlavi script: *pylwk'* (as given here and in DkM 421.6; 434.18), and the more archaic spelling *ptlwk'* (Zātspram V, 3; XXXV, 40).

[6] M. Molé, in *RHR*, 155 (1959), p. 150f., gives a different translation of this passage.

[1] See above, note 38 (p. 70), and the text from Dēnkard III, chapter 123.

being, a person or a thing. As there are a number of other terms for existence in Middle Persian, it would be of interest to try and define the meaning of *stī* more closely, in a way which would distinguish it from *astīh*, *astišn*(*īh*), both of which designate 'being, existence'. The term *astīh* has a negative counterpart, *nēstīh*, and so it can be taken to imply the positive fact of being as against non-being. It occurs also in contrast to *paydāgīh*, the two forming the pair of notions 'being' and 'manifestation', in Dēnkard III, chapter 132 (DkM 132 f.; facsimile edition, p. [99] f.; cf. Zaehner, *BSOS*, 9 (1937–39), p. 871 f., 880):

> *abar astīh ud paydāgīh ud juttarīh ī astīh az paydāgīh.*
>
> "On being and manifestation, and the difference between being and manifestation".

The text of the chapter also contains a nice contextual contrast between *astīh* and *stī*:

> **astīh hamāyīg ohrmazd-dādār, ud dēn-dānāgīh ī-š pad nērōg, ud *gāh ud gyāg ī-š stī abar, ud zamān ī-š ast hamāyīgīh.*
>
> *paydāgīh ī-šān astīh hān ī ohrmazd-dādār az dahišn kardagīh, hān ī dēn-dānāgīh saxwan ī kāmīg ud dānāgīhā kār, hān ī zamān ud gāh pad zamān andar gyāg dādan šāyastan-ez ī dahišn.*
>
> *ud juttarīh ī astīh az *paydāgīh ēn-ez ka hān astīh [ī] abē-paydāg *be ō mardom pad-xwadīh būd, was būdan šāyēd: a-bun, bun ud bunōmand ast ī a-paydāg ō mardom, ud ne hēc paydāgīh ī abē-astīh būdan šāyēd.*
>
> "Being is: the eternal Ohrmazd, the Creator; the knowledge of religion which he has in his power; space and place upon which his *stī* is found; time which is his eternity.
>
> The manifestation of their being is: as for Ohrmazd the creator, from the activity of creation; as for the knowledge religion, speech which expresses will and action done with knowledge; as for time and space, to be able to create in time and place.

> The difference between being and manifestation is this: when a non-manifest being belongs to a man's selfness, it can be of many (kinds): it is either without root, (being itself) a root, or having a root, and is non-manifest to man.
>
> There can be nothing manifest which lacks being."

The term *astīh* clearly refers to the fact of being: *stī* can be said here to imply the being of a particular individual: this meaning will be discussed further in this Appendix.

If *astišn* has a characteristic connotation which would differentiate it from *astīh*, it probably is the fact of being in a place or in time: *astišn* does not seek to affirm the existence of an object or a person, but rather to define and attach or relate it.[2] The contrast between *astišn* and *stī* is seen in the following passage:

> *abar astišn ud winārišn ī harw* 2 *mēnōg pad xwēš stī* (DkM 831.17–18): "On the existence and the arrangement of the two *mēnōgs* in their own (mode of) being".

The term *stī* ought, apparently, to be taken in a more restricted meaning than that of *astišn*: it seems to designate a manner or mode of being. A similar meaning can be noticed in the following passage:

> *bawišn stī ī pad hamīh ī nērōg ī waxš ud zōr ī mēnōg gōhr az dādār mēnōgīg bawēnīdārīh* (DkM 345.6–8): "*bawišn* is a (mode of) being which the creator brings into existence in *mēnōg* form through the conjunction of the power of *waxš* and the force of the *mēnōg* substance". *

A definition using similar terminology is given to *ham-bawišn* (DkM 345.8–10). In the passage quoted above, Dk III, chapter 123 (DkM 120.15 ff.), the word *stī* is used in the same manner.[3]

[2] In the term which occurs in the theological discussions of the process of creation, *bawišn-astišnīh*, and which comes in opposition to *bawišn-rawišnīh* (see further below in this Appendix), the element *astišn* can be taken to imply the stage in which 'becoming' comes to be established and fixed, whereas in *bawišn-rawišnīh* the movement and change are probably implied.

[3] Likewise in *Škand-gumānīk Vičār* IV, 16, 21: *stī i rōšanā* in the Pazand text (in the edition of J. de Menasce transcribed in both case *stīh* but translated *gētīh*,

As *stī* seems to designate a mode of being, it is often qualified by an adjective or some other qualifier which specifies the particular kind of existence intended. Thus several occurrences of the combination *rōšn stī* 'luminous entity' are recorded:

> *abar drōzanīh ī arš dēw ud jud-bunīh ī rōšn ud tam, ud wehīh ī hān ī rōšn stī pad wizīn ud waršt ud wadīh ī hān ī tam* (DkM 829.5–7):
>
> "On the deceit of the demon Arš, and the separate origin of light and darkness, and the goodness of the luminous being through choice and action, and the evil of the dark (being)".[4]

The soul of man is also said to be *rōšn-stī* 'of luminous existence', or 'luminous entity' (DkM 18.13; 286.6, 14f.).[5]

Another adjective which is found to qualify *stī* is *gētīgīg*:

> *ud ka ō gil-paymōgīh*[6] *ī stī ī gētīgīg paydāgīh frēstihast* (DkM 434.12–13, facsimile ed., p. [493]):[7] "when he (sc. Zoroaster) was sent to appear in a garment of clay, which is *gētīg* (mode of) being".

The same process is described in similar terms with regard to a different subject in the following passage:

> *u-š brihēnīd be ō pitān-paymōzīh ī xwad ast stī [ī] paymōgīh-ez gil ī *tanīg ahlawān frawahrān* (Dd XXXVI, 25; cf. H.W.

---

probably an error of oversight. The term is properly interpreted in the glossary and the detailed commentaries).

[4] The term is somewhat differently translated in M. Molé, *Culte, mythe et cosmologie*, p. 205.

[5] Cf. J. de Menasce in his edition of *Škand-gumānīk Vičār*, p. 157, 237f.

* [6] The reading *gil-paymōgīh*, literally 'being clothed in clay', is undoubtedly right. H. W. Bailey reads *karp-palmōkīh* (cf. following note), but the text has only one *-p-*. The reading *gil-* is confirmed by DkM 816.13 *gil-karb* (cf. H. W. Bailey, *Zoroastrian Problems*, p. 29), where the word *gil* is written by the ideogram *TYNA*. Cf. also *Pahlavi Rivāyat*, ed. Dhabhar, p. 136.12f.: *u-š mardom az hān gil ke-š gayōmard az-eš kard . . .*, and the expression *gil-šāh*, used as an epithet of Gayōmard (DkM 29.1f.), which survives in NPersian (cf. *Burhān-i Qāṭiʿ*, ed. Moʿīn, III, Tehran 1342, p. 1826f.).

[7] Cf. H. W. Bailey, *Zoroastrian Problems*, p. 33.

Bailey, *Zoroastrian Problems*, p. 33, note 1, p. 112, note 2; G. Widengren, *The Great Vohu Manah*, p. 51; M. Molé, *Culte, mythe et cosmologie*, p. 106).

"He fashioned forth the righteous *frawahrs* towards being clad in flesh, which by itself is a (mode of) being whose garment is the bodily clay".

The text goes on to describe the process by which the *fravaši* come to material existence:

> *u-š payrāst ku zamānag zamānag pad xwēš gōhrag ēstēnd ud rasēnd be ō gētīg paymōgīh, hān ī gilān-ramag-ez, tā bawandag ō hān ī zamānag kār zāyēnd* . . . (Dd XXXVI, 26; Molé, loc. cit.). "He established that from time to time they should stand by their own substance and come to the garment of *gētīg*, that which is of the flock of clay, until there are born in order to accomplish the work of the time (the following persons:) . . .".

In these two passages *stī* and *paymōgīh* stand in close proximity to each other and seem to correspond to *gētīg-paymōgīh*, but the best sense of the text seems to be obtained when we do not try to emend one of the two expressions so as to conform to the other, thus achieving perhaps a superficial parallelism.

The term *stī* occurs also in a Pahlavi summary of the lost Spand Nask of the Avesta as one of the aspects of the human existence of Zoroaster, in the series *stī, frawahr, xwarr*,—a series of notions from which it is obvious that *stī* cannot be taken to denote merely 'existence'. Each of these notions was first created in *mēnōg* and then transferred into *gētīg* (DkM 690.12–14).[8]

The concept of *stī* is clearly and sharply defined in chapter 194 of Dēnkard III (DkM 207–208). The process of the world's creation is analyzed as consisting of four stages, starting from *bawišn*, which is defined as unformed, primary matter. The simile for this stage in the organic world is the parent with regard to his offspring; in the human world the simile is that of the raw material from which the artisan fashions an object. The second aspect in this process is the one called *bawišn-rawišnīh*, defined as the

[8] Cf. Molé, *Culte, mythe et cosmologie*, p. 276f.

form (*dēsag*) given to the offspring inside the parent and to the object by the artisan. The next stage, or aspect, in this process is *bawišn-astišnīh*, which seems to signify, by a simile, the embryonal stage in the organic world and the elementary stage of fashioning forth a material object by an artisan. The whole process is finished by the emergence of *stī*, which is the completed, individuated, fully-qualified being:

> *ud stī wimandīg ēw-tāgīg tanān, ce'ōn wahmān ciš wahmān kas, cihrīg, ce'ōn bawandag nigārdagīh ī zahag andar burdār uruθwar,*[9] *ud kirrōgīg, nāmcištīg abisar ud dēm ī kirrōg zar-rēgar az zarr, ud nāmcišt taxt ud dar ī kirrōg dōrgar az dār kunēd; ud stī būdag ast ī az bawišn-astišnīh, [ce'ōn dēn gōwēd ku az bawišn-astišnīh]*[10] *be stī frāz būd. ud az stī nāmcištīg ciš ud kas ud kār ī hān ciš ud kas, ce'ōn dēn gōwēd ku az stī be hān ī andar harw* 2 *mēnōg ō ham būd, frārōnīh ud abārōnīh* (DkM 208.14–22, cf. facsimile ed. p. [162].17–[163].3): "The definition of *stī* is the individual bodies, like such-and-such a thing, or such-and-such a person; (as regards) nature, as the complete acceptance of form of an offspring in the womb, (as regards) craftsmanship, a particular crown or diadem which a skilled goldsmith makes of gold, or a particular bed or door which a skilled carpenter makes from wood. *Stī* comes into being from *bawišn-astišnīh*, [for the Religion says that from *bawišn-astišnīh*] *stī* was fashioned forth. From *stī* the particular things and persons (come into being), and the work of those things and persons, as the Religion says: From *stī* those which are in the two *mēnōgs* were constituted, namely righteousness and wickedness".[11]

---

[9] The double designation for 'womb': *burdār uruθwar*, in which the first term is the Middle Persian word and the second a transcription of the Avestan word, occurs also in DkM 496.3–4.

[10] The phrase in brackets can be supplemented with some confidence by the parallelism with the other sections in this chapter. Without it the sentence is incomplete.

[11] [Cf. J. de Menasce, *Pratidānam*, p. 195 f., n.] R. C. Zaehner, *The dawn and twilight of Zoroastrianism*, p. 201 ff., discusses this chapter as well as chapter 191, mentioned further below. His approach calls for some reservations. I do not think it is justified to call the views presented in this chapter "a purely mechanistic

A quotation from the 'Religion', i.e., the Avestan tradition, regards *stī* as being the final stage of differentiation, after which comes only the stage of moral divisions between righteousness and wickedness.

A parallel text to the one just quoted, chapter 191 of Dēnkard III, presents the process of creation from a different point of view: it describes how the world moves from *mēnōg* to *gētīg* in two stages, called *āfurišn* and *dahišn*. But that text, though using traditional terminology, tries to harmonize it with philosophical ideas, chiefly Aristotelian, it seems:

> "The word *āfurišn* is: the creation (is) first in *mēnōg*, that is, matter and *mēnōg* seed; and it is shown in *gētīg* in potentiality" (cf. Appendix D).

The word *dahišn* is defined further in the text as the transference of creatures from *mēnōg*-being to *gētīg*-being, or in other words as a realization of that which was *in potentia*. This Aristotelian view is then brought into syncretism with the former scheme, which seems to be a traditional Zoroastrian one. Thus the stage called *bawišn* is equated with the state of being *in potentia* (*padnērōg*), and is further said to be called 'the seed of seeds, unformed *stī*'. The following stages, *bawišn-rawišnīh* and *bawišn-astišnīh*, are then defined in terms which conform to this approach. The last stage, which in chapter 194 of Dēnkard III was called *stī*, is here, in chapter 191, named *tan*, 'body', person' (DkM 203.14), which reminds one of the definition given above to *stī*

---

and atheistic doctrine which was grafted on to the Avesta" (op. cit., p. 203). The fourfold scheme: *bawišn*, *bawišn-rawišnīh*, *bawišn-astišnīh*, *stī*, seems to me to belong to the original Zoroastrian tradition. This can be seen from the constant references to *dēn*, which usually designates a quotation from an Avestan source. These quotations contain all four terms. Besides, the effort made in chapter 191 to harmonize between the twofold Aristotelian conception of potentiality and actuality and our fourfold scheme strengthens the view that this scheme is part of the local tradition. The harmonizing attempt of chapter 191 is not crowned with striking success. The two views are presented there side by side and are not interwoven into a single system. It is true that the creator is not mentioned in chapter 194 of Dēnkard III, but this does not yet prove that the conception is atheistic: the chapter's concern is merely to describe the mechanism of creation. The creator is mentioned in chapter 191 (see Appendix D).

by the phrase *ēw-tāgīg tanān* 'the individual bodies'. (The whole chapter is given in Appendix D).

stī, "the differentiated being, the existent person", gives meaning also to the following passage, which has been elucidated by J. de Menasce:

> *u-š tawān pad hān ī andar šāyēn frawastag kanāragōmand, ud pad hān ī a-brīn a-kanārag; ce'ōn kanāragōmandīh-ez ī-š pad stī, ud a-*kanāragīh ī-š pad zamānag* (DkM 199.4–6; facsimile edition, p. [155]; cf. R. C. Zaehner, *BSOS*, 9, 1937–39, p. 872, 880; J. de Menasce, *ŠGV*, p. 42). "His being powerful is limited as regards that which is included within that which is possible, it is unlimited as regards that which is undecreed. Similarly, that which he has in individual existence (*stī*) is limitation, and that which he has in time is limitlessness".

Another text where the word *stī* signifies 'individuated existence' seems to be the following:

> *zamān xwad hamē, u-š xwadīh drang, ud pad-eš ast kardārīh ī nērōg ī stī. ast hamāyīg hān ī-š pad nērōg. u-š kanārag jumbišn ī stī andar wāy pad spāš, ce'ōn rōšnān wāzišn ud wād wāyišn ud āb tazišn ud urwar rōyišn ud harw wīr kār andar wāy . . .* (DkM 207.3–7; facsimile edition, p. [161]; Cf. Zaehner, *BSOS*, 9, 1937–39, p. 872, 880f.).
>
> "Time by itself is eternal. Its selfness is of long duration. The effectiveness in it is the power of individuated being (*stī*). It is eternal as regards that which is in its power, its limitation is the movement of an individuated being (*stī*) inside the atmosphere (?) through space. Such is the procession of the luminaries, the blowing of the wind, the flow of water, the growth of plants, and the action of every man inside the atmosphere (?) . . .".

This passage, connected as it is to the previously quoted one, sheds some light on it and is in its turn made intelligible by the aid of this comparison.

This definition of *stī* as an individuated being stands very close to the use of the word *stī* in order to designate separate entities, whether *mēnōg* or *gētīg*. Thus, in chapter 51 of Dēnkard III, the Amahraspands are said to belong to the class of 'invisible beings' (*a-wēnišnīg stīān*, DkM 42.11 f.), and the sun is mentioned as an example of 'visible beings' (*wēnišnīg stīān*, DkM 42.20 f.),[12] cattle and men are enumerated among '*gētīg* beings' (*gētīg stīān*, DkM 43.9–11), each of which classes has various characteristics which do not concern us here. *

The following text seems also to use the term *stī* in the sense of an individual being, although the translation of the passage is not certain:

> *ud andar hān ī būd pahlomān hu-xwadāyān hu-xwadāy yim pahlom būd, kardār-tom stī pad ruwān ī mardom ud pad tan, ud az pahlomān dēn-dastwarān spitāmān zardušt pahlom būd, kardār-tom stī pad ruwān ī mardom* (DkM 334.6–10, facsimile ed., p. [256]).
>
> "Among those who were best beneficent rulers, the beneficent ruler Yima was the best, the most effective entity as regards the soul of men and their body. Of the best authorities of religion, Zoroaster the Spitamid was the best, the most effective entity as regards the soul of men".[13]

APPENDIX C

dmšn

The reading of the word *dmšn*, which occurs in the passage *Dādestān ī Dēnīg* XXVI, 3–5,[1] is not known to me. The contexts in which the word occurs seem to favour an interpretation which would connect it to a theoretical verb *dam-* (probably unconnected with 'to breathe') or *jam-* (which could be Old Iranian *gam-*), with a meaning 'to have an evil effect, to come forth, to issue (in a bad sense)'.

[12] The sun seems according to this scheme to belong to *mēnōg*, although it is visible.

[13] M. Molé, *Culte, mythe et cosmologie*, p. 38 f., gives a different translation of this text.

[1] See above, p. 73.

The word occurs in the following passages:

I. The text already mentioned above, Dd XXVI, 5:
u-š dmšn *az bun-kadag ī anāgīh*, "its evil effect is from the source of evil".

The whole of that passage (quoted above, p. 73) gains in clarity by comparison to the parallel text in Dd XXV, 3–5, where the goodness and pleasure of paradise are described:

> *u-š andar ast hamāg āsānīh ud rāmišnīh ud urwahm ud šēdāyīh ud nēwagīh ī wēš ud weh az-ez hān ī mahist ud abardom nēwagīh ud rāmišn ī pad gētīg. u-š nēst hēc niyāz ud dard ud bēš ud duš-xwārīh. u-š xwašīh ud nēwagīh jahān az hān ī hamēšag-sūd gāh ud ganz ī purrr ī a-kahišn an-absihišn a-kanārag.* "There is in it all ease and joy and happiness and brilliance and goodness which are more and better even than the greatest and highest goodness and joy which are in this world. There is no want, pain, affliction or unpleasantness. Its sweetness and goodness spring from the place of everlasting benefit, from the full treasure which never diminishes, which is undecaying and unlimited".

The precise parallel to *dmšn* in XXVI, 5 seems to be *jahān* in XXV, 5.[2] In both cases the words in question signify the movement from the source to the places of goodness or evil.

II. *xwad ka xwad wattarīh pad abārīgān tawānīgān meh-zōrān wēš-*dmšnyx *ī az-eš anāgīh rāy gēhān ziyān-tar ud wattar pāyag pāyag tā hān ī abardom, *ce pad hān ī abar anāgīh ud ziyān az-eš frāy *ku pad hān ī azēr* (DkM 41.14ff.; facsimile ed., p. [30]f.). "The same evil in highly-placed people, in mighty ones and in those endowed with great power, is more

* [2] *jahān*, 'arising from, originating from', is connected to the verb *jastan, jah-* 'to jump, spring, come about'. In the same chapter of Dādestān ī Dēnīg there occurs also an adjective derived from it: *jahānīg* (Dd XXV, 7), 'inconstant, ephemeral', or perhaps 'originated', like Arabic *muḥdath* (?). G. Widengren, *The Great Vohu Manah*, p. 84, reads here *yazdān*. [Both passages are now given by P. Gignoux in *JA*, 1968, p. 230 f., 236 f.]

harmful to the world and is worse, advancing by degrees up to the highest one, because evil issues more from them. For evil and harm are more from those above than from those below".

The phrase *wēš*-dmšnyx *ī az-eš anāgīh rāy* in this passage has a good counterpart in the same chapter of Dēnkard III: *nēwagīh wēš-waxšišnīh rāy* (DkM 41.4): "because goodness grows more".

III. Our word occurs twice more in the same chapter (Dēnkard III, Chapter 50):

garān-dmwštl *ud wēš ziyān-tar* (DkM 41.21 f.). "having graver evil effect and more harm".

abāg kast ud winast wehīh grāy *dmwšntl [written: *xmwšntl*] *ud garān ziyān-tar az harw wadīh* (DkM 42.5 f.). "When good diminishes and becomes defective, there is more evil effect and graver harm from every evil".

IV. *u-š ō hayyārīh ī hān razmīgān ēstēnīd dōgān-ez wasān parīgān tamīgān-gōhrān, ke-šān paymuxt rah ī rōšnīgān, ku padēnd ud dwārēnd ud gardēnd azēr rōšnān wāzišnīgān pad rāh-dārīh ī andak* (?) *mēnōgān, ud gētīgān nihumbišn hān ī awē-šān rōšnīh ud xwarr, ud *apparēnd hān ī az awē-šān xwarr-baxšišnīh, ud* dmšnyx *az xwēš ō dāmān xīndagīh-ez ī ast dard ud mard hammist anāgīh ī mān ō-šān dēw* (Dd XXXVI, 44; Anklesaria ed., p. 90). "In order to assist those doing battle, he (sc. Ahreman) stationed very many parī-s of dark substance, who clothed themselves in the carriage of the luminaries, so that they might revolve and run and turn round underneath the rotating luminaries, by robbing the lesser (?) spirits, and hiding from material beings the light and splendour which is theirs, and so that they might snatch away the dispensation of splendour which comes from them, and issue from their own to the creatures disease, namely pain and death, together with (other) evil which is appropriate (?) to those demons".

APPENDIX D

A selection of texts for the relationship of mēnōg and gētīg

I. Dēnkard III, Chapter 191.

DkM 202.16–203.15, corrected by aid of the facsimile edition, p. [157]f.; cf. H. Junker, *Vorträge der Bibliothek Warburg*, 1921–22, p. 158, n. 25.

See above, note 55, p. 76, and Appendix B (p. 95 f.).

TEXT

abar ('w') āfurišn ud dahišn ī dādār-ōhrmazd dām. az nigēz ī weh-dēn.

(1) hād āfurišn ēwāz dām fradom pad mēnōgīh ī ast mādag ud tōhmag ī mēnōgīg, ud pad nērōg gētīg nimāyišn, ce'ōn *pašm ke rištag *wahān-ez, ud zarr ke abisar-ez, ud sēm ke jām-ez, ud āhen ke bīl-ez, ud dār ke dar-ez, ud bun ke bar-ez, ud zahāg ke zahag, ud abārīg mādag ke xwēšīg dahīg pad-nērōg.

(2) ud dahišn ēwāz dām az mēnōgīh ō gētīgīh wardēnīdan, ī ast dahīg az mādag ī-š pad nērōg būd, ce'ōn rištag az pašm, ud abisar-ez az zarr, ud jām-ez az sēm, ud bīl-ez az āhen, ud dar-ez az dār, ud bar az bun, ud zahag az zahāg, ud abārīg dahīg az hān ī-š xwēš mādag.

(3) ud bun mādag ī dahīg pad nērōg xwānihēd-ez tōhmagān tōhmag ud a-dēsīdag stī ud dahīgān bunyašt, u-š dēnīg nām bawišn-ez.

(4) ud miyānag-ez mādag ast dahīg [ī] pad nērōg, ce'ōn ādur ud āb, ke-šān pad nērōg zīndag-ez dēsagān, xwānihēd tōhmag dēsag-ez, fradom azešīh, stī bunyašt, u-š dēnīg nām bawišn rawišnīh.

(5) ud abdom mādag pālūdag az-eš dahīg, ce'ōn mardom az-eš mādagīh hān ī xwad ham-karb, ce'ōn pid mādag ast ī hān ī xwad ham-karb pus, xwānihēd-ez *sōhišn (?) dēsag, u-š *dēnīg nām bawišn-astišnīh, ke-š azēr ēwāzīg tan ī ēd and mardom u-šān kār ī and *gōnīh (?).

TRANSLATION

On *āfurišn* and *dahišn* of the creation of Ohrmazd the Creator. From the instruction of the Good Religion.

(1) The word *āfurišn*[1] (means): the creation is first in *mēnōg*, that is matter and *mēnōg* seed, and it is shown in *gētīg* in potentiality, like the wool which is the cause of the thread, gold of the crown, silver of the goblet, iron of the spade, wood of the door, root of the fruit, the parent of the offspring, and the other kinds of matter whose own products are (in them) in potentiality.

(2) The word *dahišn* (means:) to turn creation from *mēnōg* existence to *gētīg* existence, which is the product (emerging) from the matter where it was in potentiality, just like the thread (coming) from wool, crown from gold . . . (etc.), and the other products from that which is their own matter.

(3) The root matter, (in) which the product is in potentiality, is called 'seed of seeds', 'unformed (mode of) being', the foundation of the products'. Its religious[2] name is *bawišn*.[3]

(4) The middle matter is potentially the product,[4] like fire and water, to whom belong in potentiality the living forms. It is called 'the seed of form', 'the first production', 'the foundation of existence'. Its religious name is *bawišn-rawišnīh*.

(5) The last matter is one from which its product is refined, like a man whose matter is of the same shape as himself, just as a father is the matter of his son who has the same shape as himself. It is called *perceptible[5] form. Its religious name is

---

[1] On the distinction between the verbs *āfrīdan* and *dādan* see above, p. 67 f., note 30.

[2] The term *dēnīg* refers presumably to the Avestan name, the Pahlavi equivalent of which is given, just as the formula *ce'ōn gōwēd pad dēn*, "as he says in the Religion", regularly introduces a quotation from the Avesta.

[3] *bawišn* means literally 'becoming'. The connection between this term and the concept of 'root-matter' seems somewhat far-fetched, and this fact may strengthen the impression that we are faced here with two systems whose origins are different and which are only being harmonized with some effort. The formal justification for connecting *bawišn* with *bun-mādag* may lie in the potential quality of the latter, i.e. that it can be realized only in its products.

[4] The formula here resembles closely that which is found in the previous paragraph, in both cases the text has *dahīg pad nērōg*. The translation reflects an attempt to interpret the phrase in two different ways according to the context.

[5] **sōhišn*: the text has *dyn' xw-*. The normal reading of the phrase as written

bawišn-astišnīh, under which appellation (?)[6] are the bodies of so many people[7] and their work of so much variety (?).

II. Dēnkard III, Chapter 206.

DkM 225f.; facsimile edition, p. [176]f.

See above, p. 78, note 62. Owing to the difficulty of the text, the translation should be regarded as merely tentative.

TEXT

abar ohrmazd xwad, xwadīh, u-š mēnōg ud gētīg nām, ud paydāgīh, ud ane[8] jud, ud az-eš. az nigēz ī weh-dēn.

(1) hād ohrmazd xwad abzōnīg mēnōg, wisp-wehīh nērōg stī.

(2) u-š xwadīh passazag. *xwad-ē[9] harw mēnōgīg ud gētīgīg weh, wehīh azešīh.

(3) u-š mēnōg andar azešīh ī harw a-wēnišnīg a-gīrišnīg ciš ī weh. pad hamāg mēnōg, mēnōg-tomīh ī mēnōg menēnd.

(4) u-š gētīg andar azešīh ī harw wēnišnīg gīrišnīg ciš ī weh. pad hamāg gētīgīg ī weh, gētīg-tomīh ī gētīgān xwad-ē.

(5) u-š mēnōg-gētīg andar azešīh ī harw wēnišnīg a-gīrišnīg, gīrišnīg a-[wēnišnīg] ciš ī weh. pad hamāg mēnōg-gētīgīh ī weh, mēnōg-gētīgān mēnōg-gētīg.

(6) u-š xwadīh arzānīgīh ī spanāg-mēnōg ī dādār-ōhrmazd, ud yazd ī abārīg ham passazag.

(7) u-š paydāgīh xwadīhā.

(8) ane jud hamāg azešīg ī jud az awe azešīh, ud ō awe azešīh xwad a-passazag pad azešīh.

(9) harw azešīh pad xwadīh winardan šāyastan rāy hān azešīh az ane ī aweš ham-passazag, xwad sazēd, ī-š nām xwadīh arzānīg.

---

could be *xwānihēd ce'ōn hu-dēsag*, which conveys nothing intelligible. For *sōhišn* cf. H. W. Bailey, *Zoroastrian Problems*, p. 97, n. 2, and p. 229, and the passages collected by J. de Menasce, *ŠGV*, p. 239 (see also there, Addenda et Corringenda, ad p. 284). Also *Transactions of the Philological Society*, 1959, p. 111, n. 2 (H. W. Bailey).

[6] Both reading and translation of the whole sentence are doubtful.

[7] An alternative translation may be: "so many individual people", taking *tan* as signifying 'an individual person'.

[8] *ane*: written *ZK'd*. Cf. other examples for this spelling in *Pahlavi Yasna and Visperad*, ed. B. N. Dhabhar, Bombay 1949, p. 115.

[9] *xwad-ē*: Ms *xwtwkw'd*.

(10) gannāg-mēnōg marzēnīdārīh, ud dēw ud druz ī abārīg ham-passazag.

(11) u-š paydāgīh az xwad azešīh.

(12) kēš-dārān ke wad jumāy nēwag yazd azešīh kēš ī-šān, abar yazd gannāg-mēnōgīh-ez guft, ud spanāg-mēnōg azeš be guft bawēd.

TRANSLATION

On Ohrmazd himself, his selfness, the name of his *mēnōg* and *gētīg*, the manifestation, that which is different,[10] the product. From the instruction of the Good Religion.

(1) Ohrmazd himself is the beneficent *mēnōg*, an entity endowed with the power of doing all-good.

(2) To his selfness the individual self of every good *mēnōg* and *gētīg* being corresponds. Goodness is the product.

(3) His *mēnōg* is (found) in the product of every invisible and intangible good thing. In the whole of *mēnōg*, it is considered to be the most endowed with *mēnōg*-ness of *mēnōg*.

(4) His *gētīg* is (found) in the product of every visible and tangible good thing. In the whole of *gētīg*, it is a self most endowed with *gētīg*-ness of *gētīg* beings.

(5) His (compound) *mēnōg-gētīg* is (found) in the product of every visible and intangible, (or) tangible and in[visible] good thing. In the whole of (compound) *mēnōg-gētīg* existence, it is the *mēnōg-gētīg* (par excellence) among *mēnōg-gētīg* beings.[10a]

(6) His selfness is the worth of the Bounteous Spirit of the Creator Ohrmazd. The other gods are similar.

(7) His manifestation is according to the self.

(8) 'The other' is all product that is different from his own product, and that by itself does not correspond to his product for being (his) product.

(9) In order to be able to arrange every product through selfness, that product, (as distinguished) from 'the other' which

[10] *ane jud*: both words signify approximately the same thing. The addition of *jud* may be a gloss to help in identifying the uncommon *ane*, written with an ambiguous spelling. The more regular spelling of *ane*, with the ideogram *AXRN*, is no less ambiguous.

[10a] Cf. G. Gnoli, *AION*, N.S. 13 (1963), p. 189 n. 82, who refers to GBd 194.8 for this concept.

resembles it, is by itself suitable. Its name is 'worthy of the selfness'.

(10) The Evil Spirit is destruction; the *dēw* and the other demons resemble him.

(11) His manifestation is the product which comes from himself.

(12) Those who hold the view that the product of the gods is bad together with good, apply (in fact) the nature of the Evil Spirit to the gods, and say (in fact) that the Bounteous Spirit derives from him.

* III. Dēnkard III, Chapter 365.

DkM 349f.; facsimile edition, p. [268]f.

This chapter presents the 'evolutionary' process of the creation of the world. See above, p. 69, n. 35. Cf. R. C. Zaehner, *Zurvan*, p. 371–374.

TEXT

abar bun bawišn ī gētīg dahišn (dahišn). az nigēz ī weh-dēn.

(1) hād abzār ke dādār az hān ī anaγr-rōšnīn brihēnīd ud dām andar hangerdīgēnīd paydāgīh ī-š abastāgīg nām āθrō. kəhrpa 2. ēwag hān ī mēnōg dahišn, ēwag hān ī gētīg dahišn andar hangerdīgēnīd.

(2) andar hān ī mēnōg dahišn andar hangerdīgēnīd mēnōg ī waxš-nērōg, ud andar hān ī gētīg dahišn andar hangerdīgēnīd mēnōg ī cihr-nērōg.

(3) wēšišt abzār ī mēnōg dahišn hangerdīgīh kard spurrīg, ud pad-eš kār ī pad dahišn ī andar hān abzār abāyišnīgīh. u-š wizārd waxšōmand mēnōgān yazdān ēwag ēwag ō hān ī-šān ('*w*) xwēškārīh.

(4) ud andar abzār ī gētīg dahišn hangerdīgīh pad dādār kām warzēn cihr-*nērōg mēnōg pad dādan ī waxš-nērōg mēnōg *hamīgīhā[11] ō dārmag-tom gētīg grīw paydāgīh.

(5) fradom nihang ī-š abastāgīg nām kut, ud pad ēwāz ī gēhān *kyš* (*slyšk'*) srišūdag-ez xwānd.

[11] The Ms has *xmxyx'*. The emendation is supported by analogy with *hamūg*, which occurs below, § 8, as an epithet of *mēnōg*.

(6) az nihang ī kut srišūdag-ez nām wahānag (?), ī-š abastāgīg nām xwardagīh ud gabrīh-ez ud pad ēwāz ī mardom stunag (?) *kyš*-ez (?) xwānēnd. ud xīg ast ī kut u-š kut [kard][12] andar.

(7) ud az wahānag ī xwardagīh ud gabrīh ud stunag-*kyš*-ez nām *wašn ī-š abastāgīg nām *wiškīdōmandīh, ud pad ēwāz ī mardom wistardagīh-ez xwānēnd. ud xīg ast ī wahānag u-š wahānag kard-ez andar.

(8) ud az wašnīh ī *wiškīdōmandīh ud wistardagīh-ez nām waxš-nērōg ī hamīg ī fradom tan ī-š abastāgīg rah ud spahr-ez nām, ud pad ēwāz ī mardom spahr-ez xwānēnd, ī-š zahag andar hēnd.

(9) rōšnān xwaršēd ud māh ud starān ham-bun ō wisp dām ī-š ēr, rāyēnīdār ast ī cihrān, ud xwad cihrān abardom.

(10) ud az rah bawišn ī garm-xwēd ī wādōmand, pad ham-bastagīh ī druz ī mēnōg-waxš, ham-zōrīhā zahag ī gētīg dahišnān ī tōhmagān tōhmag.

(11) az bawišn [bawišn-]rawišnīh ī zahāgān ī dahīg ī bawišn ī xwānihēd ristagān-ez.

(12) az [bawišn-rawišnīh] bawišn-astišnīh ī zīndagān ī-š andar gōspand ud mardom stī ke hēnd gētīg *dahīg karb.

TRANSLATION

On the original 'becoming' of material creation. From the instruction of the Good Religion.

(1) The manifestation of the powers which the Creator fashioned from Endless Light and with which he accomplished the creation, —the Avestan name of which is 'the form of fire',[13]—is twofold. One is that with which he accomplished *mēnōg* creation, and one is that with which he accomplished *gētīg* creation.

(2) In that with which *mēnōg* creation was accomplished, the *mēnōg* of spiritual force (is found), and in that with which *gētīg* creation was accomplished, the *mēnōg* of substantial force (is found).

---

[12] *kard* was probably omitted here by haplography, after *kut*, both words being written identically *kwt'*.

[13] There can be little doubt that this much debated word (which occurs also in GBd 12.7–11) should be read in the form given here. Cf. J. Duchesne-Guillemin, *Dr. J. M. Unvalą Memorial Volume*, Bombay 1964, p. 14–17.

(3) He made perfect mainly the power with which *mēnōg* creation is accomplished, and through it (he carried out) the work of creation suitable for that power. He assigned each one of the gods residing in *mēnōg* to his particular task.

(4) In the power of accomplishing *gētīg* creation there was manifest, by the will of the Creator, the marvellous *mēnōg* of substantial force by the creation of the *mēnōg* of spiritual force, by association to the finest[14] *gētīg* self.

(5) First (proceeded) *nihang* ('a little'), the Avestan name of which is *kut*,[15] called in the language of the world *kyš slyšwtk'*.[16]

(6) From *nihang*, the name of which is also *kut*, *slyšwtk'*, (proceeded) *wahānag* ('cause' ?), the Avestan name of which is 'embryo'[17] and 'hollowness';[18] it is called in the language of the people 'a trunk'[19] (?)-*kyš*. It is the container[20] of *kut*, and he made *kut* inside it.

(7) From *wahānag*, whose name is also *xwardagīh*, *gabrīh*, *stunag-kyš*, (proceeded) *wašn*,[21] the Avestan name of which is 'having ramifications' (?);[22] it is called in the language of the people 'being scattered'. It is a container for *wahānag*, *wahānag* was made inside it.

---

[14] For *dārmag* cf. H. W. Bailey, *JRAS*, 1934, p. 511f.

[15] This word, which is apparently connected to Avestan *kutaka-*, 'small', could also be read as the Pahlavi **kōd*, like *kōdag*. The other *dēnīg* words in this chapter have all Pahlavi forms.

[16] I can find no explanation for these words. *kiš* may be the word for 'circle'.

[17] For *xwardagīh*, which describes a stage in the development of the embryo, cf. GBd 16.4: *pas az gumēzagīh xwardagīh bawēd, daštag humānāg*, "after the mixture there is the (development of) the embryo, resembling *daštag* (= 'foetus')". This reading of the word seems to me preferable to Zaehner's *āvartakīh* (cf. *Zurvan*, p. 305, note to line 173).

[18] I.e., the stage in which the hollowed areas in the body are formed. Cf. GBd 16.6.

[19] Or 'a column, pillar'. Cf. DkM 242.1: *ce'ōn ka stun ī kadag *škanihēd, kadag hanbahēd*. "Just as when the pillar of the house is broken, the house collapses".

[20] *xīg* means properly 'a water skin'.

[21] *wašn* could mean 'the male', cf. NPersian *gušn*. The NPersian word means also, by extension, 'conception', and this meaning might also apply here, although this does not seem the proper place for the concept.

[22] The spelling in line 22 of DkM 349 allows the reading *wiškōmandīh*, or possibly **wiškanōmandīh*. On the word in the form as emended here cf. R. C. Zaehner, *BSOS*, 9 (1937–39), p. 318.

(8) From *wašn*, whose name is also 'having ramifications' and 'being scattered', (proceeded) the *mēnōg* of spiritual force, the associate, the first body, the Avestan name of which is 'the wheel' and 'the sphere'. It is also called 'sphere' in the language of the people. Its offspring are inside (it).

(9) The luminaries: the sun, moon and stars, are the common origin of all the creatures which are underneath them. They[23] control the substances, and are themselves the highest of the substances.

(10) From 'the wheel' (proceeded) hot and moist 'becoming', possessed of wind; for arresting the demons residing in *mēnōg*, it is, with assembled forces, the begetter of *gētīg* creations, the seed of seeds.

(11) From 'becoming' (proceeded) the 'movement of becoming', which is the begetters of the product of 'becoming'. It is also called 'the elements'.

(12) From ["the movement of becoming"] (proceeded) 'the stable existence of becoming', which is the living beings which are in it; the entities of cattle and man, which are the *gētīg* shape of the product.[24]

---

[23] The verb in the text is in the singular.

[24] The text remains largely obscure, but it is hoped that this attempt may have contributed something towards understanding it.

[This article was completed in 1967. Some additions and changes made in the proof stage in 1970 are marked by brackets.]

III

SOME NOTES ON AHREMAN, THE EVIL SPIRIT, AND HIS CREATION

One of the utterances concerning Ahreman in the Zoroastrian Pahlavi books is the following surprising statement: "Ahreman has never been and will never be".[1] In a religion which has at its centre the strife betweeen the Good Lord, Ohrmazd, and the Evil Spirit, one would not expect one of the two rivals to be non-existent. Admittedly, non-existence can be regarded as a term of abuse towards a hated deity, and one is used to seeing almost any adjective deprecating the devil and showing his inferiority to God being levelled against him. Some of the commonest attributes used in this connection are ignorance or hindsight, lie, bad smell, cruelty.[2] The devil is often portrayed as working against his own interests, bringing about his own destruction, and even put in the somewhat paradoxical position of one who carries out the ultimate punishment on those who have fulfilled his own desire in the world. The epithet of non-existence seems, however, illogical, unless we can discover the structural connection which makes it possible.[3]

It is proposed to connect this statement to another one, which occurs in the Dādestān ī Dēnīg (= Dd.) and according to which Ahreman has no material (*gētīg*) existence. The statement occurs in answer to

1 "*u-šān ēn-ez a'ōn dāšt ku ahreman hamē ne būd ud ne bawed*" (DkM. 534, 5–6 = Dk. VI, 278). The idea occurs in other places as well: cf. DkM. 493 = Dk. VI, 98; *Pahlavi Texts*, p. 42. 9ff.; p. 87, §4.

2 These and a selection of further attributes of Ahreman can be conveniently seen, for example, in the Index to R. C. Zaehner, *Zurvan: A Zoroastrian Dilemma* (Oxford 1955), p. 478, *s.v.* Ahriman.

3 It is not enough to dismiss it, as R. C. Zaehner does (*The Dawn and Twilight of Zoroastrianism*, London 1961, p. 216), by connecting it to texts which according to Zaehner display "pure Zurvanism in philosophical rather than mythological form". The connection to those texts certainly exists, as we shall try to show, but the imputation of Zurvanite heresy lacks foundation, in my opinion, either here or there.

the question whether the souls of men, righteous and wicked, will be able to see either Ohrmazd or Ahreman "when they go over to the spirits" (*ka be ō mēnōgān šawend*), viz. after death. The answer to this question is:

> *ahreman rāy guft ēsted ku-š gētīg nēst, ohrmazd-ez andar mēnōgān mēnōg, pad hān ī gētīgīg hān-ez ī mēnōgīg *šnāsišn ī karb-*wēnišnīh spurr ne, be pad xrad ud zōr ī hangōšīdag wēnihēd*
>
> It has been said of Ahreman that he has no material being. Orhmazd is a spirit even among spirits: neither in the material nor in the spiritual world is there complete knowledge [of him] by seeing [him] as a form,
> * but he is seen by wisdom and by the power of comparison (Dd. XVIII, 2–3 [p. 41]; cf. XXXVI, 51).

Both Ohrmazd and Ahreman, it is clear from this answer, are spiritual beings in themselves, and so neither of them can be seen in the proper sense of the term. They differ, however, on the plain of *gētīg*, of material being: Ohrmazd is present in the material world through his creation, whereas Ahreman has no *gētīg* corresponding to him at all. Hence it is possible to deduce from the material world to Ohrmazd, but this is impossible to do with the Evil Spirit.

The statement about Ahreman having no *gētīg* may seem surprising at first sight, when we recall that according to the basic tenets of Mazdaism the material world is a state of "mixture" (*gumēzagīh*) of good and evil, and there is no doubt that Ahreman and his powers are constantly active in this world. When we go into the matter more closely, however, there can be no doubt that this passage about Ahreman having no *gētīg* is the common opinion of the Pahlavi books. The account of the creation in the Bundahišn, for example, gives the material creations of Ohrmazd in great detail, but passes in complete silence any similar creation by Ahreman: only a list of demons created by the Evil Spirit is given.[4] Herman Lommel, in his very thorough description of the Zoroastrian religion,[5] arranged the data he obtained from the Avesta and especially from the Bundahišn in a neat table, showing in parallel columns the creations of the good and the evil spirits. The section on the material creation of evil had to be left empty, but a long discussion follows, devoted to the attempt (a futile one, as we now see), to complete the missing items so that they should form a list parallel to that of the good creation.

4 GBd., pp. 14ff., cf. Zaehner, *Zurvan*, p. 135.

5 *Die Religion Zarathustras* (Tübingen 1930), pp. 106ff., cf. the table on p. 111, and the summary of the material creations of Ahreman on p. 120.

The same idea about evil having no material being is lucidly expressed in theological terms in chapter 105 of the third book of the Dēnkart, a translation of which follows:

> Spiritual creation is an uncompounded, singular being. Its distinctive mark is being uncompounded, invisible, intangible. Following the creation of the Creator, the creatures were first in spiritual being, which is uncompounded, invisible and intangible. By becoming compounded, the beings turned into materiality, which is visible and tangible. This is manifest also from this, that when a material thing which is visible and tangible is loosened away from visible and tangible material existence, it returns to the original being, which is the invisible and intangible spiritual existence, its origin. Luminous *mēnōg* is capable of turning from uncompounded *mēnōg* being to the composite being of that *gētīg* through the hot and moist power of living nature. Even now each individual material being is maintained in *gētīg* by the same power. The dark *mēnōg*, which has the substance of death, is incapable even of reaching compounded materiality because it has cold and dry *power. That which has come to manifest materiality is something wearing not its own substance, but an alien substance. Just as that in which it is, namely a burrow, took on the form of demons, — [so also] wolves and reptiles do not wear their own substance. [They are] not like the material luminous shapes, which are continued to the Renovation, — those forms of demons will be smashed and annihilated in the millennium of Zoroaster. The form of the wolf will be smashed at the beginning of the millennium of Ušēdar, and the form of the *frog will be smashed at the beginning of the millennium of Ušēdarmah. The other demons who rush about in the form of embodied creatures of luminous seed will be annihilated among the demons at the time when the separation of each separate form will take place, the vital soul being taken away from the body, when their material part will be joined back to *gētīg* and their spiritual part to *mēnōg*.
>
> In the millennium of Ušēdarmah, [at] the final arrival of the beneficent and victorious [= Saošyant], the form will be at once removed from the embodied creatures, and it will be smashed and annihilated together with the origin of the demons. A revelation of the Good Religion.[6]

A detailed discussion of this text would take us outside the scope of

6 DkM. 98–100. An annotated discussion of this text is to be included in another publication, where the terms *mēnōg* and *gētīg* will be discussed. I should like to acknowledge my debt to the Rev. Father P. J. de Menasce, with whom I had the benefit of reading this text in 1963. The text is summarized and discussed in R.C. Zaehner's *The Dawn and Twilight of Zoroastrianism*, pp. 204f. I should like to remark that I can see in this text no hint of "a dualism that proceeds from a primal unity", this being again "the Zurvanite heresy in philosophical disguise". The dualism is found already in *mēnōg*.

the present paper. For our purpose here it is enough to remark that the text takes material existence to be a form of actuality which evil is incapable of reaching, being by definition a negative concept. It can only reach a secondary kind of existence in the material world, the evil substance being clothed inside a material being, and taking on an alien shape. In the light of these observations it may be assumed that such expressions as "the material form of the demons" (*dēwān kālbud ī gētīg*, Mēnōg ī Xrad, Ch. 57, 15) refer similarly to an external material form into which the demons penetrate.

The presence of Ahreman in the material world has a particular relevance when the constitution of human beings is taken into consideration. The problem of human wickedness has always been one of the main concerns of Zoroastrianism, and if the wicked cannot be simply regarded as manifestations of Ahreman, the question of where this wickedness comes from must be raised again. Fortunately, we possess a clear answer to this, one which is moreover nicely in keeping with the previous text. It has also the advantage of being taken from a moralistic part of the Dēnkart, which seems to preserve fairly old traditions and has no theological pretensions:

> It is possible to put Ahreman out of this world in such a way that every person, for his own part, should chase him of his body, for Ahreman's habitation in the world is in the bodies of men. Therefore, when there is no habitation for him in the bodies of men, he is annihilated from the whole world. For as long as in this world [even] a small demon has his dwelling in a single person of men, Ahreman is in the world.[7]

Ahreman subsists in this world according to this text in so far as he can live, parasitically as it were, inside people. If such a habitation is denied him, he is "annihilated" from the world. The passage which follows in the text gives an opposite counterpart: If the gods are made to dwell in the bodies of men, then they are made to dwell in the whole world; it is possible to achieve this object only by driving the demons out of this world, and this is done by turning them out of the bodies of men.[8] This statement does not contradict the conclusion which should be drawn from the preceding one about the demons, it rather confirms it: the presence of the gods in this world is imperfect as long as the demons hold sway in the bodies of some men. The gods can

7 DkM. 530f. = Dk. VI, 264. The text is taken from an edition with translation of Dēnkart VI, which is due to be completed shortly.

8 DkM. 531 = Dk. VI, 265.

possess the whole world only when the bodies of men are purified from the demons.

The sixth book of the Dēnkart being a moralistic text, it may be suspected of the tendency, common to preachers, of exaggerating in order to drive home a point — and the implications in this case are fairly obvious: firstly, the fight against the demons' possession of this world is not a fight against "real", material, concrete beings, it is a fight against oneself, or, more precisely, against a non-material part of oneself. Secondly, every single person bears a responsibility for the success or failure of this fight; quite literally, the fate of the world may depend on the effort of the individual person whose task is to conduct an internal fight so as to get rid of the demons who "dwell" in his body. The aim of such passages in Dēnkart VI is to engender soul-searching by every person, and this can also be seen from the fact that the positive injunction to fight the demons "in one's own house" is followed by a warning *not* to fight them in other peoples' houses,[9] clearly in order to avoid the social phenomenon of witch-hunting.

There is no serious reason, however, to doubt that the conclusion which can be drawn from this passage, viz. that the demons have no existence in the world outside men, has relevance even on the cosmological plain. It is confirmed from a passage of the Greater Bundahišn (= GBd.), which, to my mind, has not yet been fully accurately interpreted:

> *pas ohrmazd pad harwisp-āgāhīh dānist ku agar zamān kārezār-ez-eš ne kunem, ēg tawān kardan pad dām ī man ce'ōn padēst abar burd, ud kōxšišn-gumēzišnīh hamēyīhā, u-š andar gumēzišn dām nišastan ud ō xwēš kardan tawān. ce'ōn nūn-ez mardom andar gumēzišn was ke abārōnīh wēš hamē warzend ku frārōnīh, ku kāmag ī gannāg-mēnōg wēš warzend* (GBd., p. 6; cf. Zaehner, *Zurvan*, pp. 279, 314, §12).

> Then Ohrmazd knew this by his omniscience: "If I do not fix a time for the battle against him, he will be able to do to my creatures even as he threatened, and the mixture through strife will be for ever; during the mixture he can settle in the creatures and make them his own." Just as even now, among the people in the mixture, there are many who commit more sins than pious deeds, as they do the will of the Evil Spirit more.

According to this text, Ohrmazd fixes a term to the battle in order to prevent Ahreman from gaining permanent possession of the world, which he can do through settling in the creatures. The implication

9 DkM. 501 = Dk. VI, 129–130.

seems to be that this is the only way by which Ahreman exists in the world. The example given from the observation of life in this world, that many people "do the will of the Evil Spirit more", shows quite clearly that the author of the Bundahišn viewed the presence of the Evil Spirit in the material world in the same light as did the authors of the traditions contained in Dēnkart VI.

The tenor of these passages is that Ahreman's presence in the world is not an ontological fact, but merely an anthropological or psychological phenomenon. This does not deny the reality of Ahreman as such,[10] it merely marks his totally negative, hence also non-material, character. The created world, *gētīg*, is entirely the work of Ohrmazd, but it also serves as a convenient breeding ground for the disruptive powers of Ahreman, a danger seen and weighed by Ohrmazd when he came to create the material world.[11]

Further on in the first chapter of the Bundahišn, the account of the parallel creation of Ohrmazd and Ahreman should be considered. The text is evidently corrupt, but the following restitution is offered as being more likely than the ones previously given:

> *ohrmazd az hān ī xwēš xwadīh* [*gētīg rōšnīh*] *ud az gētīg rōšnīh karb ī dāmān ī xwēš frāz brihēnīd ī pad ātaxš-karb ī rōšn ī spēd ī gird frāz paydāg*... (GBd., p. 11; cf. Zaehner, *Zurvan*, pp. 281, 316, §26).
>
> Ohrmazd fashioned forth from his own selfness [material light], from material light he fashioned forth the shape of his creatures which was manifest in the shape of fire, bright, white, round ...

The sequence of the creations of Ohrmazd thus begins with *gētīg*, light created from his selfness. The parallel creation of Ahreman is described in the following terms:

> *gannāg-mēnōg az gētīg tārīkīh hān ī xwēš(-tan) dām frāz kirrēnīd pad*

10 This is evident, for example, from the following: "*ohrmazd pad harwisp-āgāhīh dānist ku gannāg-mēnōg ast ud abar handāzišn kuned*" (GBd., p. 4, cf. Zaehner, *Zurvan*, pp. 279, 313, §6): "Ohrmazd knew by his omniscience that the Evil Spirit was there, and that he would attack him".

11 GBd., p. 8 (Zaehner, *Zurvan*, pp. 280, 315, §20). As a result of this realization by Ohrmazd he decided "inevitably" (*a-cāragīhā*, lit. "inescapably" or "irremediably") to create time so as to reduce the Aggressor to "inaction" (*a-kār*). The Evil Spirit, it is stated further, cannot be made "inactive" without battle (*kārezār*, historically *kārecār*, interpreted by a pun: "an action which it is necessary to do for escape", or "as a remedy": *kār ī pad cāromandīh kardan abāyed*. The full force of the triple play on words in the passage has not been brought out in the current translations). GBd., pp. 8f., cf. Zaehner, *ibid.*, §21.

> *wazag*(?) *karb ī siyāh ī āduristar ī tom-arzānīg ī druwand, ce'ōn bazag-*ēwēn xrafstar, u-š az gētīg xwad-dōšagīh waran ī wattar dad-karb kirrēnīd ce'ōn waran abāyed* (GBd., p. 11; cf. Zaehner, *ibid.*, §27).
>
> The Evil Spirit fashioned forth from material darkness his own creatures in the form of a frog (?), black, ashen, worthy of darkness, wicked, as a noxious reptile of sinful manners; from material self-love he fashioned forth evil lust, in the shape of a wild beast, as is necessary for lust.

The parallelism between the two powers is not exact. The text, at least in its present corrupt state, does not indicate from what material darkness was created.[12] It may be at least legitimate to assume that material darkness is regarded as a purely negative concept, lacking substance, and thus not an evidence of material creation, unlike light. In any case, the entire emphasis in the creation of Ahreman is on the harm done to the creatures of Ohrmazd:

> He first created the selfness of the demons, the bad behaviour: that spirit from which the foulness of the creatures of Ohrmazd came about. For he created that creature through which he made his own body worse, that is, that it will become powerless.[13]

The essence of Ahreman's creation is the corruption of the creations of Ohrmazd. The satisfying point in this for the Zoroastrian is the realization that Ahreman works in this unwittingly against himself and undermines his own existence.

One of the points of opposition between Ohrmazd and Ahreman is, as we have seen, that the former does exist (in *gētīg*), while the latter does not. This point, although it completes the symmetry between the two powers, also underlines the radical impossibility of attaining a real equality of parallelism in such a dualistic religion. In the older religion, in the Gāthā, the dualistic structure consisted of three terms: Ahura Mazdā with Spenta Mainyu (the Bounteous Spirit) at his side, both scaled against Angra Mainyu, the Evil Spirit, who structurally had to be posed against the Bounteous Spirit, and not against the "Wise Lord"; Ahura Mazdā remained, as it were, without rival. The balance was thus heavily tipped in favour of the good powers. This does not change the dualistic nature of this religion, as W.B. Henning

12 R. C. Zaehner's emendation of the text does not seem likely, and it conflicts with the rule that Ahreman has no *gētīg*.

13 GBd., pp. 11f., cf. Zaehner, *ibid.*, §27, where the translation given does not bring out what seems to be the essential point.

pointed out in his Ratanbai Katrak lectures, referring to a similar lack of symmetry in Manichaeism.[14]

In the Pahlavi texts the older triangular structure was substituted by a straightforward dualism, but there, too, evidence of the inherent lack of balance between the two powers is visible. This is due to the fact that evil can only be viewed as negative; it is not a creative force in its own right, but is bent upon destroying the positive creation of the good power. It is thus essentially secondary in the cosmic order; whether it is conceived as an aggression or as an imperfection, it implies the priority and ontological superiority of the good power. In the Zoroastrian cosmological myth it is at the same time essential to the creation of the world: it brings the good god to self-awareness, and it also brings about the creation of the world which is done as a defence against evil. It thus takes part, though in a negative manner, in the realization of what previously was merely a potentiality. The coming into being of the material world out of the conceptual, *mēnōg*, state is only made possible through the negative participation of the evil principle. Only in eschatology can the world be conceived to exist without the fermenting presence of evil.[15]

14 *Zoroaster: Politician or Witch-Doctor?* (Oxford 1951), pp. 47f. The lack of balance between the powers is attributed by Henning to the missionary zeal of the protagonists of these religions, but the reason is apparently more fundamental. U. Bianchi (*Zamān i Ōhrmazd*, Torino 1958, p. 88, n.) criticized Henning's interpretation with some justice, although his own conception of Gathic religion is not entirely convincing.

15 An important question, which cannot be discussed here, concerns the relationship of this conception of Ahreman to the older religion. There seems to be no sign of it in the Avesta; on the contrary, Angra Mainyu is a creating divinity, as is clear from Yasna 57, 17 and from Vendidad I. It is on the other hand firmly embedded in the theological complex of ideas at the centre of which we have the interplay between *mēnōg* and *gētīg*. This pair of concepts has its unmistakable origins in the Avesta, but by the Sasanian period it had absorbed a certain amount of foreign influence, though it preserved what seems to be a peculiarly Iranian view of the world. A consistent application of this view required considering Ahreman and the evil powers as "non-existent". Whatever date we assign to the one set of ideas would also have to be applied to the other.

IV

Mihr the Judge

1. Middle Persian *miyāncīg*

In Classical and modern Persian the term *miyānjī* is quite well established. It designates an arbiter, a go-between, an umpire. In the Sasanian period, and possibly earlier, the corresponding Middle Persian term seems to have designated a more formal kind of judicial function, that of a judge, as well as a position of administrative responsibility. We may consider, for example, its occurrence in *Ardā Virāf Nāmag*:

[I] *u-m dīd ruwān ī mard-ē ke pad pay-ē pad tārīkīh [ī] dušaxw āwīxt ēstād u-š pad dast dās-ē āhenēn dāšt ud war ud kaš ī xwēš hamē brīd ud mēx-ē āhenēn pad cašm andar zad ēstād. u-m pursīd ku ēn ruwān hān ī ke u-š ce wināh kard. gōwēd srōš ī ahlaw ud ādur yazd ku ēn ruwān ī awe druwand mard ke šahr pad miyāncīgīh aweš *dād*[1] *ēstād ud hān ī sazēd kardan ud framūdan ne kard ud ne framūd ud sang [ud] kapīz ud paymānag keh dāšt u-š az driyōšān ud az kārwānīgān garzišn ne niyōšīd* (AVn 67).[2]

> And I saw the soul of a man who was suspended by one foot in the darkness of hell, and who held an iron sickle in one hand, cutting his own breast and arm-pits and striking an iron wedge against his eye.[3] I asked: 'Whose soul is this, and what sin did he commit? Srōš the Just and the god Ādur say: This is the soul of that evil man to whom the city was given in *miyāncīgīh* and who did not do or order that which should have been done and ordered, and who kept deficient weights and measures, and who did not hear complaint from poor people and travellers'.

In a context like this, *miyāncīgīh* cannot mean 'arbitership'. Haug and West translated it, presumably by a guess from the context, 'administration'. There are two specific faults which the text of *Ardā Virāf* imputes to the man in this section: lack of fairness in weights and measures, and failure to listen to the complaint of the poor. As will be seen from other examples, the office, title or function of *miyāncīg* is associated with the notion of fairness, to which deficiency in measures is the obvious antithesis; listening to the complaints of the poor is in Iran a prime characteristic of judges, the defence of the poor having been made a formal attribute of *mōbads*, particularly those of Pārs province.[4]

---

[1] Ms. has *dāšt*.

[2] *Ardā Virāf*, ed. Hoshangji Jamaspji Asa, revised by Haug and West, p. 96f.

[3] The expression is possibly connected to the NPers. idiom *mīx-i čašm-i kas-ī būdan* 'to annoy, vex'.

[4] Cf. *Monumentum H.S. Hyberg*, II (Acta Iranica), Leiden-Teheran-Liège 1975, p. 215ff., and the literature referred to there.

That the word *miyāncīg* belongs to the sphere of the administration of justice can be seen from further passages:

[II] *ud andar hān ī xwadāyīh ud rāyēnīdārīh ud dastwarīh ud dādwarīh ((Y)) ud miyāncīgīh ud hān ī *hamīh*[5] *ud āštīh ud mihr-dārīh [ud] ce andar im-dar* (*Dk* VIII 9. 4–5; *DkM* 685.18–20; no B text, but cf. p. 69 of Dresden's facsimile edition; West, *SBE* 37, 21).[6]

Concerning lordship, administration, (priestly) authority, judgeship, *miyāncīg*-function; union, peace, love, and whatever (else) there is on the subject.

This passage is an extract from a Pahlavi summary of *Bariš Nask.*

[III] *ud abar miyāncīg*[7] *ī abar dādestān ī pad duz wābar*[8] *kard [ud] abar band ud drōš hištan pašn kard ud ce andar im dar* (*Dk* VIII 20.43; DkM 710.4–6; B 538).

Concerning a *miyāncīg* who gave credence in a judgement to a thief, and gave an agreement to let (him) away without imprisonment and punishment, and whatever (else) there is on this subject.[9]

Although the passage, from a summary of Nikādom Nask, is not unequivocally clear, it does seem to suggest that we have to do here with a *miyāncīg*, i.e. a judge, who acquitted a thief without proper evidence.

The word occurs in other contexts in a somewhat looser connotation. Such, for example, is the following passage, which occurs in an answer to a long question about a dispute between an *ērbad* and a *hāwišt* over who will be hired to perform for a gentleman who wants a competent person to recite for him the five *fragards* of the Avesta with Zand. A financial remuneration of 350 drahms is promised for the person selected to perform this pious duty. The *hāwišt*, it transpires, has the whole Avesta required, but no Zand; he claims, however, that the other fellow, the *ērbad*, possesses none of the two, and that he would act merely as a contractor, hiring other people to do the actual recitation of Avesta and Zand. It is preferable, the *hāwišt* argues, to hire someone who recites on his own, even if this does not cover both Avesta and Zand, rather than let the remuneration go to a priest who does the recitation through others. The *hāwišt* offers to go over the recitation of the whole Avesta twice, as a balance against the *ērbad*'s offer of the recitation of both Avesta and Zand. The answer given to this question begins as follows:

[IV] *passox ēd ku hān *ēw*[10] *weh-dēn ke hamāg dēn warrawist*[11] *[ud]*

---

[5] *DkM* has **AMTš**; Meherji Rana has **xmyx**, which is also West's reading.

[6] Translation in J. de Menasce, *Encyclopédie*, 38, where *miyāncīgīh* is rendered 'arbitrage'.

[7] Ms. has **myd'nykcyk.**

[8] A reading **W 'pl** = *ud appar* 'and a robber' has also been considered, but the structure of the sentence would be less satisfactory if we adopted that reading.

[9] West, *SBE*, XXXVII, p. 59f., gives a different rendering of the text.

[10] Ms. has **Y.**

[11] Ms. has **HYMNWyt´**, but an ending **st´** is inserted between the lines, above the phonetic complement of the verb.

framūd[12] *hān *ēw*[13] *kāmag [ī] wehīh [rāy] ud pad-eš pursišnīhā wizīdārīhā. hān ērbad ke-š guft ku pad 350 drahm ce'ōn-tān pēš ciš hamē dād hēd be ō man framāy, *xwad*[14] *ne dēnīg kār bahr bawēd dastwarīhā dahišn ce'ōn raft bawēd guft šahrīg-barišnīhā miyāncīg-kārīhā* (*Dd* pursišn 65; in West's division 66:19–20; K35 fol. 180r).

The answer is this. That person, follower of the Good Religion, who believed in the whole scripture and ordered (to recite it), – that was out of desire for good, and it is necessary to investigate concerning that question. The *ērbad* who said: As you have given before the 350 drahms, order (to give them) to me – this will not be, by itself, the portion of the work of religion to give (to him) with authority, as was said before,[15] according to the custom of the country and in the action of a *miyāncīg*.[16]

The translation of this difficult text is not certain. I cannot give a rendering of the rest of the reply, which contains three unfamiliar words.[17] However, with regard to the two juxtaposed expressions, *šahrīg-barišnīhā,* and *miyāncīg-kārīhā* it is possible to assume that the former refers to the custom of the people while the latter talks about fairness or justice. We seem to have here the contrast 'custom'/ 'law'. The meaning of *miyāncīg*, obtained from other texts, fits in well with such an interpretation. The meaning so far gained for this word can be usefully applied to a passage in the early part of *Zādspram*, where the creation of the world is dealt with:

[V] *u-š be az-eš zamān be ō hayyārīh xwāst, ce-š dīd ku ahreman pad miyāncīgīh [ī] hēc rōšnīh abar ne ēstēd. zamān *ēdōn harw dō-ān *pad ham-hayyārīh ud rāst-rāyēnīdārīh aweš niyāz, u-š pad 3 zamān kard ī harw zamān-ē 3 hazārag ud ahreman abar ēstād* (*Zs* 1.9–11).

Therefore[18] he asked Time for help. For he saw that Ahreman would not abide by the judgement of any luminary.[18a] Thus both parties need Time for help and for right ordering. He made it into three times, each one of a thousand years, and Ahreman accepted.[19]

We have preferred to translate *miyāncīgīh* in this passage by 'judgement,' but it

[12] Ms. has **plmwtn** .

[13] Ms. has **Y.**

[14] Ms. **NPŠH.**

[15] Literally: 'as the saying has gone'.

[16] I.e., presumably, 'in justice'.

[17] These are **dwl, 'mtl, xwpyl.**

[18] *be az-eš* seems to have the meaning "proceeding from it", which I believe is also attested for the 'sandwich' combination *az . . . be*. On this construction cf. Appendix A.

[18a] One may possibly suggest that this is a refutation of the variant myth, attested chiefly in Zurvanite sources, according to which the "angels", i.e. Mihr and others, served as judge or intermediary between the two contestants. The myth is discussed further below.

[19] Zaehner, *BSOS*, 9 (1937/9), 574, 577, and *Zurvan*, 341; Molé, *Culte*, 404. Both these authors offer translations which differ from the one given here.

may be possible to think also of 'government, rule'; using the term 'jurisdiction' might cover both these meanings. With a slightly different construction the relevant phrase may be translated as follows: "For he saw that no light would be able to overcome Ahreman by justice," in this case without supplementing an *iẓāfa* after *miyāncīgīh*. All of these alternative renderings assume that *miyāncīgīh* has a juridical or administrative sense. The plain sense of the passage as rendered above is that Time is asked to assume authority, as a judge or arbiter, because Ohrmazd realizes that his own jurisdiction would not be accepted by Ahreman. Putting Time in the role of judge makes it possible to restrict the scope of the battle, and therefore eventually to win it, even though this involves letting Ahreman have sway for a period.

The judicial connotation of the word comes out well in a number of passages of the Pāzand text *Škand gumānīg wizār*:

[VI] *nūn ažašą pursə̄t ku yazat̰ hamə̄šaa xᵛāβar aβaxšāiṇd u kərbagar dāestąnī u haravist hast būt̰ bahōt̰ dānət̰ pa har ciš kām kām-raβā ēca ku dāestąnī myąžaī ayå ka ə̄duṇ ə̄duṇ nə̄* (XI 6–7).

Now ask of them: Is God always benevolent, merciful, virtuous and just? Does He know all that is, was and will be? With regard to whatever His will is, does He carry out His will? and this too: Is He a just judge? Or is He (once) thus and (another time) not thus?

dāestąnī myąžaī, in Pahlavi probably *dādestānīg miyāncīg* 'a judge who judges by the law,' is rendered into Sanskrit *nyāyatvaṁ mādhyasthaṁ* 'propriety (and) mediation.' In the answer we read the following:

agaraš nə̄ kāmast anāī u vat əž dąmą aβāž dāštan u har kas ə̄ugānaa nə̄kī dādan ąš dāestąnī u myąžaī ku (XI, 10).

If He did not want to prevent evil and wickedness from the creatures, and to give to every person only[19a] goodness, where is His justice and judgeship?

[VII] *agaraš manišni i bažaa nə̄ xᵛat̰ ō mardumą dāt̰ ąn kə̄ hast kə̄ jat̰ əž farmąn u kām i ōi manišni i bažaa dahət̰. agaraš xᵛat̰ dāt̰ nun āhō aβar dārət̰ ąš rāstī u myąžaī əž ci* (*ŠGV* XI, 109f).

If it was not He Himself who gave sinful thought to people, who is it who gives sinful thought without His command and desire? If it was He Himself who gave (it), [and who] now sustains (?) the fault, what is His rectitude and justice?[20]

[19a] *ə̄ugānaa*, like NPers. *yagāna*, possesses, among other meanings, the sense of 'only'. The translation "à chacune et à toutes ensemble" (de Menasce) is inaccurate. The two words *dāestąnī u myąžąī* represent here abstract forms: *dādestānīh ud miyāncīgīh*.

[20] Among the meanings of *abar dāštan* 'to withdraw, take away' is recorded in Yavišt ī Friyān I 21, 28, and in NPers. usage. It seems however to be used here in the sense indicated. West's translation of the phrase "and he now considers them a fault" seems to be based on mere guess. The Sanskrit version has *upari dadhāti*, which is a mere imitation of the Pāzand. For the

[VIII] *īn əž kadąm myąžaī-kunišnī ku šnāxtan i aržamandī i nōkī i han rā dard marg anāī aβar hanō i agunāh hōlō̤t* (*ŠGV* XI, 204).

Of what (kind of) doing of justice is this, (namely), to let death and evil come on an innocent one, in order to make known to another one the value of good life?

The use of the word *miyāncīh* in the following passage is not free from some ambiguity:

[IX] *ku ašnaw az man ke hān man gōwēm ke-š*[21] *āmurzīdār ast tō rāy ohrmazd ((ku wināh be āmurzēd ud kirbag az tō padīrēd))*[22] *ke hān man zardušt rāy dēn nimūd ēstēd ohrmazd hān dēn tō-z padīr ke abāg miyāncīh ī amahraspandān pad dawāgīh*[23] *ī man *āmadag*[24] *ast awe pēš [ī] tō andar ēn gēhān ((ku amahraspandān pad dawāgīh ī man *āmadag ast andar ēn gēhān pad padīrēnīdan ī dēn pēš tō hān dēn tō be padīr ke anōh mizd [ī] mēnōg be ayābēd))* (*ZXA* 199, Višt. Yt. 32; cf. Dhabhar, *Transl. of ZXA*, 374; Molé, *Culte*, 362, 364).

Listen to me, for I say (the following): Ohrmazd is compassionate with regard to you, ((that is to say, he forgives sins and accepts good deeds from you)). Ohrmazd showed that religion to me, to Zoroaster. Accept you that religion, which has come together with the judgement of the Amahraspands by my apostleship before you in this world. ((That is to say, the Amahraspands came to this world through my apostleship so as to cause you to accept the religion. Accept you that religion, for there one finds the reward of *mēnōg*)).

The Pahlavi text departs here so considerably from the Avestan passage to which it is supposed to be a *Zand*, that very little use can be made of the parallel

---

two words *myąžaī əž* I prefer to read in restituted Pahlavi *miyāncīgīh-ez*, with the enclitic conjunction. This may be a good opportunity to correct a wrong translation in the next section of the book: *ci ka mardum . . . šər u gurg aβarō xaraβastar cạndašą tvą ō rōdagą āβastąn i xᵛōš ạndar nō hōlōnd anda kušą taβāhinənd* (XI 111f.), where E.W. West, followed by de Menasce, translates: "For when mankind . . . so far as they are able, do not let the lion and wolf (and) other noxious creatures in among their own young ones (and) pregnant (females) so long as they (can) destroy them". The 'pregnant females' are incongruous here, and in fact there is little doubt that the correct reading of *āβastąn* in Phl is *abastān* 'shelter, refuge'. This was already recognized by Neryosang, who rendered the word into Sanskrit *gosthāna* 'enclosure for cattle'. The translation of the main part of the sentence should thus be: "as far as they are able, they do not let the lion etc. into the shelter of their young ones lest they destroy them".

21 Here and in other places in this passage *ke* stands for *ku*.

22 The editor's square brackets, indicating passages which he believes to be Zand glosses on the Avestan text, are here rendered by double parentheses. These markings should however be treated with some scepticism.

23 Spelled **dwp'kyw**. The words renders Av. *dūta-*, cf. *AirWb* 749, and Dhabhar, *Transl. ZXA*, 374.

24 If the reading is correct, the word is written in this passage twice in an irregular manner: **YATWNytk'**.

between the two. It is in fact not very clear what prompted the late editor of the Pahlavi text, Ervad B.N. Dhabhar, to set aside certain sentences as glosses (these are marked here by double parentheses), in contrast to other sentences which are supposed to be straight translations. He presumably relied on the word *ku*, which normally precedes such glosses. However, the whole passage can be regarded as a loose paraphrase of the Avestan text, with considerable amplifications. The meaning of *miyāncīh* is unclear. It does not seem to signify 'mediation,' as rendered by Molé, or 'intercession,' as given by Dhabhar. 'Judgement,' 'jurisdiction,' or 'authority,' which go together with the other passages where this word occurs (or rather, its cognate, *miyāncīgīh*), may give better sense.

[X] *nūn wizīdār ī cim dast abar nihād ī ham-ēdonīh [i] warrawišn, ud miyāncīgīhā pad rāh ī xrad be abē-gumānīhā sazēd dānistan ku az mēnōg mad hēm ne pad gētīg būd hēm . . .* (*PhlT* 42.1ff.; cf. Nyberg, *Manual of Pahlavi*, I, 62).[25]

Now he who discerns the reason has indicated the manner of faith. In a *miyāncīg* manner, by way of wisdom, one ought to know without doubt (as follows): I came from *mēnōg* and was not (originated) in *gētīg*; I am created, not originated (*būdag*); . . .

The expression *miyāncīgīhā* cannot be translated 'by mediation, mediately' (Nyberg), which gives no sense in the context.[26] Basing ourselves on the parallel usage of *miyāncīg* in other passages, it is possible to suggest one of two translations: 'in a manner of a *miyāncīg* judge,' i.e. 'fairly, justly,' or 'in an authoritative manner, with authority.'

The legal sense of *miyāncīg* is perhaps derived from a specific legal connotation which the word *miyān* 'middle' seems to have possessed: 'trial, legal proceedings.' The word is attested in this meaning, if our interpretation is correct, in the following passage, which gives a model of formulas of praise addressed to the recipient of a letter:

[XI] *ō [hān ke pad] tan āfrīdag, pad zāyišn burzišnīg, pad jahišn abēzag, pad gōhr padīriftag, andar yazdān wābarīgān, andar xwadāyān . . . *nēw, andar āwām abāyišnīg, pad cihr brēh ud xwarr bawandag, pad miyān rāst buxtag, pad gōwišn wuzurg-nām pērōzgar, pad framān xwābar, pad hu-pādexšāyīh dānāg, pad rāyēnīdārīh an-abaxšāyišnīg ud a-nang, ud pad mardom-dōstīh kišwar-ummēd wehān-pērāyag, hamēyīg-pērōzgar xwadāyīgān wahmān ī wahmānān* (*PhlT* 137 §29; cf. differently Zaehner, *BSOS*, 9, 1937/39, 95, 99).

---

[25] Cf. in particular H. Corbin, in *Prof. Poure Davoud Memorial Volume* II, Bombay 1951, 129-160, where our passage occurs on p. 144 ("par la médiation de la Sagesse"); M.F. Kanga, *Čītak handarž i pōryōtkēšān*, Bombay 1960, 20 ("by way of intervention").

[26] The latest quotation of this phrase, by G. Lazard, in *Monumentum H.S. Nyberg*, II, (*Acta Iranica*), Leiden-Teheran-Liège 1975, 9, renders it: "on peut savoir médiatement par la raison, mais de science certaine".

> To [him who is in] body praised, in birth honourable, in fortune pure, accepted in descent, reliable with regard to the gods, *brave . . . with regard to rulers, comely among the populace (?),[27] perfect in nature, fortune and splendour, true and acquitted in law (?), illustrious and victorious in rhetoric, benign in command, wise in good government, unstinting and respectable in arranging affairs, the hope of the world and the ornament of the good in love of people, the ever victorious, the princely, M. son of N.

The adjectives which go with *miyān* in this passage, *rāst* and *buxtag*, are such as fit a judicial context, especially *buxtag* (legally) 'innocent, acquitted,' the opposite of *ēraxtag.*[28] If *miyān* means simply 'legal strife, trial,'[29] then *miyāncīg* properly means "the man who sits in a trial, a judge." There is thus no need to assume for *miyāncīg* the semantic development: 'mediator' → 'arbiter' → 'judge.' The existence of *miyāncīg* 'judge' is also confirmed by its occurrence as a loan-word in Jewish Babylonian Aramaic, recently discussed by E.S. Rosenthal.[30]

A Zoroastrian text in New Persian demonstrates the use of *miyānjī* both in the sense of 'a leader,' in particular a religious leader, and in that of a dispenser of justice, though the latter meaning is less prominent in this text. As the text, which occurs in the first of the two treatises called *ʿUlamā-i Islām*, is quite accessible,[31] only a translation of it need be given here:

> Some people say: There ought to be a leader (*miyānjī*) who would say what is right and what is false. This statement is true for (the following reason): a man holds a book in his hand, and people have two eyes in their head; still, as long as there is no leader (*miyānjī*) between his eyes [and] the book,[32] he cannot read the book. The leader (*miyānjī*) is light, for in

---

[27] Or "in the world"? *āwām* seems to possess in this text this peculiar meaning. Cf. Appendix B.

[28] Cf. Shaked, *Monumentum H.S. Nyberg*, II, (*Acta Iranica*), Leiden-Teheran-Liège 1975, 216ff.

[29] In *AVN* 15.9-10 we have a word which the editors read *miyān* and translate 'mediation'. The text can be read in more than one way. E.g.

> *u-m dīd hān ī was zarrēn gāh ud wistarg ī xūb ud bālišn abāg bōb* [*ī*] *passazag ke-šān pad-eš nišast hēnd kadag-xwadāyān ud dādagān ruwān ī deh* [*ud*] *dūdagmān ud miyān (ud) dast kard.* "I saw a throne with much gold, and a beautiful bedding, and a cushion with a fair carpet, on which were sitting souls of chiefs of houses and judges, who judged (*miyān-dast kard*? or governed?) provinces and families (*dūdagmān* like New Persian *dūdmān*)".

It seems, however, that we ought to prefer recognizing here the phrase *mān ud mēhan* "house and family", in which case we are left with an otherwise unknown idiom *dast kardan* 'to rule'. Other possibilities of reading need not detain us.

[30] E.S. Rosenthal, "Talmudica Iranica" (in Hebrew), in: S. Shaked, ed., *Irano-Judaica*, Jerusalem 1980 (Publications of the Ben-Zvi Institute).

[31] *PersRiv*, II, 76.13-77.1; cf. translation by B.N. Dhabhar, *The Persian Rivayat of Hormazyar Framarz*, Bombay 1932, 444f.

[32] Read: [*va*] *kitāb*, and cf. further below.

> darkness it is not possible to read the book. Now, just as it is necessary to have a leader (*miyānjī*) in reading a book, so is it also necessary to have a leader in the true faith and path. As the Jews say: Our leader (*miyānjī*) is *allūf,*[33] and the Christian say: Our leader is **kaššīšā*,[34] and the Muslims say: Our leader is *imām* and the Shīʿa[35] say: our leader is **ṣāḥib-i zamān,*[36] so[37] do the Zoroastrians say: Our leader should be a person endowed with great wisdom, high mind and luminous soul, more powerful than all people, more just in dispensing justice than all persons. At the time of (performing his) leadership he looks to the Creator. Now in spite of all that high mind and splendour (*farr*), some people believe in him and others do not. When Ahreman's time comes even those who have believed in him withdraw from his command. A person who wishes to give justice knows that it is as we have said.

If the simile of the light which enables people to see, and which guides the vision to the object of sight, strikes us as peculiar in association with 'leader', we should nevertheless resist the temptation to regard it as demonstrating a further sense of the word *miyānjī*, namely that of a means or a link, coming between the eye and the object of sight. The author of the New Persian text himself, though he evidently found this term in the traditional source which he used, may have fallen a victim to such a misunderstanding. This is perhaps why he wrote: *tā dar miyān-i cašm-i vay [va] kitāb miyānjī na-bāšad* "as long as there is no *miyānjī* between his eye [and] the book", apparently taking *miyānjī* to mean 'a mediator, means'. That this is not the correct understanding of the word can be seen from a passage in Pahlavi which speaks of light as a 'leader' of sight:

> Whenever a man thinks, speaks or acts something righteous, at the same time a brightness ('light', *rōšnīh-ē*) grows from it and it becomes in him his leader (*parwānag*) towards religion. Whenever a man thinks, speaks or acts something sinful, a darkness rises from it and stands between the man and religion, and the man sees the religion less (*Dk* VI 290; cf. *Wisdom of the Sasanian sages*, 113f.).

The term *miyānjī* in the New Persian text equals *parwānag* here.[38] It seems that by

---

[33] On *allūf* as a Jewish Babylonian title of dignity cf. J. Mann, *The Jews in Egypt and in Palestine under the Fātimid caliphs*, I, 1920 (reprinted, New York 1970), 114ff.; S.D. Goitein, *A Mediterranean Society*, II, Berkeley-Los Angeles-London 1971, p. 22, 199.

[34] The text has *kš'*, although the division could also be *kš-'st*, which should be emended to **kašīš*, as in Standard New Persian. Cf. the corresponding *pīr* in Pahlavi used by Christians: *Studies in memory of Gaston Wiet*, Jerusalem 1977, 29.

[35] Written *rafīḍān* for *rāfiḍān*.

[36] Written ṣḥf *zamān*.

[37] The text has here *va-zarātuštiyān*, where the *va* seems out of place.

[38] The expression *miyānjī* occurs for light also in Nāṣir-i Xusrau's *Xwānu l-ixwān* (ed. Yaḥya el-Khachab, Cairo 1940, p. d). In a Zoroastrian New Persian inscription dedicating a fire-temple we read: *ba-miyānjī va kūšiš-i bihdīn-i sitūda-āyīn manekjī* (M. Boyce, *AO* 30,

the time of the redaction of the New Persian text the sense of the word *miyānjī* was partially lost, and that it was re-defined in terms of a derivative from *miyān* 'middle'.[38a]

An unambiguous use of the word in a judicial sense occurs in a text which deals with the administration of oaths (*sōwgand nāma*) in the Persian *Rivāyat* of Dārāb Hormazyār. In the first of two such texts which are given consecutively the person who seems to be in charge of this function is a *miyānjī*: he is mentioned as the one who should prevent the oath from being administered in too much haste (*miyānjī bāyad kard tā zūd zūd sōwgand na-dihand, PersRiv*, I, 45; cf. Dhabhar's * translation, p. 39). In the second of these texts, the person who administers the oath, and of whom the same injunction is said, is a *dāvar*, 'judge' (Op. cit., 47ff.; cf. in particular: *dāvar bāyad ki zūd bar zōwgand dādan dilīrī na-kunad*, p. 53.14f. "It is necessary that the judge make not bold to administer the oath in haste"). The correspondence between the two texts does not make it necessary to conclude

---

1966, p. 66), which, in the light of our new understanding of the word *miyānjī* we may perhaps translate: "under the leadership and by the effort of the Zoroastrian Manekji, of praiseworthy manners". In *Xwānu l-ixwān* p. 11 there is talk of five *miyānjī* who are: *asās, imām, ḥujjat, dāʿī, maʾḏūn.*

[38a] The Middle Persian expression *andar* or *ō miyān šudan* may have meant 'to be in the lead, to be in command', like a general who commands his army from within. Such a military usage occurs with regard to the deity Wahman. He is said to be good (*weh*), powerful (*amāwand*), and a giver of peace (*āstīh-dādār*). His second epithet is explained in the following manner:

> *u-š amāwandīh ēd ku gund ī yazdān hān-ez ī ērān ka āštīh kunēnd be abzāyēnd pad rāy ī wahman ka-šān andar miyān šawēd, ud gund ī dēwān hān-ez ī an-ērān ka-šān anāštīh be abaxšēnd wahman rāy ka-šān ō* (**mtdy'n**) *miyān ne šawēd* (*GBd* 163.13-164.2; *Zand-ākāsīh* 212; TD_1 fol. 68r; cf. Gignoux, *JA*, 1968, 231f.) "His being powerful is this: when the troops of the gods and those of the Iranians make peace, they increase because of Wahman, as he commands them (lit. when he goes in their midst); when the troops of the demons and those of the non-Iranians have a conflict, they diminish because of Wahman, as he does not command them (literally, he does not come to their midst)".

abaxšēnd can not mean 'elles se repentent'; if it is not a mere error for *absihēnd*, which seems unlikely, we ought to recognize here a verb *abaxš*- 'to diminish (intr.)', in contrast to *abzāyēnd*. An expression which is attested once, to my knowledge, in New Persian may belong here, though the connection is doubtful. Xusrau Abarwēz, pursued by Bahrām Cūbīn, comes to a monastery. When it is evident that he is going to fall in the hands of his adversary, his minister, Bandūya, devises a strategem. The king changes garments with his minister and flees, while the minister, clad in the king's attire, causes the pursuers to think that the king is still there. After a day the minister admits that he was only masking as the king, and explains his motive: *tā šumārā īnjā bidāram va ū miyāna kunad* "so that I should keep you here and that he should gain a distance" (Ibn al-Balxī, *Fārs Nāma*, ed. Le Strange and Nicholson, London 1921, 101.22. The parallel accounts, Tabarī, *Ta'rīx*, II, Cairo 1961, 179; Tha'ālibī, *Ghurar al-siyar*, ed. Zotenberg, Paris 1900, 667; Dīnawarī, *Al-axbār al-ṭiwāl*, ed. Guirgass, Leiden 1888, 93, do not give a literal correspondence). The expression *miyāna kardan* may, by a guess, be a development of 'to take the lead, be in charge'. [However, Nizām al-Mulk, *Siyar al-mulūk* p. 92 bottom, has *miyāna kunīd* "you should gain a distance".]

that *miyānjī* has the same sense as *dāvar*; there may be a distinction of function between them, but they both form part of the administration of justice.

Another legal use of the word *miyānjī* in early New Persian is attested in the sense of 'surety, pledge', in the Cambridge *tafsīr* of the Qur'ān (cf. E.G. Browne, *JRAS*, 1894, p. 489).

The term *miyānjī* is applied in Classical New Persian to a judge. Two examples may suffice:

[XII] *tīγ-i tu kard miyānjī ba-miyān-i daδ-u dām* (G. Lazard, *Les premiers poètes persans*, Teheran 1964, II, p. 13 line 5) "Your sword has made justice between wild and tame animals", or, as Lazard translates it: "[Dieu] a fait de ton sabre l'arbitre entre les fauves et les gazelles".

[XIII] *miyān-šān cu ān dāvarī šud dirāz // miyānjī bar āmad yakī sar-firāz* (*Šāh-Nāma*, III, Moscow 1965, p. 9, line 49; ed. Dabīr Siyāqī, II, Tehran 1335, p. 465, line 53). "When that quarrel drew long between them, a noble judge appeared".

These two quotations from Classical Persian literature show the word to be used in the sense of a judge who decides an issue between two parties. Here too it is possible that the word was re-created or re-defined in New Persian as deriving from *miyān* 'midle'.[38b]

We seem to have in Syriac too the corresponding term used in a judicial sense. It occurs in the codex of Išoʿbuxt, which reflects a fair amount of Sasanian influence.[39] When a Christian man contracts to marry a Christian woman not in front of (*d-lā maṣʿiyūθā*, literally "without the mediation") priests and Christian laymen, but by written deed, or in front of (*b-maṣʿiyūθā*, "by the mediation of") heathens, afterwards changing his mind and refusing to marry her, there is no compulsion on him to conclude his marriage. The Syriac term used here, *maṣʿiyūθā*, literally means 'mediation', but the situation seems to require a judicial connotation, such as the legal presence (as witnesses), or the jurisdiction, of priests or laymen.

2. *Miyāncīgīh ī Mihr*

We have evidence that the term *miyāncīg* was applied to Mithra. As one of Mithra's frequent epithets in Iran is 'judge', this is not at all surprising, though it is

---

38b A curious use of this expression occurs on an Arab-Sasanian copper weight recently published by R. Curiel and Ph. Gignoux (*StIr* 5, 1976, 165-169). It has a Koranic text in Arabic on the obverse, which reads: *i'dilū huwa aqrabu li-l-taqwā*, written in Kufic script. The Pahlavi legend on the reverse has caused trouble to the editors, but I believe it can be plausibly read as a fairly close rendering of the Arabic: **mdy'n wl(y)x / nzdyktl / 'L l('st)' / Y MN yzdt'**. This may be read as follows: *miyān-warīh nazdīk-tar ō rāst ī az yazad* "Carrying the *miyān* (= doing justice) is closer to the truth which is from God". Here *miyān*, if the reading is accepted, would be an Iranian equivalent of *'adl* 'justice'. The last word may be read *dād* 'law'. It is noteworthy that the qāḍī Abū l-Ḥasan 'Alī b. Ḥasan, who was judge in Hamadān, bore the *nisba* al-Miyān(a)jī, attributed to the town of Miyāna in Azerbayjān. Cf. Yāqūt, *Mu'jam al-Buldān*, s.v. "Miyāna"; *Ta'rīx Baghdād*, II, 275. (I owe this observation to M.J. Kister. Further numerous references exist for both the place-name and the *nisba*.)

39 Cf. E. Sachau, *Syrische Rechtsbücher*, III, Berlin 1914, p. 78 §9.

remarkable that the term has not so far been noticed, to my knowledge. Mithra, with his two companions, Srōš and Rašn, who together form the triad of judges in Zoroastrian eschatology, are thus described in the following terms:

[XIV] *pad anāg-kāmagīh ī xešm ī xrvi-druš ud astvihād ke hamōyēn dām ōbārēd ud sērīh ne dānēd ud miyāncīgīh ī mihr ud srōš ud rašn ud tarāzēnīdārīh ī rašn ī rāst pad tarāzūg ī mēnōgān ke hēc kustag hu-grāy*[40] *ne kunēd, ne ahlawān rāy ud ne-z druwandān, ne xwadāyān rāy ud ne-z dehbadān* (*MX* II:117–120).[41]

With the evil desire of Xešm, who carries a bloody weapon, and Astvihad, who swallows all the creation and does not know satisfaction, and the judgment of Mihr and Srōš and Rašn, and the weighing in the scales of the just Rašn by the scale of the spirits, which does not make any side its *favourite,[40] neither the righteous nor the wicked, neither lords nor rulers.

In this context, which talks of the eschatological judgement carried out by the three deities, it makes no sense to translate *miyāncīgīh* as 'mediation', though this is what the various editors and translators of the text have done,[42] beginning with Neyosang who, in his Sanskrit version, true to his consistent method of literal rendering of the Pahlavi, used for *pad miyāncīgīh* the instrumental form *madhyastatā*. The Indian term could, however, also denote the state or function of an umpire or arbiter, close enough to the sense required by our passage. The Sanskrit term incidentally indicates a development similar to that which took place in Iranian. Thus perhaps Neyosang's choice of the word is justified.

[XV] *stāyēm ud azbāyēm dādār ohrmazd ī rāyōmand ī xwarrōmand ud amahraspandān. spāsdār hēm az ohrmazd mēnōg ī afzōnīg, xwadāy ī xwābar ī kirbakkar, dādār ī wisp dām ud dahišn ī mēnōg ud gētīg, ī xwarr dādār, ka-š frāz brihēnīd tō kirbakkar mihr ī frāxwgōyōd ka rāst-dādwar *ī azeš-mānd hēh, ku pad mēnōgān ud gētīgān dādwarīh ud miyāncīgīh rāst kunēh* (*ZXA* 241f.; Pâzend Texts, p. 258; cf. Zaehner, *Zurvan*, 101 n. 5; Dhabhar, *Transl. of ZXA*, 447 n. 16).[43]

---

[40] Pāzand has here *a-rāst*, Sanskrit *aśuddhat*, both obviously based on a different manuscript reading. The Pahlavi word in this text has been read by previous scholars by conjecture *ōgrāi* "declination, dip" (H.S. Nyberg, *Manual of Pahlavi*, II, s.v., and similarly by D.N. MacKenzie, *A concise Pahlavi dictionary*, s.v.). The word was taken to be made up from the verbal element *grāy-* "to incline", with a preverb. It is however desirable to connect this word with the one attested in *Dd*, K35 fol. 133v: *ud frazand* [*i*] **az awēšān zāyēnd hān ī anōšag ēd ce dēr-pattāy ud *hu-grāy karb dārēnd* (cf. Nyberg, *Manual*, I, 105) "The children who will be born to them will be eternal, that is, they will be long-lasting and will have attractive shape". Nyberg reads the puzzling word, spelled here **'nndl'd**, as *x*^{v}*andrāi*, a non-existent word. West (*SBE*, XVIII, p. 77) has *khûn-girâî* "blood-exhausted". M. Shaki, *ArOr*, 43 (1975), 262, reads *hu-wirāy*.

[41] Cf. Nyberg, *Hilfsbuch*, I, p. 40; *Manual*, I, p. 72.

[42] Cf. West, *SBE*, XXIV, p. 18; Nyberg, *loc. cit.*; A. Tafazzoli, *Vāže-nāme-ye Mīnū-ye Xerad*, Tehran 1969, 209; Widengren, *Hochgottglaube*, 118f.

[43] This text forms part of a Ph.D. thesis by Hamid Mahamedi (Harvard University, 1971), which I had the occasion to consult.

> I praise and invoke the Creator Ohrmazd, possessing splendour and fortune, and the Amahraspands. I am thankful to Ohrmazd, the beneficent spirit, the benevolent and virtuous lord, the creator of all creation, both spiritual and material, creator of fortune(?). Who, when he created you, the virtuous Mihr, of wide pastures, who are a just judge of the defaulter(?),[44] that is, you perform (the functions of) *miyāncīg* and judge in truth among both *mēnōg* and *gētīg* beings.

Here again, the parallels in the text are so explicit as to exclude any possibility of ambiguity. Mihr is regarded as a judge, which is indicated by a variety of nearly-synonymous terms: *rāst dādwar, dādwarīh, miyāncīgīh*, with the specifically legal term *azeš-mānd*. It seems reasonable to suppose that the individual terms denote separate judicial functions, but it is not possible, in our state of knowledge, to distinguish more closely between them.

Another interesting reference to the function of Mithra as judge, where a different expression is used, occurs in the *Bundahišn*:

[XVI] *mihr xwēškārīh wizīrīh ī gēhān pad rāstīh kardan ceʾōn gōwēd ku mihr ī frāxw-gōyōd 1000-gōš bēwar-cašm u-š frāxw-gōyōdīh ēd ku ka pad dašt abē-bīmīh be šāyēd madan ud šudan pad rāy ī mihr. u-š 1000-gōšīh ēd ku-š 500 mēnōg kār ī gōšīh hamē kunēd u-š bēwar-cašmīh ēn ku-š 5000 mēnōg kār ī cašmīh kunēnd ku mihr ēn *niyōš*[45] *ud hān-ez niyōš, ēn wēn ud hā-ez wēn. harw rōz tā nēm-rōz abāg xwaršēd pad ēn kār. ēd rāy dādwar pad gētīg tā nēm-rōz wizīr kunēd* (*GBd* 171f.; TD_1 facs. fol. 72r.; *Zand-ākāsīh*, p. 222).[46]

* [44] One may recognize here the legal term *azeš-mānd*. Christian Bartholomae explained the word as indicating some kind of legal proceedings, without committing himself to a definite reading or to a precise definition; cf. *SRb*, p. 17; *ZSR*, IV, 11; *Zendhandschriften*, p. *35. Antonino Pagliaro, *RSO*, 24 (1949), 120-135, translated the term as *interdictum*. The tribute for recognizing the correct meaning of the legal term and for offering a plausible reading should go to Anahit Perikhanian, "Le contumace dans la procédure iranienne et les termes pehlevis *hačašmānd* et *srāδ*", *Mémorial Jean de Menasce*, Louvain 1974, 305-318; and her *Sasanidskij sudebnik*, Erevan 1973, 482. Perikhanian suggests that the term means "contumacy, delay of trial due to failure to appear in court". It should however be noted that this narrow definition does not do justice to all passages where it occurs, including our own text. *MHD* A9, 3-5, also seems to require a broader definition of the term. A close reading of the passage makes it possible, I believe, to suggest that the English-language equivalent might be "defaulter", covering both meanings: (1) "one who fails to appear in court", and (2) "one who fails to comply with a court order"; possibly even more loosely (3) "one who does not comply with the law, a trespasser, a sinner". The last suggestion would make best sense here, and it goes well with the structure of the word. A similar word from the same verb, also denoting sin, is *māndag*, on which cf. my *Wisdom of the Sasanian Sages*, p. 264. Our word was traditionally read in this pasage *hōšmānd*, as can be seen from the Pāzand version and the New Persian gloss (cf. variants to the passage in *ZXA*, p. 403). An alternative reading of the word in this context, *abd-amāwand* "possessing amazing strength", which would be acceptable as to the sense (cf. "Mihr Niyāyisn", *ZXA*, 25 §15), seems less satisfactory. [Cf. the latest discussion in W. Belardi, *Studi mithraici e mazdei*, Rome 1977, 41ff.]

[45] The parallel text in "Xwaršēd Yašt" (cf. the following note) has *ašnaw*.

[46] Cf. G. Widengren, *Hochgottglaube in alten Iran*, Uppsala-Leipzig 1938, p. 121.

Mihr the Judge

> The function of Mihr is to perform the judgement of the world in truth as He says: "Mihr of wide pastures, having a thousand ears, ten thousand eyes". His being of wide pastures is this: when it is possible to walk about in the desert without fear, it is due to Mihr. His being possessed of a thousand eyes is this: five hundred spirits do for him the work of the ear. His being possessed of ten thousand eyes is this: five thousand spirits do for him the work of the eye, (saying): listen to this and listen to that, look at this and look at that. Every day he is with the sun in this work till noon. Therefore the judge in this world decides in judgement until noon.

It is noteworthy that the judgement implied in this passage is not one in which the judge merely decides between two sets of claims and counter-claims, but that the judge is here active in finding out the truth by his "eyes" and "ears" – a simile which is of course taken from the Mihr Yašt. This is an activity characteristic of a ruler, who holds a host of spies and informers,[47] rather than of a mere expert in law. The idea of authority is expressed with particular force by the term *wizīr* (which has been mentioned as a possible candidate for being the Iranian antecedent of the Arabic *wazīr*[48]). The term *miyāncīg* itself, as we have seen, often contains the semantic element of "power, authority".

Of the many references to Mihr as a judge it is perhaps useful to quote only one more, where our specific term is not mentioned, but where Mihr is presented as the god who redresses injustice:

[XVII] *mihr rōz agar-et az kas mustōmandīh-ē abar mad ēstēd pēš[ī] mihr ēst az mihr dādwarīh xwāh ud garzišn kun* (*PhlT* 70 §134; cf. Nyberg, *Texte zum mazdayasnischen Kalender*, Uppsala 1934, 50f.; Hampel, *Die Kopenhagener Handschrift Cod. 27*, Wiesbaden 1974, p. 12f.)

> On the day Mihr, if violence has come to you from someone, stand in front of Mihr, request judgement, and make a complaint.

Mihr's functions tend to be shared by him with his two associates, Srōš and Rašn.[49] In the Pahlavi Propitiation texts, from which we have quoted a passage relating to Mihr (text XV above), Srōš is represented primarily as a fighter of evil and benefactor of the good, while Rašn assumes the specific functions of a judge. Indeed, the term *miyāncīgīh* occurs in connection with him as well:

[XVIII] *ka-š frāz brihēnīd tō rašn ī rāstag ō rāst dādwarīh ī gētīgān ud xwad tan ī rāstīh hēh ud pad kirbag ud bazag āmār kunēh ud az hān ī rāst pand hēc*

Essentially the same text occurs also in "Xwaršēd Niyāyišn", *ZXA*, 21; *Transl. of ZXA*, 36f. It also occurs in "Xwaršēd Yašt", published in transcription by J. Darmesteter, *Etudes iraniennes*, II, Paris 1883, 287ff., where a New Persian and a Sanskrit versions follow. The variants in these texts are not very significant for the sense.

[47] Cf. the discussion in my article in *Irano-Judaica*, Jerusalem, 1980.

[48] Against this view cf. S.D. Goitein, "The origin of the vizierate and its true character", in his *Studies in Islamic history and institutions*, Leiden 1966, 168ff., especially 194ff.; M.M. Bravmann, *The spiritual background of early Islam*, Leiden 1972, 220-226.

[49] For Sraoša in particular cf. B. Geiger, *Die Aməša Spənta*, Wien 1916, 110. Cf. further E. Benveniste, *The Persian religion*, 91.

ēwēnag ne cafsēh, ne pad mēnōgān ne pad gētīgān. pad hu-cašmīh mar pad kas-ez ne druzēh ud miyāncīgīh ud dādwarīh pad rāstīh kunēh ud dēwān ud druzān pad rāstīh wānēh ud druzīh az dāmān ī ohrmazd pad rāstīh be barēh (*ZXA* 245; cf. Dhabhar, *Transl. of ZXA*, 453f.)

When he (= Ohrmazd) created you, the truthful Rašn, for right judgeship of *gētīg* creatures. You are yourself the entity[50] of truth, and you do the account of good deeds and sins, and you do not incline[51] in any manner from the right path, neither with regard to *mēnōg* beings, nor with regard to *gētīg* beings. You do not falsify the account of any one out of good will, and you perform (the functions) of *miyāncīg* and judge in truth, and you vanquish demons and *druj*-s in truth, and you remove *druj*-ship from the creatures of Ohrmazd in truth.

The cumulative evidence of the various passages quoted seems to indicate that the term *miyāncīg* denotes a judiciary function, and that it tends to imply also a position of authority in a rather vague sense. It is applied to Mihr (as well as to Rašn) among other terms that describe him as a judge, just as he is known in Zoroastrian New Persian by the epithets *Dāvar Mihrīzad, Mihr-i Īrān Dāvar,*[52] or the like. Thus, in a foreign source, in Syriac, we have what seems to be an evident reference to Mithra, uttered by the Sasanian king Shapur II, who says, addressing the Christian martyr Shemᶜon: "I swear by the Sun, the judge of the whole earth."[53] One should of course assume a certain syncretism with the Babylonian Shamash, whether we attribute it to the king himself, or, what seems more likely, to the Syriac writer who transmitted the story.[54]

This brings us to the famous crux in Plutarch, where Mithra is called the mediator (*mesitēs*) between Ohrmazd and Ahreman.[55] It seems to me very probable

---

[50] Literally, "the body", which can of course also mean "the person".

[51] The verb *cafs-, caft-, casp-* is amply attested in Judaeo-Persian in the sense of "to incline", in both a transitive and an intransitive sense.

[52] M. Boyce, in J.R. Hinnells (ed.), *Mithraic Studies*, Manchester 1975, 118 and note 11, where reference is also made to A.V.W. Jackson, *Persia past and present*, New York 1906, 372, for a similar formula. Cf. also J.J. Modi, *Religious ceremonies and customs of the Parsees*, 2nd ed., Bombay 1937, 80.

[53] *Sahdūθā d-qaddīšā šem'ōn qāθōlīqā bar šabbā'ē*, in Paul Bedjan, *Acta martyrum et sanctorum*, II, Paris 1891, 166. Cf. also Mani's appeal to the sun as witness of the injustice done to him at the time of his Passion (H. Puech, *Le manichéisme*, Paris 1949, 51). An oath by the sun occurs also in the Acts of St. George, cf. *Le Muséon*, 38 (1925), 88 (text), 109 (translation); Sogdian version, *BST I*.

[54] Cf. F. Cumont, *RHR*, 103 (1931), 32f.

* [55] Plutarch, *De iside et osiride*, 369E (ed. J.G. Griffiths, University of Wales Press 1970, 190f., 474). Of the many discussions of the passage mention may be made here of Duchesne-Guillemin's interpretation of Mithra, Sraoša and Rašnu's role of eschatological judges, which he regards as a transference of Mithra's 'intermediary' position between the two worlds: *La religion de l'Iran ancien*, Paris 1962, 203. E. Benveniste, *The Persian religion according to the chief Greek texts*, Paris 1929, 87 ff., insists that we should take Mithra's mediation between the two deities literally, and that this should be a Zurvanite feature of Plutarch's (or perhaps

that the term in Greek is a direct rendering of the Iranian predecessor of the Pahlavi *miyāncīg*, applied to Mithra, as we have seen, in his function of a judge. It can be shown that in certain versions of the Iranian myth Mihr indeed is supposed to act as a judge in the cosmic battle between the two deities. This need not imply that Mihr in any variety of Zoroastriniasm or at any stage of the mythical narrative is ever considered to be impartial, or that he holds, in a literal sense, a 'middle' position between the two deities. All known varieties of Zoroastrianism uphold the absolute righteousness of Ohrmazd, and it seems natural, from the mythical point of view, that the just judge who is Mihr should be firmly and unequivocally on the side of justice, that is on that of Ohrmazd. The situation as it is conceived by traditional Zoroastrian literature is given colourful expression in the eschatological story of *Zand ī Wahman Yašt*:

[XIX] *ud man dādār ohrmazd abāg amahraspandān ō gar ī hukairyāt āyēm ud framāyēm ō amahraspandān ku gōwēnd ō hamāg yazdān ī mēnōgān ku rawēd rasēd ō hayyārīh ī pēšōtan ī bāmīg. ud mihr ī frāxw-gōyōd ud srōš ī tagīg ud rašn ī rāst ud warhrām ī amāwand ud aštād ī pērōzgar [ud] xwarr ī dēn ī mazdēsnān [ud] nīrang ī rāyēnīdārīh ī gēhān ārāstār pad framān ī man dādār ō pušt rasēm ō hayyārīh ī pēšōtan ī bāmīg. be zanēnd dēwān ī tam-tōhmagān. wāng kunēd gannāg-mēnōg ī druwand ō mihr ī frāxw-gōyōd ku pad rāstīh ul ēst tō mihr ī frāxw-gōyōd. pas mihr ī frāxw-gōyōd wāng kunēd ku ēn 9000 sāl pašt-ē ī-š kard tā nūn dahāg ī duš-dēn ud frāsyāb ī tūr ud alaksandar ī hrōmāyīg ud awēšān dwāl-kustīgān dēwān ī wizārd-wars 1000 sālān-āwām wēš az paymān xwadāyīh kard. stard bawēd hān druwand gannāg-mēnōg ka ēdōn *ašnawēd.* (*ZWY* III.31-35; ed. B.T. Anklesaria, VII.27-33.)[56]

And I, the Creator Ohrmazd, shall come with the Amahraspands to the mountains of Hukairyāt and I shall order the Amahraspands to say to all the *mēnōg* deities: 'Go, get to the help of the luminous Pēšōtan.' Mihr of wide pastures, Srōš the courageous, Rašn the truthful, Warhrām the powerful, Aštād the victorious, the Fortune of the Mazdaean Religion, the Arrangement of ritual which is the adorner of the world, we shall come to the aid, to assist the luminous Pēšōtan, by an order from me, the Creator. They will smite the demons of dark seed. The deceitful Evil Spirit will raise his voice to Mihr of wide pastures: 'Rise up by truth, you Mihr of wide pastures.' Then Mihr of wide pastures will raise his voice (saying): 'Of these nine thousand years of contract which he concluded (with you), till now Dahāg of evil religion, Frāsyāb the Turanian, Alexander the Greek

rather, Theopompus's) account. This view is accepted in principle by H.S. Nyberg, *Die Religionen des alten Iran*, 1938 (Reprint: Osnabrück 1966), 385ff. A recent discussion is by J. Hansman, in *Etudes Mithriaques* (*Acta Iranica*), Leiden-Teheran-Liège 1978, 226.

[56] Cf. E.W. West, *SBE*, V, 227f.; Zaehner, *Zurvan*, 102; G. Widengren, *Iranische Geisteswelt*, Baden-Baden 1961, 204; W. Sundermann, in *Etudes Mithriaques* (*Acta Iranica*), Leiden-Teheran-Liège 1978, 494.

> and those demons with leather belts and dishevelled hair have held dominion for a period of a thousand years beyond the measure.' The deceitful Evil Spirit will become stupefied when he hears thus.

Mihr stands at the head of a whole cohort of *mēnōg* deities who rush to the help of Pēšōtan when he is attacked by the powers of evil, and Ohrmazd the Creator himself takes part in this joint action, if we can trust the form of the verb *āyēm*, in the first person. Here the Evil Spirit tries to use an argument designed to cause Mihr to withdraw from the fight. He cries to him: *ul ēst*, "Rise up", that is (if my interpretation is correct), desist; *pad rāstīh*, "By truth", for Mihr, as a judge and upholder of righteousness, should abide by the truth and avoid siding with one of the parties. Mihr's answer establishes that truth is with Ohrmazd, since Ahreman has broken the contract, and has no right to invoke truth. Thus we have the paradoxical (but not illogical) situation that in the morally unequal battle between the two deities, the judge is completely identified with one of the two parties.

The Arab theologian ʿAbd al-Jabbār, in the valuable account of various heresies and religions which he gives in the book *Tathbīt dalāʾil al-nubuwwa,* refers twice to an Iranian myth, attributed to the *majūs*, according to which God was overcome by Satan and enclosed in Paradise with his angels. The angels then mediated a truce between the two powers. In one of ʿAbd al-Jabbār's reports the angels take the swords of both antagonists and make them equal (*fa-ʿaddalūhumā*).[57] In Shahrastānī's account of the Zurvāniyya the two antagonists give their swords to two trustworthy witnesses (*ʿadlayni*), who may kill the party that breaks the covenant.[58] The angels in ʿAbd al-Jabbār's account are expressly stated to be members of Ohrmazd's camp, and could therefore well be the same deities which we know from the eschatological account in Pahlavi, that is, those headed by Mihr or by the group Mihr-Srōš-Rašn. In one of the two verision of ʿAbd al-Jabbār the episode forms part of the Zurvanite story, and the same episode occurs also in the account of the Zurvāniyya given by Shahrastānī. The same basic conception of angels mediating between the two antagonists forms also part of the faith of the Kayūmarthiyya as given by Shahrastānī.[59] In this latter myth the birth of Ahreman is the result of a thought of Ohrmazd (Ohrmazd himself is uncreated). The Kayūmarthi myth has thus certain points in common with Zurvanism: the two antagonistic deities are kins in both accounts, though in the Zurvanite story they are brothers, that is, they have a parallel and horizontal relationship, while in the Kayūmarthi one their relationship is one of father and son, that is, hierarchical and vertical. In the Kayūmarthi myth Ohrmazd fulfils both the function of Zurvan (= father and supreme deity) and that of Ohrmazd himself (= the just but wronged party).

The two myths, the Zurvanite one and the Kayūmarthi one, although close to each other, belong to two different types of dualism: the Zurvanite story presents a

[57] 'Abd al-Jabbār, *Tathbīt dalā'il al-nubuwwa*, Beirut (n.d.), pp. 105f., 331.

[58] Shahrastānī, *Al-milal wa-l-niḥal*, ed. Muḥammad Sayyid Kīlānī, I, Cairo 1967, 235.

[59] Op. cit., 233f.

triangular kind of dualism, where a supreme, but otiose deity – Zurvan – stands above the dualistic division; while the Kayūmarth story describes the dualistic split in terms of a cleavage within the deity itself. The orthodox Mazdean conception (at least as we know it from the Pahlavi books, since the view of the Gatha is open to more than one interpretation) belongs to a completely different, third, type of dualism: it denies any kinship or affinity between the two powers, and describes them in terms which are as equal as possible within a dualistic system.[60] The two powers are 'principles', not subordinate to each other or to a third power. Typologically the 'orthodox' version seems different and equally remote from both the positions of the Zurvanites and that of the Kayūmarthiyya.

The function of the mediating angels is common to the Zurvāniyya and the Kayūmarthiyya of Shahrastānī's account. It is possible that the three deities Mihr, Srōš and Rašn fulfilled this function there too, as they do in the orthodox version of the eschatology (text XIV above). The surviving texts which describe the creation, for example in the *Bundahišn* and *Zādspram*, have the negotiations between the two powers carried out directly, without intermediaries. It may however be surmised that the eschatological description which places mediators between the two antagonists preserves a detail which occurred in an older version of the cosmogonical myth, in which Mihr, with his associates, did indeed preside, as a judge, over the contract between the two powers, and that this trait was generally omitted from later Mazdaean accounts as the dualistic system of thought hardened and became more rigorous, while it stayed on in some of the more popular versions of the Zurvanite and the Kayūmarthi myths.[61] The Manichaean story too, dependent as it seems to have been on a Zurvanite form of Iranian religion, may have imitated its Iranian model also in its conception of intermediaries. As in Iran, where the angels belong to Ohrmazd, so in Manichaeism the confrontation with the Prince of Darkness is done through a series of spiritual creations of the Father of Greatness. It must be added, however, that gnostic systems earlier than Manichaeism already had such a notion of a series of emanations which conduct battle on behalf of the deity.

---

[60] Cf. my remarks in *Studies in mysticism and religion presented to G.G. Scholem*, Jerusalem 1967, 227ff.

[61] This is how al-Mas'ūdī presents the situation, in a manner which holds good at least for his own period: "The apologetics of Islam (*mutakallimū l-islām*), authors of books concerning (theological) opinions, as well as those who have tried to refute these people (scil. the Zoroastrians), both early and late (writers), report about them (the following) claim that they make: God reflected, and from His reflection there originated evil, which is Satan. He (= God) negotiated with him (= Satan), and granted him a respite for a period of time, by which means he enticed him. (They tell these stories) as well as other things concerning their (= the Zoroastrians') religious views, which the Magians reject, to which they do not submit themselves, and which they do not recognize. In my view this (story comes) from some of the common folk, who were heard to be believing in it, and it was attributed to the generality (of the Zoroastrians)" (*K. al-tanbīh wa-l-išrāf*, ed. de Goeje, Leyden 1894 [reprint Beyrut 1965], 93f.). In the manner in which the story is presented here it is a reflection of the Kayūmarth version of the myth, though it might also be supposed to be a simplified account of the Zurvan story.

A popular variant of the Iranian myth of creation mentions the sun, i.e. Mihr, as the arbiter between the two adversaries. Eznik tells that Ahreman invited Ohrmazd to a feast, and that, at the latter's suggestion, the sons of both fought each other. Ahreman's sons vanquished Ohrmazd's, and in order to decide of the victor, they jointly created the Sun, in default of another judge, to decide the issue.[62] Benveniste[63] rightly compares here the Manichaean episode in which the Primal Man and his sons fight for the Father of Greatness and are vanquished by the powers of darkness. Mihr's middle position of a judge is brought out in this story by his being made to be a joint product of the two powers.

Eznik himself noticed the conflict between this story which he reports and another one, which occurs in other sources as well.[64] According to this latter story the birth of the sun is the result of an incestuous intercourse between Ohrmazd and his mother, a device which he learnt from a disciple of Ahreman. The two stories, though widely divergent, have in common the point that the origin of the sun comes as a result of some kind of collusion between the two antagonists.

The sun, identified with Mihr already in the early Sasanian period,[65] was thus often represented as being in the middle between the two opponents.[65a] Franz Cumont tried to explain these stories by associating the notions which they carry with Babylonian ideas: "Cette 'médiation de Mithra' . . . avait probablement été confondue avec la théorie chaldéenne suivant laquelle le Soleil attire les âmes des défunts vers les sphères supérieurs".[66] There is however little evidence for this theory in Iran, save, vaguely, in Manichaeism. Widengren[67] adduced a Pahlavi sentence according to which Mithra's field of action is supposedly between the sun and the moon. However, the sentence on which Widengren's explanation is based occurs as a *Zand* on Yašt 6.5, where the Avestan text contains no allusion to any

---

[62] Eznik, *De deo*, ed. L. Mariès and Ch. Mercier, Paris 1959 (Patrologia Orientalis, XXVIII, fasc. 3, 4), 460f. (text), 597f. (translation); V. Langlois, *Collection des historiens anciens et modernes de l'Arménie*, II, Paris 1869, p. 380; Zaehner, *Zurvan*, 419ff., who refers to earlier studies.

[63] *The Persian religion*, p. 89ff.

[64] Cf. the Acts of Adhurhormizd in Syriac, in P. Bedjan, *Acta martyrum et sanctorum*, II, Paris 1891, p. 578; Benveniste, *The Persian religion*, p. 89; Bidez-Cumont, *Les mages hellénisés*, II, Paris 1938, p. 109 and note 3.

[65] Cf. J. Darmesteter, *Le Zend-Avesta*, Paris 1892-93, (Reprint 1960), II, 442. I. Gershevitch, in his contribution to *Mithraic Studies*, Manchester 1975, 68-69, at first denied, but subsequently admitted, the possibility of a pre-Manichaean Iranian notion of Mithra as the sun.

[65a] The sun as a middle entity is a current notion in hellenistic literature. It is a central theme in Julian the Apostate's Hymn to Helios, to which Prof. S. Pines drew my attention (cf. *The works of the Emperor Julian*, with an English transl. by W.C. Wright, London-New York 1913, I, 353ff.). Dr. G. Stroumsa has shown me a whole list of further references.

[66] Cf. *Textes et monuments relatifs aux mystères de Mithra*, Bruxelles 1896-99, II, 40.

[67] G. Widengren, *Hochgottglaube*, 99; cf. *op. cit.*, 107. He refers to J. Darmesteter, *Etudes iraniennes*, II, Paris 1883, p. 288, 290. The same text occurs also in *ZXA*, p. 38.

mediating position of Mithra.[68] Neither is the Pahlavi text, although it speaks of Mihr as being between the sun and the moon, concerned with Mihr's mediation. It reaches its conclusion by a twist of the Avestan original, perhaps done innocently, by misunderstanding. It tries to place Mihr locally or temporally by saying (if our reading is correct) that Mihr's activity spans both night and day; or by implying that Mihr's period is at the end of the night, just before dawn.[69] The Pahlavi text makes no attempt to connect the place (or time) of Mihr with the idea of mediation, or with Mihr's middle position, and betrays no affinity with any of the popular stories discussed above.

It may be concluded that Plutarch was not all that wrong when he described Mithra as a mediator between the two powers. Mihr is indeed said to be a 'mediator' (*miyāncīg*), in the technical sense of a judge. He seems to have held the position of a judge between Ohrmazd and Ahreman in the story of the creation not only in sectarian or popular accounts, as attested in the foreign sources, but also, if we may deduce from eschatology to cosmogony, at least in certain versions of the standard Zoroastrian myth. The fact that he is not mentioned in such a role in orthodox Zoroastrian texts may be due to a tendency to reach stricter dualism by eliminating the presence of a third force.

Late Zoroastrianism knows of another middle principle which exists primordially between the two antagonistic deities, though with little relevance for our topic. According to the classical account of the *Bundahišn,*[70] void (*tuhīgīh*),[71] also called Wāy ('air, wind'), was between the two powers. It is possible to conclude from the somewhat elaborate explanation attached to this notion in the *Bundahišn* that this void has several functions: it serves as a dividing line, a border (or rather, a no-man's-land), while it does not constitute a third entity, since it is, by definition, a void, a non-entity; it serves to blunt the edge of the paradox that while both entities are unlimited, each is spatially limited by the presence of the other. The void thus serves as both a limit and a non-limit. It also makes it possible to resolve (though we are not told how) the temporal paradox, for although both principles are eternal, the evil spirit will be eliminated in eschatology.[72]

The ancient deity Vayu may well have served in one early version of the myth as a middle entity, although it does not seem to have ever served as an active mediating agent. Otherwise in Mazdaism Vayu was split into two

---

[68] Cf. Gershevitch, *The Avestan hymn to Mithra*, Cambridge 1959, 227f. The last gloss in the Pahlavi text is not clear: *ā-š rawišn* [*ī*] *3-gāhīh anōh* "his three-period movement is there" (i.e. between sun and moon?).

[69] Vend. XIX.28. On the specific time of Mithra cf. I. Gershevitch, *The Avestan hymn to Mithra*, 31, 291f.

[70] Cf. a discussion of the relevant text in Appendix C.

[71] In *Zādspram*, I, 1, the term used is *wišādagīh* 'openness, void'; cf. Zaehner, *BSOS*, 9 (1937/39), 581.

[72] Cf. Appendix C, note 7.

persons, the good and the evil Wāy.[73] Manichaeism could well have borrowed this notion of the border from Zoroastrianism, though it also has gnostic antecedents.[74]

There are three types of 'third principle' attested in late Iranian religion:

1. The third principle as middle region, as neutral and inactive factor: the void, Wāy (a survival of a once personal ambiguous deity).
2. The third principle as otiose supreme god, the origin of the two antagonists: Zurvān.
3. The third power as a judge-mediator, the embodiment of justice: Mihr and his associates.[75]

All three types of "third principle" are independently attested, and may have had separate historical origins, but they have in common the feature that they all present a dualistic system which contains within it a mitigating element. None is attested before the late Parthian or early Sasanian period, but the Zoroastrianism of the Pahlavi texts (which represent at best late Sasanian ideas) seems to have striven towards a pure kind of dualism, from which the notion of a third principle, or of any kinship between the two principles, would be eliminated. The theology of the Pahlavi books often contains passages which sound like a polemic against such notions which upset the conception of a pure dualism.[76] That the theological consensus was not all that clear-cut may be seen from the fact that references to such notions can still be culled from the Pahlavi books themselves. The deviant accounts of the creation may well have been treated with leniency since they could have been regarded as representing popular, as opposed to theological, versions.

---

[73] Cf. Louis H. Gray, *Foundations of the Iranian religions*, Bombay: K.R. Cama Oriental Institute Publications, 1930, 169-170. Cf. also H.S. Nyberg, *Die Religionen des alten Iran*, (Reprint: Osnabrück 1966), 75, 300f.; G. Widengren, *Hochgottglaube*, 188ff.; Zaehner, *Zurvan*, 80ff., 125ff. S. Wikander, *Vayu*, Uppsala 1941, has not been available to me at the time of writing.

[74] Cf. H.-C. Puech, *Le manichéisme*, Paris 1949, 75, and note 293 on p. 162f. On comparable notions in the Valentinian and other gnostic systems cf. W. Bousset, *Hauptprobleme der Gnosis*, 1907 (Neudruck, Göttingen 1973), 129f.

[75] The notion of the just as a middle entity in the late Marcionite system presents a parallel to this idea. Cf. Bousset, *Hauptprobleme*, 130ff.

[76] Apart from *Škand Gumānīk Vicār*, examples of such passages are: *Dk* III, ch. 119 (against monotheists), 263, 193, 383.

Appendix A (Cf. note 18 above)

az . . . be

The combination of the preposition *az* with a postposition *be* has more than one sense. It can be established that one of its meanings is "proceeding from, coming from", hence "based on, on the authority of". This is, in my view, the correct meaning of the combination in the much debated passage on the transmission of the Avesta in the beginning of the fourth book of the *Dēnkard*:

[XX] *šābūr ī šāhān-šāh ī ardašīrān nibēgīhā-z ī az dēn be abar biziškīh ud star gōwišnīh . . . ud abārīg kirrōgīh ud abzār [ī] andar hindūgān [ud] hrōm [ud] abārīg-ez zamīgīhā pargandag būd abāz ō ham āwurd ud abāg abastāg abāz handāxt . . .* (*Dk* B 321, M 412).[1]

Shapur the King of Kings, son of Ardašīr, brought together again the writings (derived) from the religion concerning medicine, astrology . . . and other skills and capacities which were scattered in India and Byzantium and other lands, and considered them again together with the Avesta . . .

The tenor of the whole passage suggests very clearly, I believe, that in the view of the author of the *Dēnkard* the wisdom contained in those Indian, Greek and other books is part of the original Iranian knowledge, dispersed and then, at the time of Shapur, brought back to Iran and considered[2] together with the Avesta again. The phrase *az dēn be* is thus unlikely to mean "en dehors de la Dēn, étranger à la Religion" (Molé), but ought to mean "that which comes from the Religion, that which is based on the Religion (= on the Avesta)".[3]

The phrase *az . . . be* was discussed at length by Christian Bartholomae,[4] in connection with a formula which recurs several times in the legal treatise *Mādigān ī hazār dādestān* in more than one form: *az dastwarān be* "On the authority of the *dastwars*", *az siyāwuš be, az rād-hormizd be* etc., i.e. "(it is reported) on the authority of . . . , as coming from . . ." Bartholomae, it is true, did not quite see the precise meaning of the phrase, which he translated: "In dem [Buch] '*Dastəwarān*' wird eine Stelle angeführt". It is all the more a pity that Anahit Perikhanian, in her important translation of *MHD*,[5] does not seem to have been aware of Bartholomae's comments, and emends in some of the passages *be* to *pad* (she does not do this consistently in all the passages where this formula occurs). Once the meaning of this phrase in *MHD* is established, it helps in reaching an acceptable translation of the one passage in the book where Bartholomae believed it to have a different usage:

---

1 Cf. Nyberg, *Religionen*, 418; Bailey, *ZorPr*, 81; Zaehner, *Zurvan*, 8; Molé, *RHR*, 162 (1962), 196f.

2 *handāxtan* is best taken here in its most common meaning, 'to consider, judge'. A somewhat less satisfactory way of explaining the word is by taking it in the meaning 'to throw', very rare in Pahlavi, giving a possible translation: "and he threw them together again with the Avesta", that is, he combined them again with the Avesta.

3 This seems to be the way in which Bailey also takes this construction.

4 *Zum sasanidischen Recht*, II, Heidelberg, 1918, 47ff.

5 A.G. Perikhanian, *Sasanidskij sudebnik*, "*Kniga tysjači sudebnyk rešenij*", Erevan 1973.

[XXI] *pad ēn wāzag was kas hamdādestān, be-š juwān-jam az-ez wahrām-šād be pad-eš jud-dādestān būd* (*MHD* A 11.15-17; cf. Bthl., op. cit., p. 48, n. 1).

Many people agreed on this matter, but Juwān-Jam, according to Wahrām-šād, held a different view concerning it.

It seems wrong to translate "aber Yuvān-yam hatte darin eine von der des Vahrāmšāt abweichende Ansicht" (Bthl.) or "but Yuvan-Yam together with Vahramšat held a different view" (Perikhanian).

The phrase *az . . . be* has the sense of 'derived from, on the authority of', while it also possesses the meaning 'outside, away from' in some passages.[6]

For *az . . . be* in the sense of 'outside' cf. the unusual phrase *az-eš be guft bawēd* (*Dk* B 306.15) "was said to be absent, was removed, was denied".[7]

At the same time *az . . . be* also retains the primary meaning 'from', e.g. in *Vd* III.14 *nåŋhanat hača, čašmanaṯ hača*, etc. which is translated in Pahlavi *az nā(y) be, az cašm be*, etc. The combination *be az* occurs, e.g., *Vd* VII.79, and cf. E.W. West and M. Haug, *Glossary and Index of the Pahlavi texts of the Book of Arda Viraf. . .*, Bombay-London 1874, 80. The survival of this combination in early New Persian is attested in the Qur'ān commentary discussed by E.G. Browne, *JRAS*, 1894, p. 439. Similarly we have in early New Persian the combination *az . . . bērōn* 'outwards' in the Lahore *Tafsīr* (cf. *Tafsīr-i Qur'ān-i pāk*, p. 55.9-10 *va-sulaymān rūy az šahr bērōn nihād*).

---

6 Cf. H.W. Bailey, *BSOS*, 6 (1930/32), 75, on *ZN* §27.

7 For the context one may compare the translation by J. de Menasce, *Le troisième livre du Dēnkart*, Paris 1973, 367 (*Dk* III, chapter 408).

Appendix B (cf. note 27)
āwām

Apart from the usual meaning 'time, period', the Middle Persian word *āwām* * is said to possess the meaning of 'torture, torment', and the form *āwāmīh* has been shown to mean 'joy, ease'.[1] In the following, I should like to put in doubt the existence of a separate word meaning 'torment', while showing that we ought to define the use of *āwām* sometimes in a new sense, that of 'world', 'people', or the like.

[XII] *frāz-tom pad dānāgīh ud stūdag pad cihr ud brēh brāzišnīg andar āwām ud friyādišnīg andar harw 2 axwān wahmān ī wahmānān* (*PhlT* 134 §11)

N. son of N., foremost in knowledge, praised in nature and fortune, radiant in *āwām* [i.e. among people?], provided with help in both worlds.

Zaehner[2] translates "splendid in your time", which seems inadequate.

[XXIII] *ō ke āzād-tom pad gōhr, (. . .) kardār-tom pad šnāyēnišn ī yazdān, burd-ranj-tom pad dēn ī mazdēsnān, hayyārēnīdār-tom pad kadārce xīrān ī āwāmān *ceōn-eš āfrīn, *hamē bārestānīg ud xwarr[ōmand]* (*PhlT* 138f. §34)

To him who is most noble in lineage, (. . .), most active in propitiating the gods, most strenuous in the Mazdaean religion, most helpful in all matters whatsoever (concerning) people(?) as is his praise [i.e. the praise given to him], always patient and endowed with splendour.

Here we have a plural form *āwāmān* which seems to denote 'people'. Zaehner's translation[3] goes, I believe, off the mark: "most public-spirited in all secular matters and all forms of worship". This seems to be an unjustified transposition of Christian terminology into a Zoroastrian text.

[XXIV] *šēbišn ud āšuft ī āwām ud anāgīh ud wizand ī gēhān* (*DkM* 252.7f.)

the confusion and turmoil of the world (?), and the evil and damage of the universe.[4]

[XXV] *ka abāz az bazagīh ud frāz ō kirbagīh (ī) mardom *amaragānīh az rāh pākīh ud widarg frāxwīh ī az wēš zanišn ī dēwān, hān [mēnōgān] yazdān *āzādīh ō gētīgān wēš-rasišn-tar az abzōn ī yazdān pērōzīh, ud āwām pad hu-xwadāyīh ud hu-dēnīh [ud] dānāgīh ud dād wirāstag, ud hambāstag mardom kāmag zīšnīh buxtagīh abēr-tar bawēd hamē bawēd, hamē tā cārag (ud) rasišnīh ī dēwān pad nōg wahānēnēd (ī) āwām ī anāgīh az frēftan (ud) frāz-ez ō bazagīh. ud ka abāz az kirbagīh ud frāz ō bazagīh [mardom ī] andar gēhān amaragānihēd dēwān frāz-dwārišn-tar ud rāh ī az yazdān pad rasišn ī āzādīh az-ešān ō gētīgān bastag-tar, ud āwām pad*

---

[1] D.N. MacKenzie, in *K.R. Cama Oriental Institute Golden Jubilee Volume*, Bombay 1969, 106 note 4. Cf. also my remarks in *Wisdom of the Sasanian sages*, Boulder, Col. 1979, 292f., of which this appendix is an enlargement.

[2] *BSOS*, 9 (1937/39), 98.

[3] *Loc. cit.* p. 100.

[4] Cp. de Menasce, *Le troisième livre*, 239: "déclin et révolution de l'époque, misère et destruction du monde"

*sāstārīh ud ahlamōgīh ud kēgīh ud karabīh ud ag-dēnīh ud duš-āgāhīh [ud] a-dād ud awērān-tar ud wišuftag-tar ud mardom tangīh ud ērang ud *dušxwārīh wēš bawēd* (*DkM* 55.9ff.; B 40f.).[5]

When people in their totality (turn) back from sin and towards virtue, (then), because of the clearness of the road and the wideness of the passage, (which is) due to the fact that the demons have been smitten much, the bounty of the *mēnōg* gods comes with more abundance to *gētīg* people by the increase of the victory of the gods. The world (*āwām*) is (then) in good rule and in good religion and knowledge, the law is well-ordered, and all men's desire and life and innocence will be for ever, until a stratagem for the demons to arrive again causes the world (*āwām*) to be evil, by deceit which leads to sinfulness. When [the people of] the world (*gēhān*) all of them turn back from virtue and go forth into sinfulness, the demons come forth more, and the way from the gods for bringing bounty from them to the people of *gētīg* is more firmly blocked. The world (*āwām*) (then) becomes more subject to tyranny, heresy, sorcery, wizardry, evil religion, negative knowledge, lawlessness. It becomes more destroyed and turbulent, and the distress, guilt and hardship of people increases.

[XXVI] *abar āmadan ī dēn ō āwām* (*Zs* IV, title). "On the coming of the religion into the world."

[XXVII] *abāz-eš az awe pursīd ku ast ēdōn ēdar andar āwām ī dēn ī mazdēsnān gētīg-paydāgīh pahlom ((ku dēn ī mazdēsnān mehmānīh pad kas)) ast. u-š guft ohrmazd ku ast ēdōn andar awēšān mardom-*ez, zardušt, ce ēdar hēnd *āsrō ī guftār* . . . (*Dk* VII, 8.28-29; B 513, 17-21).[6]

Again he enquired of him: Is there here, in the world (*āwām*), one whose material manifestation of the Mazdaean religion is perfect? ((Does the Mazdaean religion inhabit any person?)) He spoke, Ohrmazd: There is thus even among those men, Zardušt, those who are here eloquent priests . . .

[XXVIII] *ud az āwām-ārāstārān ardašīr ī pāpakān* . . . (*Dk* VII, 7.12; B 503.11f.).

Of those who embellish the world, Ardašīr son of Pāpak . . .

This phrase has as parallels such expressions as: *ārāstārīh ī dēn ud gēhān* (VII, 7.4); *wišuftārīh ī dēn ud xwadāyīh ud gēhān* (ibid.); *dēn-ārāstār ādurbād ī mahraspandān* (VII, 7.19).

Two relevant passages may be quoted from the book of Ardā Virāz:

[XXIX] *u-m dīd hān ī šubānān ruwān ke-šān pad gētīg cahār-pāy ud gōspand warzīd ud parward (. . .) u-š was meh šūdīh ud bar ud nēwagīh ud xwarišn ud jāmag ī mardomān ī āwām dād* (*A Vn* XV 1-6).

And I saw the soul(s) of shepherds who fostered and nourished in the material world cattle and sheep (. . .). It (scil. the cattle) gave much good

---

5 Compare, with minor differences, the translation in J. de Menasce, *Le troisième livre*, 71f.

6 Cf. E.W. West, *SBE*, XLVII, 100; Molé, *Légende*, 84f.

benefit, fruit, material goods, food and the clothing of the people of the *world.

[XXX] *ku mardomān ī andar ēn āwām hēnd be dānēnd ku ēn yazišn ud drōn ud āfrīnagān ud nīrang ud pādyābīh ud yōšdāhrīh ī amāh pad kardag āwarēm ō yazdān rasēd ayāb ō dēwān, ud ō friyād ī ruwān ī amāh rasēd ayāb ne* (*AVn* I 25-27).

So that people who are in this *world should know (the following): this worship, *drōn, āfrīnagān, nīrang,* the *pādyāb* and *yōšdāhr* purifications which we perform,[7] do they reach the gods or the demons? do they come to the help of our souls or not?

This section, taken from the preamble of the book, describes the purpose of the mission which constitutes the theme of the book, to clarify the realities of the invisible world to the people down here, who are tormented by doubts.

Two further passages where the sense of *āwām* 'world' is apparent may be quoted. In the "Poem in praise of Wisdom"[8] we should translate, correcting my previous translation:

[XXXI] *ce was raft hēm andar āwām, was-am wazīd kustag kustag* "For I have much travelled in the world, I have moved[9] much (into) region after region".

[XXXII] *mardomān ud gōspandān ud harw ciš ī*[10] *āwām winārišn az wād* (*GBd*

[7] For the phrase *pad kardag āwarēm* cf. *Suppl. Texts to ŠnŠ* XII 32: *pad kardag aōn dāštan.*

[8] *PhlT* 165, cf. *Henning Mem. Vol.*, 400f.

[9] The reading *wazīd* has been put in doubt by A. Tafazzoli, *StIr*, I (1972), 216, n. 2. The verb *wazīdan*, like its Avestan antecedent *vaz-*, can be used both transitively and intransitively. In the former instance its object may be the object of the destination of the movement, or it may be the direct object in the sense of 'to traverse, to go through'. It is also used transitively as a causative, 'to carry, cause to move'. Used intransitively, and applied to the wind, it occurs in company of *kust* 'side': *ceōn pad harw kišwar ī āyēd az harw kust ī wazēd pad harw ēwēnag* [*ī*] *wazēd* . . . (*GBd* 133.1-2; TD_1 fol. 54r), which is somewhat reminiscent of our *was-am wazīd kustag kustag*. A similar expression is in *Wizīrkard ī Dēnīg*, p. 36 l. 6. *wazīdan* is close in usage to *taxtan* (the same is true of Av. usage; cf. e.g. Yt. 10.20): *kardag kardagīh rāy az kust kust tazēd pad nām nām xwānēnd* (*GBd* 133.9-10; TD_1 fol. 54r) "Because it is divided into sections, it moves in different regions, and it is called by different names", where the subject is the wind. Conversely, for the water, we have *wazīdan* in a transitive sense: *tan ī wād burd, āb wazīd, az ku abāz *gīrihēd, ristāxēz ceōn bawēd* (*Jāmāspī*, Phl III 2, p. 10; *GBd* 221.13; Justi, *Bd*, 71.7. *GBd* has here *wāzīd*, the other sources *wazīd*). "The body, carried away by the wind, carried off by the water, whence will it be taken again? How will the resurrection take place?" I believe, incidentally, that this transitive usage of *wazīdan* can be applied to a Manichaean passage where the verb was read *wizīdan*: **cwnwm hš'gy(r)[d]'n 'c šhr wzyd 'w '(rd'wn)** (*MirMan* II, 318; cf. M. Boyce, *A reader in Manichaean Middle Persian and Parthian*, Acta Iranica 9, p. 112) "You lead me like a disciple from the town to the righteous ones". The simile is probably that of a young student taken to a place of learning. Similarly in *Zs* 8.8: *ahreman spahbadān wazīd* may mean: "Ahreman sent forth generals."

[10] Thus in TD_1; *GBd* has **-1.**

133.7; TD_1 fol. 54v) "The organization of people, cattle and everything (else) which is in the world is from the wind".

The Pāzand equivalent of *āwām* is *ōγąm*, also attested in the sense of 'world':

[XXXIII] *ci vatarī aṇdar ōγąm nīrōtar ku vahī* (*ŠGV* XI, 97). "For evil is more powerful in the world than goodness".

Translating "dans le siècle", as done by de Menasce, seems again to transpose a Christian concept into the text.

Here also belongs the expression:

[XXXIV] *az āwām be šawēd* (*REA* V, 5; p. 14) "he dies" (literally: he departs from the world).[11]

It seems safe to establish that *āwām* tends to be used in contexts where the meaning required is broader than 'period, epoch, time', and where, perhaps by extension of meaning, it is used somewhat loosely in the sense of 'people (of the period?)'; 'world', hence sometimes the plural *āwāmām*, besides *āwāmīgān,*[12] which denotes the same. There is perhaps room to conjecture that *āwām* broadened its meaning from 'time' to 'world' just as the Greek *aeon* underwent a similar transformation (particularly in the gnostic writings), or as the Hebrew *'ōlām* and the Latin *saeculum* combine both senses. One might however, also suppose that *āwām* occurs in certain cases as a shorthand expression for *āwāmīgān* 'people of the period', hence more generally 'people of the world'.

The expression *āwām-xwadāyān*, commonly taken to mean 'rulers of the time',[13] seems to correspond to the notion in the Arabic historical writings of *mulūk al-ṭawāʾif*, applied principally to the Arsacids, who were said to conduct a decentralized system of government, where considerable power was in the hands of provincial rulers.[14] The literal sense of the expression *āwām-xwadāyān* may thus perhaps be 'rulers of peoples', or 'rulers of the world' or 'of lands', in conformity with the sense of *āwām* which emerges from the various passages quoted. It seems indeed to be synonymous with *gēhān xwadāy* (attested e.g. *Dk* B 36.8).

* As stated above, *āwām* is said to have in certain texts the meaning of 'torment, hardship'. Only two such passages are known to me, one in Zoroastrian Pahlavi, the other in Manichaean.

---

[11] A similar expression occurs in *Zādsprām*, where the text requires some reconstruction. I propose the following reading: *pad tuxsāgīhā *abzāyēnīdan ī weh dahišnān šnāyēnīdan ī ahlawān* (**MNW**) *ka az āwām-widīr *āgnēn frāz rawēd* (*Zs* 30.41; differently Bailey, *ZorPr*, 214). "By increasing the good creations with diligence, causing satisfaction to the righteous when he goes forth together (*az . . . āgnēn*?) with one who departed from the world". The following section says: *agar ahlaw baxt pad pērōzīh u-š harwisp ham-gōhrān ī mēnōg-cihrān abāg frāz rawēnd* (*Zs* 30.42) "If he is righteous, his fortune is victorious, and all those of *mēnōg* nature who have the same *gōhr* as he go forth together with him".

[12] Cf. *MX* 56.8; *Dk* VII, 4.63.

[13] *KN*, ed. Anklesaria, III.4; *PhlT* 86f., §3, 4, where the Arabic equivalent is *wulāt al-umūr*.

[14] E.g., Ṭabarī, *Ta'rīx*, I, Cairo 1960, 580ff.; Tha'ālibī, *Ghurar al-siyar*, ed. Zotenberg, Paris 1900 (Reprint, Teheran 1963), 456ff. Cf. Fr. Spiegel, *Einleitung in die traditionellen Schriften der Parsen*, I, Wien 1856, p. 9; F. Justi, in *GIPh*., II, 1896-1904, p. 511.

[XXXV] *agar ēdōn ku az xwarr amāh ne brihēnīd ēstēd xwadāyī [ī] ērān-šahr kardan, hunsand ud *bāristān abāyēd būdan, ēn kārezār [ud] xūn-rēzišnīh be abāyēd hištan, ud xwēš[-tan] az ēn ranj-āwām*[15] *āsān kardan* (*KN* 12.2; cf. Nyberg, *Manual*, I, 13.10-14).

If it is thus that by fortunes we have not been decreed to exercise sovereignty over the kingdom of Iran, one ought to be content and patient, one ought to abandon this battle and bloodshed, and to alleviate from ourselves this toil and trouble.

[XXXVI] **fr'y 'wd wyš pd ṯwxš'gyy rnz 'w'm bwrdn 'y nxwrygrwšn** (M1 lines 215ff.; Müller, *Ein Doppelblatt*, p. 17; cf. Boyce, *A reader in Manichaean Middle Persian and Parthian*, Acta Iranica 9, Leiden-Teheran-Liège 1975, p. 53). "Furthermore, by the exertion of diligence and hardship[16] by Naxurēg-rōšn . . ."[17]

It cannot be asserted from these contexts that *āwām* in the combination *ranj-āwām* means by itself 'hardship, torment'. It may very well be a development from a compound which originally meant 'a period of hardship'.

The form *āwāmīh*, as noted above, means 'joy, ease'. In a sentence of the Pahlavi model marriage-contract there occurs the word *āwām* which, it has been suggested, may be connected to *āwāmīh* 'ease'. It seems to me however that it might be better to take it with the new sense established here for the word, namely 'people'. The text in question reads as follows:

[XXXVII] *šōywarīh-sārārīh tawān-sāmānagīhā ud āwām-passazagīhā xūb [ud] pad āzarm dārēm* (*PhlT* 142. 6-8).[18]

And I shall keep my husband's authority well and with respect, to the utmost of my ability and as befits (our) people (i.e. as befits people like us).

An alternative interpretation of this phrase may be based on the observation that the preceding sentence talks of the husband's undertaking to provide food and clothing for his wife. The present sentence could thus allude, in a euphemistic style, to the husband's duty of cohabitation with his wife. This interpretation may find support in the fact that the next phrase talks of "the children born from her". If this interpretation is correct, the word *āwām* would be used in a literal sense, 'time, period'. Jewish matrimonial law also defines the three basic duties of the husband with regard to his wife as those of providing her with food, clothing and cohabitation. The Hebrew term for the third item, derived from Biblical usage, is *'ona*, literally 'period'. It should however be noted that Jewish marriage contracts, whose

---

15 The spelling of the manuscript tradition is with an *iẓāfe*: *ranj ī āwām.*

16 Or, possibly, 'effort'.

17 Cf. W.B. Henning, "'Verbum", *ZII*, 9 (1933), 251.

18 Cf. D.N. MacKenzie, *loc. cit.* (above, note 1 to this Appendix).

formulae may have been established at about the early Sasanian period, do not contain an allusion to cohabitation, but have a phrase which mentions the husband's duty to treat his wife with respect.

It may be noticed in conclusion that in a number of passages in *Dk* III where there is an opposition *zamānag* – *āwām*, the first has a good association, while the latter has a bad one. Cf. *DkM* 334.4-6: *hu-xwadāy dehbad dānāg ud dēn dastwar ī zamānag ud wattom duš-xwadāy sāstār ud ahlamōg ī āwām* "a good ruler, chief, wise, and an authority of religion of the time, and the worst ruler, tyrant, and heretic of the period".

Appendix C (cf. note 70 above)

Wāy

The position of Wāy occurs in detail in *GBd*, p. 3; TD_1 fol. 1r-2r; DH 160r-v; Justi, *Der Bundehesh*, Leipzig, 1868, 1; E.K. Antiâ, *Pâzend texts*, Bombay 1909, 14f.; B.T. Anklesaria, *Zand-ākāsīh*, Bombay 1956, 4f. Cf. H.S. Nyberg, *JA*, 214 (1929), 206-209; Zaehner, *Zurvan*, 278; Molé, *JA*, 1959, 433f.

I believe that the relevant text should be read in a number of points somewhat differently from the way it has been rendered hitherto by scholars. A reading of the text is therefore offered in the following.

[XXXVIII] *ohrmazd bālistīg pad harwisp-āgāhīh ud wehīh zamān ī akanāgrag andar rōšnīh hamē būd. hān rōšnīh gāh ud gyāg ī ohrmazd, ast ke asar-rōšnīh gōwēd. ud hān harwisp-āgāhīh ud wehīh *hāmag ī ohrmazd, ast ke gōwēnd dēn. ud hān harw 2 wizārišn ēwag. hān *hāmag zamān ī akanārag. ce'ōn ohrmazd wehīh ud dēn zamān ī ohrmazd, ī būd ud ast ud hamē bawēd.*

*ahreman andar tārīkīh pad pas-dānišnīh ud zadār-kāmagīh zōfāyag būd. ud ast ke ne bawēd [gōwēd]. u-š zadār-kāmagīh *hām, ud hān tārīkīh gyāg. ast ke asar-tārīkīh gōwēd.*

*u-šān miyān tuhīgīh būd. ast ke wāy *gōwēd, ke-š gumēzišn pad-eš harw 2 hēnd kanāragōmandīh ud akanāragōmandīh. ce bālistīh hān ī asar-rōšnīh gōwēd, ku ne sarōmand, ud zōfāy hān ī asar-tārīkīh [gōwēd], hān ast akanāragīh. ud pad wimand harw 2 kanāragōmand, ku-šan miyān tuhīgīh, ud ēwag ō did ne paywast hēnd. did harw 2-ān mēnōg pad xwēš-tan kanāragōmand. did harwisp-āgāhīh ī ohrmazd rāy harw 2 ciš andar dahišn ī ohrmazd kanāragōmand ud akanāragōmand, ce ēn hān ī andar harw 2 hēnd paymān dānēnd. did bawandag pādexšāyīh ī dām ī ohrmazd pad tan ī pasēn tā hamē hamē rawišnīh, ud hān ast akanāragīh. ud dām ī ahreman pad hān zamān be absihēnēd tā ka tan ī pasēn bawēd. hān-ez ast kanāragōmandīh.*

Ohrmazd was on high within the light, with omniscience and goodness, [which is] infinite time.[1] That light is the throne and place of Ohrmazd; some call it infinite light. That omniscience and goodness is the *year(?)[2]

---

1 *zamān ī akanārag* should no doubt be taken as an apposition to *harwisp-āgāhīh ud wehīh*, in view of the phrase *ce'ōn wehīh ud dēn zamān ī ohrmazd*, and particularly if it is close in meaning to **hāmag* which follows.

2 **hāmag* is a notorious crux. It has been read as *jāmag* ('garment'), *xēmag* ('character'), *hāmag* ('all'), *niyāmag* ('sheath'), and otherwise. The Pāzand has here *hami, ham*. The context seems to require a word which designates time, as it stands parallel to *gāh ud gyāg*, and is actually defined as *zamān ī akanārag*. The translation offered here at a guess assumes that the word has something to do with Av. *ham-* 'summer', Phl. *hāmīn*; OInd. *samā-*; Armenian *am* 'year'. There may however be a different and simpler solution. The term *hamēyīg, hamēyīgīh*, which looks not too different from the word which comes here, occurs in *Dk* III, chapter 132 (*DkM* 132f.; B 99f.) in company with the same terms which occur here. It is identified there with *zamān* and comes parallel to *dēn-dānāgīh* (like *harwisp-āgāhīh* and *dēn* here), and to

of Ohrmazd; some call it religion. The two explanations are one and the same. That *year is infinite time. Just as the goodness and the religion are the time of Ohrmazd, who was, is, and will (always) be.

Ahreman was deep under within the darkness with late knowledge and contentiousness. Some [say] he is not.[3] His contentiousness is his *year, and that darkness is his place. Some call it infinite darkness.

Between them was void. Some call it Vāy, in which is the mixture of the two, infinity and finitude. For being high above, that which is called infinite light, means that it is not limited, and being in depth below, which [is called] infinite darkness, that is infinity. At the border both are limited, because in between them is void, and they do not touch each other.[4] Another (explanation): each one of the two spirits is by itself limited.[5] Another (explanation): Because of Ohrmazd's omniscience both things are within the creation of Ohrmazd, both that which is finite and that which is infinite, for they know this, which is within both (i.e. the finite and the infinite), as the measure.[6] Another (explanation): the perfect sovereignty of the creation of Ohrmazd in the Future Body is for ever; that is infinity. The creation of Ahreman will be destroyed at that time, when there will be the Future Body; that is finitude.[7]

---

gāh ud gyāg, as here. **x'mk**, if it is not a hitherto unidentified word meaning 'perpetuity', may thus simply be a misspelt *hamēyīg*. For a full text and translation of chapter 132 of *Dk* III cf. *Acta Orientalia*, 33 (1971), 90f. [The latest discussion of this term is in W. Belardi, *Studi mithraici e mazdei*, Rome 1977, 101ff.].

3 For this idea cf. *Studies . . . presented to G.G. Scholem*, Jerusalem 1967, 227ff.

4 This explanation seems to be based on the assumption that the void, though limiting the two spirits, for they are stopped by it, does not restrict them in reality, because they do not touch each other.

5 This explanation admits that limitation does apply to the two primeval spirits, though it stresses the fact that they are limited by themselves, not by an external border. Menasce sees the point of this phrase somewhat differently, not as an alternative explanation, but as a complementary aspect of the same explanation; he translates: "En outre, les deux entités sont limitées par elles-mêmes (et non pas l'une par l'autre)". Cf. *ŠGV*, ed. J. de Menasce, p. 247, n. 2.

6 The text here is based chiefly on the reading in Justi's edition. The sentence is not entirely clear, but it may mean that the conjunction of the two notions of finitude and infinity is within the creation of Ohrmazd, as represented by his omniscience, and that they achieve their balance by the fact that they are governed by the measure.

7 This last explanation transfers the notion of the contrast between the finite and the infinite from space to time, and resolves the paradox by assigning infinity to Ohrmazd, finitude to Ahreman. It thus differs from the previous explanations by the fact that it breaks the parallelism between the two divine powers.

Mihr the Judge

Addendum

The substance of this article was to be presented to the second international congress of Mithraic Studies in Teheran in 1975, and an abstract of it was sent to the organizers, but I was prevented from attending. When this article was in the press I learned, during a visit to Rome in the summer of 1979, of the book by Walter Belardi, *Studi mithraici e mazdei* (Biblioteca di ricerche linguistiche e filologiche, 6), Rome 1977, which discusses at length some of the materials on which the present article is based. I am grateful to Professor Gherardo Gnoli and to Professor Ugo Bianchi for their kindness in enabling me to get acquainted with Belardi's book. Had I known of that book in time, I might have abridged some of my discussion, though I believe the book does not fully recognize the purely juridical and administrative senses of *miyāncīg*. Thus, in the context of the judgement of the soul after death in *MX*, Belardi puts himself into the forced position of having to explain the use of the term by remarking: "il ponte è intermedio tra il mondo terreno e il celeste, e Mihr, Sroš e Rašn sono le divinità del passaggio, del transito" (p. 39). Once we recognize that the term has to do with judgement, its use does not call for additional comments. By making this remark I do not wish to diminish the great interest which I attach to many observations in that book.

An instance of NP. *miyānjī* as a synonym of *rahnumāy* "leader" may be quoted: *xirad bī miyānjī u bī rahnumāy / bi-dānad ki hast īn jahān-rā xudāy* (*Tuḥfat al-mulūk*, Tehran 1317, p. 4).

V

The Myth of Zurvan Cosmogony and Eschatology[1]

The status and social structure of the Zoroastrian church and religion during the Sasanian period are something of a puzzle. This statement may sound paradoxical. The Sasanian period is one of the best-documented epochs in Iranian religious history, and it may seem strange that there should be any uncertainty about such a prominent issue related to it. Nevertheless, the fact remains that a central aspect of Sasanian culture and society – its official religion – is clouded by ambiguities.

To present the main problem in simple terms: We know from a variety of foreign sources that a very widespread form of belief in that period adhered to the myth of Zurvan. According to that myth the God of Time, Zurvan, was the parent of twin brothers, Ohrmazd, the creator of the world, and Ahreman, the Destructive Spirit. The local Iranian sources, however, seem to know nothing of the myth; this applies both to contemporary inscriptions on stone, and to theological and exegetical compositions (surviving in most cases in books written in the Islamic period). We are thus left with the need to decide the reason for this discrepancy. This could be done in one of two ways. One may resolve the difficulty by discrediting the foreign reports, a procedure which is hardly warranted in view of the fact that these reports are both numerous and independent of each other, and that many of them are authentic compositions of the Sasanian period, often written within the domain of Sasanian rule. Another procedure would be to assume that the indigenous literature is consciously selective in its presentation of the religious ideas of the period. Put in other words, this explanation implies that systematic editorial censorship caused all references to Zurvan's position as parent of the two major spirit to be deliberately deleted from the books. I shall

[1] This article was essentially written in 1985. References to studies published in the intervening years are not complete. I am glad to dedicate it to David Flusser in token of my admiration and affection.

try here to present the point of view that neither of these two approaches is acceptable, and that a third way is available which seems to make better sense.

Other problems arise as a result of the discrepancy between the information culled from indigenous sources and that which may be gained from foreign accounts. As a rule the Zurvan myth is all but totally ignored in the indigenous sources, while in the foreign accounts it looms much larger than the form of Zoroastrianism which we are in the habit of regarding as orthodox. Should we conclude from this discrepancy that faith in the myth of Zurvan as the god who engendered both antagonistic spirits was a major heresy in the Sasanian period? Was it perhaps the main form of religion in that period, a form banished and stamped out of existence by the survivors of that religion after the Arab conquest of Iran? Or should we, alternatively, regard it as of minor consequence and importance, a fairy tale told only to foreign observers, but by no means generally admitted? Again, we shall try in what follows to present a third approach to this problem.

* * *

The best and most succinct formulation of what is probably nowadays the most commonly accepted scholarly opinion on the question of Zurvanism may be found in a recently published book by Professor Mary Boyce, the foremost historian of Zoroastrianism. One cannot do better than quote this short passage in full:

> [Zurvanism] is the only considerable Zoroastrian heresy, evolved probably by Persian magi in the late fifth century B. C. It was a monism, based on a new exegesis of Y. 30, whereby Ahura Mazda and Angra Mainyu were seen as twin sons of Time, Zurvan (a minor divinity of late Younger Avestan texts). The earliest reference to it, by the Greek historian Theopompus, shows it linked with a special version of the 'world year'. The heresy was, it seems, adopted as the true orthodoxy by the late Achaemenian kings, and was adhered to by their Persian successors, the Sasanians; but its teachings have nevertheless to be pieced together from scattered sources. Because the Zurvanites regarded Ahura Mazda as Creator of all things good, under the remote Zurvan, they were able to worship together with the orthodox in full orthopraxy, using the same liturgies; and this seems to have prevented serious schism. The heresy disappears after the tenth century A. C.[2].

Professor Boyce's words reflect and summarize a line of thinking and scholarly investigation into the problem of Zurvanism which has extended over a period of several decades, and to which many prominent scholars in the Iranian field have contributed[3]. Zaehner, in his extensive work on this

---

[2] Boyce 1984: 96.

[3] The following scholars who contributed to this discussion up to the Second World War may be noted: Spiegel (1873: 184–187), Blue (1925), Christensen (1928: 45–59; 1944:

subject[4], took it up again for thorough consideration, completing and adding to the conjectures of his predecessors. It must, however, be said that it was not infrequently Zaehner's tendency to be carried away by far-fetched speculations, and that his textual editions and translations, although generally acceptable, are not always flawless. His work has had the merit of reopening the discussion of this question, and the fifties and sixties were indeed a period in which a great deal of fresh thinking was done about the questions connected with Zurvanism[5].

It is the purpose of the present article to take up the question again, and to try to examine the sources in order to establish whether the presentation of Zurvanism as a "considerable Zoroastrian heresy", a characterization which had already been put in doubt by a number of scholars in the past[6], is indeed tenable.

We may begin our discussion with some comments on the passage quoted from Professor Boyce's book. It must be remarked that her use of the term "heresy" calls for reservation. Heresy, it must be recalled, is not an absolute term, and cannot be determined by a historian of religion by his simply adopting the point of view of either the founder or of the present-day adherents of the religion under discussion, nor can it be defined as a deviation from a religious norm favoured by the scholar. Heresy can possess no meaning except in relation to orthodoxy, but orthodoxy itself acquires its meaning only from its position within the society or the religious community. In other words, we cannot speak of orthodoxy except as a

---

59ff.), Nyberg (1929; 1931; 1938: 380ff.), Schaeder (in Reitzenstein and Schaeder 1926; Schaeder 1941), Benveniste (1929a; 1929b; 1932), and von Wesendonk (1933: 261ff.).

4 Zaehner's work, begun with a series of articles (1937/39, 1940/42), was continued in his book *Zurvan* (1955a), and a supplementary article (1955b). He summarised and amplified his views in his more general book *The dawn and twilight of Zoroastrianism* (1963).

5 One should note in particular Duchesne-Guillemin (1956; 1962), Boyce (1957, and more recently 1990), and Frye (1959). Two individual notes of scepticism have been heard, from two different points of view. One was from Molé (1959; 1961; as well as 1963: 8ff., 28ff.), and the other from Bianchi (1958). The line of discussion begun by Nyberg was pursued and pushed to an extreme by some members of the Scandinavian school, notably Widengren (1938: 266ff.; 1955; 1965), Wikander (1946: 177ff.), and Hartman (1953: 97ff.). Gnoli (1984) referred to Zurvanism as "the second phase of Iranian dualism", although it is not entirely clear from Gnoli's presentation how he fits the historical data regarding Zurvanism into his conception of the development of Iranian dualism. Where does the dualism of the Pahlavi books come in, e.g. in his table on p. 136? Does he regard it as a different phase of that development?

6 Notably Spiegel 1873; Schaeder (in Reitzenstein and Schaeder 1926: 239); Bidez and Cumont (1938 I: 63), Bianchi 1958; and Molé 1959. A sceptical attitude is voiced also by Frye 1984: 321 n. 97, and Asmussen 1983: 939 (although on p. 941 he seems to accept Zaehner's view that there was antagonism between the orthodox and the Zurvanites).

term describing the accepted form of religion in a given period, whether it be accepted by a majority of adherents, by the social or religious establishment, or at least by a group of people who have a particular prestige. Professor Boyce, however, seems to judge as heresy any deviation from what is acceptable to her as normative for Zoroastrianism.

Is it logical to say that this heresy "was adopted as the true orthodoxy by the late Achaemenian kings"? Such a statement seems to be based on the assumption that even if a religious community, with its recognized leaders, opts for a certain form of religion, that form may still be labelled a heresy merely because it is at variance with what the scholar considers to be orthodoxy. The problem becomes even more acute when we remember that Professor Boyce regards Zurvanism as the form of religion which was dominant throughout the Sasanian period[7]. Are we the entitled to declare that throughout one of the most significant periods in Zoroastrian history the commonly held belief, i.e. the orthodoxy of the time, was in fact a heresy? Surely this would be a statement which strips our terminology bare of any sense, and which is in danger of falling into the trap of using an arbitrary system of values for judging historical phenomena. It is clearly advisable to avoid using this term except as reflecting the judgement of a specific individual or group in the society under discussion; it should not be used as a term we as scholars regard as applicable[8].

The proper use of the terms "orthodoxy" and "heresy", important as it is, is not, however, the aim of our discussion. Professor Boyce's presentation, and in this she represents a widely held view, implies essentially that there was an established school of thought, an organized group or movement, which upheld the supremacy of Zurvan. This movement stood in opposition to orthodox Zoroastrianism, which regarded Ahura Mazda and Angra Manyu as the only two cosmological and religious principles. It should be our task to try to find out whether such a model is applicable to Iranian religious history. It would be advisable to confine our discussion to the Sasanian and early Islamic period, which is the only one for which we possess sufficient documentation from a variety of complementary sources, and in which faith in Zurvan as high god is unequivocally attested. Any insights gained from this analysis may help us in reconstructing the earlier history of the Zoroastrian religion.

---

[7] Cf. Boyce 1957; 1979: 112ff., 118ff. The chapter heading for this last section is "Upholding a Zurvanite orthodoxy", where the relative value of these notions is implicitly recognized, although in the body of the chapter Zurvanism is still called a heresy.

[8] Professor Boyce goes so far as to apply the term "heresy" to modern European interpretations of Zoroastrianism; cf. Boyce 1982: 233 n.; 1979: 194f., 197, 201ff.

Once the existence of Zurvanism as a complete and independent religious system is established for the Sasanian period, even in the mild version suggested by Professor Boyce, namely, a heterodoxy that did not advocate heteropraxy at the same time[9], it should be possible to discuss whether the arguments used by Benveniste[10] and Boyce[11] for proving the antiquity of Zurvanism are convincing. These arguments are based on Plutarch's description of the Iranian religion. Benveniste suggested that this description, attributed by Plutarch to Theopompus, represents the Zurvanite, rather than any other form of the Iranian religion, but this hypothesis has not gained wide acceptance[12]. Another piece of evidence for the antiquity of Zurvanism in Iran is found, according to several scholars, in the famous inscription of Antiochus I of Commagene (69-c. 31 B.C.E.)[13]. There we seem to have evidence for the recognition of Unlimited Time[14] as a central power in the destinies of humanity. This is hardly evidence for the presence of a Zurvanite religion, for the concept of Unlimited Time is present also in the Avesta, and must have been widespread in Iranian culture. Another hint to its presence is found in the echo we have of the twin concept of time in the Jewish (or Jewish-Christian) apocryphal writing, the Slavonic Book of

---

9 This explanation of Zurvanism (first suggested by FRYE 1959, and accepted by DUCHESNE-GUILLEMIN 1962 and BOYCE 1984), which posits a Zurvanite church without a distinctive body of practice, tends to make the whole notion of a separate Zurvanite church rather questionable, for analogies to this kind of religious organisation, which is devoid of distinctive ritual, are not easy to find. Benveniste's idea of Zurvanism as a religion associated with demon worship would make better sense if one sought to reconstruct a purely theoretical possibility, without regard for historical evidence.

10 BENVENISTE 1929: 69ff.

11 BOYCE 1984: 96.

12 This interpretation of the text of Plutarch was rejected, rightly to my mind, by CHRISTENSEN 1931: 29–34; NYBERG 1931:223, 234; BIDEZ and CUMONT 1938 I: 65f.; SCHAEDER 1941: 273f. Another attempt at treating Zurvanism as an ancient belief in Iran was made by GHIRSHMAN 1958, using a pictorial representation of one of the bronzes of Luristan as evidence. It is, however, clear that an interpretation of a pictorial motif, which by the nature of things can be interpreted in more than one way, should depend on a relevant text, which in this case is totally lacking. See now BOYCE 1990: 21, who rightly, to my mind, rejects Ghirshman's hypothesis, but uses the following argument, which I find hard to accept: "That Iranians should have chosen to make representations of their own gods at so early a date appears unlikely." It is true that ancient Iran has yielded very little in the way of divine iconography, but an a priori rejection of any inclination on the Iranian part to do so strikes me as too sweeping.

13 The inscription has often been discussed in scholarly literature. One of the most illuminating of these discussions is SCHAEDER's (1927: 138ff.). There is a thorough recent analysis of the problems by BOYCE (1990: 24, with further references in n. 45), where a different stand is taken on the issues.

14 It is not clear whether this is conceived as a personal deity or as an abstraction; but if the inscription is imbued, as it seems to be, with Iranian spirit, the distinction is quite irrelevant, for the passage from one mode of reference to the other would be easy.

Enoch. There, it has been pointed out[15], a distinction is made between "the great Aion", eternal time, and "the Aion of creation", time divided into "times and hours"[16], which is the time of the created world. This is strikingly similar to the Zoroastrian conception of time, and serves in the Slavonic Enoch, as in Zoroastrianism, to explain the workings of both the creation of the world and its end. Despite the prominence of time here, there is no hint of what we may call Zurvanism.

Our first concern should, however, be to examine the evidence for Sasanian Zurvanism in order to determine whether it has historical validity in the sense that it was an organized body of religion. The evidence for Zurvanism rests on three groups of material:

(a) Reports in Greek, Armenian and Syriac sources of the Sasanian period, unequivocally available only from the end of the fourth century C.E. onwards[17], according to which the Persian myth of creation started with Zurvan, a deity that existed before anything else, and from whose sacrifice and the doubt about its outcome arose respectively the god Ohrmazd and the devil Ahreman. These reports are fortified by a number of incidental references in Syriac hagiographies and doctrinal compositions which show clearly that Zurvan was considered by these foreign authors to be the high god of Iran[18].

(b) Manichaean texts in Middle Persian, which, although they do not report directly about the faith of the Zoroastrians (except in one or two cases)[19] show, by the use they make of the name Zurvan for rendering their own high god, the Father of Greatness, that in Mani's period Zurvan was considered a supreme deity in Iran. The fact that Zurvan holds this position only in the Middle Persian and not in the Parthian or Sogdian texts may support the idea that faith in Zurvan as supreme god was held in certain areas only, namely, those in which Persian was the current language[20].

(c) Post-Sasanian reports in Arabic and Persian sources. This class of material raises some peculiar problems. It must not necessarily be assumed that what the Islamic authors report concerning the religion of the Majūs is based on direct observation and oral interrogation. In other words, we should not necessarily assume that they report

---

15 Pines 1970.

16 Slavonic Enoch, short recension, Ch. 17; ed. Vaillant, p. 60ff. Quoted and discussed Pines 1970: 77f.

17 The earliest being by Theodore of Mopsuestia, quoted by Photius, *Bibliotheca* 81 (for which cf. Clemen 1920: 108; Bidez and Cumont 1938 II: 87; Christensen 1944: 150; Zaehner 1955: 445). The Manichaean fragment published by Henning 1951: 50 n. 1, may be earlier than Theodore of Mopsuestia, but its relevance to Zurvanism is not established beyond question. See further on this in the following discussion.

18 An important passage of this kind is the one from Mar Bar-hadhbshabba, discussed by Benveniste (1932/3) and Bidez and Cumont (1938 II: 100f.; cf. also Zaehner 1955: 439f.; reproduced in Boyce 1984: 98). All the material is given in Christensen 1928: 47–54; Bidez and Cumont 1938 II: 63ff.; Zaehner 1955a. A survey of the material is in Schaeder 1941: 278f.

19 Cf. the Middle Persian Manichaean fragment M28, published by Henning 1951: 50 n. 1 (partly reproduced by Zaehner 1955a: 439), as well as the Turkish text T II D 178; the relevant passage is reprinted in Zaehner 1955a: 432. Cf. also Asmussen 1965: 168f., 194.

20 This was suggested by Boyce 1957.

on the state of the Zoroastrian religion in their own time. Some of the Arabic reports may well derive from written documents going back to the Sasanian period, and it is impossible to distinguish contemporary accounts from those of Sasanian origin. We may note in passing that the Pahlavi literature, which we inevitably use for reconstructing ideas of the Sasanian period, and which we sometimes quote as evidence for earlier layers of the Zoroastrian religion, was mostly composed in a period which is not much earlier than that of the main classical accounts in Arabic.

Apart from the question as to the source and chronology of the information contained in the Arabic books, we must also be aware of the problem that these writers do not report on things from inside the tradition to which they refer, for they report on the Iranian religion from the point of view of an alien religion, and often incorporate critical comments on the beliefs of the Persians. In this they are not much different from the Christian writers of the Sasanian period who wrote in Armenian and Syriac. In some ways, however, they may be in a better position to serve as reliable witnesses. Their writings often derive, as can be shown, from authentic Zoroastrian sources. In addition, it should be observed that the Islamic writers in Arabic and Persian were often themselves of Persian origin, and may be assumed to have been quite close to the Zoroastrian traditions by virtue of their original environment, and sometimes their own upbringing. Examples of such background affinity with the Persian material are provided by Ibn al-Muqaffa‘ (whom one may suppose to be the source of some of the information contained in the later books)[21], al-Bîrûnî, ‘Abd al-Jabbâr, al-Shahrastânî and others.

Another argument in favour of these Arabic reports is the fact that the Islamic literary and scholarly tradition developed a style of objective reporting, in which wide erudition and accurate knowledge were considered great virtues. Even theologians who set out to debate the tenets of the Zoroastrian faith in virulent terms regarded it as their duty to start off by reporting the views of their opponents with a fair degree of precision and completeness[22].

One interesting fact should be mentioned. Although the authors of Arabic books on the opinions of the sects are among those who report on the Zurvanite myth, and some, like Shahrastânî, create the impression that this myth may have been connected to a group called “Zurwâniyya”, the historical information conveyed by the totality of Islamic literature is that there were only two major deviant movements in Iran during the Sasanian period, namely, those connected with the names Mani and Mazdak. It so

---

21 For my views on Ibn al-Muqaffa‘'s background see SHAKED 1982.

22 For a survey and evaluation of the Arabic material cf. CHRISTENSEN 1944: 59 ff.; NYBERG 1958; BOSWORTH 1983.

happens that these two movements are not only described as two religious movements, with full details about faith and practice, but their reality is confirmed by a variety of complementary sources[23]. This is absolutely and conspicuously absent in the case of Zurvanism: there is no reference whatsoever to a historical sect called Zurvanism, and no details about its founder or about events connected with its existence, as we have with regard to Manichaeism or Mazdakism.

We have already stressed the fact that one source of information is conspicuous by its almost total absence: Zoroastrian literature. We may look in vain in the Pahlavi writings for the term "Zurvanism", or for any allusion to a belief in Zurvan as supreme god. No reference of this kind will be found anywhere. It is instructive to read Zaehner's book on Zurvan, with its wealth of quotations, and to find no quotation from Pahlavi which refers, whether approvingly or disapprovingly, to the Zurvanite faith, apart from a single quotation in *Dênkard* VIII which condemns the idea that Ohrmazd and Ahreman were brothers[24]. This idea occurs in the myth of Zurvan, but is not necessarily restricted to it, as we shall try to show further on. Zaehner, it must be said, was not discouraged by this absence of explicit evidence. Following in the footsteps of Nyberg, he valiantly set out to declare that a large portion of Pahlavi literature is nothing but Zurvanism in disguise. The fact that no explicit reference to Zurvanism or to any of its acknowledged elements occurs in the Pahlavi writings was circumvented by enlarging considerably the definition of Zurvanism and by selecting various criteria other than clear references to Zurvan as constituting evidence for the presence of Zurvanite ideas. Thus, for example, since Zurvan is associated with fate, any reference to the prominence of fate is automatically considered Zurvanite; since Zurvanism is deemed to be anti-woman (because the creation myth in which the Primal Whore Jeh[25] figures has been pronounced, on the basis of questionable evidence, to be Zurvanite), negative references to women are also considered to be Zurvanite[26]. As a consequence, the whole text is most often relegated to the realm of Zurvanism[27]. We shall come back to these questions at a later stage in this

[23] A discussion of Mazdak, which casts doubts on his historical existence, is to be found in Gaube 1982. The reality of the movement need not be put in doubt, although there is some confusion as to the identity of its founder. Cf. the recent and thorough presentation by Yarshater 1983.

[24] *DkM* 829, given with earlier bibliography by Zaehner 1955a: 429f. Cf. especially Schaeder 1930: 288f.; Benveniste 1932/3: 209.

[25] Cf. Benveniste 1932/3; Widengren 1967b.

[26] Cf. Benveniste 1932/3: 187ff.

[27] As an example of a liberal use of such a procedure we may quote Hartman 1953: 14. According to him, Y. 65:11 is Zurvanite because it contains the epithet *daregô.xvadâta-*

discussion, but it must be stressed that the procedure employed by Zaehner and Widengren, besides using circular arguments, leaves hardly any room for the expression of what may be termed "orthodox" Zoroastrianism, and one wonders in that case where the distinction between Zurvanism and Zoroastrianism would be found. One wonders, in the face of such pan-Zurvanism, when and how "orthodoxy" started to assert itself. Thus, for example, it is by no means clear what the "orthodox" conception of women in the story of creation would be, when all disparaging implications are considered to be of Zurvanite origin. "Orthodox" Zoroastrianism, stripped bare of its "Zurvanite" features, would emerge as a rather puritanical philosophy, having a consistently high regard for women and extolling individual responsibility which is in no way limited by fate or predestination. Such a view of Zoroastrianism seems, however, too one-sided and selective, and presents a picture of a religion which smacks of modern rationalism, and which is not readily credible in historical terms. Needless to say, in such a case we would have no evidence for the expression of orthodoxy, according to the narrow definition which emerges from this.

To come back to our main point: If, in Professor Boyce's words, Zurvanism was the major heresy of Zoroastrianism, how is it possible to explain the fact that orthodox Zoroastrian writers did not deem it necessary to dedicate more than a single line of polemic to it? It must be emphasized that generally the Zoroastrian writers were by no means reticent about their opposition to other forms of religion. The third book of the *Dênkard* is full of chapters dedicated to controversy, which are often formulated in very strong terms. The opponents are referred to by a variety of terms: *ahlamôg, zandîg, agdên*[28], *sâstâr, dêw-yasn*, and other derogatory designations. Some of the antagonists at whom these polemics are directed are explicitly named, while others are defined only as holders of particular views; among those named are Jews and Christians, Manichaeans and Mazdakites, but none of those names, and none of the views attributed to the unnamed sectarians, conforms to anything which we may identify as Zurvanite, not even according to the loose and wide definitions mentioned above. Much the same is true of the polemics contained in other Zoroastrian books, notably the major work of apologetics and polemics, *Shkand Gumânîg Wizâr*. This striking fact, viz. the absence of references to Zurvanites as the objects of religious or theological polemics, cannot be brushed aside lightly.

---

applied to Vayu. This is an epithet employed in Y. 65:8 with regard to Zurvan. "Par conséquent", Hartman concludes, "ce texte a un caractère zurvanite".

[28] A discussion of these terms will be found in Schaeder 1930: 274 ff.; Zaehner 1955b: 234 ff.; Shaked 1969: 187 ff. For the term *zandîk* cf. Molé 1961: 14 ff.

The argument used or implied, namely that passages reflecting Zurvanite views were struck out by some kind of censor, does not apply here. It was the universal practice of the period, in Jewish, Christian and pagan, as well as Zoroastrian and Manichaean texts, to quote at length from the writings of religious adversaries in order to refute their ideas. This Zoroastrian reticence with regard to Zurvanism can have only one explanation: that Zurvanism as an organized religious system is a scholarly invention which lacks historical substance.

The same conclusion may be drawn from another rather surprising fact. The name of the god Zurvan occurs often enough in Zoroastrian texts, both in the Avesta and in Pahlavi. If any cult or faith which was considered dangerously heretic had been associated with his name, one should have expected some note of caution, some warning, to be attached to this name, perhaps to the effect that Zurvan may indeed be worshipped and adored, but not in the manner in which this is done by certain people, who abuse his name and make a travesty of the Zoroastrian religion. Again, nothing like this is found anywhere. One has no sense of either the name or the person of Zurvan being associated with any tension or conflict, something one might expect had Zurvanism been as dangerous a heresy as it is made out to be.

One further piece of evidence should be mentioned. There is a composition in New Persian which professes faith in Zurvan as the deity who preceded both Ohrmazd and Ahreman. The composition I am referring to is the Zoroastrian book known as *'Ulamâ'-i Islâm* II[29]. The remarkable thing

[29] Printed in several places; cf. *Persian Rivayat* II: 80ff. Translation and bibliographical data are given in Zaehner 1955a: 409ff. More recent discussion of the text is in Bianchi 1958: 165ff.; 1977. It should be noted that the first *'Ulamâ'-i Islâm* also contains phrases that may be regarded as Zurvanite. Let us quote a passage from this composition:

> Know that the Creator is one and His religion is one. Neither the Creator nor His religion shall expire. The way is one, waylessness is several. The Creator is one, seekers are many. Each party [*1] invokes (the Creator) in a different fashion. First I shall discourse of the Behdîns (i.e. the upholders of the Good religion). The Zoroastrians [*2] recognize Yazdân as great; some call him by several names. "Creator" is the true (name) [*3] in the religion.
>
> If Yazdan and all the Amahraspands with all the people of the world came together, they would not be able to bring into being a single grain of millet without Time *(bî zamâna)*, for it comes into being in time *(barûzgâr)*. We have written "time" *(rûzgâr)* for this reason, namely because many people do not know that time *(rûzgâr)* is Time *(zamân)*. It is possible to learn the religion by time *(ba-rûzgâr)*, it is possible to learn a trade by time, it is possible to learn good manners *(adab)* by time, it is possible to cultivate a vineyard and a field by time, a tree grows by time and gives fruit by time, it is possible to make a craft by time, and the existence [*4] of every thing is repaired by time. One cannot say that there was a Creator when there was no time. If any one says that the work of time *(rûzgâr)* is night-and-day, it should be known that there was much when night-and-day was not, while Time *(zamân)* was.

about it is not that it regards Zurvan as a primordial deity, but that it has entered the collections of Zoroastrian literature without causing any stir: it was evidently not considered by the writers and compilers of Zoroastrian literature to be a piece of writing which should be banned or hidden. It occurs in the manuscripts without any editorial comments, reservations or apologies. Again, there is no indication of religious strife being associated with Zurvan's name.

In the two treatises which go under the name of *'Ulamâ'-i Islâm*, and in other Zoroastrian writings, the tendency to accord precedence to time, not as a personal god, but as a concept, is apparent. This can hardly be regarded as a monotheistic tendency in Zoroastrianism. Time is a neutral and undifferentiated entity, and even as late as the late Sasanian period it seems to have been an accepted variant within the range of Zoroastrian religious thinking that the dualism of Ohrmazd and Ahreman was preceded by undifferentiated time. The Sasanian story of Zurvan is evidently a mythologized and personalized version of the same type of thinking. Although it is possible that this time speculation was secondarily associated with the Gathic verse Y 30:3, where the two spirits are called "twins", in order to attach this idea to the sacred text, the discussion of Zurvan, both as a myth and a theological speculation, indicates that the conception of Zurvan as originator of the two spirits had in all likelihood an origin different from Y 30:3. In other words, it seems possible to conclude from the style and formulation of the various surviving fragments that there was a current of thinking that tried to explain the origin of dualism against a background of undifferentiated and impersonal time, and that this explanation was popularly translated in the myth of Zurvan into the scene of the deity that sought a son and had instead a son and a non-son through an accident. That the mythical story is late and derivative is also suggested by the echoes of other cultures which seem to have made their impact on the shaping of this story. The similarity of the story on the one hand to the Upanishads, where

---

As for Ahreman, some people call him by name and recognize evil to be from him. He cannot do any thing without Time *(zamân)*. It is a strange thing that by this deed you should become [*5] evil-doers, and it is not proper that you should call [*6] him (i.e. Time?) an evil-doer [*7]. It is even more strange that there should be such a command for you to do evil, and that the reward [*8] for the evil which you do should be punishment and torture to the soul before [*9] the resurrection *(Darab Hormazyar's Rivayat*, II: 75, lines 15 ff.; cf. DHABHAR 1932: 443 f.).

Notes to the translation: *1. MS has **kwhy**; read **grwhy**. *2. MS has **mrzrtsty'n**, which seems like a cross between *mazdayasnân* and *zardushtiyân*. *3. Literally "the truth" *(ḥaqq)*. *4. MS has **vdr vjvd**, for which read **vvjvd**. *5. MS has **myb'snd**, for which read *mîbâshîd*. *6. MS has **xv'nnd**, for which read *xwânîd*. *7. MS has **yd krd'r**. *8. MS has **svy**, read *thavâb*? *9. MS has **vpys**, read *pêsh*.

a plurality is born out of the *âtman* or Brahman[30], and on the other to the biblical story of Isaac and his twin sons, representing good and evil[31], is quite striking and can hardly be fortuitous.

Time as well as space is fairly widely attested in reports about Zoroastrianism and in the original Zoroastrian texts[32]. Together they constitute the two basic notions out of which the structure of the cosmos comes into being by the work of creation, and they are perhaps also the two basic concepts out of which the differentiation into good and evil, into the two divine beings, comes about. The earliest reference to this idea is found in the report given by Damascius (late fifth – early sixth century C.E.) on the authority of Eudemos of Rhodes, Aristotle's pupil. According to this report, there are among the Magians "some" who "call the whole of that which is Intelligible and Unique Place, while others call it Time. From this there is made the distinction either between a good god and an evil demon, or between light and darkness." The same source has the Magians placing at the head of one group of elements Oromazdes, and at the head of the other, Areimanios[33].

As Bidez and Cumont[34] already pointed out, attributing to the Iranian religion use of the term "place" as a designation for the substratum which preceded creation is not far-fetched in terms of Zoroastrian literature. As a parallel to Zurvan, who represents Time, we find references in several places in the Avesta to Thwâsha, the deity of Space[35]. But the basic equivalent of the idea contained in Damascius' report is presented through use of terms such as Way, *gâh, gyâg*, which figure in the first chapter of the *Bundahishn*, which is devoted to cosmogony[36].

---

30 For a plurality born out of thought, cf. especially Brihadâraṇyaka Upanishad 1:4.

31 Gen. 25:21 ff.

32 As an example of the occurrence of these two concepts as primordial entities cf. *SGV* XVI: 54 *thihi u jamân*. Zaehner 1955a: 388 reads in *DkM* 567 *zamân, gâs* ... "Time, Space ...", but the reading is unacceptable; see Shaked 1982: 199. On Middle Persian Way and other terms see further below. The terms *zamân* and *gyâg* occur also among the notions which were dicussed by the writings brought together by Shâpûr I in the account of *DkM* 412: 17 ff.

33 Damascius, *Dubitationes et solutiones*, ed. Ruelle, 125bis. Cf. Clemen 1920: 95; Bidez and Cumont 1938 II: 69 f. n. 15; I: 62 f.; Zaehner 1955a: 20, 447 (text G1). Schaeder 1941: 273, regards this as the oldest witness for Zurvanism.

34 1939 I: 62 n. 4.

35 The theme is discussed and developed by Zaehner 1955a: 89.

36 Cf. Zaehner 1955a: 88 ff. My understanding of the *GBd* text which deals with Way is given in Shaked 1980: 19, 29 f. It may be remarked that Spiegel 1873: 189 f. suggests that in the description of Herodotus I: 131, where he speaks of the veneration by the Persians of Zeus, identified with the whole vault of the sky, Zeus should not be understood as a rendering of Ahura Mazda, since that deity is never identified with the sky, but rather as an equivalent of Thwâsha, the god of space. An echo of the twin concepts of Time and

It seems that from the preceding discussion we may draw the conclusion that ideas of Time existing at the basis of the cosmos and even at the roots, of the division into good and evil were known and current in Zoroastrianism, with Time sometimes being supplemented by the notion of Space or Place. These notions, although they bear a theoretical resemblance to what has been called Zurvanism, were apparently not considered deviant in any way, and we find them in Zoroastrian writings without a hint of reservation, just as they are found in the reports of foreign observers like Eudemos of Rhodes[37]. On the other hand, the myth of Zurvan, in its straightforward formulation (as opposed to the philosophical ideas about the special position of Time and Space), is never found in Iranian sources.

There is thus a clear discrepancy between the information which may be gained from the bulk of the extant Zoroastrian literature and that presented to us by the majority of the Greek, Armenian, Syriac and Arabic writers reporting about the Sasanian period, a discrepancy which has caused Zurvanism to be labelled "a Zoroastrian dilemma". The discrepancy results from the fact that while in the Zoroastrian writings Zurvan merely precedes creation, constitutes the substratum or framework within which the creation took place[38], or sometimes as that which preceded the two entities or coexisted with them, in the foreign reports we often come across

Space occurs in a passage of Mas'ûdî, *Tanbîh*, 93 and Ibn Ḥazm, *Fiṣal*, I: 35. This passage was discussed by ZAEHNER 1955a: 210f.; STERN 1970: 413ff.; SHAKI 1970: 289. The passage speaks of a pentad of entities that are eternally pre-existent. The list is: Ohrmazd, meaning God; Ahreman, meaning Satan; **k'h**, meaning Time; **j'm**, meaning Place; and **ywm**, meaning *al-ṭîna wa-l-khamîra* "clay and dough". Using the observations of Stern and Shaki, the last three terms are probably to be read *gâh*, **jây* and *tô(h)m* respectively (Shaki's explanation of the last term seems convincing).

37 A very telling passage in the *Persian Rivayat* of Darab Hormazyar may be quoted:

> Ohrmazd and Ahreman became manifest from Time *(zamâna)*. That is to say, Ohrmazd and Ahreman became manifest in one period. But Ohrmazd became manifest of his own self in his bounty. There is no doubt concerning this. Further, Zoroaster asked Ohrmazd, "When this world came into existence, what was there?" Ohrmazd replied, "At that time the two of us were there, I and Ahunavar." Zurvan is called Ahunavar (DHABHAR 1932: 438).

It seems obvious that this passage represents an attempt to harmonise the Zurvanite myth with the mainstream Zoroastrian theology. It admits the Zurvanite story of creation, and at the same time it tries to introduce it as a commentary on a traditional statement attributed to Ohrmazd, to the effect that Ohrmazd and Ahunavar are two primordial entities. It does so by identifying Ahunavar with Zurvan, an identification which has no basis other than the wish to read the Zurvanite myth into the *zand*.

38 Already the *Vendidad* has a reference to Zurvan as the framework of creation, where the Pahlavi version interprets this as referring to the creation of water. Cf. *Vd.* 19:9, reproduced in WIDENGREN 1938: 269.

a specific myth of creation according to which the two divine entities sprang forth from Zurvan[39].

What is the significance of this discrepancy? The explanation given by the majority of scholars, which assumes the existence of a major heretical sect, suppressed and obliterated at the beginning of the Islamic period without leaving any traces, seems unsatisfactory.

The conclusion we must reach on the basis of the data is that what we have referred to as Zurvanism was never a sect nor a school of thought; but is was merely a fairly inoffensive variant form of the Zoroastrian myth of creation, one of several. There never were any Zurvanite heretics because the adherents of Zurvan as supreme god were simply Zoroastrians. This is how they must have regarded themselves, and it was in this manner that they were regarded by other Zoroastrians. It is possible that the theologians, members of the religious schools, were critical of the myth which gave Zurvan supremacy over both Ohrmazd and Ahreman, but they evidently did not regard this faith as constituting a grave danger to their faith, or as worthy of elaborate refutation. The reason for this may be sought in one of two directions, or possibly in a combination of both:

(a) Faith in Zurvan was not considered to be very important, because it was embraced not by the learned, the theological class, but by people who were theologically untrained, and who could not appreciate the finer distinctions between radical dualism and a dualism which is secondary to the existence of a single unifying principle. In the case of the myth of Zurvan, the primeval unifying principle fades away after the initial phase of the story, leaving the stage to the two main protagonists, and thus its outcome does not tarnish to any appreciable extent the fundamental dualistic view. To support the assertion that the Zurvanite variant of Zoroastrianism was not a religion of theologians we may refer to the rather naive aspect of the creation myth in which Zurvan figures, and to the fact that there was no intellectual development of the Zurvanite belief beyond this crude cosmogony (this applies to some extent also to the treatise *'Ulamâ'-i Islâm*). The fact that kings and members of the royal court may have been among those who believed in the Zurvanite cosmogony does not negate the possibility that it was theologically a naive faith. Kings and aristocrats are not usually trained theologians, and theologians may have been tolerant of deviant non-theological formulations even when they occurred in court circles.

(b) Zoroastrianism was probably much more tolerant of uncanonical views than we are prone to admit. To quote the words of those two perceptive scholars: "L'impression qui se dégage (...) c'est que le magisme ancien formait un ensemble de traditions et de rites

[39] The same problem, from the point of view of a scholar who believes in the existence of a Zurvanite sect, is formulated as follows: "In the Sassanian canon of holy writings, the Avesta, it is a priori probable that Zervanite teachings once occupied a prominent place... But in the now extant Avesta we seek in vain for Zervanite texts... This fact must be due to an epuration of the Avesta carried out to remove such doctrines... Pahlavi literature is full of Zervanite texts, though more or less tinged with Zoroastrianism" (WIDENGREN 1969: 179 f.).

plutôt qu'un corps de doctrines et que ses prêtres (...) avaient une grande liberté théologique et dissertaient sans contrainte sur la nature de l'être suprême."[40]

It is true that Zoroastrianism carries within it the prophetic message of Zoroaster, which is formulated in sharp and uncompromising terms, and that its own literature bears the mark of single-minded tenacity and fidelity to the principles of its dualistic point of view. There is, however, every reason to believe that deviant views were not always treated harshly or rejected out of hand. In such cases the question is always the borderline between tolerated and acceptable deviations, and those which must cause a rupture and which demand violent expulsion of the antagonists. It is clear that Manichaeism, and in a later period Mazdakism, were movements of this kind, calling for public disavowal and rejection, and there may have been numerous other, perhaps less spectacular, cases in Sasanian history. One only has to recall the frequent admonitions against heretics in Pahlavi literature in order to realize that the problem of heretical sects was acute and painful, at least for the royal court, where responsibility for the administration of the state and for the social cohesion of the population lay[41]. It may be taken for granted that the priests were as much concerned about heresy as the court, because it affected their religious control. This is why we have so many passages in the Pahlavi books which deal with the problems of heresy, and give advice on how to recognize it and fight it[42]. Zurvanism is never mentioned in such contexts, or indeed, as we have said, anywhere at all in the Zoroastrian texts.

Since Zurvanism was apparently not considered part of the menace of heresy[43], we must assume that it was regarded by its opponents as only mildly deviant, as a myth whose theological and political implications presented no grave danger[44].

Part of the reason for that may be that people who accepted the Zurvanite myth never sought to unite and form a movement, and thus could not be considered to be endangering the structure or cohesion of society, as did members of other movements that were "properly" heretical. It is thus quite possible that the ideas that may be derived from the myth of Zurvan were condemned by some priests. They might have told their audiences to

---

40 BIDEZ and CUMONT 1938 I: 63.

41 Cf. SHAKED 1969: 187ff., 214ff.

42 Cf. the passage collected and discussed by MOLÉ 1961: 9ff.; SHAKED 1969: 214ff.; 1979: XXXIIf.

43 This view was already expressed by SPIEGEL 1873: 184.

44 I am unable to share Schaeder's judgement concerning Zurvanism: *"Er gehört nicht in die Geschichte des iranischen Glaubens, sondern in die Geschichte des iranischen Unglaubens"* (SCHAEDER 1941: 293).

reject the notion that Ohrmazd and Ahreman were brothers, but probably no crusade was ever launched to eradicate this form of belief.

As will be clear to anyone using the Islamic sources carefully, the Zurvanite myth was in all likelihood not the only deviant Iranian version of the cosmogony. Shahrastânî, 'Abd al-Jabbâr and other Islamic authorities give us a powerful sense of the great variety of cosmogonic myths among what is called the Majûs. The main versions reported are:

(a) Ohrmazd gave rise to Ahreman as the result of an evil thought that occurred to him. An interesting variant of this myth is that Kayûmarth came into being (as a counterpart to Ahreman) from the perspiration formed on Ohrmazd's forehead from his thought concerning Ahreman[45]. Although the wording is not unequivocal, it seems that the perspiration was caused by the thought that gave rise to Ahreman. If this is correct, a new triad is seen here, similar to the trinity of Zurvan – Ohrmazd – Ahreman. The new triad consists of Ohrmazd – Gayômard – Ahreman, and places Gayômard in a position equivalent to Ahreman's on the divine scale[46].

(b) Ohrmazd and Ahreman both originated from Zurvan.

(c) Ahreman originated from Zurvan, while Ohrmazd is one of the four persons of light (cf. § 7 in Shahrastânî)[47].

(d) Ohrmazd and Ahreman are two eternal and uncreated principles.

(e) Ohrmazd is eternal, Ahreman is not.

(f) Ohrmazd has material existence, Ahreman does not.

(g) There are three principles: Ohrmazd, Religion and Speech (Shahrastânî, § 24).

(h) God died and left two sons (cf. *Tathbît*, extract II).

This is by no means a complete list of the permutations of the Magian faith as reported by Arabic writers, but it shows how many variations there were on the story of how the two spirits caused the world to be created. One has the impression that none of these versions was so prominent as to be regarded as exclusively correct. There may well have been a specific formulation which was considered by the priests and the learned to represent the

---

45 *wa-yaz'umûna anna mabda'a takawwunihi wa-ḥudûthihi anna yazdân ... afkara fî amri ahriman ... fikratan awjabat an 'araqa jabînuhu fa-masaḥa al-'araqa wa-ramâ bihi fa-ṣâra minhu kayûmarth* "They claim that the origin of the formation [of Kayûmarth] and his coming into being was that Yazdân ... reflected in the matter of Ahreman a thought which made his forehead sweat. He wiped the perspiration and cast it, and Kayûmarth was formed from it" (Ibn Abî-l-Ḥadîd, *Sharḥ* I: 104). A similar tradition is in Bîrûnî, *Âthâr*, 99: 7. It may be noted that Christensen 1918: 16 reads in *Bd.* III: 20 (this corresponds to *GBd* 44; *Zand-âkâsîh* 50 f.) that Ohrmazd caused perspiration to appear on Gayomard, but this is a sheer mistranslation of the word for sleep.

46 It was the prominence given to Kayûmarth, among other things, that led Schaeder to the conclusion (unjustified, to my mind) that Shahrastânî's account is devoid of any historical value. Cf. Reitzenstein and Schaeder 1926: 238 f. For a characterisation of Shahrastânî's work on the dualists cf. Nyberg 1958: 133.

47 References to paragraphs in Shahrastânî and to extracts from 'Abd-al-Jabbâr are to the division used in my annotated translation of these texts in a forthcoming article in *JSAI* 16.

'correct" faith, and this may have been the same as that propounded by the Pahlavi books, but there is no certainty about that. As an alternative hypothesis, one may assume that the doctrine familiar to us, which preaches a strict dualism with two independent and nearly symmetrical principles, was one of several doctrines current among the Sasanian priests, and that the ultimate victory of this doctrine was a fairly late historical phenomenon. The texts at our disposal are far from helpful in deciding these questions.

Against the "orthodox" upholders of strict dualism, both mediaeval and modern, it may be pointed out that the Zurvanite myth of origins allows for a more symmetrical representation of the divine world, and at least in this sense constitutes a more radical dualism than that contained in the current Zoroastrian conception of two deities in combat with each other. Zurvan of the myth is a typical *deus otiosus:* he has no function to fulfil after bringing the two antagonistic deities into existence. Fate, if indeed it represents the continued presence of Zurvan in the world, is not an agency of will and decision, but a mechanical and entirely impersonal interference. Christian polemic in Syriac and Armenian against the religion of the Persians, contemporary as it is with the Sasanian dynasty, is mostly a polemic against the Zurvanite myth. This is the clearest evidence that the myth of Zurvan was the most common form of Iranian belief at the time. It went largely out of fashion in the Islamic period, but did not entirely vanish. We still have prominent traces of it in the post-Sasanian period in the form of a myth as well as a theological speculation putting time before Ohrmazd and his demonic rival. The most important documents showing this persistence are the reports of the Islamic historians of religion, and, within Zoroastrianism, the two *'Ulamâ'-i Islâm* treatises and several references in Pahlavi literature. Logical and attractive as this may look, we really have no evidence to connect fatalism, which is widespread and endemic in Iranian religious life, to the Zurvanite myth specifically. Nor do we have any basis for assuming that the ascetic current in Sasanian Iran, mild as it was, was in any way connected to Zurvan. It consisted mostly in avoiding excesses of wealth and indulgence, in viewing the world as full of dangers and harmful temptations[48]. We certainly cannot declare the occasional negative representation of women or of the demonic female prototype Jeh to be "unorthodox".

Was there a Zurvanite eschatology? Zaehner, for one, thinks that there was: "Zâtspram's version [of the eschatological events], as we would expect,

[48] Cf. SHAKED 1979: xxxiii ff.

shows Zurvanite tendencies. In his account it is Zurvân himself who arms Ahriman with the weapon of Az, concupiscence and greed, who is ultimately to destroy his whole creation, and it is Az, rather than Ahriman, who dominates the whole apocalyptic scene."[49] Widengren makes much of supposed Zurvanite elements in the apocalyptic literature in Pahlavi[50]. His arguments are typically circular. He devotes considerable space to an analysis of the *Oracles of Hystaspes*, which he takes to be an example of an Iranian apocalyptic work[51]. But Flusser has shown[52] quite plausibly that this is a Jewish composition which used some Iranian motifs. It can hardly be an example of a Zurvanite work of apocalyptic; it seems indeed that this is not even Widengren's contention.

While it is likely, to my mind, that Iranian ideas did have an impact on Judaism[53], we would overstep the limits of good historical method if we tried to define those ideas as either "orthodox" or "Zurvanite". As I have endeavoured to show, the term "Zurvanite" has a very limited significance in Iranian religious history: it indicates a myth of creation, and perhaps the tendency to give preponderance to the god Zurvan, but it is impossible to attribute to it a particular body of ethics, ritual, or eschatology[54]. There is certainly no justification to talk of a Zurvanite, as opposed to a Zoroastrian, saviour. Jewish eschatology and apocalyptic may well have borrowed elements from Iran, but it seems futile to look for those elements in a Zurvanite faith which probably never existed.

---

[49] Zaehner 1961: 311. This is accepted by Widengren 1983: 133.

[50] In greatest detail in Widengren 1983. The arguments, e.g. on p. 108f., are tenuous. Among other points, the word for "contract", written in Pahlavi **ptm'n**, is claimed by Widengren to be a Parthian form, and he takes MacKenzie to task for transcribing it in the Middle Persian manner. Needless to say, the word exists in both Middle Iranian languages; its Parthian connection, if it were correct, would in any case prove nothing as to its Zurvanite character. The same observation applies to the other word for "pact", *pasht*, also claimed by Widengren, for no good reason, to be Parthian rather than Persian. Similar objections could be raised with regard to the treatment of the word for "disciple", Pahlavi *hâwisht*, which is equally assigned by Widengren (p. 112) to Parthian. For other observations on supposed Zurvanite elements in eschatology cf. Widengren 1972.

[51] Widengren 1983: 121ff.

[52] Cf. Flusser 1982.

[53] The latest attempt to put this in doubt, by Barr 1985, is far from convincing. Cf. the balanced treatment of the whole subject by Hultgård 1979.

[54] That there was no particular Zurvanite eschatology is a conclusion also reached by Boyce 1990: 25.

References

Note the following abbreviations (others should pose no problem):
JSAI = Jerusalem Studies in Arabic and Islam;
MIDEO = Mélanges de l'Institut Dominicain d'Études Orientales du Caire.
Pahlavi texts are abbreviated as in Shaked 1979.

'ABD AL-JABBÂR, Abû-l-Ḥasan al-Asadâbâdî, *Al-mughnî fi abwâb al-tawḥîd wa-l-'adl*, V, ed. Maḥmud Muḥammad al-Kudayri, Cairo 1958.

–. *Tathbît dalâ'il al-nubuwwa,* 2 vols., Beirut 1966.

ABÛ-L-MA'ÂLÎ, Muḥammad al-Ḥusaynî al-'Alawî, *Bayân al-adyân dar sharḥ-i adyân va-madhâhib-i jâhilî va-islâmî*, ed. 'Abbâs Eqbâl, Teheran 1312.

AMORETTI, B. S. 1975. "Sect and heresies", in: *Cambridge History of Iran* V, ed. R. N. Frye, Cambridge, 481–519.

ASMUSSEN, J.P. 1965. *Xuâstvânîft. Studies in Manichaeism* (Acta Theologica Danica, VII), Copenhagen.

–. 1983. "Christians in Iran", *The Cambridge History of Iran* 3 (2), ed. E. YARSHATER, Cambridge, 924–948.

BAILEY, H. W. 1943. *Zoroastrian problems in the ninth-century books*, Oxford [New edition, Oxford 1971].

–. 1983. "Note on the religious sects mentioned by Kartir (Kardir)", *The Cambridge History of Iran* III (2), 907–908.

BAL'AMÎ, Abû 'Alî Muḥammad b. Muaḥammad, *Ta'rîkh*, ed. MUḤAMMAD TAQÎ BAHÂR, 2 vols., Teheran 1353 A. H.

BARR, JAMES. 1985. "The question of religious influence: the case of Zoroastrianism, Judaism and Christianity", *JAAR* 52:201–235.

BENVENISTE, E. 1929a. *The Persian religion according to the chief Greek texts* (Ratanbai Katrak Lectures), Paris.

–. 1929b. "Un rite zervanite chez Plutarch", *JA* 215:287–296.

–. 1932/3. "Le témoignage de Theodor bar Konay sur le zoroastrisme", *Le Monde Oriental* 26/7:170–215.

BIANCHI, U. 1958. *Zamān i Ōhrmazd. Lo zoroastrismo nelle sue origini e nella sua essenza*, Torino.

–. 1977. "In che sense e l''Ulema i Islam un trattato 'zurvanita'?", *Studi iranici*, Rome, 35–39.

BIDEZ, J., and F. CUMONT. 1938. *Les mages hellénisés*, 2 vols., Paris [Reprinted, Paris 1973].

Al-Bîrûnî, Abû l-Rîḥân Muḥammad b. Aḥmad, *Al-âthâr al-bâqiya 'an al qurûn al-khâliya*, ed. Eduad Sachau, Leipzig 1923.

BLOCHET, E. 1898. "Le livre intitulé l'Oulema-i Islam", *RHR* 37:23–49.

–. 1913. *Études sur le gnosticisme musulman* (Extrait de la *RSO* 2, 3, 4, 6), Rome.

BLUE, I. F. 1925. "The Zarvanite system", *Indo-Iranian studies in honour of ... D. P. Sanjana*, London, 61–81.

BOSWORTH, C. E. 1983. "The Persian impact on Arabic literature", in: *The Cambridge History of Arabic Literature,* I., Cambridge, 483–496.

BOYCE, MARY. 1957. "Some reflections on Zurvanism", *BSOAS* 19:304–316.

–. 1984. *Textual sources for the study of Zoroastrianism*, Manchester.

–. 1990. "Some further reflections on Zurvanism", *Acta Iranica* 30 (Papers in honor of E. Yarshater): 20–29.

BUNDAHISHN *(GBd): The Bundahishn* (Facsimile of Ms. TD2), ed. T. D. ANKLESARIA, Bombay 1908.

CHRISTENSEN, A. 1918. *Les types du premier homme et du premier roi dans l'histoire légendaire des iraniens*, I (Archives d'Études Orientales, 14), Stockholm.

–. 1928. *Études sur le zoroastrisme de la Perse antique* (Det Kgl. Danske Videnskabernes Selskab. Historisk-filologiske Meddelelser, XV, 2), Copenhagen.
–. 1931. "A-t-il existé une religion zurvanite?", *MO* 25:29–34.
–. 1944, *L'Iran sous les Sasanides*, 2e éd., Copenhagen.
Clemen, C. 1920. *Fontes historiae religionis persicae,* Bonn.
Colpe, Carsten. 1961. *Die religionsgeschichtliche Schule. Darstellung und Kritik ihres Bildes vom gnostischen Erlösermythus* (Forschungen zur Religion und Literatur des Alten und Neuen Testaments, NF 60 [78]), Göttingen.
Dhabhar, Bamanji Nusservanji. 1932. *The Persian Rivayats of Hormazyar Framarz and others. Their version* . . ., Bombay.
Duchesne-Guillemin, J. 1956. "Notes on Zervanism in the light of Zaehner's *Zurvan*, with additional references", *JNES* 15:108–112.
–. 1959. "Explorations dualistes avec Ugo Bianchi", *L'Antiquité Classique* 28:285–295.
–. 1962. *La religion de l'Iran ancien* (Mana, I, III), Paris.
Flusser, David. 1982. "Hystaspes and John of Patmos", in: S. Shaked (ed.), *Irano-Judaica*, Jerusalem, 12–75.
Frye, R. N. 1959. "Zurvanism again", *Harvard Theological Review* 52:63–73.
–. 1984. *The history of ancient Iran* (Handbuch der Altertumswissenschaft, 3. Abt., 7. Teil), München.
Gaube, Heinz. 1982. "Mazdak: historical reality or inventions?", *Studia Iranica* 11:111–122.
Ghirshman, R. 1958. "Notes iraniennes VIII. Le dieu Zurvan sur les bronzes du Luristan", *Artibus Asiae* 21:37–42.
Gnoli, G. 1980. *Zoroaster's time and homeland. A study on the origins of Mazdaism and related problems* (Istituto Universitario Orientale. Seminario di Studi Asiatici, Series Minor, VII), Naples.
–. 1984. "L'évolution du dualisme iranien et le problème zurvanite", *RHR* 201:115–138.
Goetze, Albrecht. 1923. "Persische Weisheit in griechischem Gewande. Ein Beitrag zur Geschichte der Mikrokosmos-Idee", *ZII* 2:60–177.
Ḥamza b. al-Ḥasan al-Isfahânî, *Ta'rîkh sinî mulûk al-arḍ wa-l-anbiyâ'*, ed. Y. Y. al-Maskuni, Beirut 1961.
Hartman, Sven S. 1953, *Gayomart*, Uppsala.
Hultgård, Anders. 1979. "Das Judentum in hellenistisch-römischer Zeit und die iranische Religion. Ein religionsgeschichtliches Problem", in: *Aufstieg und Niedergang der römischen Welt* II, 19, 1:512–590.
Humbach, Helmut. 1984. *A western approach to Zarathushtra* (Journal of the K. R. Cama Oriental Institute, 51), Bombay.
Ibn Abî-l-Ḥadîd, Sharḥ nahj al-balâgha, ed. Muḥammad Abu-l-Faḍl Ibrāhīm, 20 vols., Cairo 1959–1964.
Ibn Ḥazm, Abū Muḥammad 'Alī b. Aḥmad. *Al-fiṣal fi l-milal wa-l-ahwâ' wa-l-niḥal*, 5 vols., Cairo 1317–1321 A. H.
Ibn al-Jawzî, Jamâl al-Dîn Abû l-Faraj 'Abd al-Raḥmân al-Baghdâdî, *Naqd al-'ilm wa-l-'ulama' aw talbîs iblîs*, ed. Muḥammad Munīr al-Dimashqi, Cairo [n. d.].
Jackson, A. V. W. 1901. *Zoroaster the prophet of ancient Iran,* New York.
Jeffery, Arthur. 1938. *The foreign vocabulary of the Qur'an*, Baroda.
Junker, Heinrich F. J. 1923. *Über iranische Quellen der hellenistischen Aion-Vorstellung* (Vorträge der Bibliothek Warburg, I, 1921/2), Hamburg.
Al-Maqdisî, Muṭahhar b. Ṭâhir, *Al-bad' wa-l-ta'rîkh*, ed. C. Huart, Paris 1899- (Publications de l'Ecole des Langues Orientales Vivantes, IVe serie, vol. XVI-).
Al-Mas'ûdî, Abû l-Ḥasan 'Alî b. al-Ḥusayn, *Al-tanbîh wa-l-ishrâf,* ed. de Goeje, Leiden 1894 [Reprinted, Beirut 1965].
de Menasce, J. P. 1937/9. "Autour d'un texte syriaque inédit sur la religion des Mages", *BSOS* 9:587–601.

–. 1942/45. [Review of Bailey 1943], *JA* 234: 334–339.
–. 1954. "Le témoignage de Kayhâni sur le mazdéisme", *Donum natalicium H. S. Nyberg oblatum*, Uppsala, 50–59.
–. 1962. "Réflexions sur Zurvan", *A locust's leg*, London, 182–188.
–. 1973. *Le troisième livre du Dênkart*, traduit du pehlevi (Travaux de l'Institut d'Études Iraniennes de l'Université de Paris III, 5; Bibliothèque des Oeuvres Classiques Persanes, 4), Paris.
Molé, Marijan. 1959. "Le problème zurvanite", *JA* 247:431–469.
–. 1961. "Le problème des sectes zoroastriennes dans les livres pehlevis", *Oriens* 13/14:1–28.
–. 1963. *Culte, mythe et cosmologie dans l'Iran ancien. Le problème zoroastrien et la tradition mazdéenne* (Annales du Musée Guimet, Bibliothèque d'études, t. 68), Paris.
Monnot, Guy. 1972. "Les écrits musulmans sur les religions non-bibliques", *MIDEO* 11:5–48.
–. 1974. *Penseurs musulmans et religions iraniennes. 'Abd al-Jabbâr et ses devanciers* (Études Musulmans, XVI), Paris, Cairo and Beirut.
–. 1980. "Pour le dossier arabe du mazdéisme zurvanien", *JA* 268:233–257.
Murtaḍa, *Tabṣirat al-'awâmm fî maqâlât al-anâm*, lithograph ed., Teheran 1304 (bound together with Mīrzā Muḥammad b. Sulaymān al-Tankabūnī, *Qiṣaṣ al-anbiyâ'*).
Al-Nawbakhtî, Abû Muḥammad Ḥasan b. Mûsâ, *Firaq al-shî'a,* ed. H. Ritter, Istanbul 1931.
Nöldeke, Theodor. 1893. "Syrische Polemik gegen die persische Religion", *Festgruss an ... Rudolf von Roth*, Stuttgart, 34–38.
–. 1896–1904. "Das iranische Nationalepos", *Grundriss der Iranischen Philologie* II, Strassbourg, 130–211.
Nyberg, H. S. 1928. "Questions de cosmogonie et de cosmologie mazdéennes", *JA* 214:193–310.
–. 1931. "Questions de cosmogonie et de cosmologie mazdéennes", *JA* 219:1–134; 193–244.
–. 1938. *Die Religionen des alten Iran*, tr. by H. H. Schaeder (Mitt. d. Vorderasiatisch-ägyptischen Gesellschaft, 43), Leipzig [New edition, Osnabrück 1966].
–. 1958. "Sasanid Mazdaism according to Moslem sources", *Journal of the K. R. Cama Oriental Institute* 39:1–68.
The Persian Rivayat: Darab Hormazyar's Rivâat, ed. M. R. Unvala, with an introduction by J. J. Modi, 2 vols., Bombay 1922.
Pines, Shlomo. 1970. "Eschatology and the conception of time in the Slavonic Book of Enoch", in: R. J. Z. Werblowsky and C. J. Bleeker (eds.), *Types of redemption* (Supplements to Numen, 18), Leiden: Brill, 72–87.
Reitzenstein, R. 1917. *Die Göttin Psyche in der hellenistischen und frühchristlichen Literatur* (Sitzungsberichte der Heidelberger Akademie der Wissenschaften, Phil.-hist. Klasse, 10. Abhandlung), Heidelberg.
Reitzenstein, R., and H. H. Schaeder. 1926. *Studien zum antiken Synkretismus aus Iran und Griechenland* (Studien der Bibliothek Warburg, VII), Leipzig–Berlin.
Sad-dar Bundahishn, in: *Saddar nasr and Saddar Bundehesh*, ed. B. N. Dhabhar, Bombay 1909.
Schaeder, H. H. 1927. "Urform und Fortbildungen des manichäischen Systems", *Vorträge der Bibliothek Warburg* 4 (1924/25):67–157.
–. 1941. „Der iranische Zeitgott und sein Mythos", *ZDMG* 95:268–299.
al-Shahrastânî, Abû-l-Fatḥ, *Kitâb al-milal wa-l-niḥal*, ed. Muḥammad Sayyid Kîlânî, 2 vols., Cairo 1967; *Book of religious and philosophical sects*, ed. William Cureton, London 1846 [Reprint, Leipzig 1923]. German translation: Th. Haarbrücker, *Abu-'l-Fath asch-Schahrastanis Religionsparteien und Philosophen-Schulen*, Halle 1850–51).
Shaked, Shaul. 1967. "Some notes on Ahreman, the Evil Spirit, and his creation", *Studies in mysticism and religion presented to G. G. Scholem,* Jerusalem, 227–254.

–. 1969. "Esoteric trends in Zoroastrianism, *Proceedings of the Israel Academy of Sciences and Humanities* 3:175–221.
–. 1971. "The notions *mênôg* and *gêtîg* in the Pahlavi texts and their relation to eschatology", *Acta Orientalia* 33:59–107.
–. 1979. *Wisdom of the Sasanian Sages.* An edition, with translation and notes, of *Dênkard*, Book Six (Persian Heritage Series), Boulder, Col.
–. 1980. "Mihr the Judge", *JSAI* 2:1–31.
–. 1982. "Pahlavi notes", *Acta Iranica* 22 (Monumentum G. Morgenstierne II), 197–205.
–. 1984. "From Iran to Islam: Notes on some themes in transmission", *JSAI* 4:31–67.
SHAKI, MANSOUR. 1970. "Some basic tenets of the eclectic metaphysics of the *Denkart*", *Archiv Orientální* 38:277–312.
Slavonic Book Of Enoch: ed. A. VAILLANT, Paris 1952.
SPIEGEL, F. 1873. *Eranische Alterthumskunde*, vol. 2, Leipzig.
STERN, S. M. 1970. "Ar̤abico-Persica", *W. B. Henning Memorial Volume,* London 409–416 [Reprinted in S. M. STERN, *History and culture in the Medieval Muslim world*, London 1984].
AL-THA'ÂLIBÎ, ABÛ MANṢÛR 'Abd al-Malik b. Muḥammad, *Ghurar akhbâr mulûk al-furs wasiyarihim*, ed. H. Zotenberg, Paris 1900 [Reprinted, Teheran 1963].
Vendidad, Avesta text with Pahlavi translation . . ., ed. HOSHANG JAMASP, I. Bombay 1907.
VON WESENDONK, O. G. 1933. *Das Weltbild der Iranier* (Geschichte der Philosophie in Einzeldarstellungen, I, 1a), München.
–. 1924. *Urmensch und Seele in der iranischen Überlieferung. Ein Beitrag zur Religionsgeschichte des Hellenismus*, Hannover.
WIDENGREN, GEO. 1938. *Hochgottglaube im alten Iran. Eine religionsphänomenologische Untersuchung* (Uppsala Universitets Arsskrift 1938:6), Uppsala–Leipzig.
–. 1955. *Stand und Aufgaben der iranischen Religionsgeschichte*, Leiden. (Reprint from *Numen* 1:16–83; 2:47–134).
–. 1965. *Die Religionen Irans* (Die Religionen der Menschheit, Bd. 14), Stuttgart.
–. 1967a. "Zervanitische Texte aus dem 'Avesta' in der Pahlavi-Überlieferung. Eine Untersuchung zu Zâtspram und Bundahishn", *Festschrift für Wilhelm Eilers*, Wiesbaden, 278–287.
–. 1967b. "Primordial Man and Prostitute: a Zervanite motif in the Sassanid Avesta", *Studies in mysticism and religion presented to G. G. Scholem*, Jerusalem.
–. 1967c. "Philological remarks on some Pahlavi texts, chiefly concerned with Zervanite religion", *Sir J. J- Zarthoshti Madressa Centenary Volume*, Bombay, 84–103.
–. 1969. "The death of Gayomart", *Myths and symbols. Studies in honor of Mircea Eliade*, Chicago and London, 179–193.
–. 1972. "Salvation in Iranian religion", in: E. J. SHARPE and J. R. HINNELLS (eds.), *Man and his salvation. Studies in memory of S. G. F. Brandon*, Manchester, 315–326.
–. 1983. "Leitende Ideen und Quellen der iranischen Apokalyptik", in: D. HELLHOLM (ed.), *Apocalypticism in the Mediterranean world and the Near East*, Tübingen, 77–162.
WIKANDER, STIG. 1946. *Feuerpriester in Kleinasien und Iran* (Skrifter utgivna av Kungl. Humanistiska Vetenskapssamfundet i Lund, XL), Lund.
YARSHATER, EHSAN. 1983. "Mazdakism", in: *Cambridge History of Iran* III (2), Cambridge, 991–1024.
ZADSPARAM (Zs): *Vichîtakîhâ-i Zâtsparam*, with text and introduction, by B. T. ANKLESARIA, Bombay 1964.
ZAEHNER, R. C. 1937/39. "Zurvanica, I–III". *BSOAS* 9:303–320, 573–585, 871–901.
–. 1940/42. "A Zervanite Apocalypse I–II". *BSOAS*, 10:377–398, 606–631.
–. 1955a. *Zurvan. A Zoroastrian dilemma*, Oxford.
–. 1955b. "Postscript to Zurvan", *BSOAS* 17:232–249.
–. 1961. *The dawn and twilight of Zoroastrianism*, London.

VI

FROM IRAN TO ISLAM
NOTES ON SOME THEMES IN TRANSMISSION

I. "Religion and Sovereignty are twins" in Ibn al-Muqaffa''s theory of government *

It is not easy to summarize the flow of ideas from pre-Islamic Iran into Islamic literature, since we have to do here not with a single encounter, which took place within a limited period of time, but with a fairly extended process of borrowing and adaptation. It certainly began a considerable time before the emergence of Islam, through intercourse between the population of Arabia and the Sasanian empire, and continued with particular vigour during the first two or three centuries of Islam. During this period some of the most conspicuous spokesmen for the new religion were themselves direct descendants of men who had been bearers of the ancient traditions of Iran. Iranian traditions and the Hellenistic and Judaeo-Christian heritage conduct within Islam a kind of internal dialogue in which it is not always easy to distinguish between the parties representing each strain of culture.[1]

To the difficulties inherent in this melting-pot situation of Islam one must add complications on two further levels of discussion. First, there are the limitations imposed by the Iranian material, which has only survived in an extremely fragmentary state. So much so, that it is impossible to dispense with the use of Arabic literature itself as one primary source for our acquaintance with Sasanian notions and literary traditions, with the obvious risk of having sometimes to argue in what may look like a vicious circle: from Arabic literature for the Iranian origin of a given theme or topos, and then from that for the Iranian influence in Arabic literature. This situation calls of course for utmost caution and restraint in one's arguments.

The second complication arises out of the open and eclectic character of the Sasanian literary tradition which has left its impact on Islam. The process of borrowing and adaptation, of mutual influences and inter-

[1] The present paper is intended to be the first in a series of similar notes.

cultural dialogue was in full force between the major civilizations of the Near East long before Islam came to the scene.[2] In some cases it is impossible to assign a given theme to a specific place of origin because it had become common property at a much earlier date, and it could have been taken up by the Islamic compilations from several alternative sources. One or two examples for this will be given in the following.

One of the most prominent and generally recognized bearers of Iranian literary traditions in Islam was Ibn al-Muqaffaʿ. He was not only an adult convert to Islam,[3] but also had an avowed interest in transferring to Islam what he deemed to be of most interest in his native culture. This he did by his well-known translations, of which *Kalīla wa-Dimna* (of Indian origin, but with a Sasanian introduction) deserves special mention. At the same time he also composed treatises of his own, and the ideas propounded in them have sometimes created the impression of originality and freshness of thought. On closer look, however, one sometimes notices unacknowledged indebtedness to Sasanian sources. This is the case, for instance, with his *al-adab al-ṣaġīr*.[4] I should like to take up here for scrutiny from this point of view some of the ideas contained in Ibn al-Muqaffaʿ's *Kitāb al-ṣaḥāba*, a treatise which has received deservedly high praise from Professor S.D. Goitein as constituting "a turning point in the history of the Muslim state".[5] I am however not entirely certain that it would be right to attribute most of the insights contained in that treatise to Ibn al-Muqaffaʿ himself, and to insist that they were reached "by close observation of the inner state of the Muslim religion and empire, and were quite contrary to the Sasanian tradition".[6] I believe that one can show Iranian parallels to quite a few sections in that book. Although these motifs are not in every case exclu-

2 The most important studies of the Greek impact on Zoroastrian theological writings are Bailey 1943 and the notes in Menasce 1945. Extensive literature exists on the impact in the opposite direction, from Iran to the Hellenistic world; much of it is speculative, but it was without doubt a very real phenomenon. A collection of material illustrating this process is in Bidez and Cumont, *Les mages hellénisés*, Paris 1938.

3 The question whether Ibn al-Muqaffaʿ was a convert from Manichaeism or from Zoroastrianism is not yet settled, though the majority of current opinion would regard him as a former Manichaean; cf. Goitein 1949; Gabrieli 1931/32 and *EI*². The question is taken up in detail in the Appendix.

4 I think it has not yet been noticed that a large part of *AṢ* is also found in Miskawayhi, *JX* in the section which is devoted to the wisdom of the Persians. Cf. *JX* 68, last line, with Ibn al-Muqaffaʿ, *AṢ*, 8 line 12ff. Badawī, the editor of *JX*, does not mention this striking fact. Some sections of that joint text have been identified in Pahlavi; cf. Shaked 1979, commentary on *Dk* VI 5, 178, 48. Further parallels: *AṢ* 28 lines 11-13 — *PhlT* 150 §59; *AṢ 29, lines 14-15* — *PhlT* 94 §108-109.

5 Goitein 1949 (1966). The latest detailed treatment of this work is by Pellat 1976.

6 Goitein 1966, p. 165, where it is also remarked that in some respects a return to the Sasanian system of government was recommended by Ibn al-Muqaffaʿ.

sively Iranian, their combined presence in one treatise shows that their origin is to be sought in all likelihood in Sasanian Iran. Some of the more prominent examples for this are presented in the following list:

1. The words of praise addressed to the caliph contain the phrase: *fa-'inna amīra l-mu'minīna... yajma'u ma'a 'ilmihi al-mas'alata wa-l-istimā'a.*[7] These words seem to echo the Zoroastrian notion of *hampursagīh*, one of the most prominently expressed virtues in Sasanian moral literature, which consists of constantly consulting with wise and good people.[8]

2. One of the first pieces of advice given by ibn al-Muqaffa' to the caliph in his epistle is to encourage people to be of assistance to the ruler: "For with desire is effort, and with despair is relinquishment of hope (*qunūṭ*). No sooner does hope (*rajā'*) weaken than ease of life (*rakā'*) departs. The seeking of a despairing man is feebleness, the seeking of a man of desire is firm decision (*ḥazm*)."[9] Anyone familiar with Zoroastrian literature will easily recognize here a theme which occurs often in religious writings in Pahlavi: the need is constantly enjoined there not to lose hope (*ummēd, ēmēd*) with regard to one's religious attainments, for losing hope means falling into the hands of the demons.[10] The idea as it is expressed in *Kitāb al-ṣaḥāba* has been transposed to the secular field; but as relatively little of the Sasanian secular literature is extant, it is not possible to tell whether such transposition had not taken place within Persian literature prior to Ibn al-Muqaffa'.

3. The constant triad expressing the three forms of human activity in the Zoroastrian religion is thought, speech and action, always used in this order. The Middle Persian form of this sequence is: *menišn, gōwišn, kunišn*, and it continues an ancient Iranian idea, already present in the Avesta.[11] In this case again we have a transformation of this idea into the secular field. In talking of the Khurāsān troops, Ibn al-Muqaffa' impresses on the ruler the need to supervise them closely and to discipline them, for it is impossible to rule over people when one uses men whose agreement is not firmly established in opinion, speech and conduct (*fī al-ra'y wa-l-qawl wa-l-sīra*),[12] where we come across the familiar Persian phrase in an administra-

7 *Ṣaḥāba* 117.

8 Some short notes on this notion are given in the introduction to Shaked 1979, pp. xxvii-xxix, though the subject deserves fuller treatment. It may be noted that *al-mas'ala wa-l-istimā'* is a perfect rendering of the pair of terms *hampursagīh* and *niyōšīdārīh* in *Dk* VI E45c. Another term which is used synonymously with *hampursagīh* is *dēn uskārišn ī wehān*, cf. *PhlT* 49 §54.

9 *Ṣaḥāba* 118.

10 Cf. for example the group of sayings *Dk* VI 167-170.

11 Cf. Lommel 1930, p. 239f.

12 *Ṣaḥāba* 120.

tive context.[13] In another composition of Ibn al-Muqaffa' we have the same notion expressed with regard to the ruler himself: "The man who should most rightfully compel himself towards justice in opinion, speech and action, is the ruler".[14]

4. For solving the problem of the Khurāsān troops Ibn al-Muqaffa' advises the ruler to give them a letter of appointment, which would specify their duties and serve for them as proof of their position. He calls that letter *amān*,[15] a term quite unfamiliar in this sense in classical Arabic, and one thinks of a possible Sasanian antecedent. The case here is not so clear; there are two Middle Persian terms which may have served as model for Ibn al-Muqaffa'. We know next to nothing about the way in which military appointments were made under the Sasanians, but the term *pādexšahr* or *pādexšīr* occurs in contexts where an appointment is made for a clerical dignity, in early Sasanian inscriptions, or for establishing a fire foundation. The literal meaning of that term is apparently "(the granting of) power, right", hence, "pact, treaty".[16]

Another term which one might consider, with more probability, as the Sasanian model for Ibn al-Muqaffa''s *amān* is the term *zēnhār* "security, pact, pledge",[17] which is very close in sense to the Arabic word used, and

[13] The same notion occurs in the same paragraph of the text in a different order: *taqwīmu aydīhim wa-ra'yihim wa-kalāmihim* (p. 119); this was pointed out already by Goitein 1966, p. 156 and note 2.

[14] *wa-aḥaqqu l-nāsi bi-ijbāri nafsihi 'alā l-'adli fī l-naẓari wa-l-qawli wa-l-fi'li al-wālī*, Ibn al-Muqaffa', *AK* 52.

[15] *Ṣaḥāba* 120. Goitein 1966, p. 157, renders the term by "catechism". Pellat 1976, p. 6 suggests "règlement".

[16] Cf. Gignoux **p'tḫštly, p'tḫštr, p'tḫštry** (Phl), **ptyḫštr** (Pth.). The Book Pahlavi form attested is **p'txšyl**, cf. *PhlT* 112 §39. The word was discussed at some length by Herzfeld 1924, p. 231; 1938, pp. 211ff.; and Bailey 1949/51, p. 123. The same word also possesses the meaning of "powerful, mighty", or as a noun "kingship, might", and in Manichaean Middle Persian the sense of "honour". Cf. Boyce 1977, s.v. **pdyxšr**; Nyberg 1931, p. 180; Tedesco 1921, p. 196 and note 1, where the Mandaic **p'd'hš'r** is quoted.

* [17] *zēnhār* is used in the sense of a treaty or charter, just like *amān* of early Islamic usage (for which cf. Schacht, *EI*²). For this usage of *zēnhār* one may quote a number of passages in Pahlavi:

[I] *u-šān pašt paymān rāstīh ud ēwēn nēst, ud zēnhār ne dārēnd* "They have no pact, treaty, truth or (binding) custom, and they do not keep the *zēnhār*" (*ZWY* IV 11).

[II] The sin of one miserable soul in hell is described in the following terms: *ēn ruwān ī awe druwand mard ke-š pad gētīg zēnhār ī drōg abāg mardomān kard* (*AVn* 51.5) "This is the soul of that wicked man who made a *zēnhār* of lie with people in the material world".

[III] Of the three things which one should hold most firmly (*drubušt-tar*) two are said to be *dōst* "a friend" and *zēnhār* "a pact, a promise" (*Ošnar* § 24). The first item is lost in the manuscript.

[IV] *sāsān az pāpak *pašt ud zēnhār xwāst ku-m wizand ud ziyān ma kun* (*Kn*

which seems to have been used in a much broader range of meaning than that usually assigned to *amān* in Arabic.

5. Ibn al-Muqaffa' presents the position that the caliph has supreme and undisputed authority by using the phrase: Were he to say to the mountains to move, they would do so. This is followed by an Islamic phrase: Were he to reverse the direction of prayer, he would affect his desire.[18] The first phrase, if not Sasanian by origin, is nevertheless familiar from Sasanian writings.[19]

6. Human endeavour, Ibn al-Muqaffa' says, has been established by God to revolve around two concepts: Religion and Intelligence (*al-dīn wa-l-'aql*), and the idea is developed at some length.[20] The concept is

1.15) "Sasan asked a pact and a promise, namely, 'Do not cause me harm and damage'". Nöldeke 1879, p. 38, translates: "Da bat Sâsân den Pâpak um Schonung und Sicherheit", though this does not seem to be the technical meaning of the two terms. (Cf. also Bartholomae 1911, p. 261f.)

[V] *kanīzag guft ku agar-em zēnhār *dahēh pad tan [ud] jān ī man tā rāst be gōwēm. šāhpuhr guft ku zēnhār ud ma tars* (Kn 13.19-20) "The girl said: If you give me a promise (of protection) concerning my body and soul, I shall tell the truth. Shapur said: [You have my] promise, do not fear" (cf. Nyberg 1964, p. 15; Nöldeke 1879, p. 66).

A *zinhār-nāma* which contains the phrase *ma tars* occurs in the Judaeo-Persian text *Qiṣṣa-yi Dāniyāl*, p. 398 lines 18ff. (*ma- tars* as a phrase guaranteeing safety in Islamic times occurs frequently in Arabic literature).

The etymology and original meaning of *zēnhār* have been long debated. The more prominent opinions expressed are: *az ēn dār* "keep away from this!" (Horn 1893); *az ēn hār* "protect from this" (Andreas, in Mann, *ZDMG* 47, 1893, p. 704; also quoted in Hübschmann 1895, p. 60); **zaēnō-hāra-* "Waffenschuts" (F. Müller 1894, p. 96; followed by Hübschmann loc. cit.); **jīvana-hāra-* "Schutz für das Leben" (Bartholomae 1911, pp. 260-262; followed by Nyberg 1931, p. 256, and 1974, p. 231); the Aramaic root *ZHR* (Nöldeke 1892, p. 46).

None of these etymologies strikes me as entirely convincing, as I believe the primary meaning of the word in Pahlavi, or at least the one which best fits most passages, is not "security, protection", but "treaty, promise". As yet a further etymology I would suggest **zaya-ni-dāra-* "holding fast the weapon (i.e. refraining from using it)", hence "a pact" and "security", and possibly also, as an exclamation: "on your guard!" For the verb *ni-dar* cf. Bartholomae 1904, s.v. *dar-*, and Skt. *ni-dhṛ-*; for the phonetic development **ni-dār-* to **nihār-* cp. *ni-dāta-* which gives MPers. and NPers. *nihād*.

The Arabic *amān* might indeed have been formed on the model of *zēnhār*, possessing as it does the same ambiguity of usage (cf. E.I.J. Rosenthal 1962, p. 252f.). It may be added that at least in one Arabic text an underlying **pašt ud *zēnhār* seems to have been translated by *al-'uhūd wa-l-mawāṯīq*. The text concerns the story of Šahrbarāz who fled from Khusrau Abarwēz to the Byzantine emperor, after having demanded from him security (*fa-j'al lī mā aṭma'innu ilayhi*). Having got this, he defects to the Byzantine *qayṣar*, but he first received from him promises and treaties (*wa-qad akada minhu l-'uhūda wa-l-mawāṯīqa*. Bayhaqī, *Maḥāsin* I, 210).

18 *Ṣaḥāba* 120.

19 Cf. *Dk* VI 60, and my notes to the place.

20 *Ṣaḥāba* 122.

somewhat unusual in Islamic writings. The term *dīn* is used normally as an institutional concept, not so much as a notion relating to the psychology of the individual, while this is a prominent aspect in the meaning of Iranian *dēn*. The similarity of the Arabic *dīn* to the Persian *dēn* has caused some confusion in translations from Persian to Arabic in other works.[21]

The two Iranian terms obviously underlying the Arabic words *al-dīn wa-l-ʿaql* are *dēn* and *xrad*. Both are concepts which designate powers of the human soul, of the non-material aspect of the person, and they come together to form a pair in Zoroastrian religious writings.[22]

7. Ibn al-Muqaffaʿ enjoins on the caliph the need to have an effective system of intelligence, which would report to him everything which comes about in the various outlying districts and among the troops.[23] This is again a very prominent feature of Sasanian court treatises on government, though they are known to us almost exclusively by transmission in Arabic literature, the originals having been lost.[24] The idea is, however, attested for Iran already in the ancient period.[25]

8. The social division of the kingdom is said to consist according to Ibn al-Muqaffaʿ of three parts, or classes: *al-ʿāmma, al-ḵāṣṣa*, and *al-imām*.[26] The idea may seem commonplace enough in Islam (though I am not sure

[21] Two examples may be given for this. (1) In a passage which is very obviously modelled on a Middle Persian idea, Ibn al-Muqaffaʿ writes: *wa-ḍnun bi-dīnika wa-ʿirḍika ʿan kulli aḥadin* (AK 71) "keep back your *dīn* and self from every one". The Pahlavi formulation extant which corresponds to this is: *dēn andar ham-dēnān uskārišn* "consider *dēn* (only) among those of the same *dēn*" (*Dk* VI 55, and cf. Shaked 1969, p. 183f.). *Dēn* and its Arabic rendering *dīn* is not "religion" in the institutional sense of the term, but rather a disposition of the soul. The Arabic translator added *ʿirḍ* as a kind of gloss to bring out this sense of *dēn*. (2) The Pahlavi treatise *Ayādgār ī Wuzurgmihr* states: "The Creator Ohrmazd, in order to hold back those several demons and to help man, created so many watchful things of the spirit: innate wisdom, acquired wisdom, character, hope, contentment, *dēn*, and the consultation of the wise" (*PhlT* 90 § 43). The Arabic version gives the following enumeration of these spiritual powers: *al-ʿaql wa-l-ʿilm wa-l-ʿifāf wa-l-ṣabr wa-l-rajāʾ wa-l-dīn wa-l-naṣīḥa* (Miskawayhi, *JX* 31; here quoted from an unpublished typescript edition of the text in Pahlavi and Arabic, prepared in collaboration with the late S.M. Stern). Here too *dēn* is primarily a power of the soul. Without this background knowledge, the Arabic *dīn* may strike one as incongruous in this list.

[22] Cf., for example, *Dd* 2.4; *PhlT* 67 § 104-105; and Shaked 1979, p. xxvii.

[23] *Ṣaḥāba* 124, 133.

[24] Cf. e.g. Jāḥiẓ, *Tāj* 171f.; ps.-Aṣmaʿī, *Nihāya*, has an anecdote in which Kisrā asked his ministers and wise men to say a word which would be of benefit for improving his reign. He is not satisfied with their answers, and ultimately he addresses himself to Buzurjmihr asking him for his suggestion. Buzurjmihr enumerates twelve maxims, which the king accepts with such pleasure that he orders to fill the mouth of the sage with precious stones. The last two sentences are concerned with spying on external enemies and with spying on the king's officials (fol. 198b).

[25] Cf. Shaked 1982, p. 301f.

[26] *Ṣaḥāba* 133f.

whether it is attested before Ibn al-Muqaffaʿ), but one cannot help feeling that here too Ibn al-Muqaffaʿ is under obligation to his Iranian background. The threefold, or fourfold, division of society is typical of Sasanian writings,[27] though here an adaptation to the classless structure of society in Islam seems to have been made by introducing the ruler, *al-imām*, as the third power.

These points may be sufficient to confirm the contention that this treatise too, although it was obviously composed in answer to a specific situation of the Islamic state, is impregnated with ideas which its author derived from his Iranian background. One of the most interesting themes introduced by Ibn al-Muqaffaʿ in *Kitāb al-ṣaḥāba* concerns the need for the caliph to assume responsibility over the religious life of his community: it has been rightly pointed out by modern scholars that this position is unusual in the Islamic context; it has indeed been subsequently rejected in the development of Islamic ideas of government, except by Shīʿa theoreticians.[28]

The Zoroastrian idea of the proper relationship between religion and government is however in full accord with the formulation of Ibn al-Muqaffaʿ in the *Kitāb al-ṣaḥāba*. In this particular case it can be shown that secular Sasanian court literature held the same point of view.

The basic expression for the interdependence of religion and government is contained in the *Testament of Ardašīr*, preserved only in Arabic: *al-dīn wa-l-mulk akawāni taw'amāni lā qawāma li-aḥadihimā illā bi-ṣāḥibihi* "Religion and government are twin brothers, no one of which can survive without the other".[29] A different version of the same phrase in Arabic, based perhaps on another translation into Arabic of the *Testament of Ardašīr*, has: *al-mulk wa-l-ʿadl akawāni lā ġinā bi-aḥadihimā ʿan ṣāḥibihi* "Government and justice are two brothers who cannot be without each other".[30] The divergence of this version from the one quoted earlier may be interpreted as an attempt at attenuating the religious content of the saying.

27 Some references are given in Shaked 1969, 182f. n. 23, and 217f.

28 Cf. Goitein 1949. According to E.I.J. Rosenthal 1962, p. 254, Ibn al-Muqaffaʿ's theory was "real and valid, not only in the writings of jurists, but also in the formal pronouncements of caliphs, emirs and sultans".

29 *ʿAhd Ardašīr*, p. 53; translation in Shaked 1969, p. 214. Cf. the parallel adduced by I. Abbas, *ʿAhd Ardašīr*, pp. 124f., 97, 100. Ābī, *Naṯr*, fol. 28a has this saying too. An echo of this notion occurs in Firdawsī, *ŠN* I, 39 (Jamšēd line 6): *man-am guft bā farra-yi īzadī / ham-am šahriyārī ham-am mawbadī* "To me, he said, by divine glory, is both kingship and priesthood". In his important study of the theory of government in Islam, Busse 1977, p. 66, refers to this idea as an Islamic innovation: "Die Formel vom Bruderverhältnis ist ein Versuch, zu einem Kompromiss zwischen beiden Extremen zu kommen". The Iranian origins of this idea were already recognized by Goldziher 1900, p. 125.

30 Ibn ʿAbd Rabbihi, *ʿIqd*, I, p. 23. Quoted also in Abū l-Ḥasan ʿAlī, *ʿAyn al-adab*, p. 227.

If it can be maintained that two independent Arabic versions of the *Testament of Ardašīr* were in circulation, this would add some weight to the currently held opinion of scholars that the *Testament* is indeed a Sasanian composition (even though its attribution to Ardašīr, the first Sasanian king, may be apocryphal). Most of the quite numerous quotations of this phrase in Arabic do indeed relate it to the *Testament of Ardašīr*, in which it is actually to be found, one indication among many for the relative reliability of Islamic attributions to Sasanian compositions.

If there is any lingering doubt as to whether this is in fact an Iranian idea or merely an Islamic fabrication, the evidence of the Zoroastrian writings in Pahlavi may be adduced. We may start by quoting from the words of a ninth-century Zoroastrian priest, Zādspram:

> *abar āmadan ī dēn ō āwām.*
> (...) *zamānīg kōxšišn-* gumēzišnīh māyagwarīhā pad 2 abzār, [ēwag] dehbadīh ī be az ham-nāf dēn, ud ēwag dēn [ī] ō dehbadīh ham-nāfihēd* (*Zs* 4:O, 2).
>
> On the coming of religion to the world.[31]
> (...) The mixture accompanied by struggle and conducted in time is (done) in substance by two instruments: [one] is government which stems from[32] its kinsman, religion; and one is religion which is allied in kinship to government.[33]

The passage is somewhat obscure, like much of Zādspram's style. Much to our regret, the idea is not taken up again further in the chapter. Nevertheless, the term *ham-nāf* seems to provide us with the Middle Persian equivalent to our Arabic words *taw'am, ak̲*. Literally *ham-nāf* designates "one of the same family", indicating, like the Arabic terms, parity between the two items described. A term of vertical kinship might imply lack of symmetry between the two notions of religion and government.

*

The same idea and the same term, not hitherto noticed, occur in a chapter of the third book of the *Dēnkard*, a huge compilation, largely of Sasanian material, put together in the ninth century. It may be useful to offer the full passage in transcription and translation, as my understanding of it differs in some points from that of previous editors:

[31] On this meaning of *āwām* cf. Shaked 1980, 23. One may add to the material assembled in that article the analogy of NPers. *zamāna*, e.g. Firdawsī, *ŠN* I, 39 (Jamšēd line 4): *zamāna bar āsūd az dāvarī* "The world had respite from disputes".

[32] *Be az*, cf. Shaked 1980, p. 21. The phrase could also mean "devoid of, outside of", a less satisfactory possibility in this context.

[33] Anklesaria, in his translation, *Zs*, p. LXXXII, seems to me to offer a better understanding of the text than Molé 1963, p. 39.

abar xwadāyīh ud dēn. az nigēz ī weh-dēn.
hād xwadāyīh[34] *dēn ud dēn xwadāyīh [ham-] dehān*[35] *astīh. az weh-dēn nigēz.*
andar hān wāzag[36] *awēšān-ez hanbasān*[36] *kēš padeš ham-dādestānīh pad hān ī-šān xwadāyīh abar dēn, dēn abar xwadāyīh winārdagīh kēš, ōh-ez wehān-dēn fragān-bun wāzag āstawānīh abar ohrmazd-bandagīh, mehēnišn ī dēn ēwag az did *a-wisānišn.*
ēr*[37] *xwadāyīh *mehēnīdārīh az dēn, ohrmazd bandagīh mazdēsnīh [ī] dēn az xwadāyīh. u-šān abēr-tar brāzišn sūd [ī] mehēn ō dāmān. pad hamīh ī xwadāyīh *ud weh-dēn, rāst xwadāyīh; ud pad hamīh [ī] weh-dēn ud rāst xwadāyīh, weh-dēn [ud xwadāyīh] ham-nāf.
ceōn xwadāyīh dēn [ud] dēn xwadāyīh [ham-]dehān, aōn a-xwadāyīh ag-dēnīh-ez ud ag-dēnīh a-xwadāyīh-ez (*Dk* III ch. 58; B 34f.; M 47).[38]

On kingship and religion. From the instruction of the Good Religion.
Kingship and religion, religion and kingship being [fellow-] countrymen.[39] From the instruction of the Good Religion.[40]
On that matter even those of contrary opinion are in agreement, in that they hold the opinion that kingship is built on religion, and religion on kingship.[41] Thus the doctrine concerning the foundation of the Good Religion is that there is no separation between the following two: the confession of one's being a slave of Ohrmazd, and the broadening of the religion.
The broadening of the religion of the Iranians is from the religion; (causing people to be) slaves of Ohrmazd and the religion (to be) Mazdaean, is from kingship. Their highest luminosity is the great benefit which they confer on the creatures. By the combination of kingship and Good Religion, just kingship is there. By the combina-

34 Ms. adds *ī*.
35 Ms. has *MTA'n* = *dehān*.
36 Ms. adds *ī*.
37 Ms. *ērīh*.
38 Cf. Molé 1963, pp. 51f.; Menasce 1973, p. 65; Kanga 1974, pp. 222f.
39 **ham-dehān* is suggested as an emendation in an attempt to reach an acceptable text. Molé and Menasce read what we would transcribe as *mādiyān* "essence; essential", which does not seem right, as it is hardly reasonable to suppose that kingship and religion should have been said to be "in essence" identical. Kanga takes the word as written, and translates: "Religion is the existence of sovereignty in the provinces", surely an ill-founded translation. One imagines that Pahlavi literature, with all its abstruseness, does not go against common sense. Zaehner 1961, p. 296, likewise translates: "Religion is royalty, and royalty is religion", assuming a similar tautology.
40 This seems to be an alternative heading to this chapter.
41 This is reminiscent of the expression in the *Testament of Ardašīr: lā qawāma li-aḥadihimā illā bi-ṣāḥibihi*, etc.

tion of the Good Religion and just kingship, the Good Religion [and kingship][42] are kindred.

In the same way as kingship and religion, religion and kingship are [fellow-]countrymen to each other, so are also lack of government and evil religion, evil religion and lack of government (to each other).

The text here is badly transmitted. It illustrates the problems caused by the need to reconstruct a faulty text from a single manuscript, although it is certainly not the worst example of its kind in Pahlavi. We are fortunate in this case to have the key-term *ham-nāf* secured from another Pahlavi text and from the Arabic parallel. If our treatment of the text is correct, we have here two figurative expressions for the relationship of religion and kingship: *ham-nāf* and **ham-deh*, the latter denoting close neighbourly relations, though the reading is merely conjectural.

The same set of ideas is found in several other places in the Zoroastrian writings.[43] There can be little doubt that this is a genuine conception of the Sasanian period; it is attributed by Sasanian commentators to the Avesta, and may thus have had deeper roots in Iran than the Sasanian dynasty.[44] When Ibn al-Muqaffaʻ propounds the theory that the king should control everything which relates to religion so as to prevent schisms and in order to obtain uniformity of religious practice, he is actually perpetuating a typical Sasanian idea. This does not necessarily mean that it was carried out into practice by the Sasanian kings themselves with complete effectiveness. The numerous heresies and schisms of the Sasanian period, and the independent position which several *mōbaḏ*s seem to have held, suggest that the advice given to rulers to hold religion in check was timely and necessary, but that it was not normally achieved.

[42] This addition seems necessary if the sentence is to make sense.

[43] Some further examples may be quoted briefly. The ten counsels of Zardušt the Righteous to mankind, enumerated in *Dk* III, ch. 195, recommend, in the third piece of advice, to enhance the creation through putting in order (*winārišn*) in the world the force of the dignity of the leader (*axwīh*), which is kingship (*xwadāyīh*), and that of the *rad* (*ratu*, the religious authority), which is the law of the religion (*dēn dādestān*) (*Dk* B 163; cf. Menasce 1973, p. 202f.). This is an abstract religious formulation which is equivalent to the more concrete political expressions quoted above. In the counsels of the ancient sage Sēn it is said: *[dād] pad-ez hān ī fragān ī gēhān stun ī xwadāyīh winārišn ī dēn [ī] mazdēsn ōstīgān-tar mehēnīdan* (*Dk* III, ch. 197; B 166; cf. Menasce 1973, p. 206, where the translation is different). "(It is desirable) to increase more firmly [the law] even by that which is the foundation of the world, the supporting column of kingship, (viz.) the arrangement of the Mazdaean religion". My reading is based on the expressions in the parallel and opposite chapter 198, where the same advice is phrased as follows: *padīrag hān ī ahlaw sēn dād pad fragān ī gēhān stun ī xwadāyīh winārišn ī dēn stāyēd* (B 167). A collection of texts relating to this theme in Pahlavi may be found in Molé 1963, pp. 37ff., though some of the translations given there seem to me in need of modification.

[44] Cf. the phrase *az nigēz ī weh-dēn.*

II. The Four Sages

The book *al-Siyāsa la-'āmmiyya* is based predominantly on Greek authorities. It purports to contain a series of letters by Aristotle to his disciple Alexander son of Philippos, and has been dubbed, somewhat inaptly, "roman épistolaire".[1] The first passage in the book contains the following classification

> Kings are (of) four (kinds): A king who is generous with himself and his subjects; a king who is avaricious with himself and his subjects; a king who is avaricious with himself but generous with his subjects; and king who is generous with himself but avaricious with his subjects.
>
> The Greeks said: There is nothing wrog with a king who is avaricious with himself and generous with his subjects.
>
> The Indians said: Being avaricious with himself and his subjects is correct.
>
> The Persians, in reply to the Indians, said: That king is right who is generous with himself and his subjects. All of them agreed that (for the king) to be generous with himself but avaricious with his subjects is wrong.[2]

This is the opening passage not only of the *Siyāsa 'āmmiyya*, but also of another book of a similar character, the *Kitāb al-siyāsa fī tadbīr al-riyāsa*, known also as *Sirr al-asrār*, or under the title in which it enjoyed considerable circulation in the West, *Secretum secretorum*.[3] Despite the seemingly unimpeachable Greek surroundings in which it is embedded, one has the feeling that this passage is not Greek but Persian in origin. One feature of this saying is that it allows the Persians the final say on the ideal composition of the king's character, and it puts in his mouth what is obviously taken to be the most appropriate phrase. The wording seems to indicate that in a former version of this story an actual discussion took place, for the Persians speak "in reply to the Indians". We may imagine an original form of the story in which representatives of three (or four, as we shall see later) nationalities took part.

Two further considerations add some weight to the assumption that we have to do here with a Persian story. There is, first, the use of the terms "generous" and "avaricious"; and secondly, the use of the frame story of a conference of sages or representatives of nationalities. I shall try to show that both these points indicate a Persian origin to this story.

1 Cf. Grignaschi 1965/66; 1967; and 1975, and the criticism of Manzalaoui 1974, p. 162.

2 Grignaschi 1975, p. 97f. *

3 Badawī 1954, p. 73. A Hebrew version is in Gaster 1928, III, p. 249.

To take the first point first, the terms "generous" and "avaricious" are often attested in Pahlavi literature; an examination of their significance in Pahlavi may help to determine more precisely their use in this Arabic passage. In *Dēnkard* VI 78, a text of Zoroastrian wisdom literature, a list of positive and negative qualities is discussed; their presence in an individual signifies that his person serves as a habitation for the corresponding deity or demon associated with them. Thus a person whose body is inhabited by Wahman is considered to be ardent as regards good works, to have good relationship with the good, to be easy in making peace, to be an advocate of the destitute good, and to be himself generous (*ud xwad rād bawēd*). The opposite type of man, one whose body is inhabited by Akōman, is said to be cool as regards good works, to have bad relationship with the good, to be difficult in making peace, to be an adversary of the destitute good, and to be himself [avaricious] (*ud xwad [pan] bawēd*).[4] The correspondence between the Arabic passage and the Pahlavi text is particularly striking when we notice the peculiar expression *xwad rād* (or *pan*) *bawēd* "he is himself generous (or avaricious)", with which we may associate in Arabic the expression *sakiyy* (or *la'īm*) *'alā nafsihi*. To lead a miserly life when one possesses wealth is considered in Zoroastrian writings to be wrong;[5] hence a story which attributes a tolerant attitude towards avarice by Greeks and Indians has a clear ethnic implication. It may be further remarked that generosity is sometimes defined in Pahlavi literature in a transferred sense as the action of surrendering oneself to the gods solely for the sake of religion and for the love of the soul,[6] which are notions indicating religious devotion. It is therefore possible to suggest that the expression "being generous with oneself" was understood in the Zoroastrian context as denoting piety, with the opposite sense for avarice. The terms "generous" and "avaricious" are thus loaded with meaning in Zoroastrian writings, and some of this seems to be implied in the passage in Arabic which in all likelihood derives from an Iranian sources.

Another passage in Arabic literature, also undoubtedly deriving from Sasanian literature, plays on the opposition between "generous" and "avaricious", giving them a symbolic significance:

> There are four (kinds of) people: beneficent, avaricious, a squanderer, and a moderate spender. A beneficent person is one who spends the whole of his share of this world in the interest of the other world. An avaricious person is one who does not give to any of them its

4 Shaked 1979, p. 28ff., with notes ad loc.

5 *Dk* VI C32.

6 *Dk* VI 91.

share. A squanderer is one who spends it all for the sake of the present world. A moderate spender is one who gives each one its (proper) share.[7]

The scheme of this saying is typically Iranian: it is built on a four-term correspondence, in which there are two "middle" positive qualities, flanked at the two sides by the negative attributes of excess in each direction. Thus the qualities of the generous, or beneficent, person, and that of the moderate spender, or economizer (*jawād* and *muqtaṣid* respectively) are both considered positive and within the right measure (*paymān*), while on the one hand there is the excess of waste or squandering (*musrif*) and on the other that of avarice (*bak̲īl*).[8] The figurative sense given to these qualities also reflects good Iranian practice: it is the task of the good Zoroastrian to find the right middle way in conformity with the measure, so as to achieve a balance between this world (in Pahlavi: *gētīg*) and the next (*mēnōg*).[9] By its structure, the passage belongs to a group of passages which classify people into symmetrical groups. A similar saying, with four divisions, exists in Ibn al-Muqaffa''s *al-adab al-ṣaġīr*, and its Pahlavi original is fortunately extant.[10]

A further consideration for identifying the motif of the four kings as an original Persian story is the fact that it forms part of a much larger group of sayings on the same theme. A famous story of this type concerns the relative merit of speech and silence. One version of it may be rendered as follows:

> Four kings spoke four words as if they had been shot from a single bow. Kisrā said: I am better able to retrieve something which I have not said than something which I have said. The Indian king said: If I speak a word it possesses me and I do not possess it.[11] Caesar said: I have not regretted something I have not said, but have regretted something that I have said. The Chinese king said: The result of something over which words have been spoken is graver than the regret over abstention from speaking.[12]

7 Ibn al-Muqaffa', *AṢ*, p. 30; quoted also by Manzalaoui, p. 165, 206.

8 This is a subject I hope to discuss in detail elsewhere.

9 Cf. Shaked 1979, p. xxxivf.

10 *AṢ*, p. 26f.

11 Of the versions mentioned in the next note, I am here following Ibn Qutayba and Māwardī. Jāḥiẓ, Bayhaqī and Ibn 'Arabī have "It possesses me even though I possess it" (*wa-in kuntu amlikuhā*). Iṣbahānī has: "If I say it, it possesses me; if I do not, I possess it".

12 In the main this is the text of Jāḥiẓ, *Maḥāsin*, 17. Other occurrences of the passage: Bayhaqī, *Maḥāsin* II, 115; Ibn al-'Arabī, *Muḥāḍara* II, 308; *Waṣāyā*, 283; Iṣbahānī, *Ḥilya* VIII, 170; Māwardī, *Tashīl* (I am indebted to Dr. Y. Sadan for permission to use his photocopy of this manuscript); Zandawaysitī, fol. 348b, has a version which places the *

In at least one of the sources where this passage is quoted it is explicitly stated to derive from "Persian books" (*kutub al-'ajam*),[13] but even without such a statement it is pretty obvious that the story is of Persian origin. We need only observe that it places Kisrā at the top of the list,[14] almost with no textual variation, although there are numerous variants as far as the contents of what is attributed to each king are concerned.

The same pattern of four nations discussing a single topic occurs elsewhere too in the Arabic *adab* books. Thus we have them discuss rhetoric (*balāga*), where the Persian king comes prominently either first or last, and the other participants are a Greek (*yūnānī*), a Byzantine (*rūmī*), and an Indian (*hindī*).[15] In contrast we may quote another fourfold discussion, of obvious Muslim origin. It is concerned with medicine: each one of the participants tries to answer the question what medicament there is which causes no harm to health. Those taking part are an Iraqi, a Byzantine, an Indian and a Sawādī,[16] and the conference was held at the court of Hārūn al-Rašīd. The same literary pattern was thus perpetuated in the Islamic period, in imitation of the Sasanian model.

The anecdotes referred to so far are short and pithy. There are some texts however which have longer threefold or fourfold discussions, and in which larger theoretical problems were raised. One such text occurs in *Yatīmat al-sulṭān* by Ibn al-Muqaffa',[17] and it recounts a debate between three people on the relative preeminence of intelligence (*'aql*), sovereignty

final word in the mouth of the Indian king (who says something different from the other versions), and where it is noted, on the authority of 'Abdallāh b. al-Mubārak, that the Indian king spoke well. Kisrā's saying is sometimes quoted separately, outside the frame-story; cf. e.g. Ābī, *Naṯr*, fol. 26b (I am grateful to M.J. Kister for the last three references). This idea, as so many others, was used by Ibn al-Muqaffa' without attribution when he states: "It is better to retract silence than to retract speech" (*fa-inna l-rujū'a 'ani l-ṣamti aḥsanu min al-rujū'i 'ani l-kalām*. Cf. *AK*, p. 53). The four sayings, without ethnic attribution, occur in a Geniza fragment in Judeo-Arabic which contains part of an *adab* book: Jewish Theological Seminary, New York, ENA 957f. 7b. Cf. also Ja'far b. Šams al-Ḵilāfa, *Ādāb*, p. 49.

13 Ibn Qutayba, *'Uyūn* II.

14 Māwardī (the manuscript of which shows signs of poor transmission) is the only exception I have noted.

15 Jāḥiẓ, *Bayān* I, 88; Bayhaqī, *Maḥāsin* II, 119. In both these versions there seem to be traces of an original frame-story which is lost. Each one of the participants is referred to with the article *al-*, as if he has already been spoken of before. Ḥunayn ibn Isḥāq has the same story in his *Ādāb al-falāsifa*; cf. the Hebrew version in Alḥarizi, *Musre*, p. 11 (chapter 12). The distinction between "Greek" (*yūnānī*) and "Byzantine" (*rūmī*) occurs also with regard to languages and is hard to explain; cf. Plessner 1954/5, p. 62f. and 68. In the discussion of the languages no attention seems to have been paid to the fact that these designations are also used for ethnic distinctions.

16 Bayhaqī, *Maḥāsin* I, 474.

17 Kurd 'Alī, p. 169.

(*dawla*) and health (*'āfiya*). Each one of these concepts is then represented by a human form which serves as a spokesman for it, as in some kind of allegory. Finally there emerges a fourth figure, identified as justice (*'adl*), and described by various physical features corresponding to its essence, in the same way as was done with the other three figures. It serves, appropriately enough, as the arbiter in the dispute, and its judgment consists in deciding that a combination of all three qualities is the most desirable.

There are several reasons for regarding this debate as of Sasanian origin. The personification of abstract notions is an essential feature of Zoroastrian literature from the earliest period.[18] Sasanian examples for such personified concepts are intelligence or wisdom, *xrad*, most particularly in the book *Mēnōg ī xrad*, the Spirit of Wisdom. Other texts have an allegorical flavour, for example *Ardā Wirāz Nāmag,* or *Draxt asūrīg.*[18a] The figure of Justice, the judge, which stands in the middle between the extremes, is also a typical Iranian notion. It may be compared, on the one hand, to *paymān*, the right measure, but on the other it is reminiscent of such judge figures as Mihr, the ancient god Mithra.[18b] This debate seems also to be close in spirit to a group of sayings, often attributed to the Sasanian sage Buzurjmihr (or in Pahlavi Wuzurgmihr), in which the most important things in life are arranged in a descending hierarchical order: intelligence (*'aql*), brethren (*ikwān*, scil. friends), property (*māl*), to which are sometimes added *adab* "education" and *ṣamt* "silence".[19]

Two further stories may be quoted to show the wide diffusion of such stories in Sasanian literature, even though they are mostly attested in Arabic sources only. In a wisdom treatise attributed to King Bahman, three sages are asked to say what in the opinion of each is the most virtuous thing. Their answers are: belittling a favour you do to another, while putting much weight on the small gratitude received; giving favours to a person without being asked; not to be overjoyous at a good thing which has come, and not to be envious by such a thing which has not come (to oneself).[20] The king then adds a fourth word of wisdom, which is supposed to surpass the other three: to withhold oneself from overcoming (one's

[18] Cf. the remarks made on this subject in Shaked, *Acta Orientalia* 33 (1971), 77.

[18a] For these works cf. Boyce 1968, pp. 48f., 55, and for *MX*, op. cit., p. 54.

[18b] Cf. Shaked 1980.

[19] Jāḥiẓ, *Bayān* I, 221, 7; Māwardī, *Adab*, 31; Abū l-Ḥasan 'Alī, *'Ayn al-adab*, 103. A somewhat similar frame-story is in ps.-Aṣma'ī, *Nihāya*, fols. 197b-198b, where it is said that after other wise men failed to satisfy the king, he turned to Buzurjmihr for his words. Cf. above, Section 1, note 24.

[20] This idea is expressed in *Dk* VI 2.

foe), even though one has the power. A further and more excellent phrase is then added: to accept with forbearance an offensive word from lowly people, and to be merciful when one has the power.[21] Our final example is taken from Ḥunayn ibn Isḥāq's *Ādāb al-falāsifa*: Four philosophers gathered at the court of Anūširwān, each one saying a word which summarizes all wisdom. What they said is: silence is the best wisdom; the best thing is wisdom; the best thing is to distrust the good things of this world; the best thing is to acquiesce with the decree of fate.[22]

We can thus see how popular this type of saying was with Persian authors of the Sasanian period and subsequently with Muslim compilers. The number of variations within the basic frame story is endless. We have already alluded to one type within this general pattern: the stories in which the speakers represent different nations, as in the passage which served as our starting-point, and as in the debate concerning silence. In the latter instance, it may be recalled, the peoples represented were Persians, Indians, Byzantines and Chinese, a division of mankind which could not be later than the end of the Sasanian period: we may notice that the Arabs do not figure there at all. Even where they do, in some lists, their position is such as to suggest that they are not a dominant power.[23] In the fictional context of the Aristotelian correspondence with Alexander, which pretends to be Greek by origin, the world is composed of Persians, whose prominent quality is courage; of the people of the East (i.e. Chinese or Turks), whose quality is chivalry; of Byzantines, whose gift is craftsmanship; and of Indians, who excel in wisdom.[24] Here again the period is certainly pre-Islamic, and the milieu in which it was composed is in all likelihood Sasanian. An Islamic adaptation of this saying does exist. It maintains that the Byzantines excel in their brain, the Indians in their phantasy, the Greeks in their soul, and the Arabs in their tongue.[25] The Sasanian division of the world among nations is directly extant in the *Letter of Tansar*, where
* the world consists of Turks, Indians, Byzantines and Persians, each one of which is endowed with a special quality similar to those mentioned in the pseudo-Aristotelian composition.[26]

21 Miskawayhi, *JX*, 62f.

22 Cf. Alḥarizi, p. 12; Spanish version, p. 69. Parallels in Ms. Köprülü 1608, fol. 13a; Ms. Munich Arab. 651, fol. 4, according to Badawī, introduction to Miskawayhi, *JX* p. 40; Merkle 1921, p. 60, No. 19; Gutas 1975, p. 44.

23 Zamakšarī, *Nawābiġ*, fol. 71a; Jāḥiẓ, Bayān I, 384, 137.

24 Gutas 1975, p. 182 § 56.

25 Quoted by Goldziher 1967, p. 157 note 2 from al-Ṣiddīqī, fol. 148b.

26 Tansar, p. 41, and the text on p. 40, where a slightly different geographical division is given. Cf. Boyce's translation, p. 64 and 63 respectively, with the notes by Minovi and Henning on these passages. Cf. also Ibn al-Faqīh, *Buldān*, p. 197; Ibn 'Abd Rabbihi, *'Iqd*,

In addition to these passages of Sasanian literature which have survived through Islamic intermediaries, we have a text in Pahlavi which seems to preserve an authentic Sasanian version of the same theme, although the manuscript copy of it is late and the text transmitted poor:

> *ēdōn gōwēnd ku rōz-ē frazānag-ē *rōmīg* [27] *ud hindūg ud ādurbād ī mahraspandān pēš ī šāhān-šāh nišast. Framūd ud pursīd ku pad gētīg tan-ē ce weh mad ēstēd. *rōmīg*[27] *guft ku *pādexšā [ī] abē-hamēmār weh. hindūg guft ku juwān-mard [ī pad] xwāstag*[28] *weh. ādurbād guft ku awe [ī] pad gētīg ud mēnōg abē-bīm weh.*
> *didīgar ēn pursīd ku tan-ē kardār wattar. [...]*[29] *hindūg guft ku *mehādar*[30] *ī ne kas ud ne ciš [dārēd] wattar. ādurbād guft ku margīh wattar az pas [ī] druwandīh. ud šāhān-šān guft ku zih.*
> *frazaft pad drōd šādīh ud rāmišn.*[31]

> Thus do they say. One day there sat in front of the King of Kings wise men of Byzantium and of India, and Ādurbād son of Mahraspand. (The king) commanded and asked: What person in the world has come (forth) as best? The Byzantine said: A ruler without an opponent is best. The Indian said: A young man with property is best. Ādurbād said: He who is without fear[32] in this world and the next is best.
> Secondly he asked this: What person is worst (off)? [The Byzantine said:...][29] The Indian said: An old man who [has] no person and no possession is worst (off). Ādurbād said: Death is worst after wicked-

II, p. 4f. (referred to by Minovi, *Tansar*, p. 65f.).

27 MSS *lwmyx*.

28 Asmussen read *gōšn-mart ī xuāstak* "ein junger Mann mit Besitz". While the reading of the first word is faulty, the translation is justified by the parallel of the old man without possession in the second part of the passage.

29 It is obvious that a phrase is missing.

30 MSS *'ms'tww*, which gives no sense. Taking into account the expected contrast with the first part of the passage, the emendation is not too far fetched. For the reading of this word, spelled normally *ms'twl*, cf. Nyberg 1931, p. 151, who reads it *mēštar(īh)*; Henning 1935, p. 17, who suggests *masādwar(īh)*; MacKenzie 1971, p. 55: *mehtar*. My reading follows Pāzand *mehādar*.

31 Royal Library, Copenhagen, Ms. K 20, fol. 152r, published in *Codices* I, 297. Another Ms. is in Bibliothèque Nationale, Paris, Cod. persan 33, which seems to have been copied from the Copenhagen manuscript; cf. Blochet 1898, p. 65, No. XXIX, 14. The text was published in transcription and translation, with a facsimile, by Asmussen 1971, p. 275f.

32 The main connotation of *abē-bīm* is the confidence of a person who is righteous, as pointed out by Asmussen. Cf. *abē-bīmīh ud abē-āmāragīh ī pad ruwān* (*Dk* VI E30a) "lack of fear and lack of reckoning for the soul", two expressions which denote righteousness.

ness.[33] The King of Kings said: Well done!

Completed with blessing, joy and peace.

This is, as Asmussen puts it, "ein bescheidener, anspruchsloser Text". But it provides us with a valuable addition to our collection of versions of the frame-story which gives three or four nationalities the chance to express themselves on one topic, with the final, and most appropriate, word left to the Persian. It is nice to have at least one version of this text in direct transmission in Pahlavi.

The discussion of this frame-story, which has been shown to be Iranian in origin, may give us the opportunity to make two further observations on questions which concern contacts between cultures.

Another version of our frame-story, although without the division into nationalities, occurs as early as the apocryphal third book of Ezra, known also as I Esdras, chapter 3.[34] Professor David Flusser was the first to call my attention to the Persian character of that famous story, which contains statements made by three pages at the court of Darius. One of them says that wine is the strongest thing in the world, the other maintains that it is the king who is strongest, and the third asserts that women are strongest, adding however that truth is above all, and that it bears away the victory. Flusser has argued that the final victory of truth betrays the Persian origin of the story. The Iranian term underlying it may be Avestan *aša-*, Old Persian *arta-*, but is probably more likely to be the Old Persian *rāstam* (n.), continued by MPers. *rāstīh*, usually rendered into Arabic by *al-ṣidq*.[35]

It may be remarked that although only three people are mentioned as taking part in the debate at King Darius' court, four answers are given. One may suppose here an adaptation from a fourfold debate, or a conflation of two stories in which the final word was grafted on one story from another. A similar textual situation exists with regard to the debate at the court of King Bahman, quoted above,[36] where the king himself intervenes and says the final word. The contents of the discussion at the court of King Darius are not known to us from other sources, though the isolated themes themselves, wine, women, and of course the king, are by no means rare in Sasanian court literature.[37] The same would of course also be true of other

33 I.e. it is worst to die while wicked. The alternative interpretation, viz. that wickedness and death are the two worst things, seems less satisfactory.

34 Cf. Charles 1913, I, pp. 29ff.

35 The Arabic expression occurs in Buzurjmihr's list of the most important things for a king; cf. above, Section 1, note 24.

36 Cf. above, note 21.

37 A very common injunction in Sasanian *andarz* is to distrust women and not to tell them secrets; e.g. *PhlT* 59 § 11; 149 § 48f. To be moderate in drinking wine is also a very common theme.

wisdom literatures of the ancient East.[38] That the importance of truth is a prominent Iranian motif is self-evident.[39] It thus seems probable that the story in I Esdras is the oldest preserved version of our four-sages theme in Iran.

We have had occasion to refer to occurrences of a Persian four-sages story in Arabic writings of hellenistic inspiration, like the pseudo-Aristotelian letters to Alexander. These are only some of the cases in which Sasanian literary presence is noticed in those writings. It has been suggested that these are compositions of the Islamic period, written by Sālim Abū l-'Alā', the secretary of Hišām ibn 'Abd al-Malik,[40] on grounds which are not entirely convincing.[41] Without denying the importance of Sālim Abū l-'Alā' and the great share which he may have had in the transmission of this literature in Arabic, it seems probable, as we have seen in the case of Ibn al-Muqaffa', that his role was rather more that of a transmitter than of an innovating writer. It seems perfectly possible that the syncretism of Iranian motifs and stories with hellenistic writings took place in the literary activity which preceded Islam in the border areas of the two great empires, Byzantium and the Sasanians. There are some indications for such Greek-Iranian syncretism in Syriac literature.[42] The Sasanian flavour of the Iranian passages in the pseudo-Aristotelian literature in Arabic suggests a milieu where preoccupation with Greek political thought was coupled together with admiration for the political reality and practice of the Persians, when they were still in full force. By the early Islamic period, the ready presence of an amalgam of hellenistic-Byzantine literature with Iranian-Sasanian elements made it possible to enlarge the scope, and to create compositions in which Arabic and Islamic expressions were added to the existing brew. There is no evidence yet for this process in the pseudo-Aristotelian treatises we have mentioned: they seem to be mere copies into Arabic of originals composed in another language.

38 Cf. Lambert 1960, pp. 99ff., 119f.

39 On *aša* in Zoroaster's prophecy cf. Boyce 1975, 212f.

40 Grignaschi 1965/66 and 1967.

41 A criticism of Grignaschi's hypotheses is to be seen in Manzalaoui 1974, pp. 162ff. One small correction may be suggested to the interpretation of a passage in the *Fihrist* of Ibn al-Nadīm. The Arabic text is: *wa-qad naqala min rasā'ili arisṭāṭālīsa ilā l-iskandari wa-nuqila lahu wa-aṣlaḥa huwa* (p. 117, line 30). Grignaschi 1965/66, p. 12 and 1967, p. 223, translates: "Il a traduit des lettres d'Aristote à Alexandre. On les a traduites pour lui et il les a mises en état". I would rather suggest: "He translated some of the letters of Aristotle to Alexander, (while others) were translated for him and he corrected (the translation)". This does not necessarily affect Grignaschi's thesis.

42 This seems also to be the position of Manzalaoui 1974, p. 161, where extant examples are quoted. In a later date we have Bar Hebraeus, where a similar mixture exists.

APPENDIX

Notes on ibn al-Muqaffaʻ's alleged Manichaeism and some related problems

The question of Ibn al-Muqaffaʻ's *zandaqa* has been the subject of numerous studies. An important aspect of this discussion is how to judge the anti-Muslim treatise attributed to Ibn al-Muqaffaʻ, which was lost in its original but partly known through the refutation of al-Qāsim b. Ibrāhīm.[1] In his introduction to the text, Michelangelo Guidi, the editor of the refutation, accepts the attribution of the Manichaean book to ibn al-Muqaffaʻ, though he cannot decide whether the book was composed before or after Ibn al-Muqaffaʻ's conversion to Islam.[2]

The question is certainly complicated. On the one hand there are unequivocal statements imputing Manichaeism to ibn al-Muqaffaʻ,[3] but on the other other there are some indications, on which I should like to concentrate here, which seem to suggest that Ibn al-Muqaffaʻ's religious adherence before his conversion to Islam was to Zoroastrianism. Most of the writings from Ibn al-Muqaffaʻ's pen derive from, or have affinities with, Sasanian court literature, which was impregnated with the Zoroastrian spirit. This includes, for the present purpose, *Kalīla wa-Dimna*, which, though ultimately deriving from India, represents the type of literature used by Sasanian court circles. Zoroastrianism is also the religion which underlies the anecdote told of Ibn al-Muqaffaʻ according to which he performed the *zamzama*, or Zoroastrian prayer, on the eve of his conversion to Islam, "in order not to stay without a religion for even a single night",[4] as he put it. It matters little for our present discussion if we interpret this anecdote seriously or in irony, as suggested by some scholars,[5] or even if we take it as completely apocryphal; in the latter case, at least in the eyes of those who told the story he was considered to be a Zoroastrian. The term *zamzama*, like the corresponding Syriac and Aramaic *reṭnā*, so far as we know, are only applied to Zoroastrian prayers.[6] It may further be recalled, as mentioned above, that even Ibn al-Muqaffaʻ's

[1] Guidi 1927, where *Kitāb al-radd ʻalā l-zindīq al-laʻīn ibn al-muqaffaʻ* is published.

[2] Op. cit., p. XIII note 1. The question is of course also of some importance in connection with the problem of what religion Ibn al-Muqaffaʻ professed before his conversion.

[3] Bīrūnī, *Taḥqīq*, p. 123; and again, op. cit. p. 220. ʻAbd al-Jabbār, *Taṯbīt*, I, p. 71 accuses Ibn al-Muqaffaʻ of being a *majūs*, i.e. Zoroastrian. See further note 10 below.

[4] Ibn Ḵallikān II, p. 125, quoted by Gabrieli 1931/32, p. 237 note 5. Cf. also Goitein 1966, p. 151 note 1, where the story is quoted from the manuscript of *Ansāb al-ašrāf*, and where it is assumed that *zamzama* may indicate Manichaean prayers.

[5] Gabrieli, loc. cit.

[6] Cf. Goldziher 1967, p. 157 note 4. The latest comprehensive treatment of this term is by Greenfield 1974, where, on p. 65 note 8, the material relating to *zamzama* is mentioned.

original works, notably *al-adab al-ṣaġīr*, are replete with unacknowledged quotations from Zoroastrian religious literature.[7]

One of the prominent issues around the question of Ibn al-Muqaffa''s *zandaqa* is the stand one takes on the question of who composed the introduction to *Kalīla wa-Dimna*, attributed to the Sasanian physician Burzōya.[8] Nöldeke expressed the opinion that although the text of the introduction bears generally the marks of a Sasanian composition, Ibn al-Muqaffa' was not a mere translator, but incorporated in the text interpolations which reflect his own attitudes in religious matters.[9] Such an imputation had aleady been made in earlier times by al-Bīrūnī.[10] Paul Kraus has made it clear, however, that the passage about the weakness of the religions, which Nöldeke suspected of being an interpolation of Ibn al-Muqaffa', may be regarded as Sasanian no less than the rest of Burzōya's introduction, for it has a very close parallel in another composition of the Sasanian period: the Syriac treatise on logic by Paul Persa, a philosopher who was active in the court of Khusrau Anūširwān.[11] Kraus's observation can gain further support from literature written in Pahlavi, as I shall endeavour to show.

To clarify this issue it would be well first to summarize briefly the main outline of Burzōya's introduction. It may be characterized as a schematic autobiography of spiritual quest. The author undergoes a privileged intellectual education, and finds himself faced with the choice of the pursuit of one of four aims: wealth, pleasure, fame, or the other world. He opts for the fourth possibility, and selects medicine as his vocation. He strives with his soul in order to direct it towards matters of the world to come. He then

[7] Cf. above, Section 1, note 4.

[8] An extreme position would deny all historicity to Burzōya and would consequently regard Ibn al-Muqaffa' as the author of this introduction, which he attributed to a fictitious character. This is the position of E. Denison Ross in his foreward to Penzer 1968, pp. xif., xxxi. This position is untenable as has been shown by Iqbal 1926, pp. 46ff.; Iqbal however maintains that Ibn al-Muqaffa' is the author of this introduction, cf. op. cit. p. 50f. Christensen 1930 would identify Burzōya with Buzurjmihr, a suggestion which seems gratuitous on the basis of the available knowledge. Cf. also Christensen 1929.

[9] Nöldeke 1912; followed by Gabrieli 1931/32, p. 202.

[10] Bīrūnī, *Taḥqīq*, p. 123, according to which Ibn al-Muqaffa' wrote Burzōya's introduction so as to introduce doubts into his readers' hearts and to sway them towards Manichaeism. The passage was first referred to by Iqbal 1926, p. 45. As mentioned above (note 3), a similar attack was made by 'Abd al-Jabbār, *Taṯbīt* I, p. 71, where Ibn al-Muqaffa' is said to have invented writings which he attributed to the Persians, because he had been a Magian before his conversion, and he remained a partisan of his national origins and suspect in his Islamic religion. In both these cases we seem to have slanderous accusations, which are not necessarily facts.

[11] Kraus 1934, pp. 14ff.

perceives that religion can secure more permanent liberation from pain than does medicine, and notices that most people are divided into three classes in respect to religion: those who follow their forbears; those who practise religion out of external constraint; and those who pursue worldly objects through the practice of religion. He seeks direction from the leaders of the various religions, each of whom extols his own tradition. The difficulty of reconciling their conflicting claims makes it possible to feel that if one followed the wrong direction one would be badly deluded.[12] This point is sharply illustrated by the tale of the thieves who fall prey to a trick played upon them by the man in whose house they wanted to steal: he causes them to believe that he possesses a magic word, having learnt which they use it and break their necks.[13] Burzōya then recounts how he first followed the religion of his ancestors: the idea of doing so is rejected by the argument that an immoderate eater can equally well justify himself by claiming to follow his father. A story which illustrates the foolishness of blind and literal acceptance of instructions is here inserted. At this point Burzōya discovers that dedication to do good works is of lasting benefit: this is supported by the story of the man who hired a pearl-borer but distracted him from his true work by bidding him play the cymbals.[14] Despite the hardships, abstention and total dedication (*nusk*) is the only answer to his problem, Burzōya decides. This thought is fortified by a consideration of the state of the world, illustrated by a parable: a man has fled from some danger and has fallen into a pit, where he hangs by holding on to two branches which descend from above, and which are being gnawed constantly by a black and a white rat. Underneath a dragon is ready to devour him with a wide open mouth, and his feet rest on stones behind which four serpents lurk. His attention is momentarily being diverted from this horrifying situation by honey produced by a bee hive near by.[15] Such is the

[12] It must be pointed out that the tenor of this passage is not one of scepticism: the implication seems to be that there is a religious truth behind the claims superficially made by the spokesmen for the religions.

[13] The story's point is surely that one should distrust the naive claim that it is sufficient to learn a formula in order to obtain the treasures of the other world. That the author of this trick is the housemaster himself (i.e. God, or the priests), adds a tinge of irony to the story. The supposed magic word is *šūlīm*, which Nöldeke 1912, p. 16 note 2, connects with some hesitation with Hebrew *šālōm*. It seems however possible to explain it as Syriac *šōlīm* "completion, end", in which an additional ironic hint may have been intended. For the Syriac word cf. Payne-Smith, *Thesaurus*, col. 4188; Schulthess 1903, p. 208, and Black 1954, p. 71.

[14] It may be noted that the story is known in a Sogdian version, evidently used by Manichaeans (though this does not necessarily mean that it was an exclusively Manichaean story). Cf. Henning 1943/46, pp. 465ff.

[15] The same story occurs in *Bilawhar wa-Būḏasf*. A Persian version is given by Oldenburg

human condition.

In commenting on this autobiography, it may be well to note that the impression one gets from scholars' discussions of this text is somewhat misleading. It has been unjustly described as sceptical or rationalistic;[16] I believe however that it represents the attitude of a man of deep faith who is not content with the externals of traditional religion and seeks a more profound expression for his religious feelings. This he finds in abstention from the delusions of this world and in total devotion. In Islamic terms his attitude can be described as analogical to *zuhd*.

This mode of thinking does not go against the existing religion any more than does all quest for deep faith. Such quest implies an element of criticism against the ways of this world, including those of the mundane religion. Examples for this are found in Judaism, Christianity and Islam alike; they are quite characteristic of the Indian religious tradition, which may indeed have influenced the approach of the present treatise; and they are by no means alien to Sasanian Zoroastrianism. Although the language used here is somewhat stronger than that which we are accustomed to find in the surviving Pahlavi literature, certain expressions there are not far from those of Burzōya. Even the censure of carriers of the official religion for indulgence in material pleasures is not lacking in Pahlavi writings.[17] Certain passages there betray extreme distrust of the things of this world, which the deeply religious should avoid and abandon.[18] Some motifs in this text have survived elsewhere in the Islamic transmission as part of the Iranian heritage.[19]

To illustrate the point that Sasanian literature contains within it passages of pessimism with regard to things of this world, and gloomy thoughts about the short duration of man's life and the impermanence of

1889; the Ismaili Arab text is in Stern 1971, pp. 35f. (cf. pp. 12ff. for the history of the text), and Gimaret 1973. Cf. also Gimaret 1971, p. 88 and the detailed introduction on the history of the text. Philonenko 1972, p. 258, has recently dealt with the diffusion of this theme.

16 Gabrieli 1931/32, pp. 202f., calls this passage "scettico"; Guidi 1927, p. IX, speaks of "freddo razionalismo".

17 Cf. *Dk* VI D3, D5.

18 *Dk* VI B47: It is necessary to walk (in the world) with such circumspection as if one were a man without shoes, and as if the whole of this world were full of snakes, scorpions, noxious reptiles and thorns, etc. A summary of such attitudes to this world is given in Shaked 1979, pp. xxxiv ff.

19 Somewhat reminiscent of the parable in Burzōya's introduction is the riddle in the Zāl section of Firdawsī, *ŠN* I, pp. 218ff.; cf. Zaehner 1955, pp. 444ff. I do not know why Zaehner 1955, pp. 242ff., feels constrained to regard this as a Zurvanite text. It is an ancient theme, not necessarily Iranian (cf. note 15 above), and has Sasanian cognates which are not necessarily Zurvanite, like the one discussed in note 18. The time symbolism is reminiscent of the Burzōya parable, which derives from India.

his memory after death, we may quote the opening lines of a wisdom treatise attributed to the Sasanian sage Wuzurgmihr, who flourished in the court of Khusrau Anūširwān:

> ceōn xīr ī gētīg hamāg sazišnīgīh ud wišōbišnīgīh ud wardišnīgīh, awe-z ke gēhān wišād u-š jahišn pad-eš dast dahēd, tuxšišn-ez ī a-ranjīhā aweš friyādēd, stabr xīr handōzēd ud ō mahist kār ud pādexšāyīh rasēd, abar-tomīhā kunēd ud wuzurg-tom nām xwāhēd, ud nāmīgīhā-tom kār, afrōzišnīh ī mān ud mēhan kunēd, u-š drāz zīndagīh ud abzāyišn ī frazand ud paywand ī wuzurg-ummēdīh ud nēwag jahišnīh pad kār ud dādestān, ud abārīg-ez hamāg farroxīh ī andar gētīg ēwag ō did gugāh ud ham-dādestān, pad ōstīgānīh ī hān and ciš dūr-menīdār-tom. ud ka ērag-tom andar drahnāy ī 100 sāl tan ō frazām ud pādexšāyīh ō nēstīh, ud andar drahnāy ī 400 sāl dūdag ō wišōbišn, nām ō frāmōšīh ud an-ayādīh, ud mān ud mēhan ō abē-rānīh ud ālūdagīh, ud nāf ud paywand ō frōdarīh ud abaxšīh, ud tuxšišn ō abē-barīh, ud ranj ud bār ō tuhīgīh, ud pādexšāyīh ō āwām-xwadāyān, xīr ō awe ne mānēd... (*PhlT* 85f.)[20]

> For the whole matter of this world is transience, decay and changeability. Even he to whom the world is widely open, and to whom fortune gives a hand in this matter, to whom diligence helps even without effort, who amasses considerable wealth and attains to the highest degree of power, who performs supreme deeds and seeks the greatest name, who performs the deed most conducive to the preservation of (one's) name: the setting up of house and offspring, and who has long life, abundance of progeny and kinship, which is of great hope, and who has good fortune in his actions, and all other (kinds of) happiness which are witness to each other and in agreement with each other in this world — (that man) with regard to the stability of these several things thinks too far. At the lowest, within a span of a hundred years (his) body (comes) to an end, his power to nought; within a span of four hundred years his family reaches decay, his name comes to oblivion and falls out of memory, his house comes to desolation and pollution, his kin and family become degenerate and ruined, his diligence ends up in being barren, his toil and trouble become void, his sovereignty passes over to petty rulers, and the matter does not rest with him...

The Arabic version of this text, which is fortunately extant, gives a rendering which preserves its full flavour, though it is somewhat abridged.[21]

20 Full apparatus is to be given in the forthcoming edition of this text.
21 Miskawayhi, *JX*, p. 29.

Much similar ideas are reflected in the two famous political writings of the Sasanian period, preserved only through Islamic intermediaries: the *Letter of Tansar* and the *Testament of Ardašīr*. They both purport to be of the initial period of the Sasanian dynasty, but there is no unanimity among scholars whether this claim can be accepted.[22] These writings are pragmatic in tone and address themselves to concrete problems rather than to universal truths, in contrast to the *Ayādgār ī Wuzurgmihr*, from which we have just quoted the opening text, which is a religious wisdom treatise; nevertheless they contain phrases which are quite close in spirit to the ones in Wuzurgmihr's composition.

Thus, the optimistic and confident mood of Ardašīr's *Testament*, as befits a great king and founder of dynasty, gives way to apocalyptic knowledge that the end is bad (though it is hard to tell from the text whether this is considered to lie in the near future):

> I have left to you my views, as I cannot leave behind my body... If it were not certain that at the end of a thousand years perdition comes, I would think that I have left you with something which by your clinging to it would constitute the sign of your stay for as long as time continues, provided you do not prefer something else for it, and that you cling to it. However, when the time of the annihilation comes, you will obey your whims, and you will give power to your views, and you will be shifted from your ranks, and you will disobey the best ones among you, and obey the worst ones. The lesser things that you will trample underfoot will be like a ladder towards greater things, so that you will disjoin what we have made firm, and waste away what we have preserved...[23]

This is of course part of the general millennial view of the Zoroastrian religion. This is such a common theme in Zoroastrianism, that I cannot see how any one can try and deduce from it a clue to the book's date of composition.[24] The passage corresponds pretty closely to several texts

[22] Cf. Minovi 1311, pp. y'-yh, who quotes approvingly the opinions of Christensen and Marquart, placing the composition at the time of Khusrau. Boyce 1968b, pp. 11ff., has argued that the main body of the text, to the exclusion of certain interpolations, is a composition of the third century. As for the *Testament of Ardašīr*, Grignaschi 1966, p. 3, places it in the period of the last Sasanian king, Yazdigird III, by arguments which seem insufficient. I cannot see in the text any aid for positive dating, and certainly nothing against a fairly early Sasanian date. When affinities between the two documents are noted, as is done by Grignaschi and others, it is by no means evident to my mind that the *Letter of Tansar* borrowed from the *Testament of Ardašīr*, and not the other way round; the affinities can be accounted for also by assuming that both were composed in the same milieu.

[23] *Testament of Ardašīr*, ed. IA, p. 89f.

[24] For the millennial theme: *ZWY* ch. IV; *GBd* in *Zand-Ākāsīh* ch. XXXIII. Both texts were

which are extant in Pahlavi, of which the following presents some interest and has not been correctly rendered so far:

> hān ī ēn hazārag sar *ka[25] wehīh[26] nihang ud wattarīh a-mar, ud mazdēsnīh *ōzārag dēn, ud a-dādīh frahist dād, ud dēn uskārišn ī wehān ud frārōn-kunišnān [ud] xwēš-kārān šudag, ud kerdag ī ahreman ud dēwān āškārag, ceōn-šān ēn daxšag, abāz-wirāyišnīh ī zamān, absihēnišn ī mihrān-druzān ud dēw-ez-bahrān [ud] dēn-hamēstārān, rastārīh umēdīh [ī] weh-dahišnān az aždahāgān-ez *tā paywastārīh ī kišwarān (ī) ohrmazd-dēdestān, *ēdōn harw kas pad wahman āštīh mehēnīšn, ud pad dēn āfrāh ī xrad pursišn, [ud] pad xrad rāh ī ahlāyīh wizōyišn, [ud] pad rāh ī rādīh ruwān urwāzēnišn, ud pad hu-cašmīh *wehīh burzēnišn, ud pad hunar nām xwāhišn, ud pad ērmenišnīh dōst handōzišn, ud pad bāristānīh umēd *paywandēnišn, [ud] pad xēm wehīh handōzišn, ud pad ahlāyīh rāh ī rōšn garōdmān wirāyišn ...[27]
>
> The end of this millennium is *when goodness (will be) little and evil without number, (when) Mazdaeanism will be a tiny[28] religion and illegality the main law, when consultation over religion with good people, with those who perform righteousness and who do their duty has ceased, and the action of Ahreman and the demons becomes manifest. Just as this is their sign: the restitution of the time, the destruction of covenant-breakers, of demon-associates and of opposers of the religion, the hope of escape for the good creations from (the hold of) the dragons, so that the lands may perpetuate the law of Ohrmazd — so it is incumbent on every person to enlarge peace through Wahman, to enquire the precepts of wisdom through religion, to seek the way of righteousness through wisdom, to cause joy to (one's) soul by way of generosity, to elevate goodness by benevolence, to seek fame by virtue, to collect friends by modesty, to perpetuate hope by forbearance, to accumulate goodness by (good) character, and to pave the road of the bright paradise by righteousness.

The gloomy perception of the end of the millennium is here used for exhortation to the members of the communty to do their utmost to

composed in the ninth century, though they certainly conserve earlier themes.

25 MSS *MNW* = ke.

26 Here and in the following, the words marked by a cross represent a reading based on the variants in *PhlT* and in Freiman 1906.

27 *PhlT* 49, PN § 54. Translated in Zaehner 1956, p. 27; Kanga 1960, p. 29; Freiman 1906, p. 277f.; § 43-44; Nyberg 1928, pp. 28f. (an edition of the text); Corbin 1951; Nawabi 1339.

28 For *ōzārag* cf. Sundermann 1973, p. 126 s.v. *hwz'rk*.

enhance the power of good in the world. Here again it would be idle to speculate about the possible date of this composition by its allusion to the end: one imagines that at almost any point of time during the Sasanian period the rigorously devout may have harboured similar sentiments, and the same may be argued for the early Islamic period (though the optimism of the section may have found little to support it in Islamic times).

A fairly important element in the *Testament of Ardašīr* is the emphasis on the need to have no trust in the vagaries of fortune. A king may get drunk by his reign and forget "the misfortunes, failures, changes of fortune and movements of the sphere, the atrocity of the oppression of time, the stinginess of the reign of the period", the *Testament* says. "As a result he gives free rein to his hand and tongue in speech and action,[29] and our early [sages] have said: When one is confident of one's good fortune in time, the changes of fortune take place".[30] Sentiments of a similar kind are found in the *Letter of Tansar* with regard to the decay of family in time,[31] and the final thwarting of effort,[32] as well as about the strong position of fate with regard to human endeavour.[33] The expression of human frailty with regard to fate is extremely common in Zoroastrian literature as well as in the literature derived from it and influenced by it.[34] The Zoroastrian religion has a positive attitude towards human activity in this world, but it is exaggerated to characterize it, as Theodor Nöldeke once did, "das lebensfrohe Mazdajasniertum".[35]

Coming back to our starting point, there are Sasanian analogies to the spiritual quest autobiography which constitutes the structure of Burzōya's introduction to *Kalīla wa-Dimna*. Although the analogies are but partial, they help to set the composition in its Sasanian context. The analogies are: Mani's comparison of his own religion to those of his predecessors, and his claim that his religion avoids the pitfalls of the others;[36] Mardān-Farrux, in

29 We have here an echo to the well-known Zoroastrian triad of thought, speech and action.

30 IA, p. 49f.; MG, p. 46.

31 *Tansar*, p. 19; Boyce 1968b, p. 44.

32 *Tansar*, p. 44f.; Boyce 1968b, p. 67f.

33 *Tansar*, p. 45; Boyce 1968b, p. 68.

34 Particularly in *MX* and by late reflection in Firdawsī, *ŠN*. Cf. Ringgren 1952.

35 Nöldeke 1912, p. 5 note 1.

36 Cf. Andreas and Henning 1933, pp. 295f. Mani's attitude towards his predecessors is also expressed in the Cologne Mani codex, where he seems to act towards the sect he grew up in in imitation of the way Jesus acted with the Pharisees. Cf. CMC 80, 16-18 and 87, 19-21 in Henrichs and Koenen 1978, pp. 100f., 106f.; Henrichs and Koenen 1970, p. 138f.; Henrichs 1973, pp. 51f. Cf. also Waldschmidt and Lentz 1926, pp. 59f. The most distinguished example of such an autobiography is of course Augustine's *Confessions*, and, in a later period, Ghazālī's *al-Munqiḏ min al-ḍalāl*.

a Pahlavi work of the ninth century, describes how he examined the other religions with the aim of finding the truth, and how Zoroastrianism proved to be the answer;[37] the text of a "Poem in praise of wisdom" also uses the theme of the search for truth, which is ultimately found in wisdom (not in conventional religion);[38] and the beginning of *Mēnōg ī Xrad*, which contains the same motif.[39]

[37] ã mən [i] mardã-frōxa i hōrməzd-dāt hom īn pasāžašni kard cun mən dīt̰ andar ōγãm vas-sardaī vas-dīnī vas-xvaškārašnī i kəšã u *ã-um andar ham awarnāedārī haṃvār taftī-manišnihā xvāstār vazōstār i rāstī būt̰ hom. ham cim rã ō-ca vas-kəšvar u zrih vīmand farnaft hom. vaem īn angirdī gawəešnã *yaš hast pursašni i rāstī-kāmagã ažaš əž niwə̄ i ayādagār i pə̄šīnī dānāgã [u] rāstã dastūrã ud nãmcišt ã i hūfarward ādarpād [i] *ayāwandã *cīd *vazīd ō īn ayādagār ã [i] škand-gumānī-vazār nām nahāt̰ (*ŠGV* I. 35ff.; Menasce 1945, p. 26). "I, who am Mardān-Farrox son of Hormizd-dād, have made this composition, because I have seen in the world the (division) of the faiths into many sects, many religions and many opinions. I have been even in my youth a seeker and searcher for truth, constantly with fervent mind. For this reason I have travelled even to many countries and to the limits of the seas. I have collected and selected these summary sayings, from which (comes) the enquiry of those who desire truth, from books (containing) memoranda of the early sages and of the true authorities, in particular those of the venerable Ādurbād son of *Ayāband, into this memorandum, the one which I have called the Resolver of Trenchant Doubts". Asterisks denote departures from the printed text. The above rendering differs in some points from previous attempts by West and Menasce. The reading of the name *Ayābandān follows basically that of Justi, *Iranisches Namenbuch*, s.v. Ātarəpāt, Yāwand.

[38] Cf. Shaked 1969b, pp. 401f., and 1980, text No. XXXI. It begins: "I have travelled much in the world, I have moved much (in) region after region. Much have I enquired of the sacred word of the religion, much have I learned from scriptures and books".

[39] The text is as follows:

> ud ka pad ēd rāyēnišn abar nigerīd, pad xrad xwāstārīh andar ēn gēhān šahr šahr ud pāygōs pāygōs franaft, ud az was kēš ud warrawišn awēšān mardomān ī-šān pad dānāgīh abēr-tar menīd pursīd ud wizust ud abar *mad. ud ka dīd ku ēwag andar did ēdōn hanbasān ud hamēmār hēnd ēg dānist ku ēn kēš ud warrawišn ud jud-ristagīh ī pad ēn gēhān ēwag andar did ēdōn hanbasān hēnd ne az dahišn ī yazdān sazēd *būdan, ce yazdān dēn rāstīh ud dād frārōnīh. ud pad ēn abē-gumān būd ku harw ce ne pad ēn abēzag dēn ēg-šān pad harw ciš gumānīgīh ud pad hamāg cim šēbišn wēnēnd (*MX* I, 34-41).
>
> And when he observed this arrangement, he went forth in the world in search of wisdom from kingdom to kingdom and from province to province, and enquired, examined and comprehended concerning the several faiths and beliefs of those people whom he considered foremost in knowledge. And when he saw that they are contradictory and antagonistic with regard to each other, he knew that these faiths and beliefs and separate sects which are so contradictory in this world with regard to each other are not fit to be derived from reflection on the gods, for the religion of the gods is truth and their law is righteousness. He was confident as to the following, namely that people see in all those things which are not in this pure religion uncertainty in every thing and confusion in every reason.

In conclusion, I can see no evidence to suggest that Ibn al-Muqaffa' manipulated the literary Iranian materials which he used so as to introduce his own personal views into the text. Even when he addressed himself to concrete questions of his period he seems to have employed the traditional Iranian lore of which he was, in Islam, such a prominent carrier. His material, as far as it can be identified in detail, is writings which circulated in the Sasanian court. In some cases these writings can be identified as part of Zoroastrian literature. In none have they been identified as specifically Manichaean.

In the phrase *dahišn ī yazdān* the term *dahišn* seems to possess the sense "reflection", discussed by me in an article contributed to the forthcoming *Morgenstierne Memorial Volume* [*Acta Iranica,* Leiden 1982, 197ff.]

It may be remarked that the phrase *šahr šahr pāygōs pāygōs franaft* and the whole style of the passage are very close to that which is found in *ŠGV* I, 35ff. (cf. above, note 35), and also to the phrasing in the "Poem in praise of wisdom" referred to in note 36 (the translation of which gains in force by the parallels). The last sentence in our passage is probably slightly corrupt, but Anklesaria's reading of **ke* for *ce* does not greatly improve the syntax.

BIBLIOGRAPHICAL REFERENCES

Abbreviations for Pahlavi texts will be found in Shaked 1979.

Abbas, I., *'Ahd Ardašir,* Beirut 1967.
'Abd al-Jabbār
Taṯbīt dalā'il al-nubuwwa, 2 vols. [Beirut n.d.].
Al-Ābī, Abū Sa'd Manṣūr, *Natr al-durr.* Ms Reisülküttab.
Abū l-Ḥasan 'Alī b. 'Abd al-Raḥmān b. Huḏayl
'Ayn al-adab wa-l-siyāsa wa-zayn al-ḥasab wa-l-riyāsa, Cairo 1388/1969.
Alḥarizi, Yehuda b. Shelomo
Sefer musre ha-philosophim, "Sinnsprüche der Philosophen", aus dem Arabischen des Honein ibn Ishâk in Hebräische übersetzt von Jehuda ben Salomo Alcharizi. Herausg. von A. Loewenthal. Frankfurt a.M. 1896.
Andreas F.C. and W. Henning
1933 *Mitteliranische Manichaica aus Chinesisch-Turkestan* II. (Sitzungsb. d. Preuss. Akad. d. Wissenschaften, Phil.-hist. Klasse), Berlin.
(Pseudo) Aṣma'ī
Nihāyat al-arab, or *Siyar al-mulūk*. Ms. British Museum Add. 23.298.
Asmussen, Jes P.
1971 "Einige Bemerkungen zur sasanidischen Handarz-Literatur", *Atti del convegno internazionale sul tema: La Persia nel medioevo* (Accademia Nazionale dei Lincei, Anno CCCLXVIII, Quaderno N. 160). Rome, pp. 269-276.
AVn M. Haug and W.W. West, *The book of Arda Viraf*, Bombay-London 1872.
Badawī, 'Abdurraḥmān
1954 *Al-uṣūl al-yūnāniyya li-l-naẓariyyāt al-siyāsiyya fī l-islām* I, Cairo.
Bailey, H.W.
1943 *Zoroastrian problems in the ninth-century books.* Ratanbai Katrak lectures. Oxford.
1949/51 "Irano-Indica II", *BSOAS* 13, pp. 121-139.
Bartholomae, Christian
1904 *Altiranisches Wörterbuch*, Strassburg (2. unveränderte Auflage, Berlin 1961).
1911 "Mitteliranische Studien I", *WZKM* 25, pp. 245-262.

al-Bayhaqī, Ibrāhīm b. Muḥammad
Al-maḥāsin wa-l-masāwī, 2 vols., Cairo n.d.

Bielawsk, Józef
1964-65 "Lettres d'Aristote à Alexandre le Grand en version arabe", *Rocznik Orientalistyczny* 28:1, pp. 7-34; 28:2, pp. 7-12.

Bīrūnī, Abū Rayḥān Muḥammad b. Aḥmad
Kitāb fī taḥqīq mā li-l-hind, Hyderabad 1377/1958.

Black, M.
1954 *A Christian Palestinian Syriac horologion*, Cambridge.

Blochet, E.
1898 *Catalogue des manuscrits mazdéens (zends, pehlevis, parsis et persans) de la Bibliothèque Nationale.* Besançon.

Boyce, Mary
1968a "Middle Persian literature", *Handbuch der Orientalistik*, Abt. 1, Bd. IV, Abschn. 2, Lfg. 1. Leiden. pp. 31-66.
1968b *The Letter of Tansar*, translated by M. Boyce. Rome.
1975 *A history of Zoroastrianism* I. Handbuch der Orientalistik, Abt. I, Band VIII, Abschn. 1, Lief. 2, Heft 2a. Leiden.
1977 *A word-list of Manichaean Middle Persian and Parthian* (Acta Iranica 9a. Troisième série, vol. II, supplément). Leiden-Tehran-Liège.

Busse, Heribert
1977 "Der persische Staatsgedanke im Wandel der Geschichte", *Saeculum* 28, pp. 53-74.

Charles, R.H.
1913 *The Apocrypha and Pseudepigrapha of the Old Testament in English,* Oxford. 2 vols.

Christensen, Arthur
1929 "La sagesse religieuse et morale de la Perse sous Khosrau I Anōsharvān", *Actes du Ve Congrès International d'Histoire des Religions,* Lund, pp. 250-253.
1930 "La légende du Sage Buzurjmihr", *Acta Orientalia* 8, pp. 81-128.

Corbin, Henry
1951 "Le livre des conseils de Zartusht", *Poure Davoud Memorial Volume* II, Bombay, pp. 129-160.

Firdawsī, Abū l-Qāsim
ŠN *Šāhnāma*, ed. E.E. Bertels and others, 9 vols., Moscow 1960.

Freiman, Alexander
1906 "Pand-nāmak i Zaratušt. Der Pahlavi-Text mit Übersetzung, kritischen und Erläuterungsnoten", *WZKM* 20, pp. 149-166; 237-280.

Gabrieli, Francesco
1931/32 "L'opera di Ibn al-Muqaffa'", *RSO* 13, pp. 197-247.
*EI*² article: "Ibn al-Muḳaffa'".
Gaster, Moses
1928 "The Hebrew version of the 'Secretum secretorum'," in: M. Gaster, *Studies and Texts*, London 1928 (Reprinted New York 1971), II, pp. 742-813; III, 246-278.
Gignoux, Philippe
1971 *Glossaire des inscriptions pehlevies et parthes.* (Corpus Inscriptionum Iranicarum, Supplementary Series, 1.) London.
Gimaret, Daniel
1971 *Le livre de Bilawhar et Buḏasf selon la version arabe ismaélienne*, trad. par D. Gimaret. (Dentre de Recherches d'Histoire et de Philologie, IV. Hautes Etudes Islamiques et Orientales d'Histoire Comparée, 3) Genève-Paris.
1973 "A propos de S.M. Stern et S. Walzer, Three unknown Buddhist stories..." *Arabica* 20, pp. 186-191.
Goitein, S.D.
1949 "A turning-point in the history of the Muslim state (Apropos of the Kitāb al-Ṣaḥāba of Ibn al-muqaffa')", *Islamic Culture* 23, pp. 120-135. Reprinted in Goitein 1966, pp. 149-167, from where the article is quoted.
1966 *Studies in Islamic history and institutions,* Leiden.
Goldziher, Ignaz
1900 "Islamisme et parsisme", *Actes du 1er Congrès International d'Histoire des Religions*, Paris, pp. 119-147.
1967 *Muslim Studies (Muhammedanische Studien)*, ed. by S.M. Stern, I, London.
Greenfield, J.C.
1974 "Rṭyn mgwš'", *Joshua Finkel Festschrift*, New York, pp. 63-69.
Grignaschi, Mario
1965/66 "Les 'Rasā'il ariṭāṭālīsa ilā-l-Iskandar' de Sālim Abū-l-'Alā' et l'activité culturelle à l'époque omayyade", *BEO* 19, pp. 7-83 (published 1967).
1966 "Quelques spécimens de la littérature sassanide conservés dans les bibliothèques d'Istanbul", *JA* 254, pp. 1-142.
1967 "Le roman épistolaire classique conservé dans la version arabe de Sālim Abū-l-'Alā'", *Le Muséon* 80, pp. 211-264.
1975 "La 'Siyāsatu-l-'āmmiyya' et l'influence iranienne sur la pensée politique islamique", *Acta Iranica* 6 (*Monumentum Nyberg* III), Tehran-Liège-Leiden, pp. 33-287.

Guidi, Michelangelo
1927 *La lotta tra l'Islam e il manicheismo. Un libro di Ibn al-Muqaffa' contro il corano confutato da al-Qāsim b. Ibrāhīm*, Rome.
Gutas, Dimitri
1975 *Greek wisdom literature in Arabic translations. A study of the Graeco-Arabic gnomologia.* (American Oriental Series, 60), New Haven, Connecticut.
Ḥamza, 'Abd al-Laṭīf
1965 *Ibn al-Muqaffa'*, 3rd ed., Cairo.
Henning, W.B.
1943/46 "Sogdian tales", *BSOAS* 11, pp. 465-487.
Henrichs, A., and L. Koenen
1970 "Ein griechischer Mani-Codex", *Zeitschrift für Papyrologie und Epigraphik*, 5/2, pp. 97-216.
1978 "Der kölner Mani-Kodex (P. Colon. inv. nr. 4780) *Peri tēs gennēs sōmatos autou.* Edition der Seiten 72, 8—99, 9", *Zeitschrift für Papyrologie und Epigraphik* 32, pp. 87-199.
Henrichs, Albert
1973 "Mani and the Babylonian baptists: A historical confrontation", *Harvard Studies in Classical Philology* 77, pp. 23-59.
Herzfeld, Ernst
1924 *Paikuli. Monument and inscription of the early history of the Sasanian Empire* I, Berlin.
1938 *Altpersische Inschriften* (Archäologische Mitteilungen aus Iran, Ergänzungsband 1), Berlin.
Horn, Paul
1893 *Grundriss der neupersischen Etymologie*, Strassburg.
Hübschmann, H.
1895 *Persische Studien*, Strassburg.
Ḥunayn ibn Isḥāq,
Ādāb al-falāsifa: cf. Merkle 1921; Alḥarizi, *Musre.*
Ibn 'Abd Rabbihi, Abū 'Umar Aḥmad b. Muḥammad
Al-'iqd al-farīd, ed. Aḥmad Amīn and others, 3rd. ed., 7 vols. Cairo 1384/1965 .
Ibn al-'Arabī, Muḥyī al-Dīn 'Abdallāh al-Ḥātimī al-Ṭā'ī al-Andalusī
Muḥāḍarat al-abrār wa-musāmarat al-aḵyār fī l-adabiyyāt wa-l-nawādir wa-l-aḵbār, Beyrut 1388/1968. 2 vols.
Al-waṣāyā, Beyrut n.d.
Ibn al-Muqaffa', 'Abdallāh
AK *Al-durra al-yatīma aw al-adab al-kabīr*, in: Kurd 'Alī 1946, pp. 40-106.

AṢ *Al-adab al-ṣaġīr*, in: Kurd 'Alī 1946, pp. 4-37.
Ṣaḥāba *Risālat Ibn al-Muqaffa' fī l-ṣaḥāba*, in: Kurd 'Alī 1946, pp. 117-134.

Ibn al-Nadim
Kitāb al-fihrist, ed. G. Glügel, 2 vols. (Reprint, Beirut 1964).

Ibn Qutayba al-Dīnawarī, Abū Muḥ, 'Abdallāh b. Muslim
'Uyūn al-akbār, Cairo n.d. 4 vols.

Iqbāl, 'Abbās
1926 *Šarḥ-e ḥāl-e 'Abdallāh b. al-Moqaffa'-e fārsī,* Berlin.

Al-Iṣbahānī, Abū Nu'aym Aḥmad b. 'Abdallāh
Ḥilyat al-awliyā' wa-ṭabaqāt al-aṣfiyā', 2nd ed., Beyrut 1387/1967. 10 vols.

Ja'far b. Šams al-Kilāfa
Kitab al-ādāb, ed. Muḥ. Amīn al-Kānjī, Cairo 1931.

Al-Jāḥiẓ, Abū 'Utmān 'Amr b. Baḥr
Al-bayān wa-l-tabyīn, ed. 'Abd al-Salām Hārūn, 4th ed. 4 vols. Cairo [1975].
Kitāb al-maḥāsin wa-l-aḍdād, ed. Muḥ. Amīn al-Kānjī al-Kutubī, Cairo 1324.
Kitāb al-tāj, ed. Aḥmad Zakī Bāšā, Cairo 1322/1914.

Justi, Ferdinand
1895 *Iranisches Namenbuch*, Marburg. (Reprint, Hildesheim 1963).

Kanga, Maneck Fardunji
1960 *Čītak handarž i Pōryōtkēšān. A Pahlavi text*, ed. and transl. by Ervad M.F. Kanga. Bombay.
1974 "Kingship and religion in Iran", *Acta Iranica* 3 (1re série, III). Leiden-Tehran-Liège, pp. 221-231.

(al) Khurāsāni, Muḥammad Ġufrānī
[1965?] *'Abdullāh Ibn al-Muqaffa'*, [Cairo:]. Al-dar al-qawmiyya li-l-ṭibā'a wa-l-našr.

Kraus, Paul
1934 "Zu Ibn al-Muqaffa'", *RSO* 14, pp. 1-20.

Kurd 'Alī, Muḥammad
1946 *Rasā'il al-bulaġā'*, 3rd. ed., Cairo (1365 AH).

Lambert, W.G.
1960 *Babylonian Wisdom Literature*, Oxford.

Lommel, Hermann
1930 *Die Religion Zarathustras nach dem Avesta dargestellt,* Tübingen (Reprinted, Hildesheim-New York 1971).

Manzalaoui, Mahmoud
1974 "The pseudo-Aristotelian *Kitāb sirr al-asrār*. Facts and prob-

lems", *Oriens* 23/24, pp. 147-257.

Al-Māwardī, Abū-l-Ḥasan 'Alī Muḥ. b. Ḥabīb

Adab al-dunyā wa-l-dīn, ed. Muṣṭafā al-Saqā, 4th ed., Cairo 1393/1973.

Tashīl al-naẓar wa-ta'jīl al-ẓafar fī aḵlāq al-malik wa-siyāsat al-mulk. Ms. in the Library of the University of Tehran (photocopy by courtesy of Dr. Y. Sadan).

de Menasce, Jean-Pierre

1945 *Une apologétique mazdéenne du IXe siècle. Škand-Gumānīk-Vičār. La solution décisive des doutes.* Texte pazand-pehlevi transcrit, traduit et commenté par P.J. de Menasce. (Collectanea Friburgensia, n.s. XXX). Fribourg en Suisse.

1973 *Le troisième livre du Dēnkart*, trad. du pehlevi. (Travaux de l'Institut d'Etudes Iraniennes de l'Université de Paris III, 5. Bibliothèque des oeuvres classiques persanes, 4.) Paris.

Merkle, Karl

1921 *Die Sittensprüche der Philosophen. "Kitâb âdâb al-falâsifa" von Ḥonein ibn Isḥâq in der Überarbeitung des Muḥammed ibn 'Alî al-Anṣârî.* Leipzig.

Minovi, Mojtabā

1311AH *Nāme -ye tansar ba-goštasp.* Tehran.

Miskawayhi, Abū 'Alī Aḥmad b. Muḥammad

JX *Al-ḥikma al-ḵālida, Jāwīdān xirad*, ed. 'Abdurraḥmān Badawī, (Dirāsāt islāmiyya, 13). Cairo 1952.

Molé, Marijan

1963 *Culte, mythe et cosmologie dans l'Iran ancien. Le problème zoroastrien et la tradition mazdéenne.* (Annales du Musée Guimet, Bibliothèque d'Etudes LXIX.) Paris.

Müller, Friedrich

1894 "Kleine Mittheilungen", *WZKM* 8, pp. 90-100.

Nawabi, M.

1339 *RFLT* 12, pp. 513-535.

Nöldeke, Theodor

1879 *Geschichte des Artachschîr î Pâpakân.* Separatabdruck aus der *Festschrift Benfey* (Beitr. z. Kunde d. Indog. Sprachen IV). Göttingen.

1884 *GGA,*

1892 *Persische Studien II.* (Sitzungsb. der Kais. Akad. d. Wissenschaften in Wien, philos.-hist. Classe, CXXVI.) Vienna.

1912 *Burzōes Einleitung zu dem Buche Kalīla waDimna.* (Schriften der Wissenschaftlichen Gesellschaft in Strassburg, 12. Heft.) Strassburg.

Nyberg, H.S.
1928 *Hilfsbuch des Pehlevi* I. Uppsala.
1931 Idem, II. Glossar. Uppsala.
1964 *A manual of Pahlavi* I: Texts. Wiesbaden.
1974 Idem, II: Glossary. Wiesbaden.

Oldenburg, S.
1889 "Persidskij izvod povesti o Varlaame i Ioasafe", *Zapiski vostočnago otdelenija imper. russkago arxeolog. obščestva* 4, pp. 229-265.

Pellat, Charles
1976 *Ibn al-Muqaffa' mort 140/757 "Conseilleur du calife"*. Paris. (Publication du Département d'Islamologie de l'Université de Paris-Sorbonne, II).

Penzer, N.M.
1968 *The ocean of story*; being C.H. Tawney's translation of Somadeva's *Kathā Sarit Sāgara*, V. (Indian reprint, Delhi).

Philonenko, M.
1972 "Un écho de la prédication d'Asoka dans l'Epître de Jacques", *Ex Orbe Religionum, Studia Geo Widengren* I, Leiden, pp. 254-265.

Plessner, M.
1954/5 "Liqquṭim lesefer 'musre ha-filosofim' me'et ḥunayn ibn isḥāq u-l-targumo ha'ivri", *Tarbiz* 24, pp. 60-72.

Ringgren, Helmer
1952 *Fatalism in Persian epics.* (Uppsala Universitets Årsskrift 1952:13.) Uppsala-Wiesbaden.

Rosenthal, E.I.J.
1962 *Political thought in medieval Islam.* Cambridge.

Schulthess, F.
1903 *Lexicon syropalaestinum*, Berlin.

Shaked, Shaul
1969a "Esoteric trends in Zoroastrianism", *Proc. of the Israel Academy of Sciences and Humanities* 3, pp. 175-221.
1969b "Specimens of Middle Persian verse", *Henning Mem. Vol.,* London, pp. 395-405.
1979 *Wisdom of the Sasanian sages* (*Dēnkard VI*). (Persian Heritage Series 34.) Boulder, Colorado.
1980 "Mihr the Judge", *JSAI* 2, pp. 1-31.
1982 "Two Judaeo-Iranian contributions", *Irano-Judaica*, Jerusalem pp, 292-322.

Stern, S.M. and S. Walzer
1971 *Three unknown Budhist stories in an Arabic version*, Oxford.
Sundermann, W.
1973 *Mittelpersische und parthische kosmogonische und Parabeltexte der Manichäer*, Berlin.
Tansar Cf. Minovi 1311; Boyce 1968.
Tavadia, J.C.
1956 Die mittelpersische Sprache und Literatur der Zarathustrier (Iranische Texte und Hilfsbücher, 2.), Leipzig.
Tedesco, Paul
1921 "Dialektologie der westiranischen Turfanfragmente", *Le Monde Oriental* 15, pp. 184-258.
Waldschmidt, Ernst, and Wolfgang Lentz
1926 *Die Stellung Jesu im Manichäismus* (Einzelausgabe aus den Abh. d. Preuss. Akad. d. Wissenschaften, Jahrg. 1926, phil-hist. Klasse Nr. 4). Berlin.
Al-Zandawaysitī, Abū l-Ḥasan 'Abdallāh b. Yaḥyā
Rawḍat al-'ulamā' wa-nuzhat al-fuḍalā', Ms. Brit. Mus. Add. 7258.
Zaehner, R.C.
1955 *Zurvan. A. Zoroastrian dilemma*, Oxford.
1956 *The teachings of the Magi. A compendium of Zoroastrian beliefs.* London.
1961 *The dawn and twilight of Zoroastrianism.* London.
Zotenberg, Hermann
1870 "Geschichte Daniels", *Archiv für die Wissenschaftlichen Forschung des Alten Testaments* 1, pp. 385-427.

VII

FROM IRAN TO ISLAM: ON SOME SYMBOLS OF ROYALTY

Islam inherited from the civilizations which preceded it, and particularly from Sasanian Iran, the main expressions for royal authority, in the same way as it did some of the conceptions about royalty and its relation to religion, discussed in an earlier paper.[1] Quite prominent among these influences were those which expressed by way of emblems or symbols the dignity, splendour or authority of the king. In the following some concrete objects which were commonly used to represent the royal power will be discussed. When they occur in early Islamic texts it is not always clear whether they still retain their original function and meaning, or whether they crop up as a mere gesture whose meaning has been forgotten.

In his general survey of the field of Persian influence in Islam, Goldziher states: "Aux yeux de l'Arabe le tâdj est l'attribut caractéristique de la dignité royale persane".[2] The Sasanian crown was, indeed, an important attribute of royalty. Although the Persian term *tāg*, which was eventually Arabicized into *tāj*, does not occur in the surviving Middle Persian or Parthian literature,[3] it must have been a fairly common term in Iranian, to judge by its ramified descendants, which figure as borrowed words in Aramaic, Syriac and Mandaic, as well as in Hebrew and Armenian.[4] In the royal practice of Sasanian Iran the crown fulfilled the function of an individual emblem by which each king was distinguished,[5] and at the

[1] See Shaked 1984.

[2] Goldziher 1900: 124 n. 3.

[3] Middle Persian *tāg* is only indirectly attested, by means of loanwords. See next note. The architectural term *tāq* "arch" or "dome" is at any rate unrelated since the Armenian *t'ag* indicates that the final consonant of the original word must have been *-g*, not *-k*. Cf. Hübschmann 1897:153; 1895:46; Bartholomae 1904, col. 626 s.v. *takabara-*. Eilers 1969:38f. note 108; 1971:603, 613.

[4] The Arabic *tāj*, with the final *-j*, is evidently a borrowing from the Aramaic *tāg(ā)*, the Aramaic word itself being a loan-word from Persian. In addition to the references given in the preceding note cf. Lagarde 1866:83f.; Widengren 1958:33 and 102.

[5] For a discussion of the Sasanian crowns on coins one may refer to Erdmann 1951:87ff.; Göbl 1971:12f.

same time it also represented, in combination with the diadem,[6] the idea of royalty in the abstract. It often seems to contain an iconographic reference to the notion of the divine glory of royalty, the *xwarrah*, which was considered to endow the legitimate monarch with special, divine, power,[7] although the assertion sometimes heard that the Sasanian kings were regarded as being themselves divine, or as being derived from divine ancestry, is not quite accurate.[8]

It is related that the royal crown of the Sasanians was so heavy that the king could not carry it on his head. It was therefore attached to a chain hanging from the ceiling, which was made invisible to the visitors in the audience hall by means of a screen placed in front of the king. When a visitor first approached the king, he was awestruck by the sight.[9] In the Umayyad palace at Khirbat Mafjar a reference to this practice, at least as an ornamental vestige, has survived in the form of a hanging chain, as was shown by the late Richard Ettinghausen.[10] That the Umayyad princes felt it necessary to imitate the chain-motif of the crown, without apparently making it a practical feature of their own sitting in audience, is a remarkable testimony to the power and tenacity of this royal symbol.

The hanging crown motif figures with some frequency as a literary expression for dignity and high ancestry. It is mentioned in the context of the *šuᶜūbiyya* polemic and elsewhere: *wa-kunnā ahla tījānin, kunnā nuᶜalliqu l-tāja ᶜalā ru'ūsinā wayawman ᶜalā l-rimāḥi bi-l-bayti l-ᶜatīq.*[11] So important was the crown as a symbol for the office of the king that in an anecdote which is repeated in several places we have the touching story of the Sasanian king who died without leaving behind him a living offspring. His wife, however, was pregnant, and in order to ensure his dynasty the crown was placed over the belly of the pregnant wife.[12]

[6] Cf. Erdmann 1951:117–121; Göbl 1971:8.

[7] Cf. Göbl 1971:10f.

[8] Goldziher 1900.

[9] Some references: Ṭabarī I:956f.; Ibn Kaṯīr II:177; Ibn Hišām 304. When the crown was captured by the Muslims it was split in two, each section being carried in a basket on the back of a mule, so heavy it was. Cf. Ṭabarī I:2446. It had to be placed on two pillars of wood (Ṭabarī I:2454). Cf. also Erdmann 1951:114–117.

[10] Ettinghausen 1972:28ff.

[11] Ibn Hišām 182; ᶜIṣāmī I:178.

[12] Ps. -Aṣmaᶜī fol. 115b (the king who died is Hurmuz b. Narsē). Also Jamāl al-Dīn 72.

I. Sasanian and Arabic cushions

The Sasanian king and other Sasanian dignitaries used to sit on several cushions called in the Arabic books *namraq* (pl. *namāriq*) or *wisāda* (pl. *wasā'id*). Both words are of Persian origin, although none of them is attested in Iranian. The etymology of the first word is quite transparent. It is derived from *namr,*[13] which occurs in New Persian as *narm* "soft, pliable", and the verbal root of which is *nam-* "to be soft, to bend". The second word has a less obvious etymology, and has not so far been recognized as an Iranian word. It occurs not only in Arabic, but also in Syriac (*bsadhyā*), Jewish Aramaic (**by sdy'**) and Mandaic (**bisada, basada,** and **bsada**) in the sense of "bolster, pillow". These words lack Semitic etymology.[14] The etymology which may be provided from Iranian is conjectural. The word could be derived from the Old Persian root *sā-* (which corresponds to Avestic *spā-*) "to throw, build", with a preverb such as *upa* or *avi.* An Old Persian word **upa-sāta-* might well have meant "that which is placed on top of each other", or "that which is thrown on the floor". This could have quite regularly given rise to a form *basād*, as well as to a form with an initial *wa-* or *wi-*.

For the use of these cushions in the literature we have a wealth of evidence. When Khusrau Abarwēz ascended the throne, he made a speech, in the manner which is typical of the Sasanian literary convention. The text says: *wa-waḍa*ᶜ*ū lahu l-namāriqa ba*ᶜ*ḍahā fawqa ba*ᶜ*ḍin fa-*ᶜ*alāhā ṯuma qāla*... "They placed for him cushions one on top of the other. He mounted on top of them and said...".[15] While *namāriq* are cushions one steps up on in order to make a speech, *wasā'id* seem to be cushions, usually three in number, which the king leans against in a reclining position. The detailed description of Kisrā Abarwēz is instructive. He has already been deposed by his son, but he still retains his retinue and some of the appurtenances of royalty: *fa-kāna jālisan* ᶜ*alā ṯalāṯi*

[13] This is the Parthian form, while the Middle Persian form is *narm.* An Aramaic word (derived from the Parthian) in **nmrqyn**. Cf. Fraenkel, 1880:8; Eilers 1962:206.

[14] Nöldeke 1875:42, 183, suggested that Mandaic **bisada, bisadia** contains as first element a form of *baitā* "house". Similarly Payne-Smith 1879:547, 291 (v.s. *essāḏā*). Kohut 1878ff., II:52, suggested a connection with Arabic *wisāda*, but this was rejected by Geiger in Krauss 1937:85, incorrectly, I believe. Perles 1871:25n. suggested a connection with Persian *bistar.* One may wonder whether Arabic *bisāṭ* is not at least partly moulded on the same word, although it obviously derives from an Arabic root.

[15] Ps. -Aṣmaᶜī, fol. 212b, and also fols. 142b, 217a; Ṭabarī I:2270.

anmāṭi dībājin xusrawāniyyin mansūjatin bi-l-ḏahab, wa-fawqahā bisāṭu ibrīšam, muttaki'an ᶜalā ṭalāṭi wasā'idi xazzin aḥmara... [16] We have the cushions piled up under the king when he is reclining in Sasanian iconography,[17] and the practice is also mentioned with regard to Jewish dignitaries of that period.[18] The cushions are thus not only a sign of wealth and luxury, but also a symbol of high status.

The use of the *wisāda* survived in early Islam. As an expression of this continuity, as well as in contrast to Sasanian and Byzantine practice, we hear of ᶜUmar's way of travelling. He used as his *wisāda* a cloak filled with date-palm fibres, which also served as a provision-bag (*wa-ḥaqībatuhu šumlatun maḥšuwwatun līfan hiya wisādatuhu iḏā tawassada*).[19] In contrast to this we have the story of Rustam, the Persian general, who is to receive a delegation of Ribᶜī on behalf of the Muslim army calling the Persians to surrender. Rustam consults his advisers on how he should receive the visitor, whether he should vie in splendour with the enemy, or show scorn (*a-nubāhī am natahāwanu*?). They decide to show their visitor scorn, and bring out ornaments *(zibrij)*,[20] spread carpets and cushions, place for Rustam the golden throne (*sarīr al-ḏahab*) and clothe him with his decorations, which consist of felt saddle-cloth (*anmāṭ*)[21] and cushions embroidered with gold (*wasā'id mansūja bi-l-ḏahab*). Ribᶜī's appearance is coarse. He deliberately spoils the beautiful cushions and carpets (*al-namāriq wa-l-busuṭ*) which had been laid out with the purpose of instilling into him a sense of his own insignificance. In the debate which the Persian grandees conduct among themselves following Ribᶜī's visit the contrast between the appreciation of luxury by Persians and the humble clothing of the Arab is made.[22] This is a theme which plays a prominent part in the *šuᶜūbiyya* debates between the partisans of the Persians and those of the Arabs, and it is quite possible that its occurrence in the context of the wars of conquest, in the year 14 AH,

16 Ps. -Aṣmaᶜī, fol. 258a.

17 Cf., e.g., the representation of the king on a throne in the Sasanian bowl at the Walters Art Gallery, Baltimore, reproduced in Ghirshman 1962:218 fig. 259, as well as the intaglios of the British Museum, op. cit., p. 242 figs. 296, 297.

18 Sperber 1982:90ff. The Iranian term used for these cushions in the Talmud is *wistarg* (Aram. **bstrq'**).

19 ᶜAbd al-Jabbār, 335. Similar stories about ᶜUmar's modesty, without these details, are in Iṣbahānī, *Ḥilya*, I:47.

20 On the etymology of this word cf. Eilers 1971:598.

21 On this word cf. Eilers 1971:624, 629.

22 Ṭabarī, I:2270ff.

is an anachronism. However, there is no reason to doubt the authenticity of the Persian court style as described in this story.

II. Throne and stool

The throne (Persian *taxt*) is of course a major symbol of the royal status. In Arabic it is usually called *sarīr.*[23] Besides the throne there are stools, or chairs, which serve as symbols of subsidiary rank. The information about this comes again most explicitly from the Arabic sources. We read the following description of the court of Kisrā Anūšarwān: "He used to have for every king of the greatest kings of the peoples, such as Qayṣar (i.e. the Byzantine emperor), Xāqān (i.e. the Turkish monarch), the Indian king and the king of China, and those who went the same course (i.e. those who were of the same rank) a chair (*kursī*), which was placed in the name of the king in a specified spot in the audience hall (*majlis*) of Kisrā, according to the rank of that king, as well as a saddled horse, placed at the gate, as long as Kisrā was satisfied with him. If he disapproved of someone, the mark of his reproval was that he ordered the stool to be lifted from the audience hall and the horse to be removed from the gate. When that king heard of the lifting of his stool from the audience hall and of the removal of his horse from the gate, he would acknowledge his guilt[24] and submit to whatever was required of him until Kisrā was satisfied with him. The mark of Kisrā's satisfaction was that he ordered the stool and the horse to be returned...."[25] In these terms the story lacks credibility. It seems unlikely that Kisrā's greatest rivals were much concerned with the status granted to them in the court of their enemy. The list of the four kings looks very much like the popular Sasanian motif of the four kings or the four nations.[26] In brief, the story as given here makes a strong impression of being moulded after a current *topos.* But it is precisely for this reason that we may regard this story as containing a certain type of historical truth. It seems to be based on a genuine Sasanian notion that there were special chairs reserved for grandees in the audience hall of the king of kings, and this notion was apparently welded with that of the four kings.

[23] The first Arab king to sit on a *sarīr*, we are told, was Jaḏīma al-Abraš; cf. Ṯaʿālibī, *Laṭā'if,* 7.

[24] *ḥamala al-ḥumūla* seems to give the sense as translated here.

[25] Abu l-Baqā', fol. 5a–b.

[26] See Shaked 1984.

* That there was special significance attached to the chairs in the audience hall of the Sasanian king can be seen from the story of Sayf ibn Ḏī Yazan, who was seeking the help of Xusrau Anōšarwān against the Ethiopians. He was staying for a time with al-Nuᶜmān ibn al-Munḏir, and joined the latter on his annual report (*wifāda*) at the court of the Sasanian king. At al-Nuᶜmān's intercession Sayf was given permission to enter the audience hall (the *īwān*, which continued the ancient *apadana*). Sayf entered and lowered his head while approaching Kisrā, who was sitting on his throne (*sarīr*). Kisrā greeted him in the royal manner (*fa-ḥayyāhu bi-taḥiyyati l-mulūk*), and ordered that a stool of gold (*kursī min ḏahab*) be given to him. Following this reception he was allowed to voice his petition.[27]

* The idea of a highly placed person, a petty king or local dignitary, for whom a stool is reserved at court as a mark of particular favour, gains some support from older documents relating to Iran. The elusive Aramaic phrase **n'syb kwrsy'** "he who takes (or holds) the stool" occurs several times in the inscriptions of Tang-i Sarvak in ancient Elymais (south-western Iran).[28] It has been suggested that it had something to do with ascending the throne or with holding a ritual position.[29] While this expression may possibly contain an allusion to some ritual function, it may at the same time also represent a borrowing from the field of official protocol. The terminology used with regard to a worshipper in relation to the deity is often similar to that used for a slave or vassal in relation to his monarch. The local governor in Elymais may have been granted the honoured position of "holder of a stool" (in the royal court), a title he was proud to use.

A Syriac inscription at Sumatar Harabesi also talks of a ruler giving a stool to a priestly worshipper. It seems to say, if our understanding of it is correct, that a ritual pillar (viz. a *baetyl*) and a stool have been established on the mountain, the latter for the benefit of the person who takes care of the deity. The ruler, who will be *budar* (i.e. a priest or some other religious functionary) after Tiridates the ruler, shall grant the stool to

[27] Ps. -Aṣmaᶜī, fol. 180a. The parallel story in Ṭabarī I:946f. does not have the detail about the stool. The version in Dīnawarī, p. 65, is much curtailed. The same applies to Ibn al-Balxī, p. 95; Ḥamza al-Iṣfahānī, p. 52; Yaᶜqūbī, I:144; Ṯaᶜālibī, pp. 616f.; Masᶜūdī, *Murūj*, II:55.

[28] Cf. Henning 1952.

[29] For the former, cf. Henning 1952:172f.; for the latter, Bivar and Shaked 1964:287ff.

whoever takes care of the pillar, and will have his recompense from Mārelāhā. If the ruler withholds the stool, and (as a result of this neglect) the pillar is damaged, God will know.[30] If our interpretation is correct, the stool is here reserved to the priest in the same manner as it was usually granted by the king in the audience hall to one of his favoured ministers. A similar piece of furniture was apparently adopted in cultic use.[31]

The stool and its position in the court of the King of Kings is mentioned already in Esther 3:1, where the promotion of Haman at the court of Ahasuerus is symbolized by the fact that his stool is raised above those of the other princes. Although the story of Esther is not necessarily a contemporary narrative, and is likely to be a post-Achaemenid novella-type composition, the author displays good knowledge of court life. Achaemenian protocol probably survived into the Arsacid period, and sometimes continued its life even beyond that period.[32]

One cannot help feeling that in the veneration which is said to have been accorded to the chair (*kursī*) of ᶜAlī after his death,[33] the idea of

[30] The inscription was first published by Segal 1954:26ff. Some readings are corrected in Drijvers 1972:17f. A new translation is given in Drijvers 1980:126ff. I am now inclined to modify some points in my earlier effort at translation (in Bivar and Shaked 1964:288). Incorporating Drijvers' corrected readings, I would now propose the following reading for lines 5–9. An asterisk marks a suggested new reading, based on Segal's drawing of the inscription. The punctuation marks are mine, inserted in order to clarify my interpretation:

> **w'qymn krs' lmn dntrsyhy. *šlyṭ *dyhw' bwdr mn btr tyrdt šlyṭ' wytl krs' lmn dmtrs' lh prᶜnh mn mrlh' yhw'. w'n nkl' krs' wttḥbl nṣbt', hw 'lh' ydᶜ.**
>
> And we erected the stool for whoever takes care of it. A ruler, who will be *budar* after Tiridates the ruler, and who will give the stool to him who takes care of it, his recompense shall be from Marelaha. If he withholds the stool, and if the pillar is damaged, God will know.

As for the title **bwdr/bdr**, Maricq 1965:141ff. takes up a suggestion made earlier by Segal 1954 to connect it with the term **bwγdr** which occurs in the context of the Harranian mysteries in the *Fihrist* of Ibn al-Nadīm (I:326f.). If this is a title for a priest, as it seems to be, one might think of explaining it as deriving from Iranian **baγdār** "keeper of the deity". Cf. also Chwolson 1856, II:319ff. The Syriac spellings with a **-w-** do not necessarily invalidate such an explanation, as the labial **b-** could have caused a pronunciation of the first syllable with an *-u-* vowel.

[31] In the Zoroastrian ritual use is made of stool-like tables, called *xwān*. They are described in somewhat different terms by Modi 1937:254ff., 303, and Drower 1956:22. The latter's description may be quoted: "Their ritual foods are set upon a low stone table, square, four-legged, and not unlike a stool. An identical table serves the priest as a stand for the fire-vase and is used as the platform upon which the officiants stand at certain stages of the ritual".

[32] Shaked 1982:292ff.

[33] Ṭabarī II:70–73; Balāḏurī, *Ansāb*, V:241f.

ᶜAlī's legitimate royalty, or even that of his sacred associations, gets its symbolical representation. Such an idea gains force from those earlier parallels quoted above, in which a chair stands for power, either political or sacred.

This conception is linked with the fact that the order of sitting was rigidly fixed in the court, as it probably was also in other spheres of life where social hierarchy was formally observed. For the great stress which was placed on the order of sitting at the court of the Sasanian kings we have evidence from several sources. Thus *Kitāb al-tāj*, attributed to Jāḥiẓ, contains detailed instructions as to the precise order of entering the audience hall of the king by dignitaries of various classes (pp. 7ff.). Hints as to the fixed order of sitting are spread throughout the book (e.g. p. 144, 163).[34]

Jewish academies in Babylonia in the Talmudic period normally centred around a powerful person who was venerated for his learning and who held a position of authority as a leader of the Jewish community. They probably reflected Sasanian court custom by being organized according to a fixed and rigid hierarchy which expressed itself by sitting in rows according to rank and position.[35] Similar protocol prescribed the order of sitting at a meal, perhaps at the court of the exilarch, which was conducted somewhat like a royal court.[36]

* III. The quince

One further example of continuity in the symbolism of royalty from Zoroastrian Iran to Islam is again associated with the iconography of Khirbat Mafjar. The floor of the threshold of what was recognized by Ettinghausen to be the throne apse (Exedra V) in the main banquet and throne hall of the palace has a pictorial mosaic, the only one of its kind among the thirty-eight different panels decorating that floor. "It shows a

[34] It is related similarly that on the day of Nawrōz the king sits in audience, while his retinue take their seats according to their ranks (*wa-yajlisu al-nāsu ᶜalā marātibihim*. See *K. al-tāj fī sīrati Anūširwān*, in Grignaschi 1966:103).

[35] Cf. Gafni 1980:295ff. The same order seems still to be in force in the tenth century, as one of Sherira Gaon's letters refers to a person who was second in the leadership of the *yeshiva*, and who sat at the head of the "great row" (i.e. the first row). Cf. Mann 1931:103f.

[36] Cf. Bavli Berakhot 46b. In Bavli ᶜEruvin 85b–86a wealth is mentioned as a factor in connection with the order of sitting (cf. Beer 1970:61f.). Dignitaries used to "go out by a stool", apparently carried in a litter (cf. Beer 1970:172), a practice seemingly unrelated to that of the royal stool.

simple knife beside a fruit, from which a leafy shoot emanates" (Ettinghausen 1972:21–23). The suggestion that it may be understood as an allegorical representation of the caliph with his wife and her child carries little conviction, as already pointed out by Ettinghausen (pp. 23ff.). Basing himself on the location of this representation and on the fact that, in contrast to the other mosaic panels, this is a pictorial composition, Ettinghausen (p. 35) concluded that what we have here is some form of royal symbolism. Since Khirbat Mafjar was the mansion of an agricultural estate, he assumed (*ibid.*) that "the picture is most likely that of an offering made on the spot, the presentation of a highly esteemed fruit to the lord of the plantation. It may be a welcoming gift, the first produce of the season, the symbol of the tithe, or possibly a kind of local hors d'oeuvre".

I believe that the fruit in the picture, by its shape, may represent a quince. I shall try in the following to show that the quince served as a Sasanian symbol of royalty, and that its use in Khirbat Mafjar constitutes another survival of an ancient Iranian symbol in that site.

The quince figures among the offerings to the Sasanian king on the day of *mihrajān*, the feast celebrated at the time of the autumn equinox. These are brought to the king by the first person to enter his audience hall on that day, the chief priest.[37] The offerings consist of a citrus fruit (*utrujja*), a piece of sugar (cane), a fruit of the lote tree (*nabaq*), a quince, a jujube fruit, an apple, a cluster of white grapes, and seven branches of myrtle, over which Zoroastrian prayers have been recited (*qad zumzima ᶜalayhā*). There are seven kinds of fruit mentioned (if we do not count the seven branches of myrtle, which cannot be considered in the same category), and the quince occupies the middle position among them. A very similar central position is accorded to quince in certain recipes of magic in Islamic literature.[38] It may be noted that the Mandaeans also place a quince in the central position in a list of five kinds of fruit in the *masiqta* ceremony.[39]

The symbolical connection between quince and royalty comes out in a famous story of the Sasanian period, already referred to above in a dif-

[37] Nuwayrī, I:188.

[38] In Ps. -Majrīṭī, 181 lines 2–3 the sequence is: seven branches of myrtle, Egyptian willow, pomegranate, quince, mulberry, laurel and plane-tree.

[39] The list consists of: (1) pomegranate seeds, (2) a coconut, (3) a quince, (4) walnuts, (5) raisins or fresh white grapes. Drower 1962:133. The quince occurs in a similar central position in a list of the five fruits of Paradise (Majlisī 66:122 No. 13).

ferent connection. It is related that king Kisrā Abarwēz was imprisoned in a house while his son Šīrōya was made king. The old king, although in effect deposed from his throne, still held his retinue and some of the essential requisites of royal luxury, in the form of three golden embroidered carpets over which was laid a spread of silk. He was reclining on three cushions of red silken tissue, and was holding in his hand a round yellow quince. When the young king's messenger came to him, he laid the quince on a stand, but it fell on the ground and became soiled. The messenger lifted it up and brushed away the dirt, with the intention of returning it to Kisrā. The latter refused, saying, "This quince fell from the cushions to the carpet, and from there to the spreads, and from there it rolled over to the earth and became soiled with dust. This is an omen that I have been deprived of the kingship".[40]

That the same symbolical association of the quince, *safarjal,* with kingship survived into the Islamic period we can see from a story recounted by Ṭabarī. ᶜUmar ibn Hubayra appointed Muslim Ibn Saᶜīd as governor over Khurāsān in the year 104 AH. This was done in a banquet in which, after the other participants dispersed, only ᶜUmar and Muslim stayed on. Ibn Hubayra was holding a quince. He hurled it and asked: "Would it please you if I appointed you over Khurāsān?" Muslim said: "Yes", and ᶜUmar said: "Tomorrow, God willing".[41] There is a clear connection between the Sasanian story and the Muslim one. In the former, the quince, by rolling to the ground, symbolizes the loss of royal power. In the latter, it seems to symbolize the transfer of power.

An important reference to this motif occurs with regard to Muᶜāwiya. It is related that Jaᶜfar b. ᶜAbd-al-Malik presented the Prophet with four quinces. The Prophet gave three of them to Muᶜāwiya, saying: "Meet me with them in Paradise".[42] The story is loaded with tendentious symbolism. The quinces which Muᶜāwiya gets convey to him not only power but also a certain sanctity. The numbers used may be interpreted as specifying that Muᶜāwiya possessed as much as three quarters of the charisma of the Prophet.

[40] Ps. -Aṣmaᶜī, fol. 258a. Another version is in Ṭabarī I:620f.; Nöldeke 1879:367f. In the Ṭabarī version the quince is made to symbolize "the glory of the kings" (*majd al-mulūk*), which is clearly a reference to the royal *xwarrah*.

[41] Ṭabarī II:1458.

[42] Balāḍurī, IVa:107 lines 11ff. and the variants listed in the apparatus. I owe reference to this story to M.J. Kister, who has added the following variants not yet listed in his edition: Ibn Abī Ḥātim, I:116; Ibn Ḥajar al-ᶜAsqalānī, 6:127.

The fact that quinces were selected to carry this significance is not accidental. The association of the quince with the idea of prophecy in Islamic literature is attested quite unequivocally in a number of traditions. Thus, in a remark recorded by Majlisī it is said: "There was no prophet ever sent by God but that carried with him the scent of quinces" (*wa-mā baᶜaṯa llāhu nabiyyan illā wa-maᶜahu rā'iḥatu l-safarjal*).[43] Muḥammad himself was given a quince by the angel Gabriel in Paradise, and was then confronted with one of the beautiful maids of Paradise (Majlisī, 66:178).

It thus seems eminently suitable that the fruit of the Khirbat Mafjar mosaic should indeed be a quince. By apparently continuing an earlier Sasanian symbolism the quince was made to be one of the Islamic emblems of royal as well as prophetic power.[44]

IV. The seals of ᶜAlī

One final point in this discussion of the transfer of ancient Iranian royal symbolism to Islam concerns the seals of ᶜAlī. It is reported in various sources that ᶜAlī had four seals, each of which represented a different aspect of his royal power. He had a ruby seal for his nobility, on which the formula was engraved, *Lā ilāh illā Allāh al-malik al-ḥaqq al-mubīn.* Another seal was made of turquoise, for his victory, and carried the inscription *Allāh al-malik al-ḥaqq.* A third seal was made of Chinese iron,[45] for his power, with the inscription *Al-ᶜizza bi-llāhi jamīᶜan.* Yet another seal, made of chalcedony, was for his (magical) protection.[46] It had an

[43] Majlisī, 62:284. Cf. also, slightly differently, in Majlisī, 66:176 No. 37. Another formulation (*ibid.*) is: "The scent of quinces is the scent of the prophets". A long sequence of sayings in praise of the quince is given in Majlisī, 66:166ff. Burhān I:13 s.v. *ābī* says: "It is said that if a pregnant woman eats quince her child will be good-tempered".

[44] It seems to me likely that the fruit that many Muslim miniaturists draw when they wish to represent the unnamed fruit which the women in the Qur'ānic Joseph story (Sūra xii:31) cut their hands on was also the *safarjal*, with the implied association that Joseph was endowed with royal and prophetic power. See e.g. the sixteenth-century illustration to Jāmī's *Xamsa* in Binyon, Wilkinson and Gray 1971:Pl. LXXXVI and p. 129; British Library Ms. Or. 4535 fol. 104a, illustrated in Meredith-Owens 1965:Pl. VII. It is possible that we have an early representation of this fruit in Persepolis, in the reliefs of the Achaemenian palace, where some dignitaries are shown carrying "round or oval objects, presumably fruit or eggs" (Boyce 1982:107); Professor Boyce prefers to identify those objects as eggs, but in view of the evidence collected here a fruit such as quince cannot be excluded.

[45] The only other place where this substance is mentioned to my knowledge is among the seals of Xusrau II Abarwēz, cf. Masᶜūdī, *Murūj*, I:208 (as a variant of *ḥadīd ḥabašī*).

[46] *ḥirz*, which has the sense of "talisman".

engraving of three lines: *Mā šā'a Allāh. Lā quwwata illā bi-llāh. Astaġfiru Allāha.*[47]

The motif of the four seals of ᶜAlī, divided as they are by their functions, made of four different materials, and carrying four different inscriptions, is borrowed undoubtedly from the Sasanian tradition.[48] It occurs with regard to the celebrated king Xusrau Anošarwān, but the four seals attributed to him make much more the impression of a real administrative distribution than does the story of ᶜAlī's seals.[49] The four seals of Xusrau were: [1] one for the taxes (*xarāj*), of chalcedony,[50] with the engraving "justice" (*al-ᶜadl*), [2] one for the estates, of turquoise, engraved "prosperity" (*al-ᶜimāra*), [3] one for the assistance, of deep blue hyacinth, engraved "patience" (*al-ta'annī*), [4] one for the post, of red hyacinth shining like fire, engraved *"haste" (*al-waḥā'*).[51] A similar system of four seals is already attributed to the fabled Persian king Jamšīd. He established a seal for war and treaties, on which he engraved "patience" (*al-anāt*); a seal for taxes and for the collection of money, on which he engraved "prosperity" (*al-ᶜimāra*); a seal for the post, on which he engraved "haste" (*al-waḥā'*); a seal for grievances against iniquity (*maẓālim*), on which he engraved "justice" (*al-ᶜadl*). These inscriptions, we are told, were in use among the kings of Persia until the advent of Islam.[52]

Some of the words given in this passage as constituting the text of an engraving on a seal correspond to legends familiar to us from the Sasanian corpus of seals. Thus *al-ᶜadl* may correspond to *rāstīh*, as suggested

[47] *Istorija xalifov*, fol. 49b lines 7–14. A similar report occurs in Nājī fol. 87b; Majlisī 42:62 and 68; Ṭabarsī 33 (I owe the last three references to M.J. Kister). Masᶜūdī, *Tanbīh*, 297, mentions one seal of ᶜAlī, with the inscription *Al-mulk li-llāhi.* In the same book Masᶜūdī gives the text of one seal of Muᶜāwiya (p. 302), and similarly of Yazīd b. Muᶜāwiya (p. 306), Muᶜāwiya b. Yazīd (p. 307), Marwān b. al-Ḥakam (p. 312), and so on.

[48] That the seal was one of the three visible signs of royalty we may see from a story in which the king Yazdigird tries to dissemble and asks that his belt (*minṭaqa*), seal (*xātam*), and crown (*tāj*) be taken from him (Balāḏurī, *Futūḥ*, 312).

[49] Māsᶜūdī, *Murūj*, I:294. This and other related texts are discussed by Bivar 1969:30ff. An earlier discussion is in Thomas 1868:347f.

[50] A variant has: "red hyacinth shining like fire", but this is also the description of the fourth seal.

[51] The text has *al-rajā'* "hope", with a variant *al-wafā'* "fulfilment of promise". I have preferred the reading given by Masᶜūdī in the parallel section, where the nine seals of Xusrau are enumerated. The seal used for the postal answers according to that account bears the inscription *al-waḥā'* "haste" (Masᶜūdī, *Murūj*, I:307).

[52] Ibn Ḥamdūn, fol. 76b.

by Bivar, but it may also reflect *paymān* "the right measure".[53] *Al-ᶜimāra* should correspond to *ābādīh* or *ābādānīh*, which has not yet been found on seals. *Al-ta'annī* may possibly render *burdīh* or *dēr-pattāyīh* (neither of which is yet attested on seals). *Al-waḥā'*, if the reading is accepted, may render Middle Persian *zūd* or *zūdīh*. The variants of this last word have closer correspondence in seal inscriptions. *Al-rajā'*, if this reading is accepted, may be the equivalent of *ummēd*, and *al-wafā'* of *mihr*.

A Sasanian king who preceded Xusrau, Bahrām V Gōr (421–439), is mentioned as having used only one seal.[54] A king coming after Xusrau Anōšarwān, Xusrau II Abarwēz (591–628), had, in contrast, nine seals with different bezels and inscriptions.[55] Assuming, as we ought to do, that Masᶜūdī used sources which ultimately go back to the royal Sasanian chronicles, we may take it that there was an Iranian tradition which characterized kings by, among other things, the number of seals they used and their functional distribution, as well as by the message conveyed by the different formulae engraved on the seals. If this is correct, the fourfold formula used by Xusrau Anōšarwān was certainly regarded as a number of perfection, resembling as it does the fourfold division of the kingdom, for example. If this interpretation is acceptable, then the single seal of Bahrām Gōr prepares the way for Xusrau's fourfold division, and the nine seals of Xusrau Abarwēz may represent in this historiography a certain decline. That the fourfold division was adopted for ᶜAlī in the tradition of his followers is quite significant.[56]

The few emblems of royalty and power discussed in this paper do not by any means constitute an exhaustive list of such symbols. In its formative period Islam turned to ancient Iranian traditions as a source from which visual representations of the power of the ruler could be borrowed. In some cases the original significance of the symbols was lost, and it can only be reconstructed by using all the available sources.

[53] This is rendered in Arabic sometimes by the form *al-iᶜtidāl* as well as by *al-iqtiṣād*. For *ᶜadl* as possibly rendering Middle Persian *paymān* one may quote Masᶜūdī, *Murūj*, I:277, where the chief *mōbad* tells king Bahrām I: ...*wa l-ᶜadlu al-mīzānu al-manṣūbu bayna-l-xalīqati naṣabahu al-rabbu wa-jaᶜala lahu qayyiman wa-huwa l-maliku* "*ᶜadl* is the balance which is set among the creatures. It was set by the Lord who set over it a custodian — the king".

[54] Masᶜūdī, *Murūj*, I:287.

[55] Masᶜūdī, *Murūj*, I:307f.

[56] The Targum of Cant. 5:14 talks of 12 seals corresponding to the 12 tribes of Israel.

LIST OF WORKS QUOTED

Abu-l-Baqā', *Al-manāqib al-mazyadiyya,* Ms. British Library Add. 23.296.

^{c}Abd al-Jabbār, *Taṯbīt dalā'il al-nubuwwa,* ed. ^{c}Abd al-Karīm ^{c}Uṯmān, Beirut n.d.

Ps. -'Aṣma^{c}ī, *Siyar al-mulūk*, or *Nihāyat al-arab*, Ms. British Library 23.298.

Al-Balāḏurī, Aḥmad b. Yaḥyā b. Jābir, *Ansāb al-ašrāf*, IVa, ed. M. Schloessinger and M.J. Kister, Jerusalem 1971; vol. V, ed. S.D. Goitein, Jerusalem 1936.

— *Futūḥ al-buldān*, ed. Riḍwān Muḥ. Riḍwān, Beirut 1978.

Bartholomae, Christian, 1904, *Altiranisches Wörterbuch*, Strassburg. [2. unveränderte Auflage, Berlin 1961].

Beer, Moshe, 1970, *Rašut haggola be-bavel bime hammišna we-hattalmud*, Tel Aviv.

Binyon, L., J.V.S. Wilkinson and Basil Gray, 1971, *Persian miniature painting,* New York.

Bivar, A.D.H., 1969, *Catalogue of the Western Asiatic seals in the British Museum. Stamp seals II: The Sasanian dynasty,* London.

Bivar, A.D.H., and S. Shaked, 1964, "The inscriptions at Shīmbār", *BSOAS* 27: 265–290.

Boyce, Mary, 1982, *A history of Zoroastrianism*, II (Handbuch der Orientalistik, I, VIII, 1. Abschnitt, Lief. 2, Heft 2A), Leiden-Köln.

Burhān, Muḥ. Ḥusayn b. Xalaf Tabrīzī, *Burhān-i Qāṭi^c*, ed. M. Mo^{c}in. 5 vols. Tehran 1342.

Chwolson, D., 1856, *Die Ssabier und der Ssabismus*, St. Petersburg, 2 vols.

Al-Dīnawarī, Abū Ḥanīfa Aḥmad b. Dāwūd, *Kitāb al-axbār al-ṭiwāl*, ed. Vladimir Guirgass, Leiden 1888.

Drijvers, H.J.W., 1972, *Old-Syriac (Edessan) inscriptions*, ed. with an introduction etc. (Semitic Study Series, N.S. III), Leiden.

— 1980, *Cults and beliefs at Edessa* (Etudes préliminaires aux religions orientales dans l'Empire Romain, t. 82), Leiden.

Drower, E.S., 1956, *Water into wine. A study of ritual idiom in the Middle East,* London.

Eilers, Wilhelm, 1962, "Iranisches Lehngut im arabischen Lexikon: über einige Berufsnamen und Titel", *IIJ* 5:203–232; "Nachtrag", pp. 308–309.

— 1969, "Vier Bronzewaffen mit Keilinschriften aus West Iran", *Persica* 4:1–56.

— 1971, "Iranisches Lehngut im Arabischen", *Actas IV Congresso de Estudos Arabes e Islamicos*, Leiden, pp. 581–660.

Erdmann, K., 1951, "Die Entwicklung der sasanidischen Krone", *Ars Islamica* 15/16:87–121.

Ettinghausen, Richard, 1972, *From Byzantium to Sasanian Iran and the Islamic world. Three modes of artistic influence* (The L.A. Mayer Memorial Studies in Islamic Art and Archaeology, 3), Leiden.

Fraenkel, S., 1880, *De vocabulis in antiquis arabum carminibus et in Corano peregrinis*, Leiden.

Gafni, Isaiah, 1980, "Hayyešiva habbavlit le-or sugyat Bava Qama 127a", *Tarbiz* 49:292–301.

Göbl, Robert, 1971, *Sasanian numismatics,* Braunschweig.

Goldziher, Ignaz, 1900, "Islamisme et parsisme", *Actes du 1er Congrès International d'histoire des religions*, Paris, pp. 119–147.

Grignaschi, Mario, 1966, "Quelques spécimens de la littérature sassanide conservés dans les bibliothèques d'Istanbul", *JA*, 254:1–142.

Ḥamza b. al-Ḥasan al-Isfahānī, *Ta'rīx sinī mulūk al-arḍ wa-l-anbiyā'*, Beirut n.d.

Henning, W.B., 1952, "The monuments and inscriptions of Tang-i Sarvak", *Asia Major*, N.S. 2:151–178.

Hübschmann, H., 1895, *Persische Studien*, Strassburg.

— 1897, *Armenische Grammatik*, Leipzig [Reprint: Hildesheim–New York 1972].

Ibn al-Balxī, *Fārs nāma*, ed. G. LeStrange and R.A. Nicholson (E.J.W. Gibb Memorial Series, N.S. 1), London 1921. [Reprint: 1962].

Ibn Ḥajar al-ᶜAsqalānī, Aḥmad b. ᶜAlī, *Lisān al-Mīzān*, Beirut 1971. [Reprint of the edition Hyderabad 1321].

Ibn Hišām, *Kitāb al-tījān*, Hyderabad 1347.

Ibn Ḥamdūn, Abu-l-Maᶜālī Muḥ. b. al-Ḥasan, *Al-taḏkira*, Ms. Reisülküttab 766.

Ibn Kaṯīr, Abu-l-Fidā' Ismāᶜīl, *Al-bidāya wa-l-nihāya*, Cairo 1932ff.

Ibn al-Nadīm, *Kitāb al-fihrist*, ed. G. Flügel, 2 vols. [Reprint: Beirut 1964].

Al-ᶜIṣāmī, ᶜAbdallāh b. Ḥusayn, *Simṭ al-nujūm al-ᶜawālī fī anbā'i l-awā'il wa-l-tawālī*, Cairo 1380 AH.

Al-Iṣbahānī, Abū Nuᶜaym, *Ḥilyat al-awliyā'*, Beirut 1967, 9 vols.

Istorija xalifov anonimnogo avtora XI veka (Ta'rīx al-xulafā'), with introduction by P. A. Grjaznevič, Moscow 1967.

Al-Jāḥiẓ, Abū ᶜUṯmān ᶜAmr b. Baḥr, *Al-bayān wa-l-tabyīn*, ed. ᶜAbd al-Salām Hārūn, 4th ed., 4 vols., Cairo [1975].

— *Kitāb al-maḥāsin wa-l-aḍdād*, ed. Muḥ. Amīn al-Xānjī al-Kutubī, Cairo 1324.

(Ps.-) Jāḥiẓ, *Kitāb al-tāj,* ed. Aḥmad Zakī Bāšā, Cairo 1322/1914.

Jamāl al-Dīn ibn Nubāta al-Miṣrī, *Sarḥ al-ᶜuyūn fī šarḥ risālat Ibn Zaydūn*, ed. Muḥ. Abu-l-Faḍl Ibrāhīm, Cairo 1964.

Kohut, Alexander, 1878–1892, *ᶜArūḵ haššalem (Aruch completum)*, Vienna, 8 vols. [Reprint: New York 1955].

Krauss, Samuel, 1937, *Tosefot he-ᶜaruḵ haššalem (Additamenta ad Aruch completum)*, Vienna. [Reprint: New York 1955].

de Lagarde, Paul, 1866, *Gesammelte Abhandlungen*, Leipzig.

Al-Majlisī, Muḥ. Bāqir, *Biḥār al-anwār,* ed. Sayyid Jawād al-ᶜAlawī and Muḥ. al-Āxundī, Tehran, vol. 42, 1383; vol. 62, 1389; vol. 66, 1393.

(Ps.-) Majrīṭī, Abū Qāsim Maslama b. Aḥmad, *Ġāyat al-ḥakīm wa-aḥaqq al-natījatayni bi-l-taqdīm*, ed. H. Ritter (Studien der Bibliothek Warburg, XII), Leipzig-Berlin 1933.

— *"Picatrix". Das Ziel des Weisen*, tr. into German by H. Ritter and M. Plessner (Studies of the Warburg Institute, 27), London 1962.

Mann, Jacob, 1931, *Texts and studies in Jewish history and literature*, I, Cincinnati [New edition: New York 1972].

Maricq, André, 1963, *Classica et orientalia*, Paris.

Al-Masᶜūdī, Abu-l-Ḥasan ᶜAlī b. al-Ḥusayn, *Murūj al-ḏahab*, ed. Yūsuf Asᶜad Dāġir, 4 vols, Beirut 1965.

—, *Al-tanbīh wa-l-išrāf*, ed. M. de Goeje [Reprint: Beirut 1955].

Meredith-Owens, G.M., 1965, *Persian illustrated manuscripts*, London (The British Museum).

Modi, J.J., 1937, *The religious ceremonies and customs of the Parsees*, 2nd. ed., Bombay.

Mustafa, Mohammed, 1960, *Persian miniatures of Behzad and his school in Cairo collections* (The Emerald Series, 3), London.

Al-Nājī, Muḥ, b. Maḥmūd, *Al-taᶜlīq al-rašīq fī al-taxattum bi-l-ᶜaqīq*. Jewish National and University Library, Ms. Yahuda Arab. 318.

Nöldeke, Theodor, 1875, *Mandäische Grammatik*, Halle.

— 1879, *Geschichte der Perser und Araber zur Zeit der Sasaniden*, Leyden.

Nuwayrī, Šihāb al-Dīn Aḥmad b. ᶜAbd al-Wahhāb, *Nihāyat al-arab fī funūn al-adab*, Cairo 1342/1923ff.

Payne-Smith, R., 1879, *Thesaurus syriacus*, Oxford.

Perles, Joseph, 1871, *Etymologische Studien zur Kunde der rabbinischen Sprache und Altertümer*, Breslau.

Segal, J.B., 1954, "Some Syriac inscriptions of the 2nd-3rd century A.D.", *BSOAS* 16:13–36.

Shaked, Shaul, 1979, *The Wisdom of the Sasanian Sages (Dēnkard VI)*, by Āturpāt-i Ēmētān (Persian Heritage Series, 34), Boulder, Col.

— 1982, "Two Judaeo-Iranian contributions", in S. Shaked (ed.), *Irano-Judaica*, Jerusalem, pp. 292–322.

— 1984 "From Iran to Islam. Notes on some themes in transmission", *JSAI* 4, pp. 31–67.

Sperber, Daniel, 1982, "On the unfortunate adventures of Rav Kahana: A passage of Saboraic polemic from Sasanian Persia", in S. Shaked (ed.), *Irano-Judaica*, Jerusalem, pp. 83–100.

Al-Ṯaᶜālibī, Abū Manṣūr ᶜAbd al-Malik b. Muḥammad, *Gurar axbār mulūk al-furs wa-siyaruhum. Histoire des rois des Perses*, ed. H. Zotenberg, Paris 1900 [Reprint: Tehran 1963].

—, *Laṭā'if al-* maᶜārif, ed. P. de Jong, Leiden 1867.

Ṭabarī, Abū Jaᶜfar Muḥ. b. Jarīr, *Ta'rīx al-rusul wa-l-mulūk*, ed. M.J. de Goeje et alii, Leiden 1888ff.

Al-Ṭabarsī, Raḍī al-Dīn Abū Naṣr, *Makārim al-axlāq*, Cairo 1347.

Thomas, E., 1868, "Sasanian inscriptions", *JRAS* N.S. 3:241–358.

Widengren, Geo, 1958, *Iranisch-semitische Kulturbegegnung in parthischer Zeit* (Arbeitsgemeinschaft für Forschung des Landes Nordrhein-Westfalen, Geisteswissenschaften, Heft 70), Köln and Opladen.

Al-Yaᶜqūbī, Aḥmad b. Abī Yaᶜqūb, *Ta'rīx al-Yaᶜqūbī*, 3 vols., Najaf 1964.

VIII

PAYMĀN: AN IRANIAN IDEA IN CONTACT WITH GREEK THOUGHT AND ISLAM

The extent of the debt owed by Sasanian Iran to Greek literature has been the subject of fairly extensive scholarly discussion [1]. It has not always been easy to identify the Greek terminology behind the Pahlavi terms used, and some of the areas in which Greek influence is suspected are not clearly identified. Still, there is no doubt that borrowing from the Greek was an important factor in the formation of late Zoroastrian thinking, at least in so far as the Sasanian period is concerned. This borrowing was, moreover, accompanied by some sort of religious justification. It was claimed that Iranian books had been brought over from Iran to Greece during the Macedonian occupation of Iran; carrying over Greek themes into Zoroastrian writings was, as a result, nothing more than a restitution of a lost Iranian heritage [2].

One interesting area in which the dependence of Iranian ideas on Greek thought seems prominently attested is the area of ethics. The first to note the similarity between the Iranian discussions of virtues and vices and the schemes which emerge from Aristotle's *Nicomachean*

[1] See Nallino 1922; Bailey 1943. Instances of Aristotelian ideas which were adopted in the Pahlavi writings have been noticed by several scholars since. Cf., e.g., Zaehner 1955, 33; Menasce 1958, 27; Shaki 1970. More general discussions of such influences will be found in Boyce 1968, p. 36 ff., 64 f. See also M. Boyce, *Asia Major* N.S. 5 (1955), 50 ff.; *Letter of Tansar*, Rome 1964, 14 ff.

[2] This is set out in a chapter of *Dēnkard* IV, which tells the history of the transmission of the Avesta (*DkM* 412 ff.; B 320 ff.). Cf. Bailey 1943, 218 f.; Menasce 1958, 25; Wikander 1946, 134 ff.; Nyberg 1938, 415 ff.; Idem, *Cama Or. Inst.* 39 (1958), 17 f.; Widengren 1961, 311 ff.; Zaehner 1955, 7 ff., 31 ff.; Molé 1961, 5 ff. The latest detailed treatment of this text is by Shaki 1981. It may be remarked that borrowing from other cultures was not always necessarily accompanied by such pious justifications. We have in what looks like an authentic piece of Sasanian literature in Arabic transmission, *Sīrat Anūšarwān wa-siyāsatuhu*, preserved in Miskawayh, *Tajārib*, 205-207, an elaborate admission of deliberate borrowing. Anōšarwān states that he started off by studying the history of his forefathers (*wa-naẓarnā fī siyari ābā'inā*), after which he studied the history of the Greeks (*ahl al-Rūm*) and the Indians, and selected from that what was laudable in the field of government and politics, but rejected the wisdom of the other peoples, because he had reached the conclusion that they had neither intelligence nor brains. For a French translation of this passage see Grignaschi 1966, 27 f.

Ethics was J. de Menasce[3]. The similarity in treatment is undeniable. The main concept of the Aristotelian theory of ethics, the idea of the Mean, finds its echo in the Iranian concept of *paymān*, the right measure, which is also defined, like its Greek counterpart, as the middle course between the two extremes. The extremes, identified as vices, are excess and deficiency. This relationship between Aristotelian ethics and the system of the Pahlavi books is however somewhat complex, as I shall try to show.

To see how *paymān* is defined in purely Zoroastrian terms it may be best to quote *Dēnkard* III, 297:

> On the good action of the Mazdaean religion, a summary. From the instruction of the Good Religion.
> The summary of the good action of the Mazdaean religion is to bring back to the right measure the excess and the deficiency of the Attack which are in the creatures, to give salvation and well-being to the whole creation.
> Thus, Ohrmazd the Creator (created) the Mazdaean religion in order to vanquish the Attack, and to give ease to the creatures.
> He left that which is necessary for vanquishing the Attack and for purifying the creatures. His all-encompassing wisdom (consists) in putting right the creations of Ohrmazd, each one separately. In summary, (this is) the one power of all, which is the Measure.
> Their corruption by the Attack is by two (things), which hold the whole power of the demons, excess and deficiency. One (consists in) going beyond the Measure, and one (consists in) holding back the nourishment and number[4] which are according to the Measure in the creation of Ohrmazd.
> When the creation is brought back from excess to the Measure, and is led from deficiency to the Measure, every action is saved in wisdom by the Mazdaean religion from all evil, and is brought over to the all-encompassing goodness, the pure lawfulness.
> Thus indeed is it said by the Early Teachers from the instruction of the Good Religion: the religion of Ohrmazd is (but) one word, the Measure; that of Ahreman is two words, excess and deficiency (*DkM* 306 f.; B 234. Cf. Zaehner, *Magi*, 92 f.; Menasce 1973, 292).

It is clear from this passage that the Aristotelian theory of the Mean, which assumes three elements, the middle course being placed between excess and deficiency, is here wedded to the dualistic system, which recognizes but two principles. The idea that the contrast between good and evil qualities is made not by putting them against each other, but by placing good in the middle between two evils is quite incongruous in the Zoroastrian setting. The simple dualistic contrast between good and evil loses some of its force by this description. There seems to be

[3] See Menasce 1945, 30 f.; 1958, 39 ff.

[4] This is difficult. Menasce reads *āstārīh* «la faute»; *margīh* «la mortalité». The trouble is that the first word is non-existent, and the second is not written here.

no way but to decide that it was imported from the outside, with Greece as the place of origin. The use made of this idea is however by no means one of servile dependence. The Zoroastrian text blends this borrowed idea to its own view of the world and endows the Aristotelian theory with a strong Zoroastrian flavour. In the Aristotelian view the Mean is not always an absolute term. It exists on an imagined continuum at the two far sides of which are the ethical vices, and is in principle defined by being equally distant from both. Such a view would be alien to Zoroastrian thinking, which attributed *paymān* to Ohrmazd and the two extremes to the Adversary. From the Aristotelian point of view, which takes into account psychological and social factors, it may be necessary, for educational purposes, to correct a bad tendency which has got hold of a person by taking a course of action which inclines towards the other extreme, thus restoring the balance which was lacking, or to condone in certain people what is condemned in others[5]. We have no trace of such an attitude in Zoroastrianism, and it would be surprising to have it, since the two extremes are not regarded as modes of behaviour which simply lack a balance, but are inherently evil.

One may think of other factors which may make the wedding of Aristotelian ideas with Zoroastrianism extremely uneasy. Such is, for example, the prominent Zoroastrian conception of the various invisible entities, the *mēnōgs*, that inhabit a person, and are identified with the person's thoughts and actions. Such a view of man and of the world does not fit in well, in principle, with a philosophical theory which regards human actions as dependent on and connected with nothing but the person himself. This is however a kind of difficulty which arises not only with regard to Zoroastrianism, but also with regard to Judaism, Christianity and Islam, and yet theologians of these religions have found a way to reconcile Aristotelian philosophy to the tenets of their religion.

We do not have, in the Pahlavi writings, elaborate discussions of the psychological schemes as we have them in Aristotle's books. We have, in contrast, a different type of classification of the various virtues and vices, one which is not found in the Aristotelian writings. The theory is set forth as follows:

> The wise man, as he has forward-inclined and backward-inclined (virtues), his virtues are assembled through the Measure in his nature by the creation of the Creator. ... A time the governing of which is ascendance, is generally (to be treated) by forward-inclined (virtues), though for

[5] This is the position taken by mediaeval Aristotelian thinkers such as Maimonides. Cf. also e.g. Yaḥyā b. ʿAdī, *Tahḏīb al-aḵlāq*, 37: «On some qualities which are noble in some people and base in others».

> (certain) occasions and people through backward-inclined (virtues). A time whose governing is decline is (to be treated) generally by backward-inclined (virtues), though for (certain) occasions and people through forward-inclined (virtues). The governing of virtues which is done by the good bearing of the two kinds of virtue in the two sorts of time is effective in carrying out (its purpose) (*Dk* III, 68; see Appendix 1).

This passage is followed by two lists, both containing good and bad qualities, one listing qualities which belong to the category called «forward-inclined» and the other devoted to the «backword-inclined» qualities[6].

Certain details in this discussion, e.g. the remark about wisdom which knows the right time, and which can lead the qualities in the right fashion, are reminiscent of Aristotle's words in the Nicomachean Ethics (1106b.8 ff.) regarding the knowledge (*epistēmē*) which brings its action to completion by looking at the middle. In the same context it is stated that the middle is defined as being «in the proper time, in proper things, with regard to proper people, by a proper cause, and by a proper measure» (1106b.21-23). The similarity here may not be fortuitous, but the discussion in the Pahlavi contains essential elements which have no parallel in the Aristotelian writings. It contains a reference to two types of virtues, connected with two corresponding types of time, a time of ascent and a time of descent. It is not easy to determine what exactly is meant by this typology of time, whether it refers to the astrological notions, or to social conditions. The latter interpretation is closer in spirit to Aristotle's thought, although it is not found in Aristotle.

The distinction between «forward-inclined» and «backward-inclined» qualities is not rare in the third book of the *Dēnkard*. The first category represents active, outgoing, energetic, progressive qualities, such as speed or agility, effort, generosity. The second stands for qualities which are characterized by passivity, inertia, regression. Examples for the latter are patience, forbearance, economy. These two categories are two modes of action, and each of them comprises good and evil qualities. We thus get sets of double oppositions: we find, on the one hand, the contrast between «forward-inclined» and «backward-inclined» qualities, and, on the other hand, in each group, we encounter the opposition between good and bad attributes of the person. The fundamental Zoroastrian dualistic opposition between good and evil could not fail to be prominently represented in the moral

[6] In *ŠGV* I:14 we come across a pair of other terms which are allied to *paymān*: *kunišni* and *paharezašni*, but they obviously constitute a different kind of division, viz. the distinction between things to do and things that one should avoid doing (cf. in Judaism *miṣwot ʿaśe* and *miṣwot lo taʿaśe*, in Islam *al-amr wa-l-nahy*, etc.).

field. The dualistic idea preserves its predominant position despite the introduction of a new classification system. The interesting feature of this classification is the fact that it represents an attempt at reconciling between the dualistic system, so typical of Zoroastrianism, and the trinitarian system of Aristotle. The result is a set of four items in each group. It is not easy to decide what should be the order of the fourfold set which is obtained, as there is no reference to this in the Zoroastrian writings. One reasonable method could be to put the two good qualities in the middle, with the two excesses in the two extremes, thus applying the same rule which operates with the trinitarian set of qualities in the original system of Aristotle's Nicomachaean Ethics. For example, «effort» has its excess in «lustfulness», but it stands in contrast to another good quality, which belongs to the «backward-inclined» mode of behaviour, «sufficiency» or «forbearance». Its opposite, or excess, is «sloth». The two pairs of opposites form a series of four items; if we start with the most active and conclude with the most passive we shall have the following sequence:

«lustfulness» — «effort» — «sufficiency» — «sloth».

Another example may be taken from the qualities connected with the attitude towards wealth. «Generosity» is a good quality; its opposite is «wastefulness, prodigality». In the same field «economy» is a good quality, contrasted by «stinginess». The two pairs represent respectively «forward-inclined» and «backward-inclined» qualities. Arranging the four qualities in one line, and going again from the most «forward-inclined» to the most «backward-inclined» in the group, we have the following set:

«wastefulness» — «generosity» — «economy» — «miserliness».

An alternative mode of arrangement may be the following:

«generosity» — «wastefulness» — «economy» — «stinginess».

In this set the first two qualities are «forward-inclined», and the two last ones are «backward-inclined». At the same time, «generosity» has as its opposite pole «stinginess», and «wastefulness» is neatly opposed to «economy».

Such a fourfold system, under whatever arrangment, is found nowhere in Aristotle, but it is apparently not very far from the possibilities inherent in the Aristotelian system of thought. This may be gathered from the fact that at least one of Aristotle's modern interpreters[7] suggests that two sets of dualities may be supposed to exist for each category of human quality instead of the trinitarian system of Aristotle. He goes on to elaborate a fourfold scheme not

[7] W.D. Ross, *Aristotle*, London 1956, 206.

entirely unlike the one which was developed by the Zoroastrian thinkers. He says that without presumably knowing anything about the ethical writings in Pahlavi. A somewhat similar conception is found in Apuleius of Madaura, one of the group of thinkers known as the Middle Platonists. I am quoting the relevant passage from the French translation of M. Nisard:

> Il existe pareillement un milieu entre la vertu et le vice, une sorte de moyen terme d'où résultent des action méritoires ou coupables. Entre la vraie science et l'ignorance, il y a l'esprit vide et plein de jactance; entre la prudence et la débauche, il y a l'abstinence et l'intempérance; entre le courage et la crainte, il y a la honte et la lâcheté. Ces natures médiocres n'ont pas de vertus parfaites ni de vices excessifs ou démesurés; elles ne sont qu'un mélange adouci de deux natures opposées. Mais le pire de tous les vices, c'est la méchanceté. Elle provient de ce que la plus noble partie de l'homme, la raison, obéit, au lieu de commander aux autres. La colère et la luxure, ces mères des mauvaises passions, ont vaincu la raison et la dominent. La méchanceté résulte aussi de deux principes contraires, du défaut et de l'excès; elle n'est pas seulement inégale, mais encore dissemblable; car ce qui se combat soi-même à tel point, ce qui est inégal et désordonné, ne saurait avoir aucune analogie avec le bien. (Apuleius Platonicus Madaurensis, *De Platone et eius dogmate*, Liber II, 225-226; quoted from Nisard 1842, 160)[8].

There are some obvious differences between the conception set forth by Apuleius in the name of Plato and that of the Pahlavi books. In the Pahlavi scheme we have either a binary opposition between good and evil qualities repeated twice in two related pairs, or a set of four terms whose arrangement is not clear. The Apuleian scheme sets the opposite good and had qualities in the two extremes, with two «mixed» qualities, again good and bad respectively, in between. It may not be justified to talk of a direct borrowing or dependence between Apuleius and the Zoroastrian writings. Apuleius however serves to demonstrate the potential for enlarging the Aristotelian[9] scheme into a fourfold structure, just as is done apparently in the Pahlavi writings.

We are assuming that the Pahlavi theory of ethics, as developed in a group of chapters in the third book of the *Dēnkard* is a development of a basic Aristotelian conception. A number of specific points of resemblance make the Aristotelian influence on the Zoroastrian scheme almost certain. There is, for example, a quality called *wururg-menišnīh*, which literally translated means «having a great mind, or thought». This is an expression which is not otherwise prominently attested in Persian[10], and its meaning is not immediately clear. It stands in

[8] See in general on Apuleius's ethics in Dillon 1977, 328 ff.

[9] I take it that despite the declared reference to Plato it is really the Aristotelian system that is being reshaped by Apuleius.

[10] The expression *buzurg-maništī kunad* occurs in an old Qur'ān translation preserved in a

contrast to *abar-menišnīh*, which means literally «having a superior mind», but since this is a vice one should rather translate it «having an overbearing mind». The corresponding pair among the «backward-inclined» qualities has the good quality *ēr-menišnīh*, which literally means «being of a low mind», but being a virtue it obviously denotes «having a meek or modest thinking»; the opposing vice is called *ōbastag-menišnīh*, i.e. «of a base mind», «regarding (oneself) as low». Given this set of terms, it is clear that the expression *wuruzg-menišnīh* should be defined as denoting something like «possessing a view (of oneself) which is great (but not exaggerated), possessing self-respect». The puzzling terms in Pahlavi find their perfect literal and semantic equivalents in the Greek terminology of Aristotle's *Ethics*. The term *wuzurg-menišnīh* seems to be an obvious calque translation of *megalopsychia*[11], while the vice called here *ōbastag-menišnīh* (which belongs to the other pair of opposites in the same set) finds its perfect counterpart in the Greek *mikropsychia*, the vice of deficiency in Aristotle's scheme.

Another point which suggests that the Middle Persian discussion is derived from a foreign source is the fact that the qualities, virtues and vices, which form the backbone of the traditional system of ethics, from the Avesta on, are almost entirely absent from the scheme as we have it here. I mean such terms as Truth, and its opposite, Lie; the Good Mind, as opposed to Wrath, etc., terms which are often encountered in other passages in Pahlavi where good and evil qualities are discussed, but where the traditional spirit seems to prevail. Where we do have «truth-speaking» occurring in one of these philosophical lists, its evil counterpart is not «lie», but, as a vice of excess, *nāzēnagīh*, «self-embellishment, coquetry», which is reminiscent of the Aristotelian vice of excess of «truth» (*alētheia*), which is *alazoneia*, «boasting».

One of the good qualities adduced by Aristotle is *nemesis*, «seeking just revenge, having justified anger». On both sides, as vices, he lists *phthonos*, «envy», and *epikhairekakia*, «joy at someone's misfortune». To this system one may compare in Pahlavi *ēwēn-xwāhišnīh*, «seeking what one may get by custom», *waranīgīh*, «lustfulness», and in the opposite extreme *kēn-hanbārīh*, «hoarding up of vengeance». The parallel here is not in the wording of the terms, but in the general spirit of the system.

On the whole the similarity between the Iranian lists and those

Mašhad manuscript (Ravāqī, p. 8; Sūrat al-nisā': 172), where it serves to render Arabic *yastakbiru*, a negative concept. (I owe my knowledge of this publication to the kindness of Gilbert Lazard.)

[11] The Arabic rendering is likewise a calque on the Greek: *al-kabīr al-nafs* ('Āmirī, 162).

which exist in the Aristotelian canon is rather limited. Most of the items in the Zoroastrian lists of qualities have no parallel in the Greek world. If indeed we have here a real historical connection it must be assumed that the borrowing was not done by direct literal translation, but mostly by adopting the Greek principle of arrangement.

Both the absence of the traditional set of terms from these philosophical chapters of *Dēnkard* III and the close similarity of some terms to the Aristotelian scheme make the assumption of Aritotelian influence on Zoroastrian thinking very plausible. It is still an open question whether the particular line of development which turned the Aristotelian triad into two pairs of opposites (or into a set of four items) occurred in Iran or was borrowed from a Greek school of Aristotelian philosophy (such as that represented by Apuleius).

The traditional Zoroastrian notions of ethics, on which the Aristotelian ethical theory was grafted, have a fairly long history. The idea of *paymān* is almost certainly not an import from the autside. It actually occupied an important position in traditional Iranian writings. The literature about ethics in Iran, usually called *andarz*, falls into three broad categories: (a) One has pragmatic and secular character, and may be assumed to have been wisdom literature used for study and entertainment in court circles. (b) Another may be characterized as popular religious; it possesses a certain spirit of pressimism and mild asceticism. It seems to have been written for general instruction and edification. (c) A third class consists of religious texts which made use of fairly abstruse allusions and are obviously meant for people with theological training[12]. The distinction between «popular religious» and «theological» writings does not refer to distinctions in social stratification, but merely to the degree of technical training one needs in order to cope with the language and contents of the various compositions. In other words, «popular» in this context may in principle include highly placed court officials, princes and kings, whose schooling presumably seldom comprised theological training. The ethical schemes which are close to the Aristotelian system of ethics occur only in writings which belong to the third category, which is theological and philosophical is style. They occur specifically in the third and sixth books of the *Dēnkard*. In other Pahlavi writings, when discussions of virtues and vices come up, we have what is obviously the traditional Zoroastrian view of the subject[13]. It is typical of such

[12] On the classification of *andarz* works see my article «Andarz» in the *Encyclopaedia Iranica* II.

[13] This is found in such writings as the *Ayādgār ī Wuzurgmihr* (paras. 29 ff. and paras. 16 ff.), but is not entirely absent also from the theological books. See further material in Shaked 1972, 439 ff.

passages that the good qualities are not defined as being in a middle position between two vices, and that the vices are not presented as «excess» and «deficiency». Good and bad qualities are not relative terms, as in the philosophical schemes, but rather absolute notions, and are conceived of as being good and bad spirits.

We have lists of qualities which are part of the antithesis between gods and demons[14], as well as lists which strike a balance between the traditional gods/demons type of treatment and the philosophical classification[15]. In the first type we have simple antithesis between good and evil qualities. An important characteristic of this kind of list is that it contains the pair of opposites Truth/Lie[16]. In the second type we may have a definition of the good qualities as being in the middle, with the two vices representing the extremes of excess and deficiency, as in the philosophical conception, but the list that follows is arranged by paris of simple opposition, which do not seem to comprise larger units (that is to say, they are not organized in sets of four)[17].

The harmony between the Aristotelian scheme and the traditional Zoroastrian dualism of qualities is present in an interesting manner in *Dk* III, 286[18], where we are told that the demons stole the *paymān* from men, and that the mythological king Yima saved it and brought it back to men. The term *paymān* is ambiguous in Pahlavi. It indicates both a pact, contract (more especially the contract which set a limit to the fight between the good and the evil powers in the world, and which is thus crucial for the very existence of this world), and the right measure. This chapter plays on the double meaning of the term and superimposes the Aristotelian meaning on the traditional term by way of a midrashic interpretation.

The text makes use of a mythological story, not known in detail from other sources, about how Yima fought excess and deficiency and encouraged *paymān*. He afterwards descended into Hell in the form of a demon, and stayed there for thirteen years without being recognized by the denizens of Hell. From the demons in Hell he learned the secret of how they can be vanquished, and when he came back from Hell he smote the demons and overcame them by means of the secret instrument which he took from them. Afterwards the demons could no longer take full possession of the world by excess and deficiency, and

[14] E.g., *Ayādgār ī Wuzurgmihr*, as well as *Dk* III, 310.

[15] E.g. *Dk* III, 203.

[16] Cf. *Dk* III, 310.

[17] Cf. *Dk* III, 203, where among the pairs of opposites we again find Truth/Lie, the presence of which indicates that the philosophical framework was grafted on a traditional scheme.

[18] See Appendix, 2.

paymān became current in the world. It is hard to tell what elements in this mythology belong to the early Avestan layer, which the Pahlavi version purports to reproduce. The motif of the story is close to that in which the figure of Yima comes out tainted with some unspecified blemish or sin. It is never very clear what was Yima's fault in distributing meat to manking, or why he should have been sawn in two. His descent into Hell in the present story, although done with the best of motives, seems to indicate again some slight suspicion of Yima's collusion with the underworld of demons, especially as he does not shun the trick of adopting a demonic form in such a perfect manner that the demons themselves cannot recognize in him someone different from their elk.

The concept of *paymān* is indeed so deeply embedded in the Iranian consciousness that the Pahlavi writings (and their echoes in the Islamic world) often refer to this idea as the one which distinguishes Iran most perfectly from all other peoples and cultures. A very clear statement to this effect is found in *Dk* IV:

> ērān hamē paymān stāyīd, frehbūd ud abēbūd nikōhīd. pad hṙōm fīlōsōfāy ud pad hindūgān dānāg ud pad abārīg gyāg šnāsag hān abērdar stāyīd ke gōwišn nēzumānīh azešān paydāgihast. frazānagān <ī> ērān-šahr <paymān> passandīd ēstād.
> Iran has always praised *paymān* and condemned excess and deficiency. In Byzantium the philosophers, in India the wise men, in other places the knowers have praised above all else those from whom skill of speech is manifest. The perspicacious men of the Kingdom of Iran have approved of <*paymān*>[19].

Another text states very clearly:

> Sin is essentially excess and deficiency. Good works are essentially the Measure. ... Religion is the Measure (*Dk* VI, 39).

It seems quite likely that *paymān* was indeed part of the Iranian heritage, and that they selected this term to render the Aristotelian concept of the Mean (*to meson*) non because it was the closest term, for it does not render the idea of the Mean at all literally, but because it had been there as a traditional term which conceptually approximated the Aristotelian idea. There is an interesting difference between the rendering of the term *paymān* in Arabic writings (it is rendered usually by *qaṣd*, *iqtiṣād*, *iʿtidāl*[20]), and the rendering of the Aristotelian mean in Arabic (it is often rendered by *tawassuṭ*, *wasaṭ*[21]).

[19] *DkM* 429, B 335. My translation is different from Bailey 1943, 86. I have followed Zaehner 1955, 252 n. 2, on most, though not all, points. It must be assumed that the word *paymān* was omitted from the text by mistake, for otherwise the sentence remains incomplete.

[20] Cf. e.g. the words attributed to Kisrā Anōšarwān: *fa-ra'aytu al-ʿaqla akbara l'ašyā'i wa-ajallahā ... wa-l-iqtiṣād aḥsana l-afʿāli ...* «In my view wisdom is the greatest and most sublime of things ... and the right measure the most beautiful of actions ...» (Miskawayh, *Jāwīdān Ḵirad*,

Another clear case of Iranian dependence on Greek thought in the field of ethical theory can be shown to exist in *Dk* VI, 68[22]. This section shows great similarity to a passage attributed by Miskawayh to the lost treatise on ethics by Galen[23] which has a parallel in Apuleius of Madaura. Galen says that there are people who are good by nature and others who are bad by nature, and some who are in the middle. Those who are either good or bad by nature are not capable of change through education, but those who are in the middle can be made to be good or bad by their society and education. In another place Galen says that there are some people who are like angels and others who are like pigs and worms. The *Dēnkard* passage reads like a direct translation from Galen.

Arabic literature preserved fragments from all the different types of Pahlavi books of *andarz*. We have sections translated into Arabic from the books of pragmatic *andarz*, from the books of popular religious *andarz*, as well as from the theological *andarz* works[24]. We have in Arabic instances of the fourfold scheme of virtues and vices in passages which are obviously translated from a Middle Persian original. Thus we have in Ibn al Muqaffa''s *Al-adab al-ṣaġīr* a passage which is clearly derived from a Pahlavi prototype[25]:

> There are four (types of) men: a generous man, a miser, a spendthrift and a moderate spender. The generous man is one who directs the whole of his share of this world towards the world to come. The miser is one who does not give to any of the two its due share. The spendthrift is one who gathers them both for the purpose of his this world(ly pleasure). The moderate spender is one who attaches to each one of them its due share (Kurd 'Ali 1946, 30)[26].

The fourfold scheme is used in this passage, as in some Pahlavi texts, for a *midrashic* interpretation: the terms «generous» etc. are made to

---

61). The same composition says on vices: *wa-kullu ḏālika muḵālifun li-l-qaṣdi* «All of this is in opposition to the right measure» (op. cit., p. 49).

[21] E.g. 'Āmiri, 70 ff.; Māwardī, *Tashīl al-naẓar*, 17. But cf. *i'tidāl* in Yaḥyā b. 'Adī, *Tahḏīb al-aḵlāq*, 26.

[22] The following reference should be added to my notes in *Dk* VI, 68 on Sogd. *prwyδ-*: E. Benveniste, «Notes sogdiennes», *JA* 239 (1951), 121 f.

[23] See Miskawahy, *Tahḏīb al-aḵlāq*, 33; tr. Arkoun, 54. The same idea is in Apuleius, *De Platone*, II:224: *Tria genera ingeniorum ab eo sunt comprehensa, quorum praestans et egregium appellat unum. alterum, teterrimum pessimumque. tertium ex utroque modice temperatum, medium nuncupavit*. A similar idea is found in an Arabic abridgement of Galen's book on Ethics, see P, Kraus, «Kitāb al-aḵlāq li-Jālīnūs», *Majallat Kulliyyat al-Ādāb bi-l-Jāmi'a al-Miṣriyya* 5 (1937), 36-37.

[24] Cf. references in the article «Andarz» in the *Encyclopaedia Iranica* II, as well as in the notes to Shaked 1979.

[25] It closely resembles the arrangement of *Dk* VI, B14, Nos. 1 and 9.

[26] Cf. the discussion of this theme in Shaked 1984, 41 ff.

refer not simply to an attitude to wealth and money, but to the matters of religion[27]. This cannot conceal the fact that it is the fourfold scheme which is used as a starting point for this discussion. The very fact that it is used in such a manner emphasizes, I belive, the fact that it was commonly accepted as the standard way of looking at such ethical lists. Otherwise the intellectual game with the *midrashic* interpretation would be quite meaningless. Other examples for the fourfold type of lists in Arabic transmission are not difficult to find[28]. See, for example, the list given in an Arabic text which professes to be a translation from the Pahlavi:

> Know that fate brings you towards (different) situations[29], of which (some are the following):
> A state of generosity, coming close[30] to squandering; a state of bare sustenance, coming close to miserliness; a state of patience, coming close to dullness; a state of taking advantage of a chance, coming close to levity; a state of ease of tongue, coming close to babbling; a state of adopting silence, coming close to faltering speech. A king is capable of reaching the utmost in the good side of each situation. If he stops at the limit beyond which there is excess, he bridles himself from (going towards) that which is beyond that (*'Ahd Ardašīr*, 77 f., para 30).

Or the other hand, we have lists of opposing qualities on a binary basis, similar to those found in Middle Persian, again in texts which are explicitly derived from Iranian sources. Such a text occurs in the speech attributed to Hurmuzd b. Kisrā, which is quoted in at least two Arabic sources[31]. This type of lists seems to have influenced the style of independent lists of qualities which occur in Arabic literature[32].

[27] On this literary style as applied in the Pahlavi writings see Shaked 1969. A very similar *midrashic* interpretation is given to these concepts in *Ayādqār ī Wuzurqmihr* paras. 16 ff. It may be remarked that the set of four items is arranged in this section by placing the virtues at the two extremes, while the vices are placed in the middle. This constitutes a third model for the arrangment of a fourfold scheme.

[28] A sixteeen-fold scheme of qualities occurs in the composition known as *Kitāb al-'uhūd al-yūnāniyya*, cf. Badawī 1954, 44 f. The scheme is based on the qualities «generous», «miser», «capable (or incapable) of arranging matters», «having confidence (*mustarsal*)», «suspicious», «cheerfulness (*ḥusn al-bišr*)» and its opposite. By making all possible combinations among these qualities one reaches sixteen positions which characterize a person. This list clearly does not derive from an Iranian source, and has an entirely different structure.

[29] The text has *ṭabaqāt*, which normally means «classes».

[30] The text has: *ḥattā tadnuwa min* «until you come close to».

[31] The text of the speech is given in Ps. -Aṣma'ī, *Nihāyat al-arab*, Ms. Brit. Lib., fol. 201a; Ms. Cambridge, fol. 168a; Dīnawarī, *Akḇār*, 77 ff. The thrust of the passage is that one should avoid the things which (falsely) resemble each other (*tanakkabu al-umūr al-mutašābihāt*). The term *mutašābih* may very well be a reflection of the Pahlavi concept of *brādarōd* «false brother», which occurs in similar concepts in lists of qualities (cf. Menasce 1958, 39). The list comprises more than sixty pairs of «falsely related qualities», beginning with *nusk - riyā'*; *riyā' - murāqaba*; *isā'a - iḥsān*; *šarāsa - šajā'a*; *baġḍā' - ma'taba*; *ẓulm - intiqām*, etc. A very similar list occurs in

The notion of the Mean entered Arabic literature not necessarily through the mediation of Middle Persian, but from Greek sources, and it is not always easy to distinguish between the Aristotelian concept of the middle way and that which may have come to Arabic literature from Iran. But there are a number of cases where an Iranian derivation seems closer. This seems particularly in place where the context apparently has no awareness of philosophical discussions. Thus, when we read that ʿAli b. Abī Ṭālib talked about the middle way in the «first ḵuṭba» which he delivered after his ascension, where he says:

> fa-inna al-yamīna wa-l-šimāla maḍallatun, wa-l-wusṭā *al-jādda, munhajun ʿalayhi bāqī al-kitābi wa-l-sunna wa-āṯār al-nubuwwa (Jāḥiẓ, *Bayān* II, 50).
> Right and left are an error, the middle way is the main road, following which the rest (?) of the Divine Book, the Sunna and the prophetic traditions are traced.

The same idea, with the same term, *al-wusṭā*, occurs, albeit in a different context, in a text which is attributed to a Persian original:

> wa-qad kāna qawmun min ābā'inā yusammūna mamlakatana al-wusṭā, wa-sā'ira al-mamāliki al-aṭrāfa (From *Āyīn li-Ardašīr*, in Grignaschi 1966, 102).
> Among our ancestors were people who called our kingdom «the middle one», and the other kingdoms the extremes.

Another indication showing the possible Iranian origin of such a usage in Arabic is the passage in Ibn al-Muqaffaʿ's *Yatīmat al-sulṭān*, where the middle position of *ʿadl* «justice» is described in an unusual parable. This remarkable text (Kurd ʿAli 1946, 170), which seems to be derived from Persian, describes an argument concerning *ʿaql* «wisdom», *dawla* «dynastic power» and *ʿāfiya* «health» as to which one of them is best. Each one is described allegorically as having a human form and features appropriate to represent it. The argument is decided by a fourth person, representing *ʿadl* «justice», depicted as a man of mature age, with a handsome countenance, with a fourfold measure, having powerful movements and proportionate limbs, wearing white and

another text which survives in Arabic and which is attributed to the King Kisrā Anōšarwān (Miskawayh, *Jāwīdān Ḵirad*, 49). The *andarz* text *Ayādgār ī Wuzurgmihr*, which survives in both Pahlavi and Arabic, has a sequence of qualities which should be adopted provided they are not tainted by certain vices which are close to them (para. 86ff.). The Arabic terminology used to render this is *allā yašūba al-ʿaqla ʿujbun*, etc. (Miskawayh, *Jāwīdān Ḵirad*, 33). In *Dk* III we have lists built on the principle that virtues are said to be perfect when they are «pure» of certain cognate vices (see *Dk* III, 68, quoted in Appendix, 1).

[32] One exemple for such a list occurs in Jāḥiẓ, *Ḥayawān*, I, 130, where we have a somewhat similar conception, but where the contents seem to be untouched by the tradition of the Persian *andarz* books. Another example for such a list of opposite qualities arranged in pairs occurs in Tawḥīdī, *Imtāʿ* I, 149.

clean garments, and holding in one hand sugar and in the other myrrh. In front of him he has a compound medicine, and he is sitting on a chair with four legs. In answer to questions he explains the meaning of the various elements in this description: e.g. his measure and movements express the fact that as justice he is in the middle between the two extremes. He decides the arguments by combining the rivalling parties to work together and support each other. The combination of the idea of the middle course with that of law and justice seems typical of the concept of *paymān*, and since Ibn al-Muqaffaʿ is well known to have used mostly Iranian materials in his compositions[33], the assumption of an adaptation from an Iranian prototype seems quite likely in this case too.

ʿAlī is also quoted as saying in the same spirit, and apparently again reflecting a formulation which may have reached Arabic literature from Iran:

> ʿalaykum bi-awsāṭi l-umūr, fa-innahu ilayhā yurjaʿu al-ġālī wa-bihā yulḥaqu al-tālī (Ābī, *Naṯr al-durr* I, 277).
> The middle part of things is incumbent upon you (to adopt), for the one who goes beyond it should be brought back to it, and the one who lags behind it should be made to catch up with it.

The terms *wusṭā*, *awsāṭ al-umūr* in these texts seem to reflect Iranian usage, despite the observations made above[34]. When the term used is *qaṣd* or *iqtiṣād*, which seems to reflect *paymān* in a direct manner, the assumption of a borrowing from Iranian appears to be particularly strong. This is the term used by Ṭāhir Ḏū l-Yamīnayn in his testament to his son:

> *Qaṣd* is conducive to right conduct, right conduct is a witness of divine help[35], and divine help leads the way to happiness[36].

Arabic literature seems even to preserve some echoes of the Iranian distinction between «forward-inclined» and «backward-inclined» qualities. The early Muslim *mutakallim* Ibrāhīm al-Naẓẓām expressed the idea, it is said, that man is impelled by two powers from within, which «occur» (*ḵaṭara*) to him, and these two powers are called by al-Naẓẓām *al-ḵāṭirāni*. One of the two powers is characterized by the verbal noun *al-iqdām* «advancing», and the other by *al-kaff* «desist-

[33] See Shaked 1984.

[34] See notes 20-21.

[35] The Arabic term used is *tawfīq*, which in *Ayādgār ī Wuzurgmihr* (paras. 125-128) is the Arabic equivalent of *jahišn-hayyārīh*. For comments on this term see Shaked 1979, 294 f., note C82.2.

[36] I have used the text in Ṭabarī, *Taʾrīḵ*, III, 1048 f. For the text and its versions see Bosworth 1970. Our passage is given in translation by Bosworth, p. 32. Bosworth is inaccurate, I believe, when he states that Ṭāhir's moderation is the golden mean of the Greek (op. cit., p. 28).

ing»[37]. H.A. Wolfson (1967), in his discussion of these notions, tried to interpret them as reflecting a dualistic attitude, and compared them to the Jewish idea of the two inner impulses, the *yeṣarim*. The terms used by Naẓẓām do not seem however necessarily to refer to the notions of good and evil; they are merely terms descriptive of direction of movement or of the lack of it, and seem to go rather well together with the Iranian theory of the two modes of action.

According to Naẓẓām, action is motion (a notion which includes rest, viewed as a mode of motion)[38], and this concept in its turn is divided into two parts: *iʿtimād* («stopped motion»?) and *nuqla* «transition». This idea fits in nicely with the conception of the *ḵāṭirāni* as two modes, as it tends to show that Naẓẓām was thinking in terms of modes of action, rather than in terms of ethical categories.

Ibn al-Rāwandī rapports of Naẓẓām that he talked also of *ḵāṭir al-maʿṣiya* «the occurring impetus of infidelity», which also derives from God, and which is designed for the purpose of striking a balance (*li-l-taʿdīl*). This need not be identical with one of the two *ḵāṭirāni* which Naẓẓām talked about, and may be a third concept which can occur in either of the two *ḵāṭirāni*, which are modes of thinking, rather than representing a division of actions into good and bad. Ibn al-Rāwandī might well have misunderstood Naẓẓām and interpreted his two modes as referring to the ethical division. Such an interpretation occurs also in Baġdādī, *Uṣūl*, 26, where the doctrine of the *ḵāṭirāni* is referred to Brahmanical influence, and where the two powers are interpreted as of God and of Satan respectively. Naẓẓām's words were taken by Muslim interpreters to mean an ethical division into good and evil, but Ibn al-Rāwandī himself apparently held the view that «action» may be divided into such as attract the soul and those which cause aversion[39], an idea which comes close to the notion which Naẓẓām may have held — perhaps, it may be suggested, under Iranian influence.

The material discussed in this article may be summarized as follows. The Zoroastrian theory of ethics, which, in the nature of that religion, is of great prominence and importance in Zoroastrian theology, developed in the concept of *paymān* a tool for defining virtues. This is done by making virtues equal to actions performed «in the right measure». The choice of this term makes it possible to combine the idea of the right measure with that of the primeval pact between the two powers, which served, in the mythology of creation, as the constitution for the existence of the world. The two meanings of the

[37] Cf. Ašʿarī, *Maqālāt*, 427 f.: *lā budda min ḵāṭirāyni aḥaduhumā yaʾmuru bi-l-iqdāmi wa-l-āḵaru yaʾmuru bi-l-kaffi li-yaṣiḥḥa al-iḵtiyāru.*

[38] Ašʿarī, *Maqālāt*, 403.

[39] Ašʿarī, *Maqālāt*, 428.

term *paymān* seem to overlap quite consciously in the writings of the Sasanian theologian[40]. It is hard to decide whether Aristotelian influence was active in shaping this direction in the development of the concept of *paymān*. What seems to be clear is that at a subsequent stage the Zoroastrian theologians were entirely aware of the Aristotelian system and used it extensively. As a result, we have two types of lists of virtues and vices: one, which is traditional, and in which, typically, the old concepts of human qualities with a divine or demonic aspect are predominant; and one, clearly influenced by Aristotelian thinking, which is entirely based on the idea that the good qualities are in the middle between the vices of excess and deficiency, and which tends to regard virtues and vices as human qualities rather than as divine or demonic powers. We also have instances of a mixed approach, as well as passages which contain what may be a peculiar Iranian development of the peripatetic scheme, where the virtues and vices are arranged not in trinitarian groups, but in fourfold sets, with two virtues and two vices in contrast to each other in each category of action. This last configuration of the lists of virtues and vices may have developed in some otherwise unknown Greek philosophical school by way of commentary or elaboration of Aristotle's ethics. Some indications that this line of development is possible exist in the extant fragments of at least one late school of Greek philosophy.

Islamic writers derived their ideas about ethics from Arabic translations of Greek philosophical writings, as well as from reports of Greek philosophical ideas which were transmitted orally or in anthologies of words of wisdom. At the same time there was a substantial literary movement which made use of translations, summaries and excerpts of Pahlavi texts in the process of producing and compiling monuments of Arabic literature in the form of anthologies of wisdom sayings and, in general, *abad* works. This material included fragments of writings about ethics. We thus have in Arabic specimens of Iranian writings about ethics which are derived from the traditional lore of Zoroastrianism, and where the various human qualities are treated as akin to divine beings and demons, as well as fragments of Zoroastrian theological writings which tend to treat the qualities in man, under Greek influence, as psychological impeti. The division of human virtues and vices into two categories, «forward-inclined» and «backward-inclined», so far known only from Iranian sources, seems also to have had some feeble repercussions in an isolated saying of Naẓẓām, which appears to have been misunderstood by subsequent

[40] That *paymān* signifies the cosmic treaty is clear for example from the text quoted above (*Dk* III, 286), as well as from many other occurrences in Pahlavi (e.g. *ZWY* VII:32).

thinkers in the *kalām* movement. It was certainly never prominently absorbed into any widely recognized system of ethical thought in Islam.

APPENDIX I

1. *Dk* III, 68; M 57-59; B 42 f., (cf. Menasce 1958, 42 f.; 1973, 73 f.).

abar zamānag rāyēnīdārīh šōnag. az nigēz ī weh-dēn.

hād zamānag rāyēnīdārīh šōn abērdar pad xrad hunar rāyēnīdan. ud awe ī frazānag ceōn-aš frāz-āhangīg abāz-āhangīg hunarān <ī> xwēš paymānīhā az dādār āfrišn pad cihr hanbārdag, u-š xrad pēšobāy ī hunarān. pad xrad zamānag be šnāsēd. ud zamānag ī-š rāyēnišn abrāz hamārag<ān>īhā pad frāz-āhangīg, ud hangāmiha ud kasīhā pad abāz-āhangīg. hān ī-s[4] rāyēnišn nišēb hamāragānīhā pad abāz-āhangīg, ud hangāmīhā <ud> kasīhā pad frāz-āhangīg. hunar rāyēnīdan ī pad xūb-burdārīh ī 2 ēwēnag hunar andar 2 gōnag zamān ō kār kārīgēnīdār, hunarān ī sūd-kardār ī kārān ud xūb-rāyēnīdār(īh) ī zamānag handāxtār ī xwēš husrawīh ud hu-ruwānīh ud bōzišn bawēd.

ēd aōn ku hān ī-š abrāz zamānag xrad pēšobāyīhā rāyēnīdan abērdar pad

(1) abāyišn <ī pāk> az āz
(2) tagīgīh ī abēzār az xešm
(3) jumbišn ī pāk az jōyāgīh
(4) tuxšāgīh ī pāk az waranīgīh
(5) āzād-mardīh ī pāk az karabīh
(6) rāmišn ī pāk az rēdīh
(7) āzādagīh ī pāk az anēr-pākīh
(8) rādīh ī pāk az wanēgarīh
(9) *hayyārwandīh ī pāk az sturgīh
(10) *a-tarsīh <ī> pāk az stardīh
(11) dādīgīh ī pāk az *siftārīh
(12) wuzurg-menišnīh ī pāk az abar-menišnīh
(13) društ-cašmīh ī pāk az duš-cašmīh
(14) ēwēn-xwāyišnīh ī pāk az waranīgīh
(15) cābukīh ī pāk <az> *wizīnagīh
(16) amāwandīh i pāk az zišt-menišnīh

ud abārīg hunarān ī pāk az brādarōd āhang ō rāyēnīdārīh ī abarmānd ud xwadīh passazag kardan ī wuzurg ud dūr-nāmīg ud pattāy kār ud kirbag.

ud hān ī-š nišēb zamānag rāyēnīdan xrad pēšobāyīh abērdar pad
(1) nigerīdārīh <ī> pāk az spōzgarīh
(2) burdīh ī pāk az a-ēwīh (?)

(3) xāmōšīh ī pāk az tušt-menišnīh
(4) hunsandīh ī pāk az ašgahānīh
(5) driyōšīh ī pāk az škōhīh
(6) hunsandīh <ud> brahmagīh (?) <ī> pāk az rīmanīh
(7) wizīnagīh <ī> xwāyišn ī pāk az anābagīh
(8) fšōnišn ī pāk az panīh
(9) šarm ī pāk az tarsūgīh
(10) pahrēz-kārih ī pāk az wirēg az kirbag
(11) xwābarih ī pāk az bōšīh
(12) ēr-menišnīh ī pāk az ōbastagīh
(13) hu-cašmīh ī pāk az waran-cašmīh
(14) bāristānīh ī pāk az kēn-hanbārīh
(15) āwāmīgīh ī pāk az *gilag
(16) abar-passand ī pāk az wināh-hamīh

ud abārīg hunarān ī pāk az brādarōd āhang ō rāyēnišnīgīh ī za hān ī xradīg. hu-jahišn rāyēnīdār ud pahrēz ī az xurdag wināh.

Translation

On the manner of the timely governing (of things). From the instruction of the Good Religion.

The manner of the timely governing (of things) is mostly the governing of virtue through wisdom. The wise man, as he has forward-inclined and backward-inclined (virtues), his virtues are assembled through the Measure in his nature by the creation of the Creator. Wisdom is the foremost of his virtues. He knows the (right) time by wisdom. A time the governing of which is ascendance, is generally (to be treated) by forward-inclined (virtues), though for (certain) occasions and people through backward-inclined (virtues). A time whose governing is decline is (to be treated) generally by backward-inclined (virtues), though for (certain) occasions and people through forward-inclined (virtues). The governing of virtues which is done by the good bearing of the two kinds of virtue in the two sorts of time is effective in carrying out (its purpose). The virtues which carry out actions beneficially and which govern time well become that which measures out one's good fame, the possession of good soul and salvation.

One whose time is ascendance, wisdom should govern him as a leader mostly through:

(1) need <which is free> from lust
(2) swiftness which is free[1] from wrath

[1] *abēzār* is a synonym of *pāk*. It here replaces the latter presumably in order to avoid the graphic confusion which might have arisen from writing a word which looks exactly like the ending of the preceding word (*tkykyx DKYA*).

(3) movement which is free from agitation
(4) diligence which is free from greed
(5) nobility which is free from *karabīh*[2]
(6) joy which is free from filth (?)[3]
(7) freedom which is free from lack of Iranian purity[4]
(8) generosity which is free from squandering
(9) helpfulness[5] which is free from fierceness
(10) lack of fear which is free from stupidity
(11) lawfulness which is free from stiffness[6]
(12) great-mindedness[7] which is free from arrogance
(13) severity[8] which is free from cruelty
(14) desire of what is proper which is free from greed
(15) refinement[9] which is free from fastidiousness[10]
(16) strength which is free from ugly thinking[11]

and the other virtues which are free from the inclination which is their false associate. (This is to be done) so as to govern one's heritage and one's selfness, and make seemly the good deeds which are great, of lasting memeory and abiding.

One whose time is decline, wisdom should govern him as a leader mostly through

[2] The opposition *āzād-mardīh*/*karabīh* occurs also in *Dk* VI, 142, 144.

[3] Cf. also *DkM* 789.14. On the verb from which this noun is derived see Bailey, *BSOS* 6 (1930/32), 82.

[4] The translation given by Menasce 1958, 42, «pureté non aryenne» seems unacceptable. In Menasce 1973 this is left untranslated.

[5] In a parallel list, *DKM* 372.7, the word is spelt *'y'lwndyx*, which is not the normal spelling of *hayyār-*. In *DkM* 312.22 the word is spelled *arwandīh*, in 328.1 ff. both *hayyārwandīh* and *arwandīh* occur. It is clear that the former represents the same word which occurs here, as it comes in company with *sturgīh* and *šarm*.

[6] In the parallel list *DkM* 371.21 the word occurs as *kplyx*, which may suggest perhaps *dibērīh* or the like. The reading adopted here is supported by *DkM* 419.17 (*sift-kārīh*, *siftag-dārān*), 419.20 (*siftagān*), although its meaning is not entirely clear.

[7] For *wuzurq-menišnīh* = Gk. *megalopsychia* see above.

[8] *društ-cašmīh* does not mean «un regard sain» (Menasce 1973).

[9] *cābukīh* means «refinement», as can be seen from a number of contexts. See e.g. *ābādīh ud ārāyišn ud abrang ud huniyāgīh ud rāmišn* (*DkM* 337.4 f.); *ēn 3 ciš paymān dāštār ast cašm ud dahān ud uzwān ud gōš ud grīw. cašm az zanīn ud dahān az xwarišn ī anēwēn ud uzwān az halagīh ud gōš az huniyāgīh ud grīw az cābukīh* (*DkM* 160.21 ff.; cf. Bailey 1943, 114, n., where the translation is somewhat different). «He guards these 3 (r. «5») things in measure: the eyes, the mouth, the tongue, the ear and the neck; the eyes from women, the mouth from eating food against custom, the tongue from vain speech, the ear from music, and the neck from refinement».

[10] If the word is read as given here, the meaning is presumably «selectiveness, choosiness», hence «fastidiousness». The reading *cīnagīh* is also possible, with the sense of «the passion for collecting, amassing (nice things)»; this is evidently what de Menasce had in mind when he translated «esprit de lucre».

[11] I.e. aggressiveness (?).

(1) circumspection[12] which is free from rejection
(2) patience which is free from disobedience (?)[13]
(3) taciturnity which is free from dumbness[14]
(4) contentment which is free from sloth
(5) poverty which is free from misery
(6) contentment and (good) form (?) which is free from filth
(7) discernment of desire which is free from rejection
(8) thrift which is free from avarice
(9) shame which is free from fear
(10) avoidance which is free from fleeing from good deeds
(11) benevolence which is free from vanity (?)[15]
(12) humility which is free from self-abasement
(13) good disposition which is free from greed
(14) long-suffering which is free from the storing of vengeance
(15) ease[16] which is free from complaint[17]
(16) approval of things which is free from complicity in sin
and the other virtues which are free from the inclinations which are their false associates. (This is to be done) so as to govern that which is from wisdom. A man of good fortune is one who governs and abstains from the small(est) sin.

APPENDIX II

2. *Dk* III, 286; B 225 f.; M 295 ff. (cf. Zaehner 1955, 262 f., 250 f.; partly translated in Zaehner 1956, 91 f.).

Concerning the fact that the demons took the *paymān* away from men, and that Yima brought it back to men. From the instruction of the Good Religion.

The benefit of every action and thing is through *paymān*. Their destruction and bad keeping is from excess and deficiency.

[12] *nigerīdārīh* is no doubt connected to the expression *pad nigerišn*, *nigerišnīg* «deliberate(ly), careful(ly)», on which see Shaked 1979, 257 ff., note 91.3.

[13] The reading and translation of this word are not certain. Cf. also *DkM* 67.5; 329.3; 371.18. The positive form of this word is found in *DkM* 329.5 (?).

[14] For *tušt-menišnīh* cf. *DkM* 140.14; 201.4 (*tuštīh*). See also Dhabhar, *PhlY*, Glossary, 97.

[15] *bōšīh* is found with the same contrast in *DkM* 371.21; 329.2. The translation here is based on NP *bauš*, defined in *Burhān-i Qāṭi'*: *karr u farr va xvad-namāī*, although the sense obtained is not quite appropriate.

[16] For *āwāmīgīh* see Shaked 1980, 23 (but I should like to retract what I said there about *āwām* «hardship, pain»). See also on this word MacKenzie 1984, 388 f.

[17] The word is written *gl'n*, but is obviously the same as *gilag* in the combination *gilag-ōbār* (itself often written *gl'n*, see Shaked 1979, 196, textual note E30a. 1).

The arrangement of *paymān* is through the innate wisdom which the Creator [placed] within the creations. The deviation from *paymān* is precisely excess and deficiency, the demonic lust, which is the antagonist of innate wisdom.

Whenever divine innate wisdom is winner over demonic lust, there is victory of the law of *paymān* in men and downfall for excess and deficiency, and to the creation there is good existence. The Creator made innate wisdom among men most highly placed in the ruler, so that He may vanquish through it the fiercest demon, lust, and that, by bringing benefit and good government to men in a powerful manner, He may rouse the innate wisdom which is in them from the extinction caused by the base lust. All this is done so that the precepts of innate wisdom should be acceptable among men, and that the law and the measure should be current among them, and that the creation should be governed in goodness.

Before Yima came to power innate wisdom was weak among rulers, because the *dēws* had taken it away, and lust was predominant. Such was the law of *paymān*, based on innate wisdom, under the extinction caused by the lustful excess and deficiency which belongs to the *dēws* that men resemble beasts. By departing from the precepts they got into corruption, by the harsh prevalence which excess and deficiency had over them they became estranged from the measure in acting, eating, giving, possessing and other deeds and the world was disrupted.

But, as it is revealed, by the fact that the divine innate wisdom is corrupted from among people, that demonic lust become predominant, and that the law of *paymān* which conforms to innate wisdom is weakened in the world, the lustful lawlessness of excess and deficiency comes to inhabit more among people, and the world comes to destruction and decay.

When Yima came to the world by the desire and indication (?) of the Creator, he first removed the demons from rule over men and saved the divine innate wisdom from the waylessness and lust of the demons.

He examined means for releasing *paymān* of innate wisdom from the lustful excess and deficiency of the demons, by which the demons would be made to lose their sway over people and waylessness would become weak, and by which divine innate wisdom would grow again and demonic excess and deficiency would be vanquished, and the law of *paymān*, based on innate wisdom, by vanquishing the lawlessness of excess and deficiency, (would cause) in the world supreme luminosity of power.

By this the world will become ordered and decorated and will attain breadth. By the great miraculous powers and splendour of the Creator he (scil. Yima) was transported, came in bodily form to Hell, and for thirteen winters he was in Hell in the shape of a demon. He took by magic and by skilful stratagems from the demons the secret means through which the demons may be vanquished and made powerless over people. He smote and vanquished the demons by their own means and made them powerless with regard to people and removed from them (i.e. from people).

From that time on he stopped the domination of demonic lust over people, lustful excess and deficiency was weakened, and divine innate wisdom increased among people, the law of *paymān*, based on innate wisdom, became victorious among the creatures, and by this the creation of Ohrmazd became immortal.

The Religion says in connection with Yima, concerning the fact that he brought back, made manifest and explained the law: he took away from the demons the benefit of every non-sacrificed (service), of every non-cultivated herd, as well as all prosperity and growth which the Creator of innate wisdom (gave) to people, every ease and *paymān*, the descendant of the law[1]. He took away from among them that which causes among them wayless lust, all evil (which is) excess and deficiency ...[2].

REFERENCES

[For abbreviations of Phalavi texts not listed here see Shaked 1979.]

Al-Ābī, Abū Sa'd Manṣūr b. Ḥusayn, *Naṯr al-durr*, ed. M. 'Alī Qarna and 'Alī M. al-Bajawī, Cairo 1980.

'Ahd Ardašīr, ed. Iḥsān 'Abbās, Beirut 1967.

al-'Āmirī, Abū-l-Ḥasan Muḥammad, *Al-sa'āda wa-l-is'ād*, ed. M. Minovi, Tehran-Wiesbaden 1957.

(Ps.) Aṣma'ī, *Nihāyat al-arab*, Ms. British Library 23.298; Ms. Cambridge University Library Qq 225.

Aš'arī, Abū l-Ḥasan 'Alī b. Ismā'īl, *Maqālāt al-islāmiyyīn wa-ḵtilāfu l-muṣallīn*, ed. H. Ritter, Istanbul 1929 (Bibliotheca Islamica, I).

Ayādgār i Wuzurgmihr: J.M. Jamasp-Asana (ed.), *Pahlavi texts*, Bombay 1897, 85-101. (Quoted from a typescript edition of the Pahlavi with the corresponding Arabic version from Miskawayh, *Jāwīdān Ḵirad*, to be published shortly.)

Badawī, 'Abdarrahman, 1954. *Al-uṣūl al-yūnāniyya li-l-naẓariyyāt al-siyāsiyya fī l-Islām* I, Cairo (Dirāsāt Islāmiyya, 15).

Al-Baġdādī, Abū Manṣūr 'Abd al-Qāhir, *Uṣūl al-dīn*, Istanbul 1928.

Bailey, H.W., 1943. *Zoroastrian problems in the ninth-century books*, Oxford. [New edition, Oxford 1971.]

[1] The sentence is not clear. An alternative translation may be: «the originator (*zāyag*) of the law».

[2] The last words do not make clear sense.

Bosworth, C.E., 1970. «An early Arabic mirror for princes: Ṭāhir Dhū l-Yamīnayn's epistle to his son ʿAbdallah (206/821)», *JNES* 29, 25-41.

Boyce, M., 1968. «Middle Persian literature», in *Handbuch der Orientalistik*, Abt. 1, Bd. IV, Abschn. 2, Lfg. 1, Leiden-Köln.

Dēnkard, *Dk*: *Dk* III, quoted by chapter; cf. Menasce 1973.
Dk VI, quoted by section number; cf. Shaked 1979.
Dk B, facsimile edition by M.J. Dresden, Wiesbaden 1966.
DkM, ed. D.M. Madan, Bombay 1911.

Dillon, J., *The Middle Platonists*, Ithaca, N.Y., 1977.

Dīnawarī, Abū Ḥanīfa Aḥmad, *Al-Akḇār al-ṭiwāl*, ed. V. Guirgass, Leiden 1898.

Grignaschi, M., 1966. «Quelques spécimens de la littérature sassanide conservés dans les bibliothèques d'Istanbul», *JA* 254, 1-142.

Jāḥiẓ, Abū ʿUṯmān ʿAmr. *Al-bayān wa-l-tabyīn*, ed. ʿAbd al-Salām Muḥammad Ḥārūn, Cairo 1975.

—, *Kitāb al-ḥayawān*, ed. Fawzī ʿAtwī, Beirut 1978.

Kurd ʿAlī, Muḥammad, 1946. *Rasāʾil al-bulaġāʾ*, 3rd. ed., Cairo.

de Menasce, J.P., 1945. *Une apologétique mazdéenne du IXe siècle: Škand-Gumānīk Vičār, La solution décisive des doutes*, Fribourg en Suisse.

——, 1958. *Une encyclopédie mazdéenne: Le Dēnkart*, Paris (Bibliothèque de l'École des Hautes Études, Sciences Religieuses, LXIX).

——, 1973. *Le troisième livre du Dēnkart*, Paris (Travaux de l'Institut d'Études Iraniennes de l'Université de Paris III, 5; Bibliothèque des Oeuvres Classiques Persanes, 4).

Al-Māwardī, ʿAlī b. Muḥammad, *Tashīl al-naẓar wa-taʿjīl al-ẓafar fī akḇlāq al-malik wa-siyāsat al-mulk*, ad. Muḥyī Hilāl al-Sarhān and Ḥusayn al-Sāʿātī, Beirut 1981.

Miskawahy, Abū ʿAlī Aḥmad, *Jāwīdān ḵirad*, ed. ʿAbdarrahman Badawī (under the title: *al-ḥikma al-ḵālida*), Cairo 1952.

——, *Tahḏīb al-akḇlāq*, ad. Q. Zurayk, Beirut 1966; tr. M. Arkoun (under the title, *Traité d'éthique*), Damascus 1969.

——, *Tajārib al-umam*, ed. L. Caetani (Gibb Memorial Series, VII, 1), London.

Molé, Marijan, 1961. «Le problème des sectes zoroastriennes dans les livres pehlevis», *Oriens* 13-14, 1-28.

Nallino, Carlo Alfonso, 1922. «Tracce di opere greche giunte agli Arabi per trafila pehlevica», *A volume of Oriental studies presented to E.G. Browne*, Cambridge, 345-363.

Nisard, M., 1842. *Pétrone, Apulée, Aulu-Gelle. Oeuvres complètes avec la traduction en français*, Paris.

Nyberg, H.S., 1933. *Die Religionen des alten Iran*, tr. by H.H. Schaeder, Leipzig (Mitt. d. Vorderasiatisch-aegyptischen Gesellschaft, 43). [New edition, Osnabrück 1966.]

Ravāqī, ʿAlī, 1362. *Āšnāyī ba qorʾān-e motarjam-e qods*, Tehran 1362.

Shaked, S., 1969. *Esoteric trands in Zoroastrianism* (Proceedings of the Israel Academy of Sciences and Humanities III, 175-221), Jerusalem.

——, 1972. «Qumran and Iran: further considerations», *Israel Oriental Studies* 2, 433-446.

——, 1979. *Wisdom of the Sasanian Sages*, (Persian Heritage Series 34), Boulder, Col.

——, 1980. «Mihr the Judge», *Jerusalem Studies in Arabic and Islam* 2, 1-31.

——, 1984. «From Iran to Islam. Notes on some themes in transmission», *JSAI* 4, 31-67.

Shaki, Mansour, 1970. «Some basic tenets of the eclectic metaphysics of the *Dēnkart*», *Archiv Prientálni* 38, 277-312.

——, 1981. «The Dēnkard account of the history of the Zoroastrian scriptures», *Archiv Orientálni* 49, 114-125.

SGV: *Shikand Gumānīk Vijār*, ed. H.J. Jamasp Asana and E.W. West, Bombay 1887. See also Menasce 1945.

Tawḥīdī, Abū Ḥayyān, *Al-imtā' wa-l-mu'ānasa*, ed. Aḥmad Amīn and Aḥmad al-Zayn, Beirut n.d.

Widengren, Geo, 1961. *Iranische Geisteswelt von den Anfängen bis zum Islam*, Baden-Baden.

Wikander, Stig, 1946. *Feuerpriester in Kleinasien und Iran*, (Skrifter utgivna av Kungl. Humanistiska Vetenskapssamfundet i Lund, XL) Lund.

Wolfson, H.A., 1967. «The *ḫāṭirāni* in the Kalām and Ghazālī as inner motive powers of human actions», *Studies in mysticism and religion presented to G. Scholem*, Jerusalem, 363-379. [Reprinted: H.A. Wolfson, *The philosophy of the Kalam*, Cambridge, Mass. and London, England 1976, 624-644.]

Yaḥyā b. 'Adī, *Tahḏīb al-aḵlāq*, ed. Murād Fu'ād Jaqī, Jerusalem 1930.

Zaehner, R.C., 1955. *Zurvan, a Zoroastrian dilemma*, Oxford.

——, 1956. *The teachings of the Magi. A compendium of Zoroastrian beliefs*, London and New York.

IX

A FACETIOUS RECIPE AND THE TWO WISDOMS: IRANIAN THEMES IN MUSLIM GARB

To M.J. Kister,
ṣāḥib al-ᶜaqlayn

I

Zurāfa, one of the companions of the caliph al-Mutawakkil, asked the famous ṣūfī Ḏū-l-Nūn al-Miṣri to write for him a prayer. Ḏū-l-Nūn did as he was requested, and Zurāfa presented him with a cup of *lawzīnaj*, a sweet dish made of almonds, saying, "Eat of this, for it stabilizes the brain and benefits the intelligence". Ḏū-l-Nūn said, "Something else benefits it". Zurāfa asked, "What does?", to which Ḏū-l-Nūn replied, "Following the command of God and abstaining from that which He forbade". Zurāfa insisted, "Do me the honour of eating it", but Ḏū-l-Nūn said, "I wish something else". "What do you wish?", asked Zurāfa. Ḏū-l-Nūn said, "This dish is meant for a person who does not know to eat it. People of knowledge guard themselves against this *lawzīnaj*". "I do not think", said Zurāfa, "that there is anyone in the world who can take *lawzīnaj* better than this one, which comes from the kitchen of the caliph al-Mutawakkil ᶜalā Allāh".[1] Ḏū-l-Nūn said, "I shall describe to you the *lawzīnaj* of a person who relies on God (*al-mutawakkil ᶜalā Allāh*)". Zurāfa said, "Please do, by God". Ḏū-l-Nūn then proceeded to give the following recipe:

> "Take the quintessence of the hidden part of the unadulterated food of gnosis, knead it with the water of religious exertion (*ijtihād*), set up the trivet of despondency, match pure fondness, then bake the bread of the *lawzīnaj* of the God-worshippers with the heat of the fires of the soul of those who have given up worldly desires (*zuhhād*), kindle it with the firewood of consolations until you see[2] the fires of its fuel in the sparks of languor, then stuff this with the sugar-candy[3] of contentment, make into the anxiety an almond stuffing of basil(?),[4] with the help of a mortar of fidelity, perfumed with the

[1] The name signifies "one who relies on God".
[2] S (=Suyūṭī) *tarā*; I (=Iṣbahānī) *tarmī*.
[3] Read *qand*, as in S; I has *qayd*.
[4] I has ***ḍwḍ'n***, which has no sense. Read perhaps *ḍawmarān*.

perfume[5] of the mercy of the love of desire, then roll it up as one rolls bags[6] with paste[7] for the people(?),[8] chop it up with the knives of sleeplessness in the hollow entrails of the starless nights, while casting away the sweetness of drowsiness, pile it up over the heads[9] of restlessness and sobbing,[10] sprinkle over it sugar which is extracted[11] from the moans of combustion, then eat it with fingers of entrusting one's affairs (to God) in the feasts of private supplication, while undergoing emotions due to mystical experiences which flash on the hearts. Having done this,[12] grief is dispelled from the hearts, and one reaches the state of the lover's joy with the beloved king". Having said this, Ḏū-l-Nūn took leave of Zurāfa and went away".[13]

The translation of the passages given above is only approximate. Apart from the difficulties inherent in a text which is poetical and metaphorical, written as it is in rhyming prose, and making as it does skilful use of the various ambiguities of everyday speech with the superimposed technical language of the ṣūfis, one is faced in this particular case with the problem of a carelessly edited text.[14]

The metaphorical, somewhat jocular, style used here by Ḏū-l-Nūn, transferring culinary concepts to the realm of spiritual experience, is not unusual in ṣūfi utterances. It became extremely popular about the time of Ḏū-l-Nūn among ṣūfis of various backgrounds, who were probably attracted to it because of its cryptical, elusive character, which served their purpose by both hiding and at the same time partly revealing the truths they wished to convey. Deciphering such an utterance requires a certain

5 S *bi-ṭīb*; I *bi-ṭīna*.

6 *ṭayya al-akyās* could also signify "as do shrewd people".

7 S *bi-l-ġarā* (?); I ***b'l'r'***.

8 S *li-l-anam*; I *li-l-ayyām*.

9 S *hāmāt*; I *jāmāt*.

10 S šahq; I *sahr*.

11 I ***bᶜml***.

12 Read *ḏālika*, as in S.

13 The passage occurs in Iṣbahānī, *Ḥilya*, IX:387f.; Suyūṭī, *Sirr*, fols. 56b–57a. Suyuṭī's text is based on *Ḥilya* (though he must have used a better manuscript than the one reproduced in the printed edition of the latter). Variants of this motif are current in Arabic literature. Nīsābūrī, *ᶜUqalā'*, has at least four different variants: (1) p. 90f., where the dish is called *fālūḏaj al-ᶜārifīn*; (2) p. 91f., where the dish is called *ᶜaṣīda*; (3) p. 110f., where it is called *fālūḏaj al-ᶜārifīn*; (4) p. 124 (a very short version describing the "best food", by Samnūn). Cheikho 1938, 226, quotes another variant from a book by Bahā' al-Dīn al-ᶜĀmilī. Variants are also found in Jewish literature, cf. Ḏāhri, *Musar*, 365f., with the editor's footnotes, where further references are given.

14 The printed edition of Iṣbahānī, *Ḥilya*, is notoriously bad.

mental, as well as experiential, effort on the part of the listener. The result, which brings about deeper understanding, imitates the manner of the mystical experience itself: having been blocked and enveloped for a period of time by obscurity and struggle, one suddenly finds the key which opens up comprehension, insight, and communion with God. Other examples of this kind of style are not rare in ṣūfī literature. Abū Yazīd al-Bisṭāmī, a distinguished contemporary of Ḏū-l-Nūn, was particularly fond of this genre of expression. He is reported as having said, for example:

> I rode in a chariot of truth-speaking until I reached desire, then I rode in a chariot of longing until I reached the sky, then I rode in a chariot of love until I reached the lote-tree of the extreme end (*sidrat al-muntahā*), and then I heard a voice calling me, "O Abū Yazīd, what do you want?" I said, "I want not to want ..."[15]

In another of his utterances Abū Yazīd says:

> I gathered together the effects of this world and tied them with a string of contentment, I placed them in the ballista of truth-speaking, I hurled them into the sea of despair, and achieved tranquility.[16]

The following piece of advice is also reported in his name:

> Go in the racing ground of (God's) unity until you reach the house of (God's) uniqueness. Fly in the racing course of (God's) uniqueness until you end up in the valley of (God's) constancy. If you thirst, He will let you drink from a cup which, whenever you recall it, you will never be thirsty afterwards again.[17]

These examples show that such a style, which makes metaphorical use of a mundane topic for deep mystical insights, was fairly widespread among ṣūfīs in the ninth century. The occurrence of the elaborate recipe for the mystical *lawzīnaj*, or (as in the variants) for the *fālūḏaj* of the gnostics, should in principle occasion no surprise. Nevertheless, it can be shown that this motif has its roots in Pahlavi literature.

We have a text in Pahlavi which contains the same theme. There is no need to give here the original Pahlavi, as the text is fairly easily ac-

[15] Ibn al-ᶜArīf, *Maḥāsin*, 7. Another version is Sahlajī, *Nūr*, 115. Further elaborations of Abū Yazīd's response "I want not to want" are in Sahlajī, *Nūr*, 96, 113.

[16] Sahlajī, *Nūr*, 67; also ᶜĀmilī, *Kaškūl*, 230.

[17] Sahlajī, *Nūr*, 89.

cessible, having been edited and discussed a number of times.[18] In the translation which is given below I have naturally benefited from the work of my predecessors; linguistic observations already made by previous editors have not been repeated, and only some points of interest have been noted.

> The remedy of contentment is not dispensed as a thing of cure, (but) the relief of the medicine of cure arises [from] this.[19] The remedy is this,[20] one[21] *drahm* by weight. "To mix contentment by thought[22] and to be aware of it by knowledge", one *dāng*[23] by weight. "From today until tomorrow it ought to be better", one *dāng* by weight. "It may have been worse than this", one *dāng* by weight. "It is easier for me when I am content with what has come", one *dāng* by weight. "It is more difficult for me when I am not content with an action which is not good",[24] one *dāng* by weight. These remedies should be placed in a mortar of patience, pound with a pestle of prayer, sifted with a silken sieve, and every day, at the point of daybreak,[25] one should toss into one's mouth two spoonfuls with the spoon of "reliance on the gods",[26] and afterwards drink the water of "What is it proper to do?"[27]. Then one ought to be content without any doubt, for (this is) much more beneficial to the body and soul.

There are a number of considerations which make it almost certain that the origin of the story is indeed in Sasanian Iran and not in Arabic literature. The theme of the Iranian story is very characteristic of the Zoroastrian attitude to life. Contentment, quiet joy and satisfaction with

18 Jamasp-Asana, *PhlT*, 154, and B.T. Anklesaria, *op. cit.*, 50f.; Dhabhar 1918; Klima 1967; Shaki 1968. In several points Dhabhar's rendering, which was not noticed by Klima and Shaki, seems more acceptable than that of the latter scholars.

19 Read: *ud hān-ez ī cārīg darmān āsanīh* [*az*] *ēn jahēd.*

20 Read: *dārūg *ēd bawēd.*

21 Read: **ēw.*

22 Read: *menišnīg* [*īhā*].

23 *dāng* is defined as one-sixth of anything; see Eilers 1983, 503f.

24 I.e., I should always try to do good things, so that I may be always content.

25 The expression *azēr* [*ī*] *bāmdād* is not clear, despite the analogy adduced by Klima 1967, 38 n. 18, with *gāh ī azēr*, which indicates the time when the sun is down (Kapadia 1953, 288). According to Klima, *bāmdād* would be a gloss on *azēr*, both terms being elliptical (apposition may be a better suggestion). Dhabhar seems to take the first words as *abēr* "very".

26 Read *abastān* [*ō*] *yazdān*, On *kapīc* cf. Eilers 1983, 503.

27 Read *ud āb* [ī] *ce šāyēd kardan az pas xwardan*. An alternative translation which may be considered is: "and drink the water of 'What is it proper to do next?'"

whatever has come, as well as avoidance of despair and dejection even under extreme hardship, are virtues which are frequently extolled in the Zoroastrian writings of the Sasanian period. Joy serves the purposes of Ohrmazd, despair those of Ahreman. The story just quoted breathes the same spirit, and it is easy to see how it could have been borrowed and adapted by ṣūfī circles in Islam to serve their purposes. A borrowing and transformation in the opposite direction seems much less likely, apart from the fact that the probability of this theme being borrowed from Iran is enhanced by the observation that we already have so many other elements from Pahlavi literature which come up in Arabic.

But apart from these considerations we have another piece of material evidence for this borrowing in the form of a variant of this Sasanian story, this time transmitted through Arabic channels. It runs as follows:

> Kisrā became angry with Buzurjmihr and had him imprisoned in a dark house. He ordered to have him fettered in iron, where he remained in this condition for days. Kisrā then sent someone to enquire of Buzurjmihr's condition, and there he was, joyful of spirit and with confident soul. (The visitors) told him: "You are in this dire situation, and at the same time we see that you are of joyful mind". Buzurjmihr said:[28] "I have prepared six mixtures (of elements), have kneaded them together, have made use of them, and they are that which has helped me to stay in the manner which you see". They said to him: "Describe to us those mixtures, so that we may perhaps derive benefit from them at a time of hardship". He said: "Yes. The first mixture is, 'Confidence in God'; the second is, 'Everything which was destined to be, is'; the third is, 'Patience is the best thing to be employed by someone who is put to the test'; the fourth is, 'If I do not employ patience, what shall I do? I shall not get help to myself by grief'; the fifth is, 'It could be worse than the situation which has befallen me'; the sixth is, 'From one hour to the next, deliverance (may be coming)'". What Buzurjmihr said reached the ears of Kisrā, who released him and bestowed honour on him.[29]

Not only are some of the elements in this story identical with elements in the Pahlavi version, but it also brings out its great resemblance to another Sasanian story, which also gained great popularity in Islam. That story is attributed to Ādurbād and it exists in Pahlavi in several versions. There too Ādurbād comforts himself at the onset of a misfortune by six conside-

[28] The text has *qālū*, which is evidently an error for *qāla*.

[29] ᶜĀmilī, *Kaškūl*, 211; an earlier version: Tanūxī, *Faraj*, 38; Tawḥīdī, *Baṣā'ir*, IV, 254. See also ᶜA. Badawī, *Rasā'il falsafiyya*, Beirut 1980, 298.

rations: that it might have been worse; that one of the misfortunes held in store for him is already spent; that he has suffered in his body, not in his soul; that he must be a good person to be afflicted thus by Ahreman; that it has come to him and not to his offspring; and that the store of afflictions which is kept by Ahreman has now been reduced by the one which has been brought upon Ādurbād.[30]

Although it is not easy to determine in every case across the Arabic versions what the exact Sasanian prototype looked like, it seems quite clear from Sasanian antecedents.

II

This is not only case in which a saying which carries a very clear Zoroastrian message was adopted by Islam and given a particularly Islamic connotation. Another striking example for such a borrowing, where it would be impossible to detect the Sasanian origin without being acquainted with the original, may be quoted from a saying of Muᶜāwiya, the founder of the Umayyad dynasty:

> Muᶜāwiya said: "If there were a single string of hair between me and the people, it would not be cut". He was asked, "How, Commander of the Faithful?", and he answered, "If they pulled it, I would let it go; and if they let it go, I would pull it".[31]

Muᶜāwiya seems to display in this saying his well-known character as an artful politician. The sense of the saying in this context is presumably that it is necessary for a leader, if he wants to be successful, to show flexibility where he meets with strong opposition, and to adopt an attitude of great determination whenever this is opportune, contriving in all cases not to let the string escape from his hand even for a moment.

The original Pahlavi saying, attributed to the sage Baxt-Āfrīd, has, it seems, a religious connotation:

> There is a single rope. If all the people in the world held one end in their hand, and I had one end, they would not be able to pull it away (from me), for whenever they pull it forth, I let go.[32]

30 *Dēnkard* VI, A5, in Shaked 1979, 130ff., with the references listed on p. 283. The Arabic versions which were described there as distorted can now be seen to belong to the other group of sayings, those which describe a "remedy".

31 Balāḏurī, *Ansāb*, IVA, 69, with variants.

32 *Dk.* VI, E22d, with notes, Shaked 1979, 305.

The meaning of this saying, in the context of the book in which it occurs, is certainly not political, as in the saying of Mu^cāwiya; it would seem rather to define a certain pious strategy of behaviour with regard to this world. It says, apparently, that under adverse conditions, when the whole world pulls away from one, it is still possible to retain one's hold by letting go for a time, but without giving up altogether. In other words, one should use a strategy which is based on flexibility and patience. This is probably an allegorical expression for behaviour in the religious sphere, advising the pious man to hold on to the religious values and at the same time to avoid clashing head-on with the material world. In this sense it conforms to several other sayings of Baxt Āfrīd, which are also formulated in an enigmatic and paradoxical style. One of these sayings runs as follows;

> Until the time of the Renovation, all those who are called in the material world "He who repels pain" let go of the material world when it holds them; and when they let go, it holds them.[33]

For Zoroastrians the material world is not bad in itself, but it is not desirable to cling to it, and one should keep far from it. By loosening one's grip of it one manages to achieve one's religious goal without at the same time losing the material world altogether. It is therefore expedient, from the religious point of view, to play a game of hide-and-seek with the material world: one lets go of it, while still holding it.

A paradoxical saying of a similar nature, but wtih a different lesson, is attributed in the Arabic transmission to Buzurjmihr. Like Mu^cāwiya's saying, this one may have also lost its original sense in the course of transmission. The text says:

> Buzurjmihr the Persian said: If this world comes forth towards you, spend away from it, for it will not perish; and if the world turns its back to you, spend away from it, for it will not stay for ever.[34]

III

One final example for the transfer of religious ideas from Zoroastrian Iran to Islam concerns the notion that there are two types of wisdom, one of which is innate, inborn, and another one which is acquired or learned.

33 *Dk.* VI, E22a, with notes on p. 304f.

34 Ibn Qutayba, *ᶜUyūn,* I, 179 ll. 17f.; Ibn ᶜAbd Rabbihi, *ᶜIqd,* I, 265, ll. 9–10.

The idea is coined in Arabic in a set of verses, which are sometimes attributed to ᶜAlī:

ra'aytu l-ᶜaqla ᶜaqlayni / fa-maṭbūᶜun wa-masmūᶜu
wa-lā yanfaᶜu masmūᶜun / iḏā lam yaku maṭbūᶜu
kamā lā tanfaᶜu l-šamsu / wa-ḍaw'u l-ᶜayni mamnūᶜu
"I have seen wisdom as two: inborn and learned-by-hearing;
The one which is learned-by-hearing is of no avail if there is no inborn one;
Just as the sun is of no avail when the light of the eye is gone."[35]

Ġazālī, one of the authors quoting these verses, uses this idea as a starting point for a division of sciences and kinds of knowledge according to his own scheme. Human perception of the truth, which is acquired by learning, depends on the capacity of the individual, on the question whether he possesses the intellectual instruments for absorbing and assimilating it.

When Ġazālī discusses this concept, he replaces the terms *maṭbūᶜ* and *masmūᶜ* by two other terms, *ġarīzī* and *muktasab* respectively.[36] A similar terminology, viz. *ᶜaql al-ġarīza* as against *ᶜaql al-tajriba*, is used in an earlier period by Jāḥiẓ,[37] who seems to say that the innate wisdom is a ladder leading to the wisdom-by-experience. In another source we encounter the same idea attributed to an anonymous "philosopher", who uses the metaphor of the earth (for innate wisdom) and the seeds and water (for acquired wisdom).[38]

It is however with the name of the Sasanian sage Buzurjmihr, and sometimes with that of the king under whom he served, Xusrau Anōšarwān, that this idea is most often associated in Arabic literature. In a collection of sayings attributed to Buzurjmihr we read: "Wisdom (*al-ᶜaql*) is of two kinds, one innate (*maṭbūᶜ*) and one acquired-by-learning (*mutaᶜallam*)".[39] In another quotation Buzurjmihr is reported as saying that wisdom (*ᶜaql*) without learning (*adab*) is like a good piece of earth which lies waste.[40] Kisrā is credited with a more detailed version of this:

35 Ġazālī, *Mīzān*, 145; Māwardī, *Adab al-dunyā*, 31; Ps.-Majrīṭī, *Picatrix*, 290, and cf. the references in the translation of *Picatrix*, p. 302.

36 This terminology is also adopted by Ṭurṭūšī, *Sirāj*, 123f.

37 Jāḥiẓ, *Bayān*, II, 14. The reference to the two "wisdoms" is here somewhat vague.

38 Zamaxšarī, *Nawābiġ*, fol. 8b. The terminology used here is *maṭbū'* and *masmū'*.

39 Cheikho 1903, 253. The same terms are used in Ibn al-Muqaffa', *al-Adab al-ṣaġīr*, cf. *Āthār Ibn al-Muqaffa'*, Beirut 1966, 318f.

40 Tawḥīdī, *Baṣā'ir*, IV, 127. In what seems like a corruption of this saying we have in Ps.-Aṣmaᶜī, *Nihāya*, fol. 197a: *lā yaḥṣulu ᶜaqlun bi-ġayri adabin wa-lā maṭarun bi-ġayri xayrin*. (MS Cambridge Qq 225, fol. 165a has *wa-lā manẓar bi-ġayri xabar*).

"Know that wisdom (*ᶜaql*) without knowledge (*ᶜilm*) is like earth which has trees and plants, but which is saline, with little water. Knowledge without wisdom is like barren land, which has no plant or tree. If it is not planted and ploughed, no use can be drawn from it."[41] Another simile used in an anonymous saying is that wisdom (*ᶜaql*) and learning (*adab*) are like soul and body: the body without the soul is a mere form (*ṣūra*)[42] and the soul without the body is a mere wind (*rīḥ*), but their combination is powerful.[43]

Although the idea that there are two types of intellect may strike us as fairly widespread, it does not occur very frequently in Islamic literature, nor does it seem to derive from Greek thinking. It is however a very important notion in Zoroastrian literature, and there is every likelihood that it was borrowed into Arabic literature from Iran, despite the awe-inspiring attribution to ᶜAlī which sometimes accompanies it. It is certainly considered Iranian by the Arabic writers who usually quote this idea on the authority of Sasanian sages.

The division of the intellect into two types, using the same terminology, occurs already in the Avesta. Thus we have the opposition *āsna-xratu-* "innate wisdom" as against *gaošō.strūta- xratu-* "wisdom heard by the ear" in Y. 22:25 and Y. 25:6. Both wisdoms are worshipped and both are given the epithet *mazdadāta-* "created by Mazda". It may be recalled that *xratu-*, Sasanian *xrad*, is a venerated concept in Zoroastrianism. The title (and contents) of the book *Dādestān ī Mēnōg ī Xrad* "The Discourse of the Spirit of Wisdom" provides ample testimony for this.

41 Ps.-Aṣmaᶜī, *Nihāya*, fol. 199b. The structure of this parable is different, although one must assume that both versions are variants of the same original text. In what seems like a conflation of this type of saying with another one, also recorded on the authority of Buzurjmihr, we have a series of questions: "What is the best thing given to man in this world and the next?", to which Buzurjmihr answers: "Innate wisdom (*ġarīzatu ᶜaqlin*)". The next question is, "And if this is not given?", to which he answers: "The search for knowledge (*ṭalabu l-ᶜilm*)". The next two items which a man must have in the absence of each one of the above are a good friend and then a quick death (Ps.-Aṣmaᶜī, *Nihāya*, fol. 197b). This is a widespread theme; without the contrast between the two types of intellect one has it, for example, in Ibn Huḏayl, *ᶜAyn al-adab*, 103; Jāḥiẓ, *Bayān*, I, 221 and p. 7; Māwardī, *Adab al-dunyā*, 31. See also Ibn Ḥātim al-Tamīmī, *Rawḍat al-ᶜuqalā'*, MS Paris Bib.Nat. arabe 5809, fol. 6a.

42 This could render Pahlavi *kālbōd*.

43 Māwardī, *Adab al-wazīr*, 30. The two wisdoms are called *ra'y* and *adab* in Miskawayhi, *Jāwīdān*, 77 ll. 2f, a text which corresponds partly to *Dk.* VI E45d; cf. Shaked 1979, 308.

The contrast between the two notions is made in very clear terms in a passage of the *Bundahišn* which describes the role of Wahman, the deity "Good Thought", in the presence of Ohrmazd. Wahman's function, we are told, is to introduce the righteous to the Best Existence and to Ohrmazd; he is the lord of power, helping the good troops against the evil ones, and he procures peace for the creations of Ohrmazd. In addition, the innate wisdom and the acquired wisdom first appear to the eyes of (*abar*) Wahman (in the after-life): he who possesses them both, comes to the Best Existence; he who has none, comes to the Worst Existence; when a person does not possess innate wisdom, he cannot be taught acquired wisdom (*ka āsn-xrad nēst, gōšōsrūd ne āmōxtēd*). A person who possesses innate wisdom but does not have acquired wisdom does not know how to put (his) innate wisdom to use.[44] These are words which are very close to those quoted above on the authority of Kisrā.[45] Another Pahlavi passage in the same spirit says: "Innate wisdom without acquired wisdom is like a female without a male, who does not conceive and does not bear fruit. A man who possesses [acquired] wisdom but whose innate wisdom is not perfect is like a female who is not receptive to a male. For a female who is not receptive to a male does not bear fruit in the same manner as one who does not have a male in the first place."[46]

A discussion of the concept of wisdom and its different divisions in Zoroastrian literature must be reserved for a separate occasion, but the material discussed here is sufficient, I believe, to show that this dual conception of wisdom is a central theme in the religious thought of the Sasanian period, and has Iranian roots going much further back in time. It is instructive for the history of Arabic literature to watch how it is quoted as a piece of Persian wisdom, and how it is also transformed into an Islamic notion. Eventually, as we have seen, it has gained the ultimate stamp of approval by being attributed to ᶜAlī.

44 *GBd.* 163f.; TD1, fol. 67a–b; *Zand-Ākāsīh,* 212ff. Cf. also Gignoux 1968, 231f., for a transcription of this passage.

45 See note 40.

46 *Dk.* VI, 262, in Shaked 1979, 102f.

BIBLIOGRAPHICAL REFERENCES

Al-cĀmilī, Muḥammad Bahā' al-Dīn, *Al-Kaškūl,* Cairo 1313.

Ps.-Aṣmacī, *Nihāyat al-arab,* Ms. British Library 23.298.

Al-Balāḏurī, Aḥmad b. Yaḥyā b. Jābir, *Ansāb al-ašrāf,* IVA, ed. M. Schloessinger and M.J. Kister, Jerusalem 1971.

Cheiko, Louis, 1903. "Ḥikam Buzurjmihr", *Al-Machriq* 6:205–207, 250–254.

———, 1938, *Majānī al-adab fī ḥadā'iq al-carab,* II, Beirut.

Al-Ḏāhri, Zacharia, *Sefer hammusar,* ed. Y. Ratzaby, Jerusalem 1965.

Dhabhar, Bamanji Nasarvanji, 1918. "A recipe for contentment", *The Dastur Hoshang Memorial Volume,* Bombay, pp. 193–195. [Reprinted in: B.N. Dhabhar, *Essays on Iranian Subjects,* Bombay 1955, 39–41.]

Eilers, Wilhelm, 1983, "Iran and Mesopotamia", *Cambridge History of Iran*, 3(1), Cambridge, 481–504.

Al-Ġazālī, Abū Ḥāmid Muḥammad, *Mīzān al-camal*, Cairo 1328.

GBd = The *Greater Bundaishn*, Facsimile of TD 2, ed. by T.D. Anklesaria, Bombay 1908.

Gignoux, Philippe, 1968. "L'enfer et le paradis d'après les sources pehlevies", *Journal Asiatique*, 219–245.

Ibn cAbd Rabbihi, Abū cUmar Aḥmad b. Muḥammad, *Al-ciqd al-farīd*, 7 vols., Cairo 1359/1940–1372/1953.

Ibn al-cArīf, Abū-l-cAbbās Aḥmad b. Muḥammad al-Ṣinhājī, *Maḥāsin al-majālis*, ed. M. Asín Palacios, Paris 1933 (Collection de textes inédits relatifs à la mystique musulmane, 2).

Ibn Huḏayl, Abū-l-Ḥasan cAlī b. cAbd al-Raḥmān, *cAyn al-adab wa-l-siyāsa wa-zayn al-ḥasab wa-l-riyāsa*, Cairo 1388/1969.

Ibn Qutayba al-Dīnawarī, Abū Muḥammad cAbdallāh b. Muslim, *cUyūn al-axbār*, Cairo 1963.

Al-Iṣbahānī, Abū Nucaym, *Ḥilyat al-awliyā'*, 10 vols., Beirut 1387/1967.

Al-Jāḥiẓ, Abū cUṯmān cAmr b. Baḥr, *Al-bayān wa-l-tabyīn*, ed. cAbd al-Salām Muḥammad Hārūn, 4 vols., 4th ed., Cairo 1975.

Jamasp-Asana, Jamaspji Dastur Minocheherji (ed.), *Pahlavi Texts*, Bombay 1897.

Kapadia, Dinshah D., 1953. *Glossary of Pahlavi Vendidad*, Bombay.

Klíma, Otakar, 1967. "The Dārūk i xuansandīh", *Yádnáme-ye Jan Rypka*, Prague and The Hague-Paris, 37–39.

———, 1968. "Einige Bemerkungen zum Dārūk i xuansandīh", *Archiv Orientální* 36:567–576.

Al-Māwardī, Abū-l-Ḥasan cAlī b. Muḥ., *Adab al-dunyā wa-l-dīn*, ed. Muṣṭafā al-Saqā, 4th ed., Cairo 1393/1973.

———, *Adab al-wazīr*, Cairo 1348/1929.

Miskawayhi, Abū ᶜAlī Aḥmad b. Muḥammad, *Jāwīdān xirad*, ed. under the title *Al-ḥikma al-xālida* by ᶜAbd al-Raḥmān Badawī, Cairo 1952.

Al-Nīsāburī, Ḥasan b. Aḥmad, *ᶜUqalā' al-majānīn*, ed. Muḥammad Baḥr al-ᶜUlūm, Najaf 1387/1967.

Nuwayrī, Šihāb al-Dīn Aḥmad b. ᶜAbd al-Wahhāb, *Nihāyat al-arab fī funūn al-adab*, Cairo 1342/1923.

Al-Sahlajī, *Al-nūr min kalimāt Abī Ṭayfūr*, in: ᶜAbd al-Raḥmān Badawī, *Šaṭahāt al-Ṣūfiyya*, I, Cairo 1949.

Shaked, Shaul, 1979. *Wisdom of the Sasanian Sages (Dēnkard VI)*, by Āturpāt i Ēmētān (Persian Heritage Series, 34), Boulder, Col.

Shaki, Mansour, 1968. "Dārūk i hōnsandīh", *Archive Orientální* 36:429–431.

Al-Suyūṭī, Jalāl al-Dīn ᶜAbd al-Raḥmān, *Al-sirr al-maknūn fī manāqib al-ᶜārif billāh taᶜāla Ḏī-l-Nūn*, Ms. Lâleli (Süleymaniya, Istanbul) 2051.

Al-Tanūxī, Abū ᶜAli al-Muḥsin b. Abī-l-Qāsim, *Al-faraj baᶜda al-šidda*, Cairo 1375/1955.

Al-Tawḥīdī, Abū Ḥayyān, *Al-baṣā'ir wa-l-ḍaxā'ir*, ed. Aḥmad Amīn and Aḥmad Ṣaqar, Cairo 1373/1953.

TD1 = *The Bondahesh, Facsimile edition of Ms. TD1*, Tehran n.d. (Iranian Culture Foundation, 88).

Al-Ṭurṭūšī, Abū Bakr Muḥammad Ibn Abī Rindaqa, *Sirāj al-Mulūk*, Cairo 1354/1935.

Al-Zamaxšarī, Abū-l-Qāsim Muḥammad, *Al-Nawābiġ wa-l-ḥikam*, Ms. Köprülü 1224.

Zand-Ākāsīh, Iranian or Greater Bundahišn, transliteration and translation, B.T. Anklesaria, Bombay 1956.

X

FIRST MAN, FIRST KING

Notes on Semitic-Iranian Syncretism and Iranian Mythological Transformations

In the original Indo-Iranian period Yima (Indian Yama) was probably a First Man figure. This trait of his personality is not preserved with any clarity either in India or in Iran, but certain hints in late Iranian literature show that he may have been considered as the originator of humanity and of civilization.[1] Several myths connected with his figure suggest that he was the first mortal, for at his time humanity knew no death. His connection with death is also a prominent feature of the Indian figure of Yama.[2] As the first mortal, he is the originator of proper human existence. If it is true that he was in one early layer of tradition the first human, he may have lost that position in Iran with the advent of Zoroastrianism. This could have been the result of a reshuffle of functions, caused, among other things, by the fact that Gaya Maretan assumed the role of the first Man.

Gaya Maretan (later Gayōmard) belongs to the specific Zoroastrian terminology, and is thus part of the novel religious conception introduced in Iran by Zoroastrianism. The main argument in favour of this assumption is the observation that his name has a structure similar to that of several other Zoroastrian innovations: Angra

---

[1] Cf. Christensen 1934:35; also the recent and interesting study by Kellens 1984.

[2] For details see lately Kellens 1984:279ff.

Manyu "the Evil Spirit", Vohu Manah "the Good Mind", Aša Vahišta "the Best truth", etc.[3] The name Ahura Mazdā "Lord Wisdom" itself falls in the same category. The structure of this divine name serves, I believe, as a powerful argument in favour of the Zoroastrian origin of this deity, although the issue is still disputed.[4]

Yima, representing an older layer of tradition, has had to be accommodated as a secondary figure, one whose function, in part overlapping with that of Gayōmard, is not entirely lucid. It is by no means clear where he fits in within the Zoroastrian history of humanity. He does not form part of the cycle of creation stories, but occurs separately, both in the Avesta and in the later literature, in a series of independent episodes.[5] Only in mediaeval texts is there an attempt

---

[3] This is an opinion already expressed by Christensen 1917:41f.; Schaeder 1926:211f.; Lommel 1930:137. Hoffmann 1957 argues that the myth of Gayōmard continues an ancient Indo-Iranian story, attested in India for the figure of Mārtāṇḍa, a suggestion which makes good sense. (He does not make the identification, but Boyce 1975:97 regards Gayōmard as identical with Mārtāṇḍa.) Hoffmann further assumes that the epithet Gaya Maretan, which became the proper name of the First Man figure in Iran, goes also back to Indo-Iranian times, since it corresponds closely to the epithets *amartya-gaya-* "immortal life", attested in the Rigveda (cf. Hoffmann 1957:100). The last point is important, but does not prove the existence of the Avestan epithet in the ancient period or of the person to which it was applied. It only shows that such an epithet was in use. The Avesta contains numerous expressions and themes which continue pre-Zoroastrian usage; for establishing the continuity of a divine figure we want to know that it existed in the Indo-Iranian period, but evidence for this is lacking. Lincoln 1975/6 assumes, on the basis of the Scandinavian parallel, that Gayōmard takes the position initially occupied by Yima. Again, whether this is correct or not, this would not affect our judgement as to whether Gayōmard is a creation of the Zoroastrian religion. If there was an ancient myth of the sacrifice and dismemberment of Yima, memory of it was no longer alive either in India or in Iran by the time of the beginnings of Zoroastrianism.

[4] Cf. Kent 1933; Konow 1937; Thieme 1970; Humbach 1957; Boyce 1975:38ff. The issue is not capable at the moment of proof, the arguments in either direction being undecisive. The fact that, like the abstractions which later became the Amešа Spenta, and similar Zoroastrian deities, Ahura Mazdā too was not yet a fixed proper-name in the Gāthās shows, I believe, that at the time of Zoroaster it was still an innovation. In the pre-Zoroastrian period an earlier process had taken place by which abstract notions had become divine proper names (cf. e.g. Mitra=Mithra, Varuna, Aryaman; Thieme 1970:402ff.). The Gathic list constitutes the beginning of a new layer of notions which were to undergo the same procedure. See also lately Lincoln in Colpe 1974:352-354 s.v. "Gayōmart".

[5] An example of the embarrassment caused to Zoroastrian commentators by the position of Yima with regard to the couple Mashye and Mashyāne may be seen in

made to combine and harmonize the various stories and bring them into a seemingly continuous narrative. This is seen in the Islamic works, and is particularly typical of the Shāhnāme, where both the harmonization process and the euhemeristic tendency are given full expression.

Yima (Jamshīd, as he is called in the later literature) is one of the most ambiguous figures in Iranian mythology. In a religious civilization where a clear-cut distinction between good and evil is so important, and which is not prone to admit the existence of intermediate shades between light and darkness, Yima, who combines in his person something of the two opposites, stands out as an unusual phenomenon. There are of course also some other subtle ambiguities in the Iranian mythical accounts. Ohrmazd himself emerges as a de facto collaborator with Ahreman in the myth of creation, for without an agreement concluded between them the world would not have come into being, and in this sense the world is in effect the result of the joint effort of both powers. Another case of ambiguity, to be discussed further on, concerns the first human couple, who are also the first sinners according to the account of the Bundahishn; the nature of their sin is also somewhat hazy. But in their case the sin is part of their human character, a result of the intervention of the demonic powers in the world, which has turned the creation of Ohrmazd into the mixture that it presents nowadays. As we shall try to show, Yima's case is different. A third type of ambiguity is caused by the occurrence of different third-party figures in the myth, whether it is Mithra as a judge and mediator, or Vayu, an ancient deity with ambivalent associations in Zoroastrianism.[6] Yima belongs to none of these categories. He is, in Iranian mythology, a semi-divine figure with a flaw.

Yima is not the First Man in Iran, but belongs rather to the type of founders of civilization and archaic heroes. He is specifically the first King;[7] indeed, he is the model virtuous king and an originator of

---

the discussion of *Dk* III 12 (French translation in Menasce 1973:36).

6 Cf. Shaked 1980:16ff.

7 Kellens 1984 has argued against taking Yima as a royal figure. He sets out from the tripartite framework of Dumézil, which I believe tends to distort the proper understanding of the texts, because it imposes on them questions which are not always demonstrably part of their own background. While it is true that some of the epithets and appurtenances of Yima have agricultural and especially pastoral associ-

religious obligations. At the same time, he is also a sinner, perhaps the first transgressor.[8] Thus he is said to have established incest marriage (*xwēdōdah*), one of the most important of religious precepts; he invented the idea of *paymān*, the Right Measure, a virtue which is considered by Zoroastrians to be a central trait of their religion;[9] he is credited (in late sources) with the foundation of the Nowrūz, the New Year holiday, which has strong associations with the beginning of human civilization and with eschatology, and which also serves as the prime symbol for the permanence of royalty and of the good order of society; and he is mentioned as the originator of the *kustīg*, the sacred belt which symbolizes one's adherence to the Zoroastrian faith. Besides, as the founder of civilization, he is said to have established the production of weapons and the weaving of textiles, the division of society into classes,[10] the hewing of stones for the construction of buildings, and similar skills and exploits.[11]

---

ations, only a firm faith in a rigid tripartite division of society and in the essential incompatibility of pastoralism with royalty can lead one to reject the numerous references to Yima's royal position as irrelevant. Other distortions which sometimes occur as a result of the way in which Dumézilian conceptions are imposed on the texts will be pointed out in the following. It may be noted that Dumézil himself gave a different interpretation of the enigmatic figure of Yima (1971:282ff.). Cf. also the remarks by Gnoli 1980:150ff.

8 Something like a concept of original sin occurs in the story of the first human couple, Mashye and Mashyāne, but this is part of a different cycle of stories, and the sense of this fall is different; cf. further on.

9 On this concept see Shaked (forthcoming).

10 This point has as its basis the Avestan text Yt. 19:34-38, which was interpreted by the later Zoroastrian literature as referring to the three classes of society. The text itself does not say that. It merely speaks of the *khvarenah*, the divine splendour, which left Yima three times (or less likely: of three splendours that left Yima) as a result of the fact that he found joy in lying words; it states that the splendour was received successively by Mithra, Thraētaona, and Kbresāspa. *Dk.* VII 1:25-37 applies these successive transfers of splendour to the three social classes, although it puts Oshnar in the place of Mithra (cf. Molé 1963:462f.). Darmesteter 1892-93, II:624ff. interpreted the Avestan passage in this light as referring to the social classes, and his idea was endorsed by Molé (ibid.) and Dumézil 1971:284ff., despite the obvious difficulties of this interpretation. Kellens 1984:275, whose approach is also Dumézilian, has had to admit that the passage defies explanation from this point of view. Lincoln 1975/6:132 n. 41 gives a new explanation which seeks to retain the idea of an original tripartite version of the myth, by assuming that one of the names was changed at a later date.

11 Cf. e.g. Ṭabarī, *History*, I:179; translation in Christensen 1934:85.

At the same time, Yima is also presented as a man who committed some grievous offence against the deity. While his virtues are manifest and clearly described, the cause or circumstances of his collapse are shrouded in some mystery. The mode of his fall is also recounted in several conflicting versions. The nature of Yima's sin is often not described at all. This is the case with the Vendidad account of his reign, where it is said that after a period of great welfare and expansion under Yima's reign, a flood was brought over humanity, and was about to annihilate a large part of it, but the reason for this is not specified. In another Avestan allusion to his person, in the single unequivocal reference to Yima in the Gathas (Y 32:8),[12] where he is mentioned as one of the early sinners, it is hard to tell what his sin consists of. The obscure Gathic verse has been the subject of numerous attempts at interpretation.[13]

When Yima's sin is mentioned in clear terms, different versions give a bewildering number of conflicting accounts of it. It is said in one place that Yima lied (Yt. 19:33). But this is hardly a specific sin, for lie is a general term for sin in Zoroastrianism.[14] The accusation

---

12 Humbach 1974 has tried to argue that Y 30:3, the famous Gathic verse which mentions the two primeval spirits as twins (yemā), is actually concerned with Yima, but this seems doubtful; see the criticism by Insler 1975:330ff. On the other hand, it does not seem excluded that the two primeval spirits were in some way related to the Indo-Iranian myth of the twins of whom one was attacked and killed by the other; a more direct echo of that myth is found in the late story of Gayōmard, as recounted in the *Bundahishn*, if the reconstruction proposed by Lincoln 1975/6 is to be accepted.

13 See lately Insler 1975:204f.; Boyce 1975:93. Apart from establishing the nature of Yima's sin, there is the problem of understanding why he was regarded as tainted by sin. It seems barely sufficient to explain Yima's sin on general grounds by stating: "In a mythology where there is already the figure of a creator, Yima...has some traits of the antagonist, in conformity with a fairly widespread phenomenon" (Gnoli 1980:150). Boyce 1975:93 regards the motif of the sin as a priestly attempt to explain in moral terms why death had to befall Yima.

14 The verb "to lie" as a general designation for sin is used, for example, in the account of the sins of the first human couple, where every sinful action committed by them is described as a lie, although some of these actions did not necessarily involve saying untruthful things (*GBd*, translation in Christensen 1917:19). That it was used in this sense not only in religious contexts, but also in the political language, may be seen from the great inscription of Darius in Behistun, where every act of disobedience to the king is called a lie. Boyce 1975:93f. assumes that the theme of Yima's sin is secondary in the story. We are here chiefly concerned with Yima's history in Iran, and the question of the origins of the various themes in the story are therefore of lesser importance in this context.

that Yima taught men to eat flesh may be merely the result of a wrong interpretation of the Gathic verse Y. 32:8 (cf. Christensen 1934:49). We have no way of telling whether the praise bestowed on Yima for refusing to make a certain substitute for cattle, as the demons wanted, has anything to do with the sin mentioned in the Gatha.[15] It is often said of Yima that he was seduced by a female demon.[16] The final outcome of this seduction story is good, for he discovers the virtue of consanguinous marriage, when he abandons the female demon and cohabits with his sister.[17] Very often he is said to have become haughty and to have regarded himself as a god.[18]

Sometimes what is wrong with Yima is not a sin deliberately committed by him, but some circumstantial association with demons. The act which entails this contact is done with the best of motives, and yet is harmful, because it carries within it a kind of contagious effect. Thus, when he descends into the realm of Ahreman and extracts from there that valuable commodity, the *paymān*, the Right Measure,[19] he acts in an outrageous manner; besides, the implication that there are certain beneficial qualities which are hidden in the realm of evil and which may be extracted from there for the good of humanity is essentially alien to Zoroastrianism.[20] Another instance for the peculiar involvement of Yima with Ahreman is provided by the episode in which he puts his hand through Ahreman's buttock in order to wring out from Ahreman's entrails his brother Tahmurath;

---

15 The passages where this episode is alluded to are *PRiv*, p. 102f.;*MX* 26:33. Early translations of the passage in *Mēnōg ī Xrad* have rendered the word **pyl** "an old man" (i.e. *pīr*). Cf. West 1885:60; Christensen 1934:24. Tafazzoli 1354H:125ff., and 1975, has recently argued that the word should be read *pīl* "elephant". In the absence of supporting textual evidence, it is difficult to accept the suggestion that the elephant was substituted to cattle as a sacrificial victim (or as provider of meat?), and one would welcome a different reading of the word.

16 *Dd* 39:16.

17 *PRiv* 14-16; cf. Christensen 1934:28f.

18 *'Ulamā-i Islām*, ed. Mohl, 6; Christensen 1934:63. Also Firdawsi, *Shāhnāma*, translated in Christensen 1934:103.

19 On this episode cf. Shaked (forthcoming).

20 Such a conception is typical of gnostic thinking, and is current in Manicheism, which may have influenced the myth under consideration. It is equally possible that this is a pre-Zoroastrian motif which re-emerges in this late story.

here again he acts unconventionally, and is accordingly punished by having his hand, where it touched Ahreman, covered with leprosy. The final point of that story is aetiological: Yima discovers the purifying effect of bull's urine, the substance considered in Zoroastrianism most beneficial for ritual cleansing, and can impart this knowledge to mankind.[21]

Running through the Yima stories is a theme with an almost tragic ring to it, since Yima's association with the powers of evil is inadvertent or inevitable, but the results are disastrous. This duplicity in his character may well be an early Iranian feature of the cycle of stories connected with his person, as allusions to it are found in the Avestan references to Yima. It was presumably suppressed, or at least toned down, in the classical Zoroastrian accounts, and has mostly survived in the more popular versions of the mythology, those which often preserve for us ancient features we might otherwise have disregarded.

As noted above, the story of the first human couple, Mashye and Mashyāne, who fell into a life of partial sinfulness (representing the actual situation of mankind), also contains within it an element of fall. But there are marked differences between the fall of Yima and that of Mashye and Mashyāne. These latter are not superhuman or quasi divine. On the contrary, they are the very models of humanity as it really is. Their story is that of the human condition: from initial innocence and purity, they fall into the ways of the actual world, where good and evil are mixed. They go through this, because this is how humanity is constituted. Yima the Luminous, in contrast, is a conspicuous solar figure.[22] During his reign, humanity does not know of death. He symbolizes divine power and presence in the world. When he falls, in the Iranian stories, his fall does not represent the devolution of human existence, but a divine failure in the world. It hints at the possibility that dualism may be inherent in the bright luminosity of divinity itself, though this is a possibility that goes against Zoroastrian doctrines, and is vehemently denied and rejected in other contexts.

---

[21] This occurs in a Zoroastrian *Rivāyat* in Persian; translation in Christensen 1917:188.

[22] Cf. Kellens 1984:277.

The extensive survival of Yima's ambiguities in the popular versions of the Iranian mythology seems to suggest an internal Iranian syncretism, a syncretism which operates vertically, between different layers of the religion, and diachronically, by letting ancient themes filter through and imbue the later formulations of the Iranian view of the origins of the world. A different kind of syncretism is seen when we consider the accounts of the Iranian religion in the Islamic books. Yima, according to the ignorant among the Persians, says Ibn al-Muqaffa‘,[23] is the same as King Solomon, son of David. "The ignorant among the Persians" may have made this identification because they wanted to integrate their mythology to that of their Arab conquerors. It seems however possible to assume that they had already made it earlier, at the time of the Sasanians, in order to harmonize their traditions with those of their Semitic neighbours. The process of syncretistic adaptation of Iranian materials to the surrounding Semitic world may have begun long before the advent of Islam.

If we turn to examine the vicissitudes of the story of Gayōmard, we find a situation which is different in certain respects. There is no pre-Zoroastrian layer here, since Gayōmard appears to be a Zoroastrian creation.[24] But within Zoroastrianism the figure underwent a series of ramifications, in addition to the changes which took place later, in the Islamic sources.

There is a marked contrast between the story of Gayōmard in the official Zoroastrian cannon and the more popular stories preserved by the Islamic authors. The figure of Gayōmard and those of Mashye and Mashyāne are presented in the Zoroastrian books as forming part of the grand scheme of divine origins from which the whole world and humanity came about. The creation of humanity fulfils a definite function within a larger plan. There is a well-defined theology which lies behind the mythological story. The name Gayōmard, interpreted to mean "mortal life", or "life and death", or "life, death and reason",[25] is certainly a direct reference to his human existence; it may

---

23 Dīnawarī, 9. A similar opinion is reported by Ibn al-Nadīm, 309; Tha‘ālibī, 10 (who objects to this opinion and remarks that Yima is separate from Solomon by a period of more than two thousand years). a discussion of these identifications is in Christensen 1934:119.

24 See above, note 3.

25 Pahlavi *zīndagīh gōwāgīh mērāg<īh>*, (*DkM* 230:8-9); and the Arabic

be noted that the cognate terms *martya, mašya* in India and ancient Iran also describe Man primarily as "mortal". Gayōmard's features are reminiscent of humanity, but his character and dimensions are super-human. He belongs however also to the vegetable world by virtue of the fact that he grew from the earth like a plant. His position is strictly parallel to that of the Bull, *Gāw ī ēwag-dād*, and in this sense he constitutes the human counterpart to the animal world. The account of Gayōmard is thus clearly that of a composite figure, carefully designed to represent, in a symbolic way, the characteristics of the main forms of existence. The germs of human existence, as symbolized in the person of Gayōmard, contain within them the chief elements of all the other forms of being, both in the material and in the divine world, but Gayōmard does not represent human existence as it was constituted after it was attacked and defiled by the Evil Spirit: he lacks nourishment, particularly the more problematic kind of food, which is meat; and he lacks sexuality (his descendants are born from his sperm, ejected at his death, but without the application of sexual differentiation and contact); and deceit, the archetypal form of sin in Iran, is never connected with his person.

The account of the first human couple, the indirect descendants of Gayōmard, Mashye and Mashyāne, is, by contrast, one of gradual development from the elements characteristic of Gayōmard (initially they have an undifferentiated, vegetable, immutable shape) to those which are identifiably human, containing movement, sexual differentiation, and the basic human cravings and failings. They grow as a single stalk of a rhubarb plant, but are subsequently separated to become a human couple, and eventually they come to discover their biological human needs. They begin to consume milk and flesh, and they discover sexuality. This, in Iran, as in the Jewish and Christian traditions, is regarded as a fall from perfection.

The accounts given in the Muslim sources, for the most part, show no familiarity with the imaginatively mythical aspects of the figure of Gayōmard, but portray him simply as one of the ancestors

---

equivalents: *al-ḥayy al-nāṭiq*, which occurs in several sources (e.g. Shahrastānī, *Milal*, 233). "The ability to speak" is an epithet attributed to Man, presumably by influence of Greek philosophical terminology, where speech (*logos*) is equated with reason. Bailey's erroneous interpretation of this phrase (1943:83f.) is corrected in the introduction to the second edition, p. xxxiv f.

of mankind. He is viewed as either a first man or a first king; in the latter version, in which his functions overlap with Yima's, he marks the beginning of human society, creating its institutions of government and civilization.

The changes which the Iranian themes underwent in Islam were probably caused by a number of different reasons. In some cases it may be assumed that Islamic writers elaborated on the material they received from their Iranian informants. Since many of them were themselves of Iranian origin, they might have actually served as their own informants. Often they may have supplemented their own answers to unformulated speculative questions which were never explicitly formulated in the Iranian material. In other cases they may have put together stories which they had received separately, and combined them into a continuous narrative.

We can occasionally spot textual errors which betray the fact that the Islamic accounts derived from literary sources written in the highly ambiguous Pahlavi script. Two examples may be quoted. The epithet of Gayōmard is recorded in two different manners: in some versions it is said to be Gil-Shāh, "King of Clay", while according to other authorities it is quoted as Gar-Shāh, "King of the Mountain". The confusion cannot be explained by oral transmission; it can only arise when one reads the epithet in the Pahlavi script, where -l- and -r- are expressed by the same letter, and where the vowels are not marked.[26] The second example is derived from the Islamic accounts of the creation of Gayōmard. This is sometimes said to be associated with perspiration coming on the forehead of Ohrmazd,[27] but one cannot help feeling that this is not an original detail of the story, but is the result of a textual error. When the pain of death was brought upon Gayōmard by Ahreman, it is said that Ohrmazd caused sleep to come to Gayōmard in order to alleviate the pain which he was suffering. In the Pahlavi script "sleep", *xwāb*, and "perspiration", *xwey*, can have an identical appearance; it seems likely, as Schaeder has shown,[28] that the perspiration of Ohrmazd owes its

26 Various confusions have taken place with regard to *gil* in Pahlavi. Cf. Christensen 1917:27; Nöldeke 1879:xxv, and, in a different context, Bailey 1944:29f. Further notes relevant to this point are in Shaked 1971:92 n. 6.

27 Bīrūnī, *Āthār*, 99:7.

28 Schaeder 1926:217 n.1 and 351f.

existence to this confusion. Once "sleep" was misread as "perspiration", it was moved to the stage of creation, where it seemingly made better sense.

Such confusions appear however to be of minor importance. They do not account for the major differences that exist betweeen the story of Gayōmard as transmitted by the Muslim authors, and that of the Pahlavi tradition. What emerges is that we have basically two kinds of reports in the Muslim sources: one, based essentially on the known Iranian literary traditions (e.g. Shahrastānī, Bīrūnī), results in the two conflicting views of the origins of humanity — the Iranian view and the Muslim (i.e. Judaeo-Christian) one — being presented side by side; and another one, the result of a harmonization, tries to reconcile the Iranian view to that of Judaism and Islam by interspersing the figures of Iranian mythology within the genealogy of the early forefathers of mankind according to the Biblical account.

Whatever the origins of the representation of Gayōmard, the fully developed Zoroastrian story, as it is given in such late Zoroastrian sources as the *Bundahishn* and the *Selections of Zādspram*, forms part of the well-conceived organic whole which constitutes the scheme of Zoroastrian cosmogony. According to this theological mythology, the world is planned by Ohrmazd as a trap, following the agreement made by him with Ahreman: it is an agreement in which both deities stand to lose, but which Ohrmazd is clever enough to turn to his ultimate advantage. The initial power of Ahreman is equivalent to Ohrmazd's, and there is no way of overcoming him, since in *mēnōg* both spirits are eternal and invincible. The pact which set a temporal and spatial Limit on the battle between the two deities may have seemed fair to Ahreman, but it contained the promise of his final destruction, because he would have to fight on alien territory, and within a time limit which was not his own. The result is that his fate is determined from the start. In another episode of the story he is said to be extremely dejected, to lie prostrate and incapacitated for a long period of time, until he is comforted and cheered up by the promise made to him by Jeh, the Primal Whore, that she would arouse sexual desire in Man — a promise that stamps sexuality with a taint of impurity. This conclusion is not invalidated by the observation that the story is directed at giving an aetiology to the demonic origin of menstruation.[29]

---

29 The statement that Ahreman suffered a total loss of consciousness following the discovery of his ultimate defeat by the hand of Ohrmazd occurs also in the main

The creation of Man in this narrative is part of the grand scheme of Ohrmazd, devised for the purpose of fighting and overcoming Ahreman. The figures of Gayōmard, of Zoroaster, and of the Final Redeemer, the Saošyant, merge into each other as we are given to understand that they are basically three different representations, or stages, of the same function in universal history, the function of vanquishing the devil. The generic term which hides behind all three is that of the Righteous Man (*mard ī ahlaw*), the potent symbol of that power which is capable of defeating evil in the world. This is associated with the idea that evil has no place of its own, indeed it has no reality of its own in the world, and so it survives in this world by clinging to mankind. Once it is cast away from humanity, it has been virtually banished from the whole world. None of this implied theology is present in the Islamic versions, where the tale of Gayōmard is given merely as a curious story.

In a monograph on Gayōmard, Sven Hartman (1953) argues that there is a distinction in the Avesta between two figures: Gaya and Gaya Maretan. In the later literature those two persons fell together, according to Hartman, in the single figure of Gayōmard. The evidence for this hypothesis is not entirely convincing. The term *gaya*, which means "life", is used in the Avesta sometimes on its own, as an abstract notion, but it also occurs in a number of passages as a shorthand designation for the full epithet "Gaya Maretan". The name Gaya, in this usage, appears as the counterpart of Gav "the Bull". The pair Gaya and the Bull are exactly equivalent to the pair Gaya Maretan and the Bull (Y. 13:7), just as in the late formulation of the cosmogonic story, Gayōmard and the Bull constitute a constant pair.[30] In the Avesta, Gaya occurs as one of the "elements" of the world, indeed as the final item in a list which contains the sky, water, earth, plants, the Bull and "Gaya" (Yt. 13:86). Its place in this list indicates quite clearly that we are dealing with the figure of the Primordial Man, whose full name elsewhere is Gaya Maretan.

version of the story, where Jeh does not figure. See *GBd*, p. 7 and *Zs* 1:24 (translation in Zaehner 1955:314, 342, respectively).

30 In the late version, which exists in several forms, both in Pahlavi and in a number of Islamic sources, Gayōmard, "Mortal Life", and the Bull (Gāw) are parallel creations of Ohrmazd and also parallel victims of the assault of Ahreman on the world.

The obvious conclusion is that the two terms are interchangeable. The assumption that there could be two such separate figures in the Avesta, each one associated with the Bull as its pair, both called by practically the same name and yet belonging to two different traditions, seems tenuous.[31]

The attempt to distinguish in the Avesta between two concepts, Gaya and Gaya Maretan, is unfortunately associated with a hunt for texts which supposedly contain Zurvanite elements. One is invited to accept the hypothesis that the Avesta as we have it is a composite of two sets of religious texts, Zurvanite and non-Zurvanite, and that even supposedly non-Zurvanite passages may contain traces of tampering by Zurvanite editors. Such a conception, evidently inspired by the hypotheses and methods used in Biblical criticism (where this approach seems also to have lost some of its glamour), has not yet proved to be useful for the study of the Avesta. No one would deny that the composition and redaction of the Avestan corpus stretched over an extensive period of time. As a result, the Avesta certainly contains several distinct chronological layers, which reflect, it may be assumed, different stages in the history of the religion. It is however far from proven that it also embodies the conflicting views of diverse theological schools.

In the course of his arguments, Hartman (1975; 1983) refers also to the fact that the name of the supreme deity of Zoroastrianism does not occur in the Gāthā in the same shape as we know it from the Younger Avesta.[32] This does not mean to say that it does not occur at all: it only means that its usage is somewhat different from that of the later period. It often consists of only one of the two elements of the name; when both are present their order is often reversed, they may be separated from each other by the interposition of other words, or they may occur in two different hemistichs separated by a

[31] Hartman's strongest argument is the observation that both Gaya and Gaya Maretan occur in the same Avestan text (Yt. 13:86-87, cf. Hartman 1953:13). This fact is however as damaging for Hartman's theory of a conflict of schools as it is for any other view of the matter; for it is difficult to explain how and why both designations are present in one text, when the assumption is that each designation belonged to a different school.

[32] This had already been noticed by Bartholomae 1904, col. 292, and Kent 1933. See also Kuiper 1976 and Kellens 1984a.

caesura. This shows, to my mind, nothing more than that it took some time for such a Zoroastrian innovation as Ahura Mazdā to become established as a proper name in the full sense of the term. Zoroaster himself apparently treated it as an epithet rather than as a proper name, and its usage in the Gāthā still displays a great deal of fluidity. The same situation may apply also to the Avestan Gaya Maretan.[33]

As developed in late Zoroastrianism, probably in the Sasanian period, the two sets of First Man figures, Yima (Jamshīd) with his associates (e.g. Thraētaona=Farīdun) on the one hand, and Gaya Maretan (Gayōmard) with the Bull and the first human couple Mashye and Mashyāne on the other, found themselves complementing each other, despite the obvious inconsistencies and duplications in their functions and symbolism caused by their divergent origins. Thus, for example, both Yima and Gayōmard are distinctive solar figures; both are associated with the major Zoroastrian festivals; both mark the beginnings of humanity; and both are said to have been the first to receive the divine message of Ohrmazd.[34] At the same time, each one of the two sets belongs to a different symbolic field. Gayōmard and his set symbolize humanity as a passive instrument in the cosmic battle. They are marked by initial innocence, by subsequent transgression (for the first human couple), and by ultimate death and suffering (for Gayōmard), without any connection between the two last points. Jamshīd represents a semi-divine presence in the world, indicated both by a superhuman splendour and abundance and by a gigantic fall. His style of action, even during his period of decline, is active and heroic. From another point of view, however, the two sets of myths developed in parallel fashion in two different Sasanian milieus. In the official, priestly, Zoroastrian religion, the roles were very much as formulated here, while in popular, non-theological circles, there developed, through a combination of euhemerism and harmonization, the tendency to describe both sets of

[33] Indeed, not only Gaya but *maretan* too may have served in the Avesta as a shorthand designation for the whole name, if one adopts the suggestion made by E. Lehmann and endorsed by Schaeder 1926:213 for the interpretation of the Gathic verse Y 30:6.

[34] This is most clearly visible in the account of Shahrastānī, *Milal*, 240, 242, which is definitely derived from a written Zoroastrian source.

figures as those of early kings and heroes, and to seek to establish for them an appropriate place in the biblical genealogies.

That there used to be considerable diversity in the mythological data transmitted in Iran is a manifest fact. Some diversity of this kind is visible even in the extant Zoroastrian sources, although they seem to represent on the whole a single school of priestly teaching, the one that prevailed and that has survived in late orthodox Zoroastrianism. Extraneous sources, however, were not bound by the same restrictions, and they often give us more than one account of various Iranian mythical events. It is from them that we can most often reconstruct some of the popular, uncanonical views of Zoroastrian mythology which we possess. On the basis of these deviant versions we may try to understand the other reality of Zoroastrianism, that of the popular religion. Although it was probably believed in and practised quite widely, very little of it survived, because it was not included in the teachings of the priests who were ultimately responsible for the transmission of the religion. If the religion transmitted to us in the literary canon of scripture and in the mediaeval Zoroastrian tradition is mainstream Zoroastrianism, it was certainly not the only form of religion, perhaps not even the most widespread one, in the Sasanian period.

Popular Zoroastrianism was apparently more open to syncretistic relationship with the neighbouring religious cultures than was the official religion of Iran. The tendency to harmonize Iranian traditions with those of the Semitic world belongs, one may assume, to this layer of religion. Under the general term harmonization, it may be useful to distinguish two types, one consisting of a genuine fusion of conflicting traditions, and the other representing a process of translation. The first one is caused by the wish to smooth over the conflict caused by divergent traditions. This may be motivated by different aims. It may, for example, reflect a desire to endow one of two cultures with the respectabibility of the more prestigious one; or it may represent the aim of creating a unified history, free from the internal contradictions caused by the different sources of transmission. As a result, one tries to combine the exclusive claims of the different versions about the origins of humanity into a unified, albeit artificial, tradition.

The other type of harmonization is not so much concerned with a fusion of two traditions, as with an act of translation. In the Islamic context it involves, for example, equating Gayōmard with Adam, which signifies that in the Iranian story Gayōmard fulfils a function similar to that of Adam. Taxmuraf is equated with Noah (Mas'ūdī; v. Christensen 1918:194). This conveys the sense that Taxmuraf is one of the ancestors of mankind, although not the ultimate beginning of humanity; it further denotes that he is responsible for the foundation of much of human civilization. This is basically the method already employed by Mani, when he caused the figures of his elaborate mythology to be translated into terms available in each one of the cultures in which his religion was propagated.[35] This is not syncretism in the proper sense of the term. It does not necessarily represent a desire to combine two cultures and does not directly affect a change of contents. Starting off from an awareness of the affinity of concepts in different cultures (and probably from the former existence of syncretism), it treats the religious language as a collection of mere labels which point at certain realities, but are not to be confused with those realities themselves. It conveys the implicit message that sheer names may be disregarded, and that one should concentrate on the meanings behind the names. The technique of translating the names of one mythology into those of another was widely practised in the Greek and hellenistic periods, but Mani may have been one of the first to use it in the creation of a whole religious system. In contrast, most prophets and founders of religions before and after Mani, especially in Judaism, Christianity and Islam, regarded the name as essential to the deity. Even when one deals with a mere translation of divine names, however, the activity probably entails also some far-reaching change. In other words, it may be assumed that some genuine syncretism takes place even though what is affected is seemingly only a set of names.

Through the data given by the Islamic authors we may form an idea of the activity of what may be labelled "les mages sémitisés".[36] Both forms of cultural contact, that of assimilation

---

35 For a penetrating discussion of this point cf. Schaeder 1926:281ff.

36 The term is used by Bidez and Cumont 1938 I:68. In the context in which they apply it, however, the grounds for attributing this particular piece of tradition to Semitized Magians seem to me erroneous. They refer to a text of Theodore of Mopsuestia as quoted by Photius, *Bibliotheca*, where the name of Zoroaster is given in the form Zarades. From this form they conclude, on the basis of the -d- which replaces the original -t- of the name, that the origin of the information received by

through harmonization, and that of name-translation, were evidently pursued in what looks like the popular forms of the Iranian religion. In fact, the two processes cannot be easily distinguished. While adopting Semitic labels which they deemed to be interchangeable with the labels carried by the Iranian mythological heroes, the character of the Iranian figures may have changed. This process seems to have had its beginnings in the Sasanian period, and it may well have paved the way to the overwhelming encounter Iran was to have with Semitic culture following the Islamic conquest.

References

[Pahlavi texts are quoted as in the abbreviations to my *Wisdom of the Sasanian Sages*, Boulder, Col. 1979.]

Bailey, H.W. 1943. *Zoroastrian problems in the ninth-century books*, Oxford. (Reprint with new introduction, 1971).

Bartholomae, Christian. 1904. *Altiranisches Wörterbuch*, Strassburg. (Reprint, Berlin 1961).

Bidez, Joseph and Franz Cumont. 1938. *Les Mages hellénisés. Zoroastre, Ostanès et Hystaspe d'après la tradition grecque*, I-II. Paris (Reprint: Paris 1973).

Bīrūnī, Abū al-Rayḥān Muḥammad b. Aḥmad, *Al-āthār al-bāqiya 'an al-qurūn al-khāliya*, ed. E. Sachau, Leipzig 1923.

Boyce, Mary. 1975. *A history of Zoroastrianism*, I (Handbuch der Orientalistik, I, 8, 1, 2), Leiden-Köln.

Christensen, Arthur. 1917. *Les types du premier homme et du premier roi dans l'histoire légendaire des Iraniens*, I (Archives d'Études Orientales, 14), Stockholm.

—. 1934. Idem, II, Leiden.

Colpe, Carsten (ed.). 1974/82. "Altiranische und zoroastrische Mythologie", in H.W. Haussig (ed.), *Wörterbuch der Mythologie*, II, Stuttgart.

Darmesteter, James. 1892-93. *Le Zend-Avesta*, I-III (Annales du Musele Guimet, t. 21, 22, 24), Paris (Reprint: Paris 1960).

Dīnawarī, Abū Ḥanīfa Aḥmad b. Dāwūd, *Al-akhbār al-ṭiwāl*, ed.V. Guirgass, Leiden

---

Theodore was Semitic, since this change, according to them, took place in Syriac (Bidez and Cumont 1938 I:37). This is a mistake. The phonetic change -t->-d- in postvocalic and postsonantic position is a feature of Middle Persian and Parthian, not of Aramaic or Syriac. It is true that the form Zarathushtra should have resulted in Middle Persian not in -d- but in -h-; and such a form is actually attested in Manichaean Middle Persian. But a form derived from a putative *Zaratushtra is also attested: it is the form underlying the spelling in Pahlavi **zltwxšt**, as well as that of New Persian, Zardušt.

1888.

Dumézil, Georges. 1971. *Mythe et épopée, II. Types épiques indo-européens: un héros, un sorcier, un roi*, Paris.

Gnoli, Gherardo. 1980. *Zoroaster's time and homeland. A study on the origins of Mazdeism and related problems*, (Istituto Universitario Orientale, Seminario di Studi Asiatici, Series Minor,VII) Naples.

Hartman, Sven S. 1953. *Gayōmart. Etudes sur le syncretismedans l'ancien Iran*, Uppsala.

—. 1969. "Les identifications de Gayōmart à l'époque islamique", in S. Hartman (ed.), *Syncretism*, Stockholm, 263-294.

—. 1975. "Der Name Ahura Mazdāh", in: A. Dietrich (ed.), *Synkretismus im syrisch-persischen Kulturgebiet*, Göttingen, 170-177.

—. 1983. "Datierung der jungavestischen Apokalyptik", in: D. Hellholm(ed.), *Apocalypticism in the Mediterranean World and the Near East. Proceedings of the International Colloquium on Apocalypticism*, Tübingen, 61-75.

Hoffmann, Karl. 1957. "Mārtāṇḍa und Gayōmart", *Münchener Studienzur Sprachwissenschaft* 11:85-103. (Reprinted in: K. Hoffmann, *Aufsätze zur Indoiranistik*, II, Wiesbaden 1976, 422-438.)

Humbach, Helmut. 1957. "Ahura Mazdā und die Daēvas", *Wiener Zeitschrift für die Kunde Süd- und Ostasiens* 1:81-94.

—. 1974. "Methodologische Variationen zur arischen Religionsgeschichte", in: *Antiquititates Indogermanicae. Gedenkschrift für Hermann Güntert*, Innsbruck, 193-200.

Ibn al-Nadīm, *Kitāb al-fihrist*, ed. Gustav Flügel, Leipzig 1871/2 (Reprint: Beirut 1964).

Insler, S. 1975. *The Gathas of Zarathustra*, Leiden-Tehran-Liège. (Acta Iranica 8).

Kellens, Jean. 1984. "Yima, magicien entre les dieux et les hommes", *Acta Iranica* 23 (Orientalia J. Duchesne-Guillemin emerito oblata), Leiden, 267-281.

—. 1984a. "Mazdā Ahura ou Ahura Mazdā?," *MSS* 43:133-136.

Kent, R.G. 1933. "The name Ahuramazdā", in: *Oriental studies in honour of C.E. Pavry*, London, 200-208.

Konow, Sten. 1937. "Medhā and Mazdā", *Jhā Commemoration Volume*, Poona, 217-222.

Kuiper, F.B.J. 1976. "Ahura Mazdā 'Lord Wisdom' ?," *IIJ* 18:25-42.

Lincoln, Bruce. 1975/6. "The Indo-European myth of creation", *History of Religions* 15:121-145.

Lommel, Herman. 1930. *Die Religion Zarathustras nach dem Awesta dargestellt*, Tübingen [Reprint, Hildesheim-New York, 1970].

de Menasce, J. 1973. *Le troisième livre du Dēnkart*, Paris (Travaux de l'Institut d'Etudes Iraniennes, 5; Bibliothèque des oeuvres classiques persanes, 4).

Molé, Marijan. 1963. *Culte, mythe et cosmologie dans l'Iran ancien*, Paris (Annales du Musée Guimet, Bibl. d'études, t. 69).

Nöldeke, Theodor. *Geschichte der Perser und Araber zur Zeit der Sasniden*. Aus der arabischen Chronik der Tabari übersetzt..., Leyden.

Schaeder, H.H. 1926. "Iranische Lehren", in: R. Reitzenstein and H.H.Schaeder, *Studien zum antiken Synkretismus aus Iran und Griechenland*, Leipzig and

Berlin, 199-355.

Shahrastānī, Abū l-Fatḥ Muḥammad b. ʻAbd al-Karīm, *Al-milal wa-l-niḥal*, ed. Muḥammad Sayyid Kīlānī, Cairo 1967.

Shaked, Shaul. 1971. "The notions *mēnōg* and *gētīg* in the Pahlavi texts and their relation to eschatology", *Acta Orientalia* 33, 59-107.

—. 1980. "Mihr the Judge", *Jerusalem Studies in Arabic and Islam* 2, 1-31.

—. (Forthcoming). "Paymān", *Studia Iranica*.

Tafazzoli, Ahmad (tr.). 1352H. *Mīnū-ye xerad*. (Enteshārāt-e Bonyād-e Farhang-e Irān, 201.) Tehran.

—. 1975. "Elephant: a demonic creature and a symbol of sovereignty", *Acta Iranica* (Monumentum H.S. Nyberg, II), Leiden-Tehran-Liège, 395-398.

Thaʻālibī, Abū Manṣūr ʻAbd al-Malik b. Muḥammad. *Ghurar akhbār mulūk al-furs wa-siyarihim. Histoire des rois des Perses*. Ed. H.Zotenberg. Paris 1900 (Reprint: Tehran 1963).

Thieme, Paul. 1970. "Die vedischen Āditya und die zarathustrischen Ameša Spenta", in: B. Schlerath (ed.), *Zarathustra*, Darmstadt (Wege der Forschung, Bd. 169), 397-412.

Zaehner, R.C. 1955. *Zurvan. A Zoroastrian dilemma*, Oxford.

XI

"FOR THE SAKE OF THE SOUL": A ZOROASTRIAN IDEA IN TRANSMISSION INTO ISLAM

In an Arabic anthology of wise sayings, compiled by Abū l-Qāsim Muḥammad al-Zamakhšarī (d. 538/1144), we have the following anecdote:

> *qāla al-mawbadh bi-ḥaḍrati l-ma'mūni: mā aḥsantu ilā aḥadin wa-lā asa'tu. fa-qāla al-ma'mūnu: wa-kayfa dhālika? qāla: li-annī in aḥsantu fa-ilā nafsī aḥsantu, wa-in asa'tu fa-ilayhā. fa-lammā nahaḍa qāla al-ma'mūnu: a-talūmūnanī 'alā ḥubbī man hādhā 'aqluhu* (Al-Zamakhšarī, *Al-nawābiġ wa-l-ḥikam*, MS Köprülü 1224, fol. 52a).

> A *mōbad* (Zoroastrian priest) said in the presence of al-Ma'mūn: "I have (never) done good to any one, nor have I (ever) done evil (to any one)." Al-Ma'mūn said: "How is that?", and the *mōbad* answered, "That is because if ever I do good, it is to myself,[1] and if I do evil, it is likewise to it". When he rose (to leave) al-Ma'mūn said: "Do you blame me for loving a man whose mind is like this?"

However much we may share al-Ma'mūn's admiration for the wit and wisdom of the *mōbad*, the truth must be said that in this case the thought which he expressed is not entirely his own. The *mōbad* may have been responsible for the form in which he expressed his idea: saying a sentence which at first strikes one as strange and incomprehensible, then smoothing the matter off by explaining his first utterance as an allusion to a moral or religious truth.[2] However, the idea on which this anecdote is based was certainly not invented by him.

---

1 Literally: "to my soul".

2 Even in form the *mōbad* seems to continue a style which was current in the Sasanian wisdom literature; cf. my remarks in the introduction to Shaked 1979, xxiii.

On the face of it, it may have derived from the Qur'ān. We have in Sūra 17: 8 a sentence which may well have served as a prototype for the words of the *mōbad* (or of the storyteller who recounted this anecdote): *in aḥsantum aḥsantum li-anfusikum, wa-in asa'tum fa-lahā*. However, despite the fact that a Qur'ānic verse contains a phrase which carries this meaning, the idea never became common usage in Arabic. The reason is probably twofold. First, there is the fact that *nafs* tends to have in Arabic the pejorative sense of the base part of the person, as opposed to *rūḥ* or *qalb*; secondly, there is the ambiguity of *nafs*, which refers to "self" as well as to "soul". For an illustration of this point we may quote the following anonymous saying: *man jamaʿa al-māla li-nafʿi ġayrihi aṭāʿūhu, wa-man jamaʿahu li-nafʿi nafsihi aḍāʿūhu* (Māwardī, *Tashīl al-naẓar*, 112). "Whoever amasses wealth for the benefit of others, people obey him, and whoever does that for his own benefit, they bring perdition upon him". "To amass wealth for the sake of one's self" is a negative activity, which explains why the *mōbad*'s statement should have caused such surprise.

It would indeed be surprising to have a *mōbad* come out with a statement which merely echoes Qur'ānic wisdom. It seems reasonable to expect that when a *mōbad* is the main figure in a story we should hear from his mouth something which was deemed to be typical of what he represented. On closer examination we do find that the *mōbad* expressed an idea which is entirely in keeping with his upbringing and tradition. Indeed, the saying of the *mōbad* relates to an idea which forms part of an important complex of beliefs in Zoroastrianism.[3]

---

3 The saying is elsewhere attributed to ʿAlī. Cf. Ābī, *Nathr al-durr*, I, 293. In the story of ʿAlī the final sentence is made to conform literally to the Qur'ān (17: 8). Such an attribution seems quite a common feature of sayings which have some Iranian association (see, e.g., the saying about the two wisdoms, in Shaked 1987, 30 ff. Another example is an Arabic counterpart to *Dk* VI, 2, where we read: "Do not worry about an evil which has not come"; a saying attributed to ʿAlī renders this thought as follows: *lā taḥmil hamma yawmika alladhī lam ya'ti 'alā yawmika alladhī anta fīhi* (Ābī, *Nathr al-durr*, I, 295).

The idea that all pious actions done by man are actually performed for the sake of his own soul is very prominent in the Zoroastrian writings of the Sasanian and post-Sasanian period. Phrases such as *ruwān ī xwēš rāy, az bahr ī ruwān*, "for the sake of the soul, of one's own soul", are used everywhere, in common parlance as well as in judicial language, to indicate that a certain action is done out of piety, and not for material gain. The equivalent Christian phrase, in Syriac, is "For the love of Christ" (*meṭul ḥubbeh da-mšīḥā*).[4] It is necessary to go in some detail into a discussion of this curious expression, viz. "doing something for the sake of one's own soul", because I believe it has not always been understood properly in the Iranian context.

The following sentence occurs in *Dēnkard* VI: [5]

> A man whose action is for the soul (*ke kunišn ō ruwān*), the *gētīg* world is his and the *mēnōg* world is even more his (*Dk* VI, A2).

The antithesis to this is a man whose action is for the body (*ke kunišn ō tan*), and who loses both the *mēnōg* and the *gētīg* worlds. The status of one's soul is such that it can be referred to as a divine being, deserving worship as a *yazad*:

> There will be (something) wonderful to him who gives every protection to one (particular) *yazad*, worships him and is reverent towards him: he (viz. the *yazad*) then saves him (viz. the man) from evil. Concerning that *yazad* it is said: it is the man's own soul (*Dk* VI, 237).

Such an utterance with regard to one's own soul (*ruwān*) is not unique. It is indeed the norm in Zoroastrian literature, and goes back to the Avesta,[6] where we read:

> *haom uruuānem yazamaide hauuām fravašīm yazamaide* (Y 71: 18).

---

4 Mšīḥā-Zkhā, in Mingana 1907, 20: 37, 25: 149f.

5 References to *Dk* VI are based on my edition, 1979. The translations given here reflect in some cases modified views on the text or its meaning.

6 On this subject cf. Lommel 1930, 169f.

This is rendered into Pahlavi:

> *hān ī xwēš ruwān yazēm, hān ī xwēš frawahr yazēm*
> "We worship our own soul, we worship our own *fravašī*".

Or, in a more extensive formula:

> We invoke and worship my own soul for protection, watching, care and inspection [Y 71: 11].

The soul comes here as part of an extensive list of entities which the community declares itself as worshipping. The list of items which one should worship is indeed so long as to be almost unlimited. Among the objects which are given in this particular list are the following: fulfilled and omitted words of the Gathas, the bounteous Gathas themselves, and other kinds of sacred words. In addition we have of course also such *yazatas* as: Ahura Mazdā, Zarathuštra, the *fravaši* of Zarathuštra, the Ameša Spenta, the *fravašis* of the righteous (*ašavan*), and a little further on: the waters, the plants, the earth, the sky, the stars, the moon and the sun, etc. Practically all components of the good creation of Ahura Mazdā are regarded as participating in his special sanctity and deserving to be worshipped. The more elevated parts of one's person, the soul (*urvan*) and the eternal *mēnōg* counterpart of Man, the *fravaši*, as well as the religious *mēnōg* person, the *daēnā*, are all part of the same group of divine beings.[7] The body of man is, however, not singled out for worship, although it is also part of the good creation. Here one must bear in mind that although the Zoroastrian religion advocates the need for striking a balance between the material and the spiritual aspects of the world, preference is definitely given to *mēnōg*. In this particular case one often comes across the demand to regard things which relate to *mēnōg* in general, and the soul in particular, as more important than the body. When the need arises to make a choice, the advice is: "leave

---

7 A short discussion of the significance of the term *ruwān* in Zoroastrianism will be found in Shaked 1971, 80. On the relationship between *ruwān* and *frawahr* see *op. cit.*, 79 n. 65.

the body and keep the soul" (*Dk* VI, 25; cf. also 26).[8]

We similarly have the following verse in the Avestan hymn to the Sun:

> He who worships the sun, the immortal radiance, of swift horses, for standing against the obscurities, for standing against the *daēvas* of dark seed, for standing against thieves and robbers, for standing against sorcerers and *pāirikas*, for standing against the danger of the *daēva* of forgetfulness (*maršavan*) - that man worships the Bounteous Immortals, worships his own soul, gives satisfaction to all the spiritual and material deities, who worships the sun, the immortal radiance, of swift horses (Yt. 6: 4).

This is why good deeds are so regularly said to be done "for the sake of the soul". The expression is so frequent, that we need do no more than quote a few instances in order to illustrate its use. A Pahlavi passage gives a description of some extreme situations in which a man behaves in the proper way, despite strong pressure or temptation to the contrary; such a person will come to Paradise (*garōdmān*). One of the three examples given for this is the following:

> ... When a woman and a man come together in an uninhabited place[9] and, having eaten, they are full and merry, and have much desire for each other, and if they fulfilled their desire no one would know, yet, solely for the sake of the soul, that man does not unite sexually with that woman (*Dk* VI, 153).
>
> That advocacy is best: One who speaks for a person who is inarticulate and cannot speak of his own oppression and complaint - that person speaks solely for the sake of his soul and for the sake of the poor and good man and of the people of this world and of these six Amahraspands (*Dk* VI, 23).[10]

---

8 Cf. also such expressions as: *tan ī was-kāmag, ruwān wēn*, discussed in Shaked 1977, 29. On the whole question see the Introduction to Shaked 1979, xxxivff., and Shaked 1971, 59–107.

9 For *wiškar* cf. *ŠnŠ*, 2: 47; Tavadia (p. 48) understands this word to mean "lonely apartment".

10 I am now inclined to read and translate this passage somewhat differently from the way I did in Shaked 1979. Note in particular my present reading: *hān kas ēwiz ruwān ī xwēš ud hān ī driyōš weh kas ud mardom ī gētīg ud ēn 6 amahraspand rāy gōwēd.*

The same expression occurs also in the inscriptions of the priest Kirdēr, in the third century C.E., where we read:

> ... *W wlxl'[n] MLKAn MLKA ZY wlxl'nkn ZY BYN štry l'ty W l'sty W mtlp'n W xwkly W klpkly PWN štry YK'YMWNt W PWN dwšlmyxy ZY 'wxrmzdy W yzd'n W NPŠH lwb'n l'dy ZKm BYN štry 'pltly g'sy W ptxštly 'BYDWN...* (KSM 10–11 with KKZ 7–8; see also KNRm 22. Cf. Gignoux 1968, 394; Gignoux 1972, 186; Brunner 1974, 104.)
>
> ... and (when) the King of Kings Warhrān, son of Warhrān, who in the kingdom is generous, just, kind,[11] beneficent and virtuous, has stood up in the kingdom, and out of love for Ohrmazd and the gods and his own soul,[12] he has made for me in the kingdom a superior position and dignity ...

The king raised the position of Kirdēr "out of love for Ohrmazd and the gods and his own soul", i.e. out of piety and dedication to religion.

It is Ohrmazd's desire that people should do everything for their own good, while Ahreman desires the opposite (*Dk* VI, 32). A wicked person can justly be called therefore "an enemy of his own soul" (*ruwān-dušman, Dk* VI, 236). The term *ruwān* can in this sense be equated to *dēn* "the religion" or "one's devotional or religious person". Thus we have the double expression: *ruwān dōšarm ud dēn rāy* (*Dk* VI, 91) "for the love of the soul and for the sake of the religion".[13] The piety of the people of Alburz is described by the epithets *weh-dēn, ruwān-dōst ud dēn-dōst* "of good religion, loving (their) soul and (their) *dēn*" (*AZam* VI: 2; Messina, p. 48). Similarly, in the Kirdēr inscription Ohrmazd and the gods are juxtaposed to the soul and make up a unified concept.

---

11 Gignoux renders this word "fidèle", but I see no reason to separate this word from the word frequently attested in Middle Persian and New Persian: *mihrabān* "kind".

12 The syntactic construction is apparently *pad ... rāy*.

13 The Manichaean expression for pious people in Sogdian is *fryrw'n nγwš'kt* (Henning 1937, 77, note to line 623). "The soul-loving hearers". Another Manichaean expression is: *kyy δynyh rw'n ptšmyrty* (Henning 1937, 37 lines 621–622) "(the five gifts) which are considered by the religion as the soul". (Henning translates: "die für das Hauptstück der Religion gehalten werden".)

There is some evidence which suggests that at least certain Islamic writers understood the significance of this phrase for Zoroastrians and regarded it as typically Persian. Thus Māwardī, *Tashīl al-naẓar*, 114, quotes a saying in which the views of different peoples as to the duties of the king with regard to himself and to his subjects are enumerated. According to the Persians, he says, a king should be generous towards himself, and may be avaricious towards his subjects, because the Persians regard it as a duty to cause (their own) souls to be in happiness (*li-annahum yarawna tan'īma l-nufūsi mina l-wājibāt*).[14]

A specific use of this expression is in the term commonly used in legal texts dealing with endowments and pious foundations, *pad ruwān, ruwān rāy*, which is used to designate a property administered by a private individual for pious purposes, and which therefore signifies a property made over for the sake of one's soul (or sometimes for that of somebody else's soul). In some cases it is specified that the property should cover the expenses of the elaborate services for the good of the soul of a deceased, but in many other cases the idea of the foundation is to serve for doing any charitable or pious deeds.[15]

The adjective *ruwānīg*, when it comes in contrast to a term designating "people", is used for referring to a sin committed in violation of purely religious prescriptions, not involving harm or damage to other people:

> *winān ī hamēmārān andar hamēmārān wizārišn ud hān ī ruwānīg andar radān wizārišn* (ŠnŠ 8: 1)

14 The reference to Māwardī should be added to the discussion of the motif of the four kings in Shaked 1984, 41ff. The version quoted on p. 41 of Shaked 1984 is from *Al-siyāsa al-'āmmiyya*. Māwardī's version is clearly secondary; it adds the Arabs, who are given here the final word, whereas in the original version the punch line is reserved to the Persians.

15 Perikhanian 1973; *Idem* 1983, 160ff.; as well as the important article by Boyce 1968. The whole material was collected by J.P. de Menasce 1964, where, on pp. 59ff., the expression is discussed (in too narrow a sense, I believe).

A sin committed against one's associates[16] should be atoned for among them; a sin pertaining to the soul should be atoned for among the (spiritual) masters.

Tavadia (p. 104) rightly refers to the sentence in *Frahang i Oīm*:

wināh ī andar mardomān wināh ī hamēmārān, hān ī abārīg wināh ī ruwānīg xwānihēd[17]

An offence among people is called "a sin against associates". Other (offences) are called "sins pertaining to the soul".

This distinction is reminiscent of the Jewish rabbinical distinction between "offences between man and the divine" and "offences between man and his fellow man".[18]

This subject is closely linked to the technical term *ruwānagān* (*ruwānīgān*), used both in Zoroastrianism and in Manichaeism. The definition of the Manichaean term as given by W.B. Henning[19] makes it refer to the services rendered by the Hearers to the Elect, e.g. by providing the latter with food, clothing and lodging. One wonders whether it is necessary to limit the definition to such narrow confines. It may be assumed that other acts of piety might also be included under the heading of *ruwānagān*, although the extant quotations do not explicitly refer to them. Such an assumption seems necessary if we consider it likely that the Manichaean term is derived from Zoroastrianism, where, as I shall try to show, it has a fairly wide range of meanings, and, as it is a cognate of the expression *pad ruwān, ruwān ī xwēš rāy*, it covers all acts of charity and piety.

It has already been noticed that the Manichaean office of *ruwānagān spasag* has its equivalent in the Zoroastrian title

---

16 *hamēmār*, from *ham-* and *āmār*, *ēmār* (cf. Bartholomae 1918, 21, n. 1), clearly denotes in this context "associate", and this may well be assumed to be its original meaning, in conformity with its etymology. The sense "adversary, opponent" is possibly a secondary development, which eventually took over and became the only meaning of the word.

17 Cf. *FrOīm*, ed. M. Haug, 33f.; ed. Reicheit 1900, 206.

18 עברות שבין אדם למקום, עברות שבין אדם לחברו (Bavli Yoma 85b).

19 *MirMan* II, 317 n. 3.

ruwānigān dibēr "the administrator of the pious foundations".[20] It has further been suggested that rather than seek the origins of the Muslim institution of *waqf* in Byzantium, which does not offer a good model for the Islamic *waqf*,[21] we might do better by looking for it in the Iranian establishment of foundations "for the soul",[22] which seems to present a system of charitable organizations which shows close similarity to that which developed in Islam.[23]

The Pahlavi term *ruwānīgān* is of rare occurrence. In fact, the only two attestations which have come to my notice occur in one chapter of the book of Ardā Wīrāz. The text recounts how the righteous Wīrāz has been selected from among the believers for the task of making a fateful passage in order to visit the other world on behalf of the Zoroastrian community and bring from there news which would confirm the faith of the Zoroastrians concerning the afterlife, reward and punishment, and other tenets of the religion. Wīrāz's departure is deemed to contain an element of danger and is felt akin to temporary death. Preparing himself for his perilous undertaking, Ardā Wīrāz adopts a posture of respect in front of his fellow Mazdaeans, putting his hands under his armpits, and says:

---

20 Cf. Benveniste 1932, 157; Herzfeld 1924, 195 (Glossary No. 429), who quotes a passage from Khwārizmī, *Mafātīḥ al-ʿulūm*, 118, where the term *rw'nk'n dfyrh* (i.e. *ruwānagān dibērīh*, in the abstract) is rendered by *kitābat al-awqāf*. In Dīnawarī, *Al-akhbār al-ṭiwāl*, 57, a certain *Panāh-Khusraw is mentioned, whose function is described as *ṣāḥib ṣadaqāt al-mamlaka* "the man in charge of the state charities", which may be a different rendering into Arabic of the same title of office. See further Schaeder 1934, 19ff.; Christensen 1944, 135. Frye 1975, 17 and 250 n. 37, is not quite accurate when he describes these foundations as "endowments established for the dead", or when he takes *ruwānikān* to be the plural of *ruwān*.

21 Cahen 1963.

22 Perikhanian 1983, 175f.

23 I am not sure whether thought has been given to the Jewish institution of *heqdeš* in this connection. Cf. on this Goitein 1971, 53, 99 ff.; Gil 1976.

> (Give me) authority[24] to perform *ruwānīgān*, to eat food, to give instructions (to my descendants). Afterwards give me wine and narcotic[25] (*AVn* II: 9;[26] ed. Haug and West, II: 22).[27]

The taking of wine and narcotic is going to induce in Wīrāz the proper state of mind for making the journey which he is required to take. Even Gignoux, in his otherwise admirable edition and translation of this text, has made a mistake in his treatment of the term *ruwānīgān yaštan*: it certainly cannot mean "to sacrifice to the souls (of the deceased)", if only for the simple reason that *ruwānīgān* is not the plural of *ruwān* "soul". Were we to have here the plural of *ruwān*, the expression should have contained a preposition (it might have read *ō ruwānān yazēm*, or the like). Besides, it may be remarked that it is not usual in Pahlavi to talk of the souls of the departed as a collective under the term *ruwānān*; the normal expression denoting in general terms the souls of the pious ancestors is *fravaši*, Pahlavi *frawahr*. It thus seems highly unlikely that *ruwānīgān* would designate the souls of the departed; on the other hand it does seem required that we should try to associate this expression with the Manichaean term *ruwānagān*. One might think of rendering the term here "a pious deed", with the implication that Wīrāz is asking for an opportunity to offer in service (*yaštan*) a pious deed (*ruwānīgān*) before departing from the world, even though his departure is hoped to be temporary. The expression could refer more specifically to acts of charity and the giving of alms.

---

24 *dastwarīh ast*, literally "there is authority". Gobrecht 1967, followed by Belardi, tries to interpret *dastwarīh* in the sense of "custom", but this does not seem convincing.

25 On the possible meanings of *mang* see the extensive discussion by Belardi, 113ff.

26 Quoted from the recent edition by Gignoux 1984.

27 Cf. also Belardi 1979, 58ff. and Vahman 1986, 193.

The second occurrence of the term follows shortly afterwards:

> Then the religious authorities chose a place of thirty paces in the abode of *mēnōg* for that good (action).[28] Wīrāz washed his head and body and put on a new garment. He perfumed himself with a good-smelling scent, and spread a new and clean bed-cover on an appropriate couch. He sat down on the couch with the clean bed-cover, performed the *drōn* ceremony, recalled the *ruwānīgān*, and ate the food (*AVn* II: 11-14; ed. Haug and West, II: 24-28).[29]

Here too it does not seem in place to assume that *ruwānīgān ayādēnīd* means "remembered the departed souls", as done by Haug and West, followed by Gignoux, or " remembered the rites for the

---

28 I have to disagree somewhat with previous translations of this sentence. "A place of thirty paces", as has already been pointed out, is clearly a reference to the requirement for ritual purity, as in the Baršnūm-gāh ceremony (for a description one may refer to Modi 1937, 112ff.). I take it to be a short-hand allusion to the requirement to keep the person who is to undergo the purification ceremony 30 paces away from fire or other sacred entities. Gobrecht 1967, 390, suggests that by *pad hān ī xūb* the *xūb* ceremony of purification is meant (cf. Modi 1937, 140). This seems to me a valid possibility. A fire temple is out of the question for such a purpose, and it is much less suitable to contain the body of a man who may be considered ritually dead, as suggested by Haug and West, followed by Gignoux. What is meant by the words *mān ī mēnōg* I am unable to tell, unless it refers here to a unique place consecrated on this particular occasion for the highly unusual experience of encounters with the spirits. The references which follow and which imply that Wīrāz's couch and bed-spread should also be in perfect purity do not tally with the assumption that he is preparing to undergo death, albeit temporarily, but rather with the realization that he is making himself ready to meet with sacred and pure spirits, which is why he has to make himself as clean and ritually pure as possible.

29 Belardi 1979, 61ff. The last sentence is rendered by Boyce and Kotwal 1971, 65: "He consecrated the *drōn* and remembered the rites for the departed, and ate his food..." (Similarly in Vahman 1986.) This translation involves forcing the language a little beyond what is normally allowed, for one does not "remember" a rite in Middle Persian, one performs (*yaz-*) it.

departed", as suggested by Boyce. I am inclined to believe that the expression means "he brought to memory the pious deeds (done by him in preparation for his perilous journey)", deeds which are evidently deemed to fortify him in facing the dangers which he is setting out to encounter.[30]

In support of this interpretation of the phrase *ruwānīgān yaštan* it may be relevant to quote a short passage from the book of Yawišt ī Friyān:

> *haštom frašn ēn pursīd ku kadām hān zīndag mardom ke astōvihād wēnēd [ud] mīrēd u-š ēdōn kāmag ku abāz *ōh zīndag šawēd. ud did-ez astōvihād wēnēd ud be mīrēd u-š xwār sahēd.*
> *yawišt ī friyān guft ku zīndagān pad škōh bāš mar ī druwand [ī] sāstār ud murdagān ō dušaxw ōft. ud sedīgar hān mardom ke zīndag ruwān ne yašt ēstēd ud ahlawdād ne dād ēstēd ud yazišn ī yazdān ne kard ēstēd u-š ahlawdād ō weh mardom (u-š) guft ku dahēm ud ne dād ēstēd. u-š [ka] mīrēd kāmag aōn ku abāz zīndag šawēd ud did-ez mīrēd ud astōvihād wēnēd u-š xwār sahēd (Yawišt ī Friyān* II: 41–48).

> The eighth puzzle. He asked this: Which is that living man who sees Astōvihād[31] and dies, whose desire is to walk[32] again alive. He sees Astōvihād again and dies, and this seems to him a light matter.
> Yawišt ī Friyān said: Be in misery while alive, wicked felon and tyrant,

---

30 A comparable sentence occurs in a seal inscription, which may be read: *ruwān ayād ēw baw[ēd]* "May the soul be remembered", i.e. let my own soul be remembered (by me), so that I may do pious deeds. Cf. Shaked 1977, 30, where a seal originally published by Mordtmann in 1877 is quoted. It may be noticed that the *drōn* ceremony is associated with an invocation to the *fravaši*, the souls of the departed; cf. *ŠnŠ* 9: 11ff. (ed. Tavadia, 120ff., and the notes).

31 The Angel of Death of the Zoroastrian tradition.

32 The usage may already be that of New Persian, where this verb signifies "to become".

fall into hell when dead. A third one[33] is a man who did not render service[34] to the soul (while) alive,[35] did not give alms and did not worship the gods. He said to a good man[36] concerning alms: "I shall give (you)", but he did not give. When he dies, his desire is that he may walk[37] alive. He dies again, sees Astōvihād, and it seems to him a light matter.

To render service" or "worship" (*yaštan*) the soul while alive is used here synonymously with giving alms, *ahlawdād*. It seems to be the basic religious conception of what one does as a service to one's own soul: helping other people by charitable deeds, or more vaguely, doing acts of piety and charity.

In concluding this short excursion into the meaning of the term *ruwān ī xwēš rāy* and its cognates in Zoroastrian writings, we may come back to our point of departure, the anecdote about the *mōbad*. The conception that good deeds are such as are done for one's own soul, with the corresponding idea that evil deeds go against one's own soul, is so very prominently and characteristically Zoroastrian, that it was only natural for a *mōbad* to be credited with it. One may well ask whether the Qur'ānic verse which heralds a similar idea was also influenced by Iranian thinking. This seems a possibility which cannot

---

33 Yawišt's answer contains three categories of men who desire to come back to life after an initial death; the first two concern (1) a man who did not perform the *yašt* and did not partake of the *haoma* ; and (2) a man who did not take a wife although he had come of age.

34 The verb used is *yaštan*, which literally means "to sacrifice, to worship".

35 *zīndag ruwān* could also be translated "the living soul", i.e. the soul of a man while alive, which would give the same sense.

36 In the numerous cases where the term *weh mard* occurs it is possible to think of reading it *wey mard* "a wise man", an adjective which has been shown to be commonly used in proper names; cf. Gignoux 1981. It seems however better to stick to the accepted reading and translation of this phrase.

37 Cf. note 25 above.

be ruled out, although I would not venture to go beyond such assertion.[38]

We have seen that the idea that one should venerate one's own living soul in Zoroastrianism has apparently left some mark on Islamic thinking. It is possible to show that the Iranian idea of the soul after death, the spiritual counterpart of man which comes to his encounter on his journey from this world to the next, the *daēnā*, or in Middle Persian *dēn*,[39] may have also had some impact on Muslim thinking. This is seen in a story which recounts how the Reward of one's prayers comes to greet one "with a bright countenance" after death. The man asks, "Who are you, as I have not seen a face finer than yours and I have not smelled a smell more fragrant than yours?" Then the Reward will reply, "O my beloved, I am the Reward of (your) prayer..."[40] This is obviously a translation into Muslim terms of the classical *daēnā* motif in Zoroastrianism. In the Iranian story we are told of a man who walks on his way to the other world after death. While walking he meets coming towards him a mysterious female

---

38 For a number of expressions and themes in the Qur'ān which may possibly be derived from Zoroastrian Iran see Bausani 1959, 138ff. The verse in the Qur'ān was commonly interpreted to mean that one's good deeds will be rewarded, and one's evil deeds punished; cf. e.g. Ṭabarī, Bayḍāwī.

39 It should be noted that this is not only a Zoroastrian, but also a Manichaean idea. According to Ibn al-Nadīm, *Fihrist* (335: 10ff.), at the time of the decease of an elect Primal Man sends towards him the leading Wise One, with three deities, together with Victory (*zakāt*), a garment, a head-band (i.e. diadem?), a crown and a garland of light. In their company comes also the Virgin, "who is similar to the soul of that elect". Cf. the analysis of this passage with the parallel versions by Polotsky in Schmidt and Polotsky 1933, 72f.; Polotsky 1933, 269ff.; *Idem* 1935, 260f.

40 See Kister 1971, 216. A similar story occurs in Ġazālī, *Durra*, 13, where a masculine figure which presents itself as the man's good action (*anā ʿamaluka al-ṣāliḥ*) presents itself to the soul after death. Ġazālī, *op. cit.*, 44, also recounts how this world (*dunyā*) comes towards the soul in the form of a hoary old hag, more hideous than can be described (*aqbaḥ mā yakūnu*). The people are asked, "Do you know this one?" And they are told, "It is this world, for the sake of which you used to envy each other and to hate each other".

figure which, as it turns out, is a reflection of his own self, beautiful, if he was righteous, or ugly, if he was a sinner while alive.

A further development of this motif may be felt to exist in a story allegedly told by the Prophet in reference to his night journey (*isrā'*) :

> When I was lifted to the sky, Jibrīl took my hand and made me sit on one of the carpets of Paradise. He placed in my hand a quince[41] and when I was turning it round it split open and a fair and black-eyed (*ḥawrā'*) maiden came out of it, of such a beauty as I had never seen the like of. She said to me: "Peace be upon you, Muhammad". I said: "Who are you?" She said: "I am the one who is pleased and who gives pleasure. The Almighty created me from three sorts (of perfume): my lower part He created from musk, my middle part from camphor, and my upper part from amber. I was kneaded from the water of the animal.[42] The Almighty then said to me: Be, and I came into being. He created me for your brother and cousin 'Alī b. Abī Ṭālib. (Majlisī, *Biḥār al-anwār* 66, 178).

The story has an obvious political aim, which finds expression in its final sentence. If we disregard this tendentious ending, which may have been attached to an existing story for the purpose of glorifying 'Alī, we may recognize in it a wedding between the *daēnā* motif and the Qur'ānic theme of the houris in Paradise.[43] Like the Zoroastrian story, we have in the *ḥadīth* a sequence of questions and answers exchanged by the man and the mysterious female figure, as a result of which her identity is revealed. As it turns out, she is not a reflection of himself, but was created to be the female counterpart of a specific individual (who, by implication, is very close to the person of the Prophet).

---

41 See my notes about the quince as a royal symbol in Shaked 1986, 82 ff.

42 The text may be corrupt. For *mā' al-ḥayawān* one should perhaps substitute *mā' al-ḥayāt* "the water of life", which would make better sense.

43 It has indeed been suggested that the motif of the houris in Paradise was itself influenced by the Iranian idea of the *daēnā* ; cf. Bausani 1959, 143.

REFERENCES

[For references to Zoroastrian texts see bibliography in Shaked 1979.]

Al-Ābī, Abū Sa'īd Manṣūr b. al-Ḥusayn, *Nathr al-durr*, ed. Muḥammad 'Alī Qarna and 'Alī Muḥammad al-Bajāwī, Cairo 1980.

Bartholomae, C., 1918. *Zum sasanidischen Recht* I (Abhandlungen der Heidelberger Akademie der Wissenschaften, phil-hist. Klasse, Abh. 5), Heidelberg.

Bausani, A., 1959. *Persia religiosa da Zaratustra a Bahā'ullāh*, Milan 1959.

Belardi, 1979. *The Pahlavi book of the Righteous Vīrāz* (Biblioteca di ricerche linguistiche e filologiche, 10), Rome.

Benveniste, E., 1932. "Un titre manichén en transcription chinoise", *Etudes d'orientalisme publiées par le Musée Guimet à la mémoire de Raymonde Linossier*, I, Paris, 156-158.

Boyce, M., 1968. "The pious foundations of the Zoroastrians", *BSOAS* 31, 270-289.

Boyce, M., and F. Kotwal, 1971. "Zoroastrian *bāj* and *drōn*", *BSOAS* 34, 56-73; 298-313.

Brunner, C.J., 1974. "The Middle Persian inscription of the priest Kirdēr at Naqš-i Rustam", in: D.K. Kouyumjian (ed.), *Near Eastern numismatics, iconography, epigraphy and history. Studies in honor of G.C. Miles*, Beirut, 97-113.

Cahen, C., 1963. "Quelques réflexions sur le waqf ancien", *Trudy 25 meždonarodnogo kongressa vostokovedov (1960)*, II, Moscow, 38-40.

Christensen, A., 1944. *L'Iran sous les sassanides*, 2nd ed., Copenhagen.

Dīnawarī, Abū Ḥanīfa Aḥmad b. Dāwūd, *Kitāb al-akhbār al-ṭiwāl*, ed. V. Guirgass, Leiden 1888.

FrOīm: Frahang ī Oīm, ed. M. Haug, *An old Zand-Pahlavi glossary*, Stuttgart 1867 [reprint, Osnabrück 1973]; H. Reichelt, "Der Frahang i Oīm", *WZKM* 14 (1900), 177-213; 15 (1901), 117-186.

Frye, R.N., 1975. *The golden age of Persia*, New York.

Ġazālī, Abū Ḥāmid, *Al-durra al-fākhira fī kašf 'ulūm al-ākhira*, Cairo 1347/1928.

Gignoux, Philippe, 1968. "L'inscription de Kartir à Sar Mašhad", *JA*, 367-418.

--, 1972. "L'inscription de Kirdir à Naqš-i Rustam", *StIr* 1, 177-205.

--, 1981. "Le nom propre Vēh en pehlevi", *Die Sprache* 27, 32-35.

--, 1984. *Le livre d'Ardā Vīrāz*, Paris.

Gil, M., 1976. *Documents of the Jewish Pious Foundations from the Cairo Geniza*, Leiden.

Gobrecht, G., 1967. "Das Artā" Vīrāz Nāmak", *ZDMG* 117, 382-409.

Henning, W.B., 1937. *Ein manichäisches Bet- und Beichtbuch* (Preussische Akademie der Wissenschaften, 1936, phil.-hist. Klasse, Nr. 10), Berlin.

Goitein, S.D., 1971. *A Mediterranean society. The Jewish communities of the Arab world as portrayed in the documents of the Cairo Geniza*, II, Berkeley, Los Angeles and London.

Herzfeld, E., 1924. *Paikuli*, Berlin.

Ibn al-Nadīm, *Fihrist*, ed. G. Flügel, Leipzig 1871 [Reprint, Beirut 1964].

al-Khwārizmī, Abū 'Abdallāh Muḥammad b. Aḥmad, *Mafātīḥ al-'ulūm*, ed. G. van Vloten, Leiden 1895.

Kister, M. J., 1971. "'Rajab is the month of God...': A study in the persistence of an early tradition", *IOS* 1, 191-223 [Reprinted in: M.J. Kister, *Studies in Jāhiliyya and early Islam*, London 1980].

Lommel, Hermann, 1930. *Die Religion Zarathustras nach dem Awesta dargestellt*, Tübingen.

Al-Māwardī, 'Alī b. Muḥammad, *Tashīl al-naẓar wa-ta'jīl al-ẓafar fī akhlāq al-malik wa-siyāsat al-mulk*, ed. Muḥyī Hilāl al-Sarḥān and Ḥusayn al-Sā'ātī, Beirut 1981.

de Menasce, J.P., 1964. *Feux et fondations pieuses dans le droit sassanide* (Travaux de l'Institut d'Etudes Iraniennes, 2), Paris.

Mingana, A. 1907. *Sources syriaques* I, Leipzig.

Modi, J.J., 1937. *Religious ceremonies and customs of the Parsees*, 2nd ed., Bombay.

Perikhanian, A.G., 1973. "Častnye celevye fondy v drevnem Irane: problema proisxoždenija vakfa", *Vestnik Drevnej Istorii* (1), 3-25.

--, 1983. *Obščestvo i pravo Irana v parfjanskij i sasanidskij periody*, Moscow.

Polotsky, H.J., 1933. "Manichäische Studien", *Le Muséon* 46, 247-271.

--, 1935. "Manichäismus", in Pauly-Wissowa, *Realencyclopädie*, Suppl. VI, 240-271.

Schaeder, H.H., 1934. *Iranica* (Abhandlungen der Gesellschaft der Wissenschaften zu Göttingen, Philol.-hist. Klasse, 3. Folge, Nr. 10), Berlin.

Schmidt, C., and H.J. Polotsky, 1933. *Ein Mani-Fund in Ägypten* (Sitzungsberichte der Preussischen Akademie der Wissenschaften, Phil.-hist. Klasse, I), Berlin.

Shaked, Shaul, 1971. "The notions *mēnōg* and *gētīg* and their relation to eschatology", *Acta Orientalia* 33, 59-107.

--, 1977. "Jewish and Christian seals of the Sasanian period", in: M. Rosen-Ayalon (ed.), *G. Wiet Memorial Volume*, Jerusalem, 17-31.

--, 1979. *Wisdom of the Sasanian sages*, a translation of *Dēnkard* VI by Ādurbād ī Ēmēdān (Persian Heritage Series, 34), Boulder, Col.

--, 1982. "Two Judaeo-Iranian contributions", in: S. Shaked, *Irano-Judaica*, Jerusalem, 292-322.

--, 1984. "From Iran to Islam. Notes on some themes in transmission", *JSAI* 4, 31-67.

--, 1986. "From Iran to Islam: On some symbols of royalty", *JSAI* 7, 75-91.

--, 1987. "A facetious recipe and the two wisdoms: Iranian themes in Muslim garb", *JSAI* 9, 24-35.

Vahman, F., 1986. *Ardā Wirāz Nāmag. The Iranian 'Divina Commedia'* (Scandinavian Institute of Asian Studies, Monograph Series, 53), London and Malmö.

Yawišt ī Friyān, in: *The Book of Arda Viraf*, ed. Destur Hoshangji Jamaspji Asa, rev. by M. Haug and E.W. West, Bombay-London 1872.

XII

SOME IRANIAN THEMES IN ISLAMIC LITERATURE

Iranian themes are so ubiquitous and so numerous in Arabic literature that it would take volumes to encompass the subject.[1] The more one reads in the vast repository of Arabic literature the more one comes across further elements that may be regarded as reflecting or continuing older Iranian ideas. The time is not yet ripe to make a definitive inventory of such themes, but it may be useful to mention some of the more prominent ideas noticed by scholars, to which I shall try to add some new points.

The first scholar to work on this subject was Blochet, who wrote several articles around the turn of the century on aspects of Islam, in which the Iranian theme was always present in his mind.[2] Ignaz Goldziher, who may be regarded in many ways as the founder of the modern scholarly study of Islam, contributed some important studies to this field. He did this in various scattered notes, especially in his *Muhammedanische Studien*, where he devoted a chapter to an analysis of the interaction between Arabs and Persians in early Islam.[3] He also wrote a special article on this theme, under the title "Islamisme et parsisme",[4] in which he promised to come back to the subject at a later period. It seems that he never did. The next important scholar who devoted special attention to this subject was Alessandro Bausani, who, in his book on religion in Iran,[5] devoted a few pages to an enumeration of some points in the Qur'an where an Iranian

[1] I should like to thank several scholars who made helpful comments on the text of the lecture in Bamberg. Among them are F. de Blois, H. Kumamoto, V.A. Livshits, B. Radtke.

[2] Cf. Blochet 1898; 1899; 1902; 1913.

[3] See Goldziher 1889:101ff., and in the English version, edited by S.M. Stern, pp. 98ff.

[4] Goldziher 1900.

[5] Bausani 1959:138ff.

ifluence seems to be visible. Part of the prolific scholarly output of Henry Corbin was also concerned with this problem.[6] In a number of previous articles I have myself tried to discuss some individual problems connected with this subject.[7] Several other scholars who treated one theme or another will be mentioned further on, but the list is far from being comprehensive.

One fairly large topic on which there is quite clear evidence of close affinity between Iranian and Islamic ideas so as to suggest probable dependence is eschatology. Islamic eschatology derived a good deal of material from Jewish and Christian sources, which in their turn were also dependent, it seems, on Iranian antecedents.[8] But there are elements in the Islamic treatment of eschatological events that derive quite clearly from Iran. This comes out already in the Qur'an and the early Hadīth, but is visible with great clarity in a book entitled *al-Durra al-fākhira* attributed to the great thinker and writer of the eleventh century, al-Ghazālī. As with several other treatises that go under Ghazālī's name, this one too may be taken to be a pseudepigraphic composition. The first scholar to draw attention to the Iranian connection of this treatise was Louis H. Gray (1902). The similarity between the eschatological descriptions in Pahlavi and those occurring in this Arabic treatise is so striking that it almost looks like a deliberate adaptation from a Zoroastrian source.

It has been pointed out that the Islamic *miᶜrāj* literature contains elements of Persian origin, although much of the discussion of this literature has focused on its possible impact on Dante's *Divine Comedy*.[9]

In the field of individual eschatology, which deals with the fate of the soul after death, certain points spring to mind as displaying a probable impact of the Iranian tradition in Islam. One telling detail that has been noticed is the injunction, often attributed to the Prophet Muhammad, not to mourn too much for a dead person, because this makes his passage through the next world more difficult.[10] Both the prohibition (which has been generally ignored in Islam) and the explanation given to it suggest a Persian background.[11] The need to avoid surrendering oneself to grief and mourning is often emphasized in Zoroastrianism.[12] The reason is that a

[6] Corbin 1951 dealt directly with a Pahlavi text, but his main contributions were in the field of mystical thinking; cf. in particular Corbin 1960; 1964:107f.

[7] Cf. Shaked 1984a; 1986; 1987a; 1987b; 1990.

[8] Cf. Shaked 1971; 1984b.

[9] Cf. in particular Levi della Vida 1949; Widengren 1950.

[10] Cf. Goldziher 1900:129; Gray 1902:169.

[11] The Zoroastrian formulation is found in *AVN* 16:7-10; further references in Meier 1973:219ff.

[12] There are many injunctions against gloom and despondency in the Pahlavi texts; for example, *Dk* VI C9, C10, D4. Contentment acts against greed, which is the fiercest demon (*Dk* VI E28). It is enjoined that one should not complain of one's misfortune (*Dk*

feeling of dejection is one of the means by which the demons try to tighten their grip on humanity. The demand to restrain one's sorrow at the bereavement of a dear member of the family is but one instance of the same attitude. Fritz Meier (1973) has made a very thorough investigation of the traditions around this subject, and has also discussed the suggestion that this may be an Iranian borrowing in Islam. In view of the many parallels in various cultures, where a similar notion exists, he has decided that there is no proof for a specific Iranian origin for it. The flow of ideas from Iran to Islam is such, however, that Iran may be regarded as a natural source for comparable Islamic ideas unless there is good reason to suppose differently.

Tor Andrae has remarked[13] on the similarity of some of the stories concerning the circumstances of Muhammad's birth in the Arabic sources to those recounted of the birth of Zoroaster in the seventh book of the *Dēnkard*.

The curious Koranic expression, which refers to a "colour" of God, has been noted by Bausani,[14] who has pointed out the striking parallel with an expression occurring in the *Dēnkard* which attributes colour to time.[15] The chapter of the *Dēnkard* where this expression occurs is somewhat problematic, and I believe the translations currently available are not quite satisfactory, but the term "colour" (in Pahlavi *rang*) quite clearly occurs there. Words meaning "colour" in Iranian tend to have a peculiar usage; this peculiarity may almost serve as a fingerprint test for establishing a borrowing from Iranian. The Middle Persian *gōnag* "colour" was used in the sense of "mode, manner", as it is still used in New Persian, and was borrowed in this sense into Aramaic and hence into Hebrew. In at least one early Judaeo-Persian text we find the Arabic word *lawn* "colour" used in the sense of "mode, manner".[16] The Koranic reference to the "colour" of God, if it reflects a borrowing from Iranian, as it is likely to do, would denote the style, mode, spiritual shape, of God.

Somewhat more doubtful in my eyes is Goldziher's assumption that the character of the Islamic Friday, as a day of assembly rather than one of rest and abstinence from work, in contrast to the Jewish Saturday or the

VI 29, 286, C46, C83c). The virtue of joy is often extolled (*Dk* VI 33, 195, 196, E30b; *PhlT* 78f. §6).

[13] Cf. Andrae 1917:30f. A further Islamic source in which similar stories are found is Ta'rīkh-i Sīstān, 58ff.

[14] Bausani 1959:142. The expression occurs in Koran 2:138.

[15] *Dk* III 27; B 15-17; M 21-24. Cf. Zaehner 1955a: 378ff.; Molé 1961:16; Menasce 1973:44f.

[16] This usage is prominent in the Tafsīr of Ezekiel from Leningrad, which I am preparing for publication. This sense is attested sporadically in Classical Arabic, and seems to be used also in some modern Arabic dialects.

Christian Sunday, was established as a result of the Zoroastrian mocking polemic against the Jewish notion of God needing a rest after the six days of creation. An echo of that polemic is certainly found in the Qur'ān.[17] The polemic is only attested in the late Zoroastrian work *Škand gumānīg wizār*, but it is of course possible that this theme was already used by Zoroastrians in their polemics with the Jews in the Sasanian period. On the other hand, the need that the early Muslim community felt to differentiate its practices from those of Jews and Christians, and indeed from those of the Zoroastrians, comes into such frequent attestation that we hardly have to have recourse to the Zoroastrian dialogue with the Jews in order to explain the character of the Muslim Friday. Still, the fact that the point of the argument against the notion of God having to rest at the end of his work of creation is attested in both Muslin and Zoroastrian sources is interesting.

There is perhaps yet another remarkable point of contact between Islam
* and Iran concerning Friday. Its name in Arabic is *yawm al-jumᶜa*, "the day of assembly", which is hard to explain from the cultural antecedents of Islam in Judaism and Christianity. The closest semantic equivalent of this Arabic term seems to be the New Persian designation, *ādīna* or *ādhīna*. This word formed the subject of an interesting and learned article by Josef Markwart (1927), who tried to show that it is essentially the same word as NP *āyīna* "mirror" and "manners, a way of conduct". The difficulties about this, both semantic and phonetic, are considerable, and in any case one fails to see why a word with such a meaning should have been introduced in order to render the Muslim concept of "Friday". I should like to assume that the word came into use in Iran in pre-Islamic times, and that it was initially used to represent the Jewish and Christian Friday, that it originally was, in other words, a loan translation of a Jewish or Christian term. The common designation of Friday in Aramaic, used by Jews as well as by Christians, is by referring to it as "the eve of the Sabbath", the "setting" or "coming in" of the holy day. In Aramaic the word used is *ᶜarōbhtā*, which may literally designate "evening", "setting", or "coming (i.e. either coming in, or coming together)".[18] These are some of the senses suggested by the root of the word. If *ādīna* is derived from the root *ay-* "to come", and is combined with a preverb that gives it the meaning of "coming in", the meaning

[17] Cf. Goldziher 1900:145f.

[18] A discussion of this word, which occurs in Palestinian Jewish Aramaic but not in Babylonian Jewish Aramaic, and of the origin of the Muslim practice of the Friday prayer, is in M.J. and Menahem Kister 1979:234, 244ff. A source quoted op. cit., p. 245f., from the *Muṣannaf* of ᶜAbd al-Razzāq, III:159f., shows evidence that in the early Islamic period it was accepted that the choice of Friday was in emulation of, and at the same time in order to be distinguished from, the Jews and the Christians. The Arabic loanword *ᶜarūba* is also quite well attested; see Goitein 1959:188.

obtained would be a fair rendering of the Aramaic concept.[19] If *ādīna* is indeed a rendering of Aramaic *ᶜarōbhtā*, the same Aramaic term could have given rise to the Arabic rendering by *jumᶜa*, which had initially some of the semantic ambiguity of the Aramaic word, the root *jamaᶜa* meaning essentially "to bring together", just as the Aramaic root *ᶜRB* has among its meanings "to mix together". The Aramaic term *ᶜarōbhtā* could well have been interpreted by some as meaning "a mixture (i.e. of people)", a meaning that could be quite adequately rendered by *jumᶜa*. If this was indeed sensed to be a prominent aspect of *ᶜarōbhtā*, it is quite possible that the Persian *ādīna* also contained an element of this meaning in it, for it could well have signified "coming together". It may be noted that *ādīna* is used in the additional sense of "the eve of a (Jewish) holiday" in several Jewish Persian dialects, particularly that of Kashan.[20] In Classical Persian[21] and in Tajik *dīna* is used in the sense of "yesterday", a possible extension of the sense of "the day before (the Sabbath)". The length of the first vowel in *ādīna* is embarrassing, but the fact that the word can occur in New Persian without an initial vowel in the form *dīna* probably shows that it had originally a short vowel. All of this is partly speculative, but it at least helps us understand the origin of the Islamic designation of the day.[22] Since it

[19] The combination *ati+i* is well attested for Iranian in the sense of "to come in", in Old Persian *atiyāish* (DB III 73), in Sogdian *tys*, in Manichaean Parthian *ʾdyh-*, and in Khwarezmian *cy* (cf. Gershevitch 1987:54; Humbach 1985:98; 1989:199). Already *Jāḥiẓ* sensed a connection between *jumᶜa* and *ādīna*, but could not explain it; cf. *Jāḥiẓ, K. al-ḥayawān*, 1:194. Another attempt at explaining *ādīna* is in Bailey 1971:4, n. 9. Bailey regards the Persian term for "Friday" as a translation from the Arabic *jumᶜa*, and he equates it with "New Persian *āēnah*, Zoroastrian Pahlavi *ādhēn*", which he derives from **adi-ayana-*. There are several difficulties with this series of identifications, but the most serious is the fact that the Zoroastrian Pahlavi form *ādhēn* is probably inexistent. It is quite doubtful that the New Persian word *āyēn(a)* "manners; mirror" is indeed related to the word for "Friday". It seems more likely that it is a development of Middle Persian *ēwēn*, from OIr **abi-daina-*; cf. Henning 1944:110, n. 1; 1958:71. An early attestation of the word for "Friday" in NP is in the Qurʾān commentary published by Browne 1894:440.

[20] I have this information from my colleague S. Soroudi.

[21] *Farhang-i Anandrāj* s.v.

[22] It may be noted that Goitein 1959, in his discussion of the origin of the Friday practice in Islam, tried to explain *yawm al-jumᶜa* "the day of the assembly" as a loan translation of the Hebrew term *yom hakkenisa* "the day of the assembly" (also, "the day of coming in"). The Hebrew term is attested in the sources quoted by Goitein for designating the weekly market-days of Monday and Thursday, and Goitein makes the plausible suggestion that it was generalized for any market-day. He also shows evidence that Friday was the market-day for the Jews of Arabia, and thus the term could have been adapted to mark Friday, eventually acquiring the peculiar Muslim connotation (see especially Goitein 1959:188f.). If this line of reasoning is accepted, it may serve as an alternative to the explanation given above, for it would very satisfactorily account for *ādīna* as the Persian equivalent to both Hebrew *kenisa* and Arabic *jumᶜa*. In that case the

makes it likely that the Persian term was not derived from the Arabic but directly from the Aramaic (with the Arabic term just possibly influenced by the Persian precedent), it shows, if we are right, that an analysis like this may be instructive for the history of the religious communities in Iran and for gaining a better understanding of the origins of Islam.

We have quite a few examples for Islamic customs that have their origin in the desire, often made explicit in the tradition, to set the Muslims apart from the habits of other peoples. Quite often those other peoples are Jews, but in certain cases we have an injunction to be different from the Persians.[23] Goldziher mentioned in this connection the Islamic attitude to dogs. In the early days of Islam dogs were tolerated even in mosques. That attitude changed partly under the impact of the need to differentiate the Muslims from the the Zoroastrian population.[24] There is an interesting passage in Jāḥiẓ, where he says: "The Prophet commanded us to kill dogs. He later prohibited us from killing them, saying, 'Beware [only] the black, dark (*bahīm*) [dog], which has two dots over its two eyes, for that one is a devil".[25] The reference to this particular description of a dog seems to add weight to Golziher's observation, for it is most likely inspired by the type of dog used by Zoroastrians for the *sag-dīd*, in the ritual for the disposal of the dead, when the corpse is exposed to a dog of similar description. At least according to this tradition, the Islamic problem with dogs is quite clealy linked with a Zoroastrian ritual custom. In another passage in the same book, Jāḥiẓ shows that he is acquainted with the Zoroastrian custom, and gives it a rational explanation. When a Zoroastrian (*majūs*) dies, he says, he is not brought to his place of burial (*nāwūs*) unless a dog comes near his body in order to smell it, for they are of the opinion that by smelling someone a dog can invariably tell whether that one is living or dead, for it only bites living persons.[26]

We have a whole list of prohibitions that are accompanied by the explicit explanation, that they are to be avoided because they are Persian. These include, for example, the obvious injunction not to write a *muṣḥaf*, a codex

Persian term would have to be considered as an Islamic coinage, as we have no evidence for Friday as a market-day among Babylonian or Iranian Jews.

[23] Examples for this are given in the following.

[24] Cf. Goldziher 1900:248ff.

[25] Jāḥiẓ, *Ḥayawān*, 1:174.

[26] Jāḥiẓ, *Ḥayawān* 1:223. In this connection Jāḥiẓ adds a piece of information concerning a Jewish funerary practice, which seems to show that he uses his own interpretation in this text, rather than faithfully reporting the tradition. Of the Jewish custom of washing the dead, he says: "The Jews seek to know the same thing of a dead person [i.e., whether he is dead or alive] by anointing his anus with oil". For Muslim attitudes to dogs, it is interesting to note the book of Ibn al-Marzubān.

of the Qurʾan, in Persian.[27] This may be obvious in the sense that the Qurʾān is considered as not liable to translation, but there is a whole range of contradictory sayings, occurring partly in the prophetic *ḥadīth*, concerning the special position of the Persian language in the divine entourage. Thus we read in a *ḥadīth*: "When God wishes (to convey) something with softness in it, he reveals it to the angels in His close presence in *darī* Persian; but when He wishes (to convey) something which has harshness in it, He reveals it in manifest Arabic".[28] Another saying formulates a similar point of view in different terms: "When God is angry, He reveals His message in Arabic; when He is pleased, He reveals it in Persian".[29] The opposite attitude is expressed however by a saying that states that Persian is the language most hateful to God.[30] The debate over the value of Persian in the eyes of God thus manifests some of the attitudes that were current about the position of Persians in Muslim society, and indirectly perhaps about the value of the older Persian civilization.

Among other rules in which attitudes to Persian customs become apparent there is a prohibition to use a Persian bow;[31] to kill frogs (the killing of these animals, deemed to be among the worst representatives of the demon, entails great merit for Zoroastrians);[32] to stay in a house where Persian luxuries are in sight;[33] and to pray in the Persian manner, which is known in Arabic, following the Aramaic precedent, as *raṭānat al-ʿajam*.[34]. Here also belongs the encouragement to use the toothpick, a Persian religious custom.[35] A somewhat puzzling point is the advice to avoid

[27] Bakrī, *Iʿānat al-ṭālibīn* I:65.

[28] The Arabic text is as follows: *idhā arāda llāhu amran fīhi līnun awḥā bihi ilā l-malāʾikati l-muqarrabīna bi-l-fārisiyyati l-dariyyati, wa-idhā arāda amran fīhi šiddatun awḥāhu bi-l-ʿarabiyyati l-jahīrati, yaʿnī al-mubīnata*. This saying occurs in Suyūṭī, *Aḥādīth mawḍūʿā*, p. 23, No. 19. Some of the Arabic quotations have been communicated to me by M.J. Kister.

[29] Dhahabī, *Aḥādīth mukhtāra*, p. 23 No. 1.

[30] Dhahabī, *Aḥādīth mukhtāra*, p. 24, No. 2.

[31] One should only use an Arabic bow, although other opinions are also quoted. al-Muttaqī, *Kanz al-ʿUmmāl*, IV:213-214, Nos. 1756-1758.

[32] *ḍafādiʿ*. Zamakhsharī, *Rabīʿ*, 4:441.

[33] Ibn Ḥanbal, *Kitāb al-waraʿ*, 83, 85.

[34] ʿUmar, for example, is reported as saying: "Beware of the mode of prayer of the Persians (*raṭānat al-aʿājim*) (Ibn Taymiyya, *Iqtidāʾ* 199f., where other sayings in a similar vein are to be found, concerning the celebration of nowrūz and mihrajān. Those who celebrate them will find themselves on the day of Resurrection in company with the impious). Cf. the Aramaic term *reṭna da-mgūšā*, on which Greenfield 1974 is the latest discussion.

[35] Goldziher 1900:246-248. The Middle Persian term is *dandān-frēš*, or *dandān-frašn* (possibly the same word as *fraš* "spear"). Cf. *ShNSh* 10:20 (and cf. the further references of Tavadia 1930:136 ad loc.); 12:13 (Kotwal 1969). *Dd* purs. 39:6 (= West 1882:135, §40:8). *PhlT* 123f. §18-19. It seems quite possible that the Arabic *miswāk*,

Persian-type asceticism, which, according to this tradition, apparently meant refraining from listening to music.[36] The question whether music is acceptable in Islamic religious practice — the question of *samāᶜ* — became, as is well known, a major theme of debate in pious Muslim circles,[37] but we know nothing from other sources of a Zoroastrian type of asceticism which may have involved abstention from listening to music or from the recitattion of poetry. The theme comes up occasionally in Byzantine literature, where notes of discontent concerning the use of music as distracting from the divine service are heard,[38] but it does not seem likely that Christian practices would be referred to in Arabic literature as "Persian asceticism". Rather than dismiss it as a piece of irrelevance, we would be well advised to keep this information in mind, for it is just possible that some further material which may explain it will eventually come to light.

The Shiᶜa treatment of unbelievers as impure has its roots in Qurʾan 9:28, as Goldziher noted. The Sunnis interpreted the Qurʾanic reference to impurity as a spiritual disparagement, while the Shiᶜites, presumably under Persian influence, accepted it in a literal sense.[39] The exercise of *taqiyya*, the concealment of one's true faith in order to avoid persecution, sanctioned by the Shiᶜites, can also be shown to have Zoroastrian parallels.[40]

Some further concrete examples, hitherto, to the best of my knowledge, not commented on, can be brought. One of these are the sayings that we find in Arabic literature against anger, Arabic *ghaḍab*. Thus, Jāḥiẓ quotes Abū Muslim Ṣāḥib al-Dawla as saying to Šahrām al-Marwazī at the end of an angry exchange of words: "Anger is a devil" (*innamā al-ghaḍabu*

siwāk is an adaptation from an original loanword from Middle Persian **sawāk* "a scraper, rubber", from the verb *sūdan*. A similar suggestion was already made by Eilers 1971:590. On the usefulness of a toothpick against forgetfulness and other matters, see the material collected by Goldziher 1903:148.

[36] Saᶜīd b. Musayyab (d. 94 AH) is told that certain pious Muslims (*nussāk*) are against the recitation of poetry, and he reacts by remarking that this is the mode of piety of the Persians (*nusk aᶜjamī*, which should therefore be avoided; Jāḥiẓ, *Bayān*, I:202).

[37] Some idea of the ambivalence towards poetry, music and dance among pious *ṣūfīs* is given in Ritter 1955:442, 491ff.

[38] Wellesz 1961:92ff., where references for a sentiment of disapproval concerning the use of instrumental music in church service are given; cf. also pp. 172ff., where criticism of chanting by monks is quoted.

[39] See Goldziher 1900:256. A Zoroastrian text for this prescription is *SDN* 38, where we read "it is necessary to make an effort so as to abstain from (using) the same cup as a man of a different religion (*jud-dēn*)"; cf. also Williams 1990, II:187.

[40] Cf. *PRiv* 33b:1. Goldziher wrote a classical short article on *taqiyya* (Goldziher 1906), where however he does not refer to the Zoroastrian parallel. The same phenomenon is also found in the Mandaean religion, see K. Rudolph in Foerster 1972/4, II:139.

šayṭān).[41] This could only be inspired, it seems, by the Zoroastrian idea of Xešm, the Old Iranian Aišma, the arch demon, that has also endowed Judaism with its demonic figure, Ashmeday, the Asmodaeus of the Book of Tobit.[42] The same idea inspired also similar expressions in Jewish and early Christian writings.[43] The concept of two types of wisdom, innate and acquired, which is quite central to Zoroastrian discussions of the subject, occurs scacttered in various places in Arabic literature, sometimes duly credited to the Iranian source, but elsewhere simply given as an Islamic concept, in at least one case on the authority of ᶜAlī.[44]

The Zoroastrians made much fuss about walking about with one shoe only, which should be strictly avoided.[45] Curiously, we find the same prohibition in the Islamic books of traditions, and it is enjoined, for example, that if the thong of one sandal is torn, one should immediately take the other sandal off until both are put right.[46] Goldziher had some trouble explaining the great attention paid to this seemingly trifling point in Islamic tradition, and hesitantly made a connection with the presumed custom of reciting curses on an enemy, as while reciting a piece of *hijāʾ* poetry in pre-Islamic society, after having taken off one shoe.[47] He quotes a parallel from a fragment of Euripides which shows that war activities were engaged in with a bare left foot. There can be little doubt that the strongly negative attitude of the Islamic tradition towards walking about with one shoe only is connected with the Persian custom. The reason for the

41 Jāḥiẓ, *Maḥāsin*, 18.

42 On Ashmeday see Boyce and Grenet 1991:414 n. 239 and p. 425, where references are given. See further Moulton 1913:252.

43 Pines 1982.

44 Cf. Shaked 1987b.

45 The Zoroastrian Middle Persian expression is *ēw-mog dwārišnīh* "running about with one shoe". Cf. *MX* 1:37; *ShNSh* 4:12; *GBd* 183:8; *PRiv* 11:2; *AVN* 25:3. Scholars have had considerable trouble in understanding this injunction. West 1885:11, n. 4, suggested to emend it to what I would transcribe *a-mōg* "shoeless", or alternatively to understand this in the sense of "a single foot-cover", i.e. without the outer boots. The former explanation is considered possible by Williams 1990 II:143, and the latter was accepted by Tavadia 1930:90. Vahman 1986:252f. expresses his incredulity that this injunction could be taken literally. According to Skalmowski 1987:501 the expression may be understood in the sense of wearing the same shoes both outdoors and indoors. The traditional understanding of the term, as we have it in the Sanskrit version of Neryosang (quoted in Tavadia *loc.cit.*) is literal, i.e. the sin consists of walking about with one foot bare. In view of the Arabic parallels, there can be no doubt that this is exactly the sense of the Middle Persian.

46 Quoted in Goldziher 1896:49, n. 4, where further material is brought together. Cf. also Haythamī, *Majmaᶜ al-zawāʾid* 5:139; Ṭaḥāwī, *Muškil al-āthār* 2:141-143; Al-Fākihī, Ms., fol. 507b; Maᶜmar, *Jāmiᶜ*, Ms., fol. 143b; Abū l-Qāsim, Ms., fol. 34b; Zarkašī, *Ijāba*, 67 [These references are due to the amiability of M.J. Kister].

47 Goldziher 1896:47ff.

Zoroastrian abhorrence of wearing one shoe only is not made explicit, but the Arabic expression that this is *ziyyu l-šayṭān* "satan's clothing fashion"[48] seems to fit in nicely with the Zoroastrian conception.

Another point which is made much of in the Iranian texts is the prohibition to urinate while standing.[49] The Zoroastrian reason given for this prohibition is that this causes too much pollution to the earth. The same prohibition occurs in Islam, and is also mentioned in Jewish writings.[50] The Jewish and Muslim explanation for it seems to be the desire to avoid the risk of the man polluting himself by his own urine. It is difficult in such a case to decide whether this is an Iranian theme perpetuated in Islam, or whether Islam took over this prohibition from Judaism; Judaism in its turn may have borrowed it from Iran, or could have developed it on its own. It should however be obvious that the rationalization of a custom is not necessarily part of the original reason for the custom being established.

One point where I would hesitate to see a Persian influence on Islam is the hypothesis formulated not long ago by Philippe Gignoux, according to which the Zoroastrian formula *pad nām ī yazdān* "By the name of the gods" gave rise to the Islamic *bismi llāhi l-raḥmān al-raḥīm*.[51] When one quotes the Islamic phrase in its entirety one notices more sharply the dissimilarity with the Iranian tradition, which sometimes has epithets of a different kind following the term *yazdān*: *rayōmand* and *xwarrōmand*, for example.[52]

On the other hand we have quite a wide range of attestations from the Jewish and Christian domains of formulae of a similar character, chiefly in the magical bowls, where the short formula in Hebrew is *bišmakh ani ʿośe* "By your name I act".[53] The very common Aramaic formulae at the beginning of magic bowls is *byšmk*, *bšmk mry ʾswtʾ*, *byšmyh dmʾry ʾswʾtʾ*, or *byšmyk mry šmyʾ wʾrʿh* "By your name", "By your name, the

[48] Quoted Goldziher 1896:50.

[49] *PRiv* 11:3; *AVN* 25:3; *MX* 2:37. Cf. the comments by Vahman 1986:253 and Williams 1990 II:144. An Arabic echo of this Persian rule, quoted from the *Kitāb al-āyīn*, is in Ibn Qutayba, *ʿUyūn* 3:221.

[50] Much Islamic material has been collected on this topic by M.J. Kister. In this connection it may be sufficient to refer to Zarkašī, *Ijāba*, 86f., where traditions for and against this custom are quoted. In the Babylonian Talmud a discussion of the subject is found in Berakhot 40a, where it seems that the requirement to be seated while urinating is based purely on the pragmatic consideration of avoiding the fall of droplets of urine on the legs. If the same aim can be acheived by other means, it is lawful to urinate while standing.

[51] Gignoux, Curiel, Gyselen and Herrenschmidt 1979:159-163. The idea had already been proposed almost a hundred years ago by Blochet 1898:40, n. 1.

[52] Quoted, for proving the opposite point of view, by Gignoux in Gignoux, Curiel and others 1979:163.

[53] Montgomery 1913:183 (No. 14), and frequently.

Lord of healing", "By the name of the lord of healings", "By your name, the Lord of heaven and earth",[54] attest to the frequency of this phenomenon, as do the similar Christian invocations "By the name of the Father, the Son, and the Holy Ghost".[55] Quite close to the Islamic formula by its reference to "mercy" is the Aramaic magic formula *brḥmy šmyʾ* "By the mercy of heaven".[56] The Mandaic formula *bšwmʾywn d-hyyʾ* "By the name of Life"[57] is of a similar nature. The Hebrew formula *be-šem...* has been the subject of a learned note by the late Saul Lieberman.[58]

A Manichaean amulet in Parthian, which may date from the 4th-6th century, reads as follows: "By your name, by your will, by your command and by your power, Lord Jesus Christ. By the name of Mar Mani the Saviour, the apostle of the gods... By the name of Michael, Sarael, Raphael and Gabriel...".[59] Here the whole range of Christian and Judaeo-Christian formulae, together with a specific Manichaean invocation, are used.

A similar formula attested in Jewish legal deeds and even in correspondence, although fairly late, seems to be a possible continuation of a pre-Islamic Jewish custom, which has not been directly preserved. The Aramaic formula frequently found on Jewish writings in the Geniza is the Aramaic *bišmākh raḥmānā*, "By your name, the Merciful one".[60] An interesting Jewish Persian usage which seems related to both the Jewish and Iranian traditions is *pnʾm, pnyy* (= *pa nām i YY*), "By the name of God".[61] In Samaritan we have the frequent formula "In the name of YHWH".[62]

It thus seems likely that Goldziher's position in his article on the *Basmala* formula for the *Encyclopaedia of Religion and Ethics*,[63]

[54] E.g. Montgomery 1913:127 (Bowl No. 3); p. 145 (Bowl No. 7); p. 154 (No. 8); p. 213 (No. 28).

[55] Cf. in the Syriac bowl published by Montgomery 1917/8:137-139. For the use of the name of Jesus see also Deissmann 1927:121ff.; Preisigke 1910:149ff.; Conybeare 1897:62ff.

[56] Montgomery 1913:193 (No. 18).

[57] Montgomery 1913:252 (No. 40). Cf. also *Ginza* I, 1, s. dextra, p. 1.

[58] Lieberman 1957/8:183f.

[59] Henning 1947:50; for the supposed date, p. 49.

[60] This occurs in early Judaeo-Arabic texts, also on papyrus; see P. Mich. 6710 (in Sirat 1985: plate 31); or ʿal šmakh raḥʾ, Österreichische Nationalbibliothek H 70 (in Sirat 1985: plate 20).

[61] This occurs in two of the Geniza letters that form part of my projected edition of this material; these are the letters that I have marked L17 and L3 respectively.

[62] Gaster 1928, III:149ff. The use of the formula "in the name of" in legal terminology of the fifth century B.C.E., not directly of relevance to our usage, is discussed by Lidzbarski 1906:3213.

[63] Goldziher 1909. The same attitude was expressed by Nöldeke 1909:116f. Cf. also the considerable material assembled by Heitmüller 1903, where he considers apparently

according to which it is derived from Jewish and Christian sources, stands a good chance of being correct. At the same time it is quite clear that a similar formula was current in Iranian, among both Zoroastrians and Manichaeans.

It is good to remember, when we are dealing with the situation of Iran towards the neighbouring cultures, that it is often far from easy to establish which one influenced the other. We are faced with a host of similar themes and motifs in Greek, Jewish, Christian, Babylonian and Iranian sources to name just some of the cultures that were in contact with each other. It is only rarely that we can prove with any conclusiveness that a specific notion did originate in one of these cultures and that it must have spread from there to the others. In most cases we have to use a kind of reasoning that is close to speculation. This applies, for example, to the question of the origins of the apocalyptic literature, which has generated a considerable amount of debate in recent years. Much depends on individual judgement, that may be subjective. I hope however to have talked of a few elements where the probability of borrowing, and the direction of borrowing, can be demonstrated in a fairly clear manner.

REFERENCES

Abū l-Qāsim ᶜIsā b. ᶜAlī Ibn al-Jarrāḥ. Juzʾ, Ms. Chester Beatty 3495.

Andrae, Tor. 1917. *Die Person Muhammeds in Lehren und Glauben seiner Gemeinde* (Archives d'Études Orientales, 16), Stockholm.

AVN: *Ardā Wirāz Nāmag*, in: *The book of Ardā Virāf*, ed. M. Haug and E. West, the Pahlavi text prepared by Dastur Hoshnagji Jamaspji Asa, Bombay 1872. [Cf. also Gignoux 1984; Vahman 1986.]

Bailey, H.W. 1971. "The second stratum of the Indo-Iranian gods", in: J.R. Hinnells, *Mithraic studies. Proceedings of the First International Congress of Mithraic Studies*, Manchester: Manchester UP, 1-20.

al-Bakrī, Abū Bakr b. Muḥammad Šaṭṭā al-Dimyāṭī. *Iᶜānat al-ṭālibīn ᶜalā ḥall alfāz fatḥ al-muᶜīn*, 4th printing, Beirut: Iḥyāʾ al-turāth al-ᶜarabī, n.d.

Bausani, Alessandro. 1959. *La Persia religiosa, da Zarathustra a Bahāʾullāh*, Milano.

Blochet, E. 1898. "Études sur l'histoire religieuse de l'Iran, I", *RHR* 38:26-63.

--. 1899. "Études sur l'histoire religieuse de l'Iran, II", *RHR* 40:1-25, 203-236.

--. 1902. "Études sur l'ésotérisme musulman", *JA* 19:489-531; 20:49-111.

--. 1913. *Études sur le gnosticisme musulman* (Extrait de la *RSO* 2,3,4,6), Rome.

Boyce, Mary; and Frantz Grenet (with a contribution by Roger Beck). 1991. *A history of Zoroastrianism*, III. Zoroastrianism under Macedonian and Roman rule (Handbuch der Orientalistik, 1. Abteilung, 8. Band, 1. Abschnitt, Lieferung 2, Heft 2), Leiden etc.: Brill.

that the Iranian formula arose independently of the Jewish-Hellenistic one, a reasonable possibility.

Browne, Edward G. 1894. "Description of an old Persian commentary on the Ḳurʾān", *JRAS*, 417-524.

Conybeare, F.C. 1897. "Christian demonology", *JQR* 9:59-114, 444-470.

Corbin, Henry. 1951. "Le livre des conseils de Zartusht", *Prof. Poure Davoud Commemoration Volume*, II, Bombay, 129-160.

--. 1960. *Terre céleste et corps de résurrection de l'Iran mazdéen à l'Iran shîʾite* (La Barque du Soleil), Paris: Bucet/Chastel.

--. 1964. *Histoire de la philosophie islamique*, I, avec la collaboration de Seyyed Hosseïn Nasr et Osman Yahya (Collection Idées), Paris: Gallimard.

Dd = *Datistan i Dinik*, ed. Tahmuras Dinshaji Anklesaria, Part I, Pursishn I-XL, Bombay n.d. [printed but not published].

Deissmann, Adolf. 1927. *Light from the ancient East. The New Testament illustrated by recently discovered texts of the Graeco-Roman world* (tr. L.R.M. Strachan), New revised edition, London.

Al-Dhahabī, Shams al-Dīn Muḥammad b. Aḥmad. *Al-aḥādīth al-mukhtāra*, ed. ʿAbd al-Raḥmān b. ʿAbd al-Jabbār al-Farīwāʾī, Medina 1404 AH.

Dk VI, see Shaked 1979.

Eilers, Wilhelm. 1971. "Iranisches Lehngut im Arabischen", *Actas IV Congresso de Estudos Arabes e Islámicos*, Leiden, 581-660.

al-Fākihī, Muḥammad b. Isḥāq. *Taʾrīkh makka*, Ms. Leiden Or. 463.

Farhang-i Anandrāj = Pādšāh, Muḥammad Šād. *Farhang-i Anandrāj*, ed. Muḥammad Dabīr-Siyāqī, 7 vols., Tehran 1335 AHS.

Foerster, Werner. 1972/4. *Gnosis. A selection of gnostic texts*, English translation edited by R. McL. Wilson, 2 vols., Oxford: Clarendon Press.

Gaster, Moses. 1928. *Studies and texts in folklore, magic, mediaeval romance, Hebrew Apocrypha and Samaritan archaeology*, 3 vols., London [Reprint, New York 1971, with a "Prolegomenon" by T. Gaster].

GBd: The Greater Bundahishn, in: *The Būndahishn*, ed. Tahmuras Dinshaji Anklesaria, Bombay 1908.

Gershevitch, Ilya. 1987. "Literacy in transition from the Anshanian to the Achaemenian period", *Transition periods in Iranian history. Actes du Symposium de Fribourg-en-Brisgau (22-24 mai 1985)* (Cahiers de Studia Iranica, 5), Leuven, 49-57.

Ghazālī [Pseudo-?].*Al-durra al-fākhira fī kašf ʿulūm al-ākhira*, ed. Muḥammad Muṣṭafā Abū l-ʿAlāʾ, Cairo n.d. [Printed in the same volume as *Sirr al-ʿālamayn* of the same author.]

Gignoux, Ph.; R. Curiel; R. Gyselen; and Cl. Herrenschmidt. 1979. *Pad nām i yazdān. Études d'épigraphie, de numismatique et d'histoire de l'Iran ancien* (Université de la Sorbonne Nouvelle. Travaux de l'Institut d'Études Iraniennes, 9), Paris: Klincksieck.

--. 1984. *Le livre d'Ardā Vīrāz. Translittération, transcription et traduction du texte pehlevi* (Institut Français d'Iranologie de Téhéran. Bibliothèque iranienne No. 30; Éditions Recherche sur les Civilisations, Cahier No. 14), Paris.

Ginza, in: Johannes Petermann (ed.). 1867. *Thesaurus sive Liber magnus*, vol. 1, 2 parts, Lipsiae.

Goitein, S.D. 1959. "The origin and nature of the Muslim Friday worship", *The Muslim World* 49:111-125.

Goldziher, Ignaz. 1889. *Muhammedanische Studien*, vol. 1, Halle a. S. [English version: *Muslim studies* (*Muhammedanische Studien*), I, ed. S.M. Stern, London: Allen and Unwin 1967]

--. 1896. *Abhandlungen zur arabischen Philologie*, Vol. 1, Leiden.

--. 1900. "Islamisme et parsisme", *Actes du 1er Congrès International d'Histoire des Religions*, 119-147. [Reprinted in: Goldziher, *Gesammelte Schriften*, Hildesheim: Olms 1967-1973, 4:232-260]

--. 1903. "Muhammedanischer Aberglaube über Gedächtniskraft und Vergesslichkeit, mit Parallelen aus der jüdischen Literatur. Beitrag zur Volkskunde", in: A. Freimann and M. Hildesheimer (eds.), *Festschrift zum siebzigsten Geburtstage A. Berliner's*, Frankfurt a.M., 131-155.

--. 1906. "Das Prinzip der *taḳiyya* im Islam", *ZDMG* 40:213-226. [Reprinted in: Goldziher, *Gesammelte Schriften*, 5:59-72]

--. 1909. "Bismillāh", *ERE* 2:666-668. [Reprinted in: Goldziher, *Gesammelte Schriften*, 5:167-169]

Gray, Louis H. 1902. "Zoroastrian elements in Muhammedan eschatology", *Le Muséon* N.S. 3:153-184.

al-Haythamī, Nūr al-Dīn. *Majma^c al-zawā$^{\supset}$id wa-manbi^c al-fawā$^{\supset}$id*, 2nd ed., Beirut 1967.

Heitmüller, Wilhelm. 1903. *"Im Namen Jesu". Eine sprach- und religionsgeschichtliche Untersuchung zum Neuen Testament, speziell zur altchristlichen Taufe* (Forschungen zur Religion und Literatur des Alten und Neuen Testaments, 1. Band, 2. Heft), Göttingen: Vandenhoeck & Ruprecht.

Henning, W.B. 1944. "Bráhman", *TPS* 108-111 [Reprinted in *AI* 15:193-203].

--. 1947. "Two Manichaean magical texts, with an excursus on the Parthian ending -ēndēh", *BSOAS* 12:39-66 [Reprinted in *Acta Iranica* 15:273-300].

--. 1958. "Mitteliranisch", in: *Handbuch der Orientalistik* I,IV,1, Leiden, 20-129.

Humbach, Helmut. 1985. "Altpersisch avaparā atiyāish", *MSS* 45:97-103.

--. 1989. "Choresmian", in: R. Schmitt (ed.), *Compendium linguarum iranicarum*, Wiesbaden, 193-203.

Ibn Ḥanbal, Aḥmad b. Muḥammad. *Kitāb al-wara^c*, Cairo 1340.

Ibn al-Marzubān, Abū Bakr Muḥammad b. Khalaf. Faḍl al-kilāb alā l-kathīr mimman labisa al-thiyāb (The book of the superiority of dogs over many of those who wear clothes), translated and edited by G.R. Smith and M.A.S. Abdel Haleem, Warminster: Aris & Phillips, 1978.

Ibn Qutayba al-Dīnawarī, ^{c}Abdallāh b. Muslim. *^{c}Uyūn al-akhbār*, 4 vols., Cairo.

Ibn Taymiyya. *Iqtidā$^{\supset}$ al-ṣirāṭ al-mustaqīm mukhālafat aṣḥābi l-jaḥīm*, ed. Muḥammad Ḥāmid al-Faqī, 2nd edition, Cairo 1369 AH.

Jāḥiz, Abū ^{c}Uthmān ^{c}Amr b. Baḥr. *Al-bayān wa-l-tabyīn*, ed. ^{c}Abd al-Salām Muḥammad Hārūn, 4th ed., 4 vols., Cairo 1975.

--. *Kitāb al-ḥayawān*, ed. Fawzī ^{c}Aṭwī, 7 vols., 2nd ed., Beirut 1978.

--. *Al-maḥāsin wa-l-aḍdād, Le livre des beautés et des antithèses*, ed. G. Van Vloten, Leiden 1898.

Kister, M.J.; and Menahem Kister. 1979. "On the Jews of Arabia -- some notes" (in Hebrew), *Tarbiz* 48:231-247.

Kotwal, Firoze M. 1969. *The supplementary texts to the Shāyast nē-Shāyast* (Det Kongelige Danske Videnskabernes Selskab, Historisk-filosofiske Meddelelser 44.2), Copenhagen.

Lidzbarski, Mark. 1906. [Review of: A.H. Sayce, *Aramaic papyri discovered at Assuan*], *Deutsche Literaturzeitung* 27:3205-3215.

Liebermann, Saul. 1957/8. "On incantations in Judaism", *Tarbiz* 27:183-189.

Markwart, Josef. 1927. "Np. ādhīna 'Freitag'", *Ungarische Jahrbücher* 7:89-121.

Ma^{c}mar, *Jāmi^c*, Ms.

Meier, Fritz. 1973. "Ein profetenwort gegen die totenbeweinung", *Der Islam* 50:207-229.

Montgomery, James A. 1913. *Aramaic incantation texts from Nippur* (University of Pennsylvania. The Museum. Publications of the Babylonian Section, III), Philadelphia.

--. 1917/8. "A Syriac incantation bowl with Christian formula", *AJSLL* 34:137-139.

Moulton, James Hope. 1913. *Early Zoroastrianism* (The Hibbert Lectures, 2nd series, 1912), London.

Muttaqī al-Hindī, ᶜAlā al-Dīn b. ᶜAbd al-Malik. *Kanz al-ᶜummāl*, 19 vols., Hyderabad 1953- 1972.

MX = *Mēnōg ī xrad*, in: Dānāk-u Mainyō-ī Khard, ed. Tahmuras Dinshaji Anklesaria, Bombay 1913..

Nöldeke, Theodor. 1909. *Geschichte des Qorāns*, 1. Teil, 2. Auflage, bearbeitet von Friedrich Schwally, Leipzig.

Pines, Shlomo. 1982. "Wrath and creatures of wrath in Pahlavi, Jewish and New Testament sources", in: S. Shaked (ed.), *Irano-Judaica*, Jerusalem, 76-82.

Preisigke, Friedrich. 1910. *Girowesen im griechischen Ägypten*, Strassburg i.E.

PRiv: *The Pahlavi Rivāyat accompanying the Dādistān-ī Dīnīk*, ed. Ervad Bamanji Nasarvanji Dhabhar (Pahlavi Text Series, 2), Bombay 1913. [See also Williams 1990.]

Ritter, Hellmut. 1955. *Das Meer der Seele. Mensch, Welt und Gott in den Geschichten des Farīduddīn ᶜAṭṭār*, Leiden: Brill.

SDN: *Sad-Dar Nasr and Sad-Dar Bundehesh*, ed. B.N. Dhabhar, Bombay 1909.

Shaked, Shaul. 1971. "The notions *mēnōg* and *gētīg* in the Pahlavi texts and their relation to eschatology", *Acta Orientalia* 33:59-107.

--. 1979. *The wisdom of the Sasanian sages*. An edition, with translation and notes, of *Dēnkard*, Book Six, by Aturpāt-i Ēmētān (Persian Heritage Series, 34), Boulder, Col.: Westview Press.

--. 1984a. "From Iran to Islam: Notes on some themes in transmission", *JSAI* 4:31-67.

--. 1984b. "Iranian influences in Judaism", *Cambridge History of Judaism*, I, Cambridge: Cambridge UP, 308-442.

--. 1986. "From Iran to Islam: On some symbols of royalty", *JSAI* 7:75-91.

--. 1987a. "Paymān: an Iranian idea in contact with Greek thought and Islam", *Transition periods in Iranian history. Actes du Symposium de Fribourg-en-Brisgau (22-24 mai 1985)* (Studia Iranica. Cahier 5), Paris: Association pour l'Avancement des Études Iraniennes, 217-240.

--. 1987b. "A facetious recipe and the two wisdoms: Iranian themes in Muslim garb", *JSAI* 9:24-35.

--. 1990. "'For the sake of the soul': a Zoroastrian idea in transmission into Islam", *JSAI* 13:15-32.

ShNSh: *Shāyast nē shāyast*, cf. Tavadia 1930.

Sirat, Colette. 1985. [Avec la collaboration de M. Beit-Arié, M. Dukan, F. Klein-Franke, H. Harrauer. Calligraphie et illustration A. Yardeni], *Les papyrus en caractères hébraïques trouvés en Égypte*, Paris: CNRS.

Skalmowski, Wojciech. 1987. [Review of Gignoux 1984; Vahman 1986], *BiOr* 44:500-601.

Suyūṭī, Jalāl al-Dīn ᶜAbd al-Raḥmān. *Al-aḥādīth al-mawḍūᶜa min al-jāmiᶜ al-kabīr* (in the same volume also: ᶜAbd al-Raʾūf b. Tāj al-ᶜārifīn b. ᶜAlī al-Munāwī, *Al-aḥādīth al-mawḍūᶜa min al-jāmiᶜ al-azhar*), ed. ᶜAbbās Aḥmad Ṣaqar and Aḥmad ᶜAbd al-Jawā, Beirut: Dār al-išrāq, 1988.

Taʾrīkh-e Sīstān, ba-taṣḥīḥ-e Malekoššoᶜrā Bahār, Tehran 1314 AH.

Ṭaḥāwī, Abū Jaᶜfar Aḥmad b. Muḥammad. *Muškil al-āthār*, Hyderabad 1333 AH.

Tavadia, Jehangir C. 1930. *Shāyast-nē-shāyast. A Pahlavi text on religious customs*, ed., transliterated and translated, Hamburg.

Vahman, Fereydun. 1986. *Ardā Wirāz Nāmag. The Iranian 'Divina Commedia'* (Scandinavian Institute of Asian Studies, Monograph Series, No. 53), London and Malmo: Curzon Press.

Wellesz, Egon. 1961. *A history of Byzantine music and hymnography*, 2nd edition, Oxford: Clarendon Press.

West, E.W. 1882. *Pahlavi texts, II. The Dādistān-ī dīnīk and the Epistles of Mānūshkīhar* (The Sacred Books of the East, XVIII), Oxford UP [Reprint, Delhi-Varanasi-Patna: Motilal Banarsidass, 1965].

--. 1885. *Pahlavi texts, III. Dīnā-ī maīnōg-ī khirad, Shikand-gūmānīk vigār, Sad dar* (The Sacred Books of the East, XXIV), Oxford UP [Reprint, Delhi-Varanasi-Patna 1965].

Widengren, Geo. 1950. *The ascension of the Apostle and the heavenly book*, Uppsala.

Williams, Alan V. 1990. *The Pahlavi Rivāyat accompanying the Dādestān ī Dēnīg*, 2 vols. (Det Kongelige Danske Videnskabernes Selskab, Historisk-filosofiske Meddelelser 60:1), Copenhagen: Munksgaard.

al-Zamakhšarī, Maḥmūd b. ᶜUmar. *Rabīᶜu l-abrār wa-nuṣūṣu al-axbār*, ed. Salīm al-Nuᶜaymī (Iḥyāʾ al-turāth al-islāmī, 13), 4 vols., Baghdad 1982.

al-Zarkašī, Badr al-Dīn. *Al-ijāba li-īrādi mā stadrakathu ᶜāʾiša ᶜalā al-ṣaḥāba*, Cairo n.d.

ADDENDA

I. Esoteric trends in Zoroastrianism

The negative judgement passed by Bailey on the conclusions of this paper (cf. Bailey 1971, in the introduction to his new edition of *Zoroastrian problems in the ninth-century books*) seems to me to be based on a somewhat careless reading of my argument.

One can quote as an analogy for a practice of 'esoteric' teaching, where the contents of the teachings do not differ radically from those of the open techings, the sceptical academy of Athens, as reconstructed by Glucker 1978:300 f.

p. 180, passage 70: An improved transcription and translation will be found in Shaked 1979.

p. 182, note 23: The Arabic material on Sasanian religious hierarchy is quite abundant. Here are some further references: Ibn Qutayba, *'Uyūn al-akhbār*, I:13; III:10.

p. 183, passage 55: This passage has an Arabic version in Ibn al-Muqaffa', *Al-adab al-kabīr* (cf. Ibn al-Muqaffa', *Āthār*, 297).

p. 187 ff.: On the restriction in the teaching of the Avesta cf. the testimony of Ibn Ḥazm, *Al-fiṣal*, I:115 f.

On the problem of Avesta and Zand cf. also Menasce 1956/7:8 f.

p. 193, note 49: Cf. also Messina 1930:80 ff.

p. 199, note 64: An improved version of paragraph 57 is in Shaked 1979.

p. 203 ff.: For the notion of *hāwišt* in the sense of a degree of priesthood, it may be noted that in the Mandaean tradition the word for "disciple" (*tarmīda*) becomes the technical term for "priest"; cf. Rudolph 1960/1, II:119 ff.; summarized in Rudolph 1968/9:234.

p. 206 ff.: On the term *rāz*. It should be noted that Frye 1967:79 treats this term with scepticism, with no good reason.

For the use of the term *rāz* in the Pahlavi literature cf. also the following quotations:

Dk VII, 4:63: *ud zardušt ēd rāz ō mardom āhuft* ...

Dk VII, 5:8–10: *āhuftan ī zardušt* ... *rāzīgīhā bawandīgīhā ī pad yazdīg dānišnīh ud mēnōg-wēnišnīh šayēd* ...

p. 218, note 9: On the relative value of silver and gold cf. the article by Sperber 1970/1.

Further evidence for an order of preference that put silver above gold in writings of the Sasanian period can be quoted. Cf. in Syriac, Bedjan 1891:567, where, in a composition of the fifth century, the order is "much gold and silver and many precious gifts". The same order occurs again on the same page.

In Ps.-Aṣma'ī, *Nihāyat al-arab*, MS British Library, fol. 142a, the gifts given to al-Mundhir are enumerated: *al-dhahab wa-l-fiḍḍa wa-l-jawāhir* "gold, silver and jewels", in what looks like an ascending order.

II. The notions mēnōg and gētīg in the Pahlavi texts and their relation to eschatology

p. 77, second paragraph: The translation of *Dd* XXX:5 should be:

> Except (in cases) when through the great consideration of the Creator, the spirits are clothed in visible *gētīg*, or when they join to *gētīg* people sight which is in the nature of *mēnōg* perception, the self (of men) can see the spirits with *gētīg* perception by that similitude, as when they see bodies in which there is soul, or fire in which there is Warhrām, or water in which its spirit is found.

p. 85, note 84: Cf. also Zaehner 1955:354 f.; Widengren 1967:94 f. (whose understanding of the text is, in my opinion, erroneous). I would now revise somewhat my translation, taking the words *ohrmazd gannāg-mēnōg* to go with the following phrase.

p. 89, end of Appendix A: Cf. also Ms. Copenhagen, Cod. 27, in Hampel 1974:26 (where the editor did not recognize the word).

p. 91, paragraph 7: For the passage *DkM* 345.6-8 cf. Molé 1963:413; Shaki 1973:147 f.

p. 92, note 6: Cf. the use of the expression *ādam-i gilīn*, with a specialized *ṣūfī* connotation, in Baqlī Šīrāzī, *Šarḥi-i Šaṭḥiyyāt*, 84, lines 6-7.

p. 97, end of the first paragraph: Zoroaster is described as *rad ī stīān* "chief of the beings" (cf. Dhabhar 1963:383, n. 3 to §42).

p. 98, note 2: Cf. Shaked 1979, note to ***13:3***.

p. 104: Add among the references for *Dēnkard* III, Chapter 365, Shaki 1970:283–286.

III. Some notes on Ahreman, the Evil Spirit, and his creation

Some further evidence for the notion of the non-existence of Ahreman in the Pahlavi texts can be adduced from the following catechism in the *andarz* literature.

> u-m warzišn ī xwēškārīh ud frēzbānīh ēn ku ohrmazd pad astīh, *hamē būdīh hamē bawēdīh ud anōšag-xwadāyīh ud a-kanāragīh ud abēzagīh, ahreman pad nēstīh ud wanēbūdīh menīdan ... (*PhlT*, Jamasp-Asana 1897/1913:42; *Pand-nāmag* §3).
>
> And my doing my duty and my obligation is this: I think of Ohrmazd as existing, having always been and being always in the future, having eternal rule, being unbounded and pure, and of Ahreman as non-existent and destined to be destroyed ...

The Persian *Rivāyat* has the following relevant phrase:

> *va čūn bā rūḥānī čīzī ba-dast na-dāšt* (Darab Hormazyar, *PersRiv*, II:82. Cf. Dhabhar 1932:452. Zaehner 1955:411 mistranslated this phrase).
>
> And as he [=Ahreman] had no control over the *mēnōg* substances.

p. 228: For *Dd* XVIII:2-3 cf. Molé 1959:453. For the lack of symmetry between the good spirits created by Ahura Mazdā and the evil demons created by Angra Mainyu cf. also Benveniste 1929:86 f.

IV. Mihr the Judge

The term "middle man, mediator" is used sometimes in Syriac literature in contexts where the notion of "judge" would seem to be in place. An example from a post-Sasanian text is the following:

> **kd mṣʻy' lšrbh 'nšyn mn 'pysqwp' dhwprky' gb'** (Chabot 1898:303, lines 179 f.)
>
> He selected as judges (?) for his affair (certain) bishops of the diocese.

An echo of the same notion with regard to the sun as the mediator, i.e. judge, of the world is found in the magical address to the sun occurring in the *Picatrix* (ps.-Majrīṭī 1933:216 (cf. Ritter and Plessner 1962:228), where the sun is called *mutawassiṭatu l-kulli* "that which stands in the middle of everything". This is rightly explained by the translators by referring to the notion of the sun as the middle of the seven planets. While this is certainly true, one cannot help feeling that the old notion of the sun as mediator/judge also plays a role in this definition of the sun as the middle.

For Mithra as mediator cf. also Imoto 1981.

p. 9: A reference to *PersRiv* II, 84:14 should be added, where we have:

> *urdībihišt amšāsfand miyānjī-i ʻuqūbat buvad*
> Aša Wahišta is the judge/ruler over punishment.

Zaehner 1955:414 translates this by "mediator".

p. 12, note 44: For the term *azeš-mānd* cf. Macuch 1981:127–135.

p. 14 f., note 55: A connection of the Greek term μεσίτης with Mithra's function as eschatological jusdge is made by Wesendonk 1924:144. Mihr, the Third Messenger of Manichaeism, is identified by Reitzenstein 1917:7 as the Mediator.

p. 23: For the reading and etymology of the word for "time" cf. Markwart 1927; Junker 1929:138 ff.

For *āwām* in the sense of "world" cf. the Pahlavi version of the Psalms, where the Syriac phrase *pārōqā d-ḵul* "Saviour of all" is rendered **p'lwk' [ZY] 'wb'm** (Andreas and Barr 1933:97, and the editors' comments, p. 117). The editors translated the Pahlavi by "Erlöser der Zeit", which seems out of place. It should be translated, in view of the sense established here and in view of the Syriac original, "saviour of the world", or "saviour of humanity".

p. 26 f.: I should like to retract my sceptical remarks concerning the sense of "torment, hardship" for *āwām*. Cf. Henning 1958:71; also MacKenzie 1984:388 f.

V. The myth of Zurvan: Cosmogony and eschatology

This discussion relies on the analysis of the reports of Zoroastrianism given by some Islamic authors. My analysis of these reports forms the main subject-matter of Shaked 1994.

VI. From Iran to Islam. Notes on some themes in transmission

p. 31 ff.: For the notion that "religion and sovereignty are twins", cf. the article by Gignoux 1984, where a radically different point of view is taken.

Biruni writes in the interesting introduction to his *Kitāb al-ṣaydana* as follows: "Our religion and the dynasty are both Arab and twins. Over one of them there hovers divine power and over the other a heavenly hand..." (Biruni's introduction to *Kitāb al-ṣaydana*, ed. Meyerhof 1933, Arabic section, 12). In the Persian edition (edited by 'Abbās Zaryāb), 14, the text is emended to read: "Our religion and the dynasty are both Arab. Over the twins, <religion and the dynasty/sovereignty>, there hovers divine power over one and a heavenly hand over the other..." Although the text is hard to interpret, the emendation does not reallly improve matters. The fact that Bīrūnī uses this theme, and the particular emphasis he puts on the Arab character of the "twins", makes one more convinced that a polemic is intended with a deeply-rooted Sasanian notion.

p. 34 f. note 17: For the use of *zēnhār* in the sense of a treaty, reference may be made to the Judaeo-Persian Tafsīr of Ezekiel, St. Petersburg MS, 79:6, where the expression **zynh'r gryptn** indicates "to conclude a pact".

p. 38, last but one paragraph: The word *ham-nāf* is also attested in Manichaean Middle Persian; cf. Henning 1936:443, line 387 (**hmn'p'n**).

p. 41, note 2: Another version of this saying is in Māwardī, *Tashīl al-naẓar*, 114, where the Arabs are added and are given the final word, which is reserved here to the Persians.

p. 43, note 12: In the printed edition of Māwardī, *Tashīl*, the text is on p. 59.

p. 46: The "intelligent peoples" according to 'Abd al-Jabbār, *Tathbīt*, 13, are the Arabs, the Persians, the Indians and the Byzantines (*rūm*).

VII. From Iran to Islam: On some symbols of royalty

p. 80: For the significance of the chairs in the audience hall of the Sasanian king we have parallels in the protocol of the Byzantine rulers. References to similar Byzantine customs are fairly frequent. Cf. in the Arabic account known as *Histoire nestorienne* (Patrologia Orientalis IV, Paris 1908, 277), with regard to Constantine and the Council of Nicea.

The language used with regard to establishing a Christian patriarch in Ctesiphon also refers to a chair (Arabic *kursī*). Cf. *Histoire nestorienne*, Patrologia Orientalis VII, Paris 1911, 149.

p. 80 f.: The phrase that establishes a ruler's dignity by the fact that he holds or has erected a stool in front of the deity has now received further confirmation by an inscription published by Aggoula 1985:66, where the text says:

> **k[ʿn h]qym krs'' znh / qdm ṣlm zy rb lmytb / šngl' w'šym' 'lhy tym'**

p. 82 ff.: On the use of quinces in folk-medicine in nineteenth-century Syria cf. Van Dyk 1851:574.

XII. Some Iranian themes in Islamic literature

p. 146 f.: For the use of Arabic *jumʿa* in the sense of "eve of holiday" and its connection with *ʿarobta*, cf. Ben-Shammai 1993.

REFERENCES

Aggoula, Basile. 1985. "Studia Aramaica II", *Syria* 62:61-76.

Aṣma'ī (Ps.), *Nihāyatu l-arabi fī akhbāri l-fursi wa-l-'arabi*, Ms. London, British Library Add 23.298.

Andreas, F.C.; and Kaj Barr. 1933. "Bruchstücke einer Pehlevi-Übersetzung der Psalmen", *Sitzungsberichte der Preussischen Akademie der Wissenschaften, Philosophisch-historische Klasse*, Berlin, 1933:91-152.

Bailey, H.W. 1943. *Zoroastrian problems in the ninth-century books* (Ratanbai Katrak Lectures), Oxford [Reprinted, with new introduction, 1971].

Bailey, H.W. 1971. See: Bailey 1943.

Baqlī Šīrāzī, Rūzbihān. *Šarḥ-i šaṭḥiyyāt*, ed. H. Corbin (Bibliothèque iranienne, 12), Tehran 1344 H / 1966.

Bedjan, Paul. 1891. *Acta martyrum et sanctorum*, II, Leipzig.

Ben-Shammai, Haggai. 1993. "'ג'מעה' בערבית-יהודית כתרגום שאילה של 'ערובתא' - היום הקודם למועד. עדויות קדומות על מנהג התרת נדרים בערב ראש השנה", לשוננו 57 (תשנ"ג): 125–136

Benveniste, Emile. 1929. *The Persian religion according to the chief Greek texts* (University of Paris. Ratanbai Katrak Lectures.) Paris.

Bīrūnī, Abū Rayḥān Muḥammad ibn Aḥmad. *Kitāb al-ṣaydana fī l-ṭibb*, taṣḥīḥ 'Abbās Zaryāb, Tehran: Markaz-e našr-e dānešgāhī, 1370.

Chabot, J.B. 1898. "La lettre du catholicos Mar Aba III", *Actes du onzième congrès international des orientalistes*, 4e section, Paris, 295–335.

Darab Hormazyar's Rivayat, by M.R. Unvala, with an introduction by J.J. Modi. 2 vols. Bombay 1922.

Dhabhar, Bamanji Nusservanji. 1932. *The Persian Rivayats of Hormazyar Framarz and others. Their version...*, Bombay.

Dhabhar, Bamanji Nusservanji. 1963. *Translation of the Zand-i Khūrtak Avistāk*, Bombay: K.R. Cama Oriental Institute, 1963.

Frye, R.N. 1967. "Iran und Israel", *Festschrift für Wilhelm Eilers. Ein Dokument der internationalen Forschung zum 27. September 1966*, Wiesbaden, 74-84.

Gignoux, Philippe. 1984. "Church-state relations in the Sasanian period", *Monarchies and socio-religious traditions in the Ancient Near East.*

Bulletin of the Middle Eastern Cultural Center in Japan, Wiesbaden, 1:72–80.

Glucker, John. 1978. *Antiochus and the Late Academy*, Göttingen.

Hampel, Jürgen. 1974. *Die Kopenhagener Handschrift Cod. 27. Eine Sammlung von zoroastrischen Gebeten, Beschwörungsformeln, Vorschrfiten und wissenschaftlichen Überlieferungen* (Göttinger Orientforschungen, III. Reihe, Band 2), Wiesbaden: Harrassowitz.

Henning, W.B. 1936. "Ein manichäisches Bet- und Beichtbuch", *Abhandlungen der Preussischen Akademie der Wissenschaften, Philosophisch-historische Klasse* (1936, No. 10), Berlin, 417–557 [Reprinted in *Acta Iranica* 14].

Henning, W.B. 1958. "Mitteliranisch", *Handbuch der Orientalistik* I,IV,1, Leiden, 20-129.

Ibn al-Muqaffa'. *Āthār Ibn al-Muqaffa'*, Beirut 1966.

Ibn Ḥazm, Abū Muḥammd 'Alī b. Aḥmad, *Al-fiṣal fī l-milal wa-l-ahwā' wa-l-niḥal*, 5 vols., ed. Muḥammad Ibrâhîm Naṣr and 'Abd al-Raḥmân 'Umayra, 5 vols., Beirut, 1985.

Ibn Qutayba al-Dīnawarī, Abū Muḥammad 'Abdallāh b. Muslim. *'Uyūn al-akhbār*, 4 vols., Cairo: Dār al-kutub al-miṣriyya 1343-1349 AH / 1925-1930.

Imoto, Eiichi. 1981. "Mithra, the mediator", *Acta Iranica* 21 (Monumentum Georg Morgenstierne), 299–307.

Jamasp-Asana, D.M. 1897/1913. *Pahlavi texts*, Bombay.

Junker, Heinrich F.J. 1929. "Mittelpers. *frašēmurv* Pfau", *Wörter und Sachen* 12:132-158.

MacKenzie, D.N. 1984. "Some Pahlavi plums", *Acta Iranica* 23 (Orientalia J. Duchesne-Guillemin ... oblata; Acta Iranica, Hommmages et opera minora, IX), Leiden: Brill, 383-391.

Macuch, Maria. 1981. *Das sasanidische Rechtsbuch "Mātakdān i hazār dātistān" (Teil II)* (Abhandlungen für die Kunde des Morgenlandes, Bd. XLV, 1), Wiesbaden: Deutsche Morgenländische Gesellschaft (Franz Steiner).

Majrīṭī (Ps.). 1933. *"Picatrix". Das Ziel des Weisen von Pseudo-Mağrīṭī*, 1. Arabischer Text, ed. Hellmut Ritter (Studien der Bibliothek Warburg, 12), Leipzig.

Markwart, J. 1927. "Np. âdhîna 'Freitag'", *Ungarische Jahrbücher* 7:89-121.

Menasce, J.P. 1956/7. "La conquête de l'iranisme et la récupération des mages hellénisés", *Ecole Pratique des Hautes Etudes. Section des Sciences Religieuses. Annuaire 1956-1957*, 3-12.

Messina, Giuseppe. 1930. *Der Ursprung der Magier und die zarathuštrische Religion* (Scripta Pontificii Instituti Biblici), Rome.

Meyerhof, Max. 1933. "Das Vorwort zur Drogenkunde des Bērūnī", *Quellen und Studien zur Geschichte der Naturwissenschaften und der Medizin* 3:157–208; Arabic text 1–18.

Molé, Marijan. 1959. "Le problème zurvanite", *Journal Asiatique* 247:431-469.

Molé, Marijan. 1963. *Culte, mythe et cosmologie dans l'Iran ancien. Le problème zoroastrien et la tradition mazdéenne* (Annales du Musée Guimet, Bibliothèque d'études, t. 68), Paris.

Māwardī, Abū l-Ḥasan 'Alī b. Muḥammad b. Ḥabīb. *Tashīl al-naẓar wa-ta'jīl al-ẓafar fī akhlāq al-malik wa-siyāsati l-mulūk*, ed. Muḥyī Hilāl al-Sarhān and Ḥusayn al-Sā'ātī, Beirut 1981.

Reitzenstein, Richard. 1917. *Die Göttin Psyche in der hellenistischen und frühchristlichen Literatur* (Sitzungsberichte der Heidelberger Akademie der Wissenschaften, Philosophisch-historische Klasse, Jahrgang 1917, 10. Abhandlung), Heidelberg.

Ritter, Hellmut; and Martin Plessner (trsl.). 1962. Majrīṭī (Ps.). *"Picatrix". Das Ziel des Weisen von Pseudo-Mağrīṭī*, translated into German from the Arabic by Hellmut Ritter and Martin Plessner (Studies of the Warbug Institute, 27), London: Warburg Institute.

Rudolph, Kurt. 1960/1. *Die Mandäer* (Forschungen zur Religion und Literatur des Alten und Neuen Testaments, 74-75; NF 56-57), Göttingen: Vandenhoeck & Ruprecht.

Rudolph, Kurt. 1968/9. "Problems of a history of the development of the Mandaean religion", *History of Religions* 8:210–235.

Shaked, Shaul. 1979. *The wisdom of the Sasanian sages.* An edition, with translation and notes, of *Dēnkard*, Book Six, by Āturpāt-i Ēmētān (Persian Heritage Series, 34), Boulder, Col.: Westview Press.

Shaked, Shaul. 1994. "Some Islamic reports concerning Zoroastrianism", *Jerusalem Studies in Arabic and Islam* 17:43–84.

Shaki, Mansour. 1970. "Some basic tenets of the eclectic metaphysics of the *Dênkart*", *Archiv Orientální* 38:277-312.

Shaki, Mansour. 1973. "A few philosophical and cosmogonical chapters of the *Dēnkart*", *Archiv Orientální* 41:133-164.

Sperber, Daniel. 1970/1. "Silver as a status-symbol in Sasanian Persia",

Persica 5:103-105.

Van Dyk, R. 1851. "On the present condition of the medical profession in Syria", *Journal of the American Oriental Society* 1:561-591.

Wesendonk, O.G. von. 1924. *Urmensch und Seele in der iranischen Überlieferung. Ein Beitrag zur Religionsgeschichte des Hellenismus*, Hannover.

Widengren, Geo. 1967. "Philological remarks on some Pahlavi texts, chiefly concerned with Zervanite religion", *Sir J.J. Zarthoshti Madressa Centenary Volume*, Bombay, 84-103.

Zaehner, R.C. 1955. *Zurvan. A Zoroastrian dilemma*, Oxford: Clarendon Press.

INDEX

A. GENERAL

Note that "A" refers to the Addenda

B. WORDS

I. Iranian

II. Arabic

III. Aramaic, Hebrew

C. PASSAGES

II. Arabic

III. Bible, Semitic inscriptions

IV. Greek and Armenian